D1117853

AMERICA IN THE FIFTIES

AMERICA IN THE TWENTIETH CENTURY

John Robert Greene, *Series Editor*

Other titles in America in the Twentieth Century

America in the Twenties
Ronald Allen Goldberg

America in the Seventies
Stephanie A. Slocum-Schaffer

AMERICA IN THE FIFTIES

Andrew J. Dunar

With a Foreword by *John Robert Greene*

SYRACUSE UNIVERSITY PRESS

First Edition 2006

06   07   08   09   10   11   6   5   4   3   2   1

Library of Congress Cataloging-in-Publication Data
Dunar, Andrew J.
America in the fifties / Andrew J. Dunar ; with a foreword by John Robert Greene.—1st ed.
p. cm.
Includes index.
ISBN 0–8156–3103–0 (cloth : alk. paper)—ISBN 0–8156–3128–6 (pbk. : alk. paper)
1. United States—History—1945–1953. 2. United States—History—1953–1961.
3. Nineteen fifties. I. Title.
E813.D86 2006
973.921-dc22   2006024107

Manufactured in the United States of America

To Jamie, Kimberly, and Michael

Andrew J. Dunar is a professor of history and chair of the Department of History at the University of Alabama in Huntsville. He is the author of *The Truman Scandals and the Politics of Morality,* coauthor (with Dennis McBride) of *Building Hoover Dam: An Oral History of the Great Depression,* and coauthor (with Stephen P. Waring) of *Power to Explore: A History of Marshall Space Flight Center, 1960–1990,* which won the History Book Award from the American Institute of Aeronautics and Astronautics (AIAA) in 2000. He has served as editor of *The Oral History Review,* the journal of the Oral History Association, and is currently working on an oral history of The Farm, a hippie commune in Summertown, Tennessee.

Contents

Illustrations

Foreword

JOHN ROBERT GREENE

"THERE JUST NEVER SEEMS TO BE ENOUGH TIME"—"The text-book is so bland; the students won't read it"—"Don't *teachers* ever write?"—"If I could only find more than one book that I feel good about assigning."

These are several of the complaints endemic to those of us who teach survey American history courses. The book series America in the Twentieth Century was designed to address these issues in a novel fashion that attempts to meet the needs of both student and instructor alike. Using the decade as its organizing scheme (admittedly a debatable choice, but it is our experience that chronology, not theme, makes for a better survey course), each book tackles the main issues of its time in a fashion at once readable and scholarly in nature. Authors are chosen by the editors of this series primarily for their teaching skills—indeed, each book proposal was accompanied by syllabi that showed the prospective author's course pedagogy. In fact, contributors have been urged to write these books from their lecture notes and limit footnote references that can often distract or intimidate the student-reader. In a departure from virtually every textbook series of note, one member of our editorial board is a presently sitting college student, whose comments on the manuscript may well be the most helpful of all. The volumes in the series have either a bibliography at the end or a recommended reading section at the end of each chapter. They are admittedly, not exhaustive, but no list of our favorite work is.

The result is a readable, concise, and scholarly series of books from master teachers who know what works in the college classroom. We offer it to college instructors and their students in hopes that they will, in the words of the Latin maxim, do the one thing that we all hope in the academy that professor and student will do together, *Tolle et Lege*—"Take and Read."

Acknowledgments

THANKS FIRST AND FOREMOST go to Bob Greene, who envisioned this series and who offered me the opportunity to write the volume on the fifties. His comments on an earlier draft of the book helped me rethink its organization and sharpen its prose. At Syracuse University Press, Mary Selden Evans offered encouragement and patience, and guided the manuscript through to acceptance. The students in my Recent American History and foreign affairs classes helped me in ways they probably don't realize. Thanks also to copyeditor Jeffrey H. Lockridge, whose careful work has improved the book in many ways. Thanks, as always, to Cathie, and to Jamie, Kimberly, and Michael, to whom I dedicate the book.

AMERICA IN THE FIFTIES

1

Origins

Postwar America and the Roots of the Fifties

DECADES ARE USEFUL but artificial divisions of time. Categorization is one way that people make sense of things, and for that reason dividing time into ten-year increments helps us understand trends, long-term developments, and themes. Yet the generalizations we derive from categorization can often be misleading. Among the more pervasive images of the 1950s are those associated with popular culture and prosperity: a golden age of television, cars with large tail fins, an abundance of consumer goods, Elvis Presley, Mickey Mantle. It seems to have been a simpler time, in which the idealized family life depicted in televised situation comedies had at least some basis in reality and crime was a less constant menace. On reflection, however, more threatening images of the first full decade in the shadow of the atomic bomb come to mind: the less than decisive U.S. victory in Korea, the Soviets' surprising launch of Sputnik, the bombast of Nikita Khrushchev, the hysteria of McCarthyism, the clash over the integration of a high school in Little Rock.

Major developments of later years have their origins in the 1950s. The civil rights movement has roots deeply planted in the fifties, for the decade witnessed the Supreme Court decision that gave federal backing to the desegregation of schools (foreshadowing the demise of segregation in other facets of public life), the emergence of Martin Luther King and the tactic of nonviolent direct action, and byplay between activists and their adversaries. Other developments that would have profound effects on people in the sixties and beyond seemed barely discernible in the fifties—but on reflection they, too, originate in that decade. The "movements" of the 1960s and 1970s—on behalf of women, Indians (as Native Americans were known in the fifties), Chicanos (or Hispanic Americans), the environment, the counterculture, and consumers—have undeniable origins in the 1950s. Few Americans would have been able to locate Vietnam on a map in the fifties, yet the Truman and Eisenhower administrations both took steps that deepened our involvement and led to the Vietnam quagmire of the sixties and seventies.

A common stereotype of the 1950s is that it was a decade of conformity: the decade of the cookie-cutter "Organization Man," of rows of identical boxes in the housing tracts of suburbia, of corporate research teams that suppressed individuality even in scientific research, of mass consumerism that led everyone to follow fads and fashion trends in unison, of "the bland leading the bland" in politics. Yet actor James Dean, the cinematic "Rebel Without a Cause," symbolized the decade's very American tendency to buck the tide. Jack Kerouac, Allen Ginsberg, and other "beatniks," or "beats," celebrated nonconformity. Elvis Presley became one of the great commercial successes in history by flaunting American musical traditions—drawing on the wellspring of black music that refused to conform to convention. Future artistic trends also originated in the fifties—in the work of talented artists such as Jackson Pollock.

Seldom can we understand a decade, development, or event without looking at its origins. Just as later developments had their roots in the fifties, so we must retreat into the forties to understand the fifties. In many ways a more natural division to employ in studying the fifties is to look at the postwar period from 1945 to 1960. Indeed, historian Eric Goldman called that fifteen-year period the "Crucial Decade" in a popular history. To understand the Cold War, McCarthyism, civil rights, and many of the other central developments of the fifties, we must begin earlier. So this examination of the 1950s begins at the end of World War II. The present chapter will trace developments of the late forties that set the stage for the fifties.

Prospects and Problems in the Postwar World

When World War II ended, Americans faced a future that seemed at once threatening and full of promise. The war ended with the birth of the atomic age, and perhaps the bomb most aptly symbolized the uncertainties of the postwar world. The dropping of atomic bombs on Hiroshima on August 6 and on Nagasaki three days later triggered little of the angst that accompanied later reflection about the meaning of the bomb. To most Americans, the fact that the war had ended seemed more important than the way it ended.

Wartime spending had brought an end to the Great Depression, and many Americans feared that the end of the war would bring economic decline and a slide back into Depression conditions. The national debt had risen five-fold, from 50.7 billion dollars at the end of 1940 to 260.1 billion dollars at the end of 1945, further contributing to concern. Could wartime price controls be lifted? Would there be jobs available for returning veterans? Would there be housing for them? Strikes in key industries in 1946 increased concern about the ability of the economy to adjust to peacetime conditions.

What would happen to America's minorities? Race riots had taken place after the end of World War I, and since there had been riots in Detroit and Harlem during World War II, wasn't it likely that they might happen again after another war? Would women who had taken jobs to support the war effort be able to keep those jobs?

The international situation seemed even more menacing. President Roosevelt's death in April thrust the untested former haberdasher, Harry Truman, into the presidency. Was he capable of filling Roosevelt's large shoes? Could he stand up to Joseph Stalin? At war's end, the Red Army occupied much of Eastern Europe; the Soviet Union, so recently the ally that had defeated Hitler in the East, now loomed as an adversary.

Despite these concerns, the overriding mood in the United States in late 1945 was one of optimism. No nation was better situated to lead the world into the postwar era. Other major nations had suffered greater loss of life and physical damage than had the United States during World War II. Americans were poised to shape the postwar world economy. The United Nations, a dream of American internationalists since the Senate rejected membership in the League of Nations after World War I, was now a reality.

Individual Americans also had reason for optimism. The Truman administration wanted to release soldiers and sailors at a moderate pace for reasons of security and because the simultaneous return of large numbers of veterans might put unacceptable pressures on American society and the economy. Veterans and their families had fought for a more rapid demobilization, and the administration had relented. Veterans returned to an enthusiastic welcome, and to a nation in which consumer goods that had been restricted during the war were now becoming available.

The nation faced the postwar world with a president who was still adjusting to his new responsibilities. Franklin Delano Roosevelt died on April 17, 1945, just weeks before the war in Europe ended on May 8. Roosevelt had been elected to four terms, and had only begun the fourth term. Harry S. Truman became vice president only in the last term, and thus had only served eighty-three days when the president died. Truman, a Missouri farmer, served as an artillery officer during World War I. After returning from the war, he became involved in politics at the county level in the Kansas City area as a part of Boss Tom Pendergast's Democratic machine. In 1934, Pendergast picked him to run for the Senate, and after his victory some of his Washington colleagues looked down on him as the "senator from Pendergast." But he was a hard worker—diligent and honest in spite of his ties to the Kansas City machine. Reelected in 1940, he made his mark during the war as the head of a Senate committee that investigated waste at military bases. The committee operated on a bipartisan basis, and issued an unbroken string of unanimous reports, saving the nation some $15 billion by Truman's estimate. This service lifted him to the front rank of senators, and made possible his selection as Roosevelt's running mate in 1944. He presided over one of the most tumultuous periods in American history. In just his first four months in office, he had to make decisions about the end of the war, both in Europe and in the Pacific, and about the use of the atomic bomb.

"Peace Is Hell"

Once the celebrations accompanying the victory over Japan came to an end, Americans faced uncertainties troubling enough to prompt President Truman, weary from battling a seeming unending series of strikes, to mutter, "Sherman was wrong. Peace is hell." Labor posed particular problems to the Democrats and the Truman administration. Labor had long looked to the Democrats for support, and during Roosevelt administration New Deal pro-labor legislation had reinforced the bonds between the party and the major unions. During World War II, however, strains had emerged, particularly over the Roosevelt administration's policy of holding inflation in check through a program of wage and price controls. In the view of labor, the administration had done a better job of holding the line on wages than on prices, which had crept up steadily.

Truman tried to react vigorously to prevent price increases, but his hands were tied. He wanted to continue the wartime agency that had regulated prices, the Office of Price Administration (OPA). Congress, however, gave him only half of what he wanted, authorizing continuation of the OPA but limiting its authority. In the summer of 1946, when price controls ended, consumer prices shot up by 30 percent, and wholesale prices went up even faster. Strikes in coal and other key industries during the war undermined public support for labor unions, but did not resolve the substance of the dispute between labor and management. Thus at war's end, labor was angry, believing that the Democrats had not kept their part of the compact, while many Republicans and the general public believed that labor had demonstrated poor judgment during the war and did not deserve special attention afterward.

Truman's own situation was equally complex. He had always had labor support, even during his early days in politics in Missouri. In fact, his selection as Roosevelt's running mate in 1944 owed much to labor's backing. Truman had been deeply disturbed by wartime strikes, however, believing that labor had placed its own interests ahead of those of the country. After the war ended, he believed that one of his crucial responsibilities was to keep inflation in check, which could not happen without putting the brakes on wage increases. Thus when the war ended, the pro-labor Democratic president and pro-Democratic labor leaders stood at odds, with intractable circumstances dividing them.

Matters came to a head in late 1945 and early 1946, when a wave of strikes in key industries rocked that country. On November 21, 1945, the United Auto Workers struck General Motors. In January 1946, the United Steelworkers demanded a wage increase larger than the 18.5-cent hourly increase the president had recommended. And on April 1, led by the irascible John L. Lewis, one of the nation's most powerful union leaders, 400,000 members of the United Mine Workers walked out.

Truman made it clear that he would respond aggressively to strikes. He called in the head of the CIO and the president of U.S. Steel to negotiate, and under his pressure they came close to an agreement, finally settling a short time later. When railroad workers walked out late in May, Truman went before Congress to ask for authority to draft the strikers, only to be handed a note as he was about to begin his speech that the issue had been settled. He moved to seize the coal mines, but also made concessions that allowed a settlement. The miners walked out again just before the fall elections, and this time Truman refused to talk to John L. Lewis, who tried to use the looming elections to pressure Truman into concessions. Truman would not budge. Lewis finally settled, but not until after the election.

The disputes had repercussions for labor and for the president. The outbreak of strikes turned many Americans against labor, and gave Congress the confidence to adopt the Taft-Hartley Act, which curtailed labor's right to strike. It provided for a cooling-off period prior to the beginning of a strike, and also forbade industry-wide strikes, and the closed shop. It gave the president the authority, through court injunction, to halt strikes against public utilities and companies engaged in interstate commerce and communications. Truman won back some of his labor support by vetoing the bill, but Congress easily overrode the veto.

Truman paid a price, too. The 1946 off-year elections, which took place in the shadow of the miners' strike, was a disaster for the Democrats. Returning the economy to a peacetime footing was proving more difficult than people had expected, and the public judged Truman's management harshly. Strikes and inflation dominated the headlines. Problems emerged within the administration that further called the president's leadership into question. Talk of cronyism, of a "Missouri gang," circulated, and stories about Truman's poker games fanned the flames of criticism. Two Roosevelt holdovers, Secretary of Commerce Henry A. Wallace and Secretary of the Interior Harold Ickes, resigned in public disputes with the president, Wallace over U.S.-Soviet relations, Ickes over control of tideland oil. Truman had pleased neither liberals nor conservatives, and found himself isolated in the political center. In one year, his popularity took a drop of unprecedented proportions; in August 1945, his approval rating stood at 90 percent; by September 1946, it dropped to 34 percent. "To err is Truman" became the mantra of the president's opponents. Truman, who ordinarily delighted in the rigors of electioneering, had no stomach for the campaign trail in 1946, and even the chairman of the Democratic National Committee suggested to him that it would not help the Democrats for him to get involved. Truman stayed close to Washington, and gave no campaign speeches.

The election seemingly brought disaster to the Democrats. For the first time since before the crash of the stock market and the onset of the Great Depression, the Republicans captured both Houses of Congress, winning the Senate by 51 to 45, and the House by 246 to 188. For the Democrats, this proved to be blessing in disguise: the 80th Congress, elected in 1946, was so conservative, so out of touch with the public's desire for change, that Truman and his party would be able to run effectively against it in 1948.

Wartime Conferences, Postwar Problems, and the Origins of the Cold War

Two conferences in the last year of the war demonstrated the strains in the wartime alliance, and set the stage for the Cold War. In February 1945, President Roosevelt traveled to Yalta, a Black Sea resort on the Crimean Peninsula, to confer with Churchill and Stalin. Roosevelt was ill, and would die only two months later. The crucial decisions the three leaders made at Yalta would shape the postwar world. Roosevelt achieved agreement on a framework for the United Nations. Other issues proved more difficult. The three leaders could only agree on the principle of dividing Germany into zones of occupation, and that the Soviet Union deserved a major portion of reparations from Germany, but they deferred settlement of the details. The issue of Poland was even more intractable. Stalin wanted to ensure that the Polish government would be friendly toward the Soviet Union, whereas Roosevelt and Churchill insisted that democratic elements be incorporated into the new regime. The final agreement left much unresolved, or so vaguely worded that the Soviets could "stretch it all the way to Washington," in the words of one member of the administration. Critics would blast Roosevelt for giving away Eastern Europe, but in reality he could not have gained more—the Red Army, after all, was occupying Poland.

The world situation had changed dramatically five months later, when the Big Three met again, in Potsdam, a suburb of Berlin. The war in Europe had ended in May, and the war in the Pacific had entered its final phase. Roosevelt had died, to be replaced by Harry S. Truman, an underestimated leader of firm resolve who had virtually no diplomatic experience. Truman knew that his early contacts with the Russians would be watched closely, and he wanted to show them he could hold his own. Hard-liners in the administration, especially the American ambassador to the Soviet Union, W. Averell Harriman, reinforced Truman's own inclination to be tough. As the leaders met in Potsdam, two dramatic developments occurred: Churchill was defeated as prime minister, to be replaced by Clement Attlee, and, even more important, scientists at Los Alamos, New Mexico, successfully tested the first atomic bomb. On learning of the test, Truman, who had indeed been holding his own, seemed to gain in confidence.

Though more substantive than the Yalta Conference in its results, the Potsdam Conference sowed the seeds of later dissent. The leaders agreed on the territorial division of Germany into zones of occupation, with the Soviet Union, Britain, the United States, and France each receiving a zone to administer. Each of the victors was to manage reparations within its zone of occupation, satisfying the Yalta provision that the Russians were entitled to substantial reparations. Berlin, the old German capital, lay deep within the Soviet zone. Rather than relinquish control of the city to the Soviets, the victorious powers divided it into zones as well, thus devising a formula that guaranteed contention and led to the city's becoming one of the major hot spots in the Cold War. Although Truman won Stalin's agreement that the Soviets would join the war against Japan, big issues—the fate of Poland, the status of Eastern Europe—remained unresolved.

On August 6, just days after the end of the Potsdam Conference, an American B-29 nicknamed the "Enola Gay" dropped the first atomic bomb on the Japanese city of Hiroshima. At least 78,000 people, and perhaps more than 100,000, died in the blast. Three days later, the United States dropped a second atomic bomb, this time on Nagasaki. On August 14, the Japanese emperor surrendered unconditionally, and the war was finally over.

The shockingly sudden end to the war meant that the Soviet Union, which had not attacked Japan itself despite a much-belated declaration of war, would be denied a role in the occupation of the defeated nation. Unlike the situation in Germany, the United States alone would occupy Japan. General Douglas MacArthur headed the occupation forces; Japan responded to MacArthur's commanding presence. The general dictated a new constitution instituting a new democratic government, and helped initiate and economic recovery that would make Japan a world economic power within a generation, and transform an erstwhile enemy into an American ally.

By most any measure, the United States emerged from the war as the most powerful nation in the world. It had not been scarred by the war as had the other leading nations. Its economy would soon prove to be the most stable and dynamic. It was the world's only atomic power. With power came responsibility, however; in the late 1940s, the United States set a course that determined how it would shoulder that burden.

Such power was awesome, but it was not absolute. World War II unleashed forces that no one could have imagined. Communism soon became the specter that most Americans feared, but it was but one of several forces that would reshape the world in the postwar era. American leaders of both parties in the late forties and the fifties viewed the international situation principally as a struggle of two ways of life, one represented by the Soviet Union, the other by the United States.

Such a bipolar worldview overlooked other influences, the most potent of which was nationalism, which would result in the worldwide retrenchment of colonial empires. The late-nineteenth-century imperial enterprises of Western European nations and (to a lesser extent) the United States gave rise to political and economic arrangements that allowed them to dominate the nations of Africa, Asia, and South America. Those arrangements included annexation, establishment of protectorates, governing through puppet rulers, creation of spheres of influence, and economic exploitation through loans, the introduction of technology controlled by the imperial power, and special agreements with local elites. The peace settlement after World War I had changed only the details of these arrangements, and in many cases had ratified earlier colonial patterns. Indeed, as Japan expanded onto the Asian continent in the 1930s, its leaders claimed their right to establish their own sphere of interest—the Asian Co-Prosperity Sphere—following the Western example, only in their own backyard.

The remnants of these old imperial patterns made the postwar world a complex place; many of the key international developments of the forties and fifties transpired in the areas affected, soon to be called the "Third World," the "lesser developed world," or the "undeveloped world" (all terms representing the biases of former colonial powers). Colonial possessions shifted allegiances or gained independence, redrawing the political map of the world at a pace that must have made mapmakers dizzy. Nations gained their independence through a variety of means, sometimes through the intentional withdrawal of the former colonial powers, which often were exhausted from their participation in World War II or could no longer afford to maintain colonies. Other nations gained independence through revolution.

From the perspective of the Cold War, none of these developments could be viewed in isolation. Were independence movements strictly nationalist uprisings? Were they inspired by Communism? The answer was seldom clear, for one spawned the other. Communist (or leftist) involvement may have given rise to genuine nationalism, or movements of nationalist yearning may have invited leftist participation. Even that question left open the issue of whether leftist political activity necessarily indicated Soviet involvement.

Where did the United States stand on these issues? Surprisingly, even though the U.S.-Soviet rivalry often overshadowed other postwar developments, there was some ambiguity in the American position immediately after the end of the war. On the one hand, as a nation born of revolution, the United States was an inspiration to other nations. Americans felt uncomfortable as an imperialist power. President Wilson had included self-determination as one of the Fourteen Points, his prescription for peace after World War I; President Franklin Roosevelt had spoken out against colonialism, and reaffirmed the principle of self-determination in the Atlantic Charter in 1941. On the other hand, 175 years after its own revolution, the United States was no defender of revolution. Indeed, given the choice between a revolution that might replace a stable authoritarian regime—even with a democracy—and the status quo, Americans had opted for the status quo, time and time again.

The most pressing international questions after the war were what to do with areas now occupied by the victors or formerly occupied by the vanquished. The answers to these questions exposed contradictions in U.S. foreign policy. As the most significant of these, even as it pressed the Soviet Union to withdraw from occupied areas and not to expand into others, the United States cooperated with Western European nations in reestablishing their colonies. Thus, in South and East Asia, the United States pressured the Soviet Union to withdraw from the northern provinces of Iran and, as a means of warding off Soviet expansion, it occupied the southern part of the Korean Peninsula; in Southeast Asia, ignoring the pleas of Ho Chi Minh in Vietnam, it assisted the French in establishing their former colony of Indo-China. In doing so, the Truman administration demonstrated U.S. willingness, first, to respond to perceived threats anywhere in the world and, second, to counter the expansion of Communist, especially Soviet, influence through the ad hoc strategy of containment—two courses of action that would characterize its Cold War foreign policy.

In Europe, several crises loomed. Having established friendly governments in Poland, Bulgaria, and Romania, the Soviet Union was moving to extend its hegemony to the whole of Eastern Europe. Still uncertain of its own economy at war's end in 1945, the United States sought to avoid a recurrence of the disastrously jerry-rigged financial arrangements that had collapsed within a decade after World War I, bringing on a worldwide economic depression. Disagreements over how to handle finances and reparations in occupied Germany, however, led to the Soviet Union going its own way in its zone, while Britain and the United States went theirs in "Bizonia."

The Origins of Containment

Events in the early months of 1946 crystallized American anti-Soviet views into policy. Warnings from the American diplomat George Kennan and former British Prime Minister Winston Churchill laid the groundwork for what became the American policy of containment.

The first regional crisis of the Cold War came in Iran. In January 1942, Russian, British, and Iranian negotiators had agreed that all allied forces would withdraw from Iran six months after the end of the war. In March 1946, six months after the Japanese surrender, Russian troops remained in Iran, and the Soviets supported separatist movements in the northwestern Iranian provinces of Azerbaijan and Kurdistan. Although the Soviet Union finally withdrew in May because withdrawal occurred when Soviet-American relations were at a delicate stage, the crisis stiffened Truman's attitude toward Iran, demonstrated the value of firmness, and taught American strategists about Russian behavior. It also drew the United States closer to the young Iranian ruler, Shah Mohammad Reza Pahlavi.

Another issue that gave the United States and the Soviet Union the opportunity to take each other's measure was atomic energy. Here the United States held all the cards. Should it maintain its atomic monopoly for as long as possible or move toward international control of fissionable materials for peaceful purposes? After some debate, the Truman administration announced that the United States would relinquish its monopoly if the Russians would submit to inspections of their defense establishments, among other significant concessions. Moderates warned that these concessions would be unacceptable to the Russians, which of course was exactly the point. As expected, the Russians refused, and the plan died.

In March 1946, Churchill visited the United States and traveled by train with President Truman to Fulton, Missouri. There, on the campus of Westminster College, Churchill delivered a warning to Americans: "From Stettin in the Baltic to Trieste in the Adriatic, an iron curtain has descended across the continent." The United States and Britain had to join together to defend against this threat, but because the United States "stands at this time at the pinnacle of world power," it bore a particular accountability to the future.

That summer, Truman asked his special counsel, Clark Clifford, and a junior naval aide, George Elsey, to prepare a report about Soviet violations of their agreements. The resulting Clifford-Elsey report painted a picture of the Soviet menace in the Middle East, Asia, and South America that amounted to a quest for world domination. To confront this challenge, the United States would have to augment its defenses and prepare to defend other nations where the menace was most threatening. The report—which Truman considered to be so politically sensitive he ordered all twenty copies circulating in the higher levels of his administration to be retrieved and locked up—allowed no shades of gray, portraying the Soviet threat in unrelenting terms, and overlooking more conciliatory actions. As the diplomatic historian Melvyn Leffler concluded, the report "simplified international realities, distorted Soviet behavior, and probably misread Soviet motivations and intentions." Truman's views were hardening. Only one member of the administration, Secretary of Commerce Henry A. Wallace, urged a more conciliatory approach to the Soviets, and Truman forced him to resign in September.

American Aid and Containment: The Truman Doctrine and the Marshall Plan

In the late months of 1946, a new challenge to the West arose in the eastern Mediterranean, in Turkey and Greece. The Soviets, seeking access to the Mediterranean via the Black Sea, demanded a role in the defense of the Dardanelles. Meanwhile, a Communist insurgency threatened the British-backed Greek government with guerilla attacks. The United States worried not only about losing Greece and Turkey, but also about having its access to Middle Eastern oil severed. Then, in February 1947, Britain informed the United States that it could no longer bear the burden of defending Greece.

On March 12, Truman went before a joint session of Congress and gave the most significant speech of his presidency. He asked not only for $400 million in aid for Greece and Turkey, but also for authority to greatly expand American global responsibilities. He portrayed the Soviet challenge as fundamental, a struggle between two ways of life, one representing freedom, the other terror and oppression. Then he laid out what became known as the "Truman Doctrine": "I believe that it must be the policy of the United States to support the peoples who are resisting attempted subjugation by armed minorities or by outside pressures." Communism would have to be contained, and the United States would have to be on the alert to confront it wherever it might seek to expand. In accepting Truman's recommendation for aid to Greece and Turkey, Congress also accepted his program for vast new American worldwide responsibilities, far broader than any nation had ever undertaken.

George Kennan, the American with the most experience in dealing with the Russians, provided a historical context and theoretical rationale to support the Truman Doctrine. He sent a dispatch from Moscow to the State Department that had such impact that it soon became known simply as the "Long Telegram." In this telegram, and later in an article in July 1947 published anonymously (but understood immediately to have been written by Kennan) in the influential journal *Foreign Affairs*, Kennan elaborated his understanding of the Soviets. The Soviet Union, he advised, bore the stamp of traditional Russian behavior as indelibly as it did Communist doctrines. The Soviets were insecure, distrusting, and patient in pursuit of their goals. They would exploit any opportunity, and attempt to move into any "nook and cranny available to it in the basin of world power." But since they operated under no timetable, the Soviets would back down if confronted with superior force. Thus the United States had to respond with "a long-term, patient but firm and vigilant containment of Russian expansive tendencies." Kennan thus laid the theoretical basis for the defense strategy of containment, and as the policy gained support in the administration, Kennan would be known as the "father of containment."

Inevitably, the question rose as to whether other areas in Europe also ought to be considered for aid similar to that approved for Greece and Turkey. Truman's cabinet mulled over the idea, and the War, Navy, and State Departments in particular began to consider plans for the reconstruction of Europe. Secretary of State George C. Marshall, convinced that the Soviets wanted to hinder the recovery of Europe, initiated planning for a program in the State Department. Undersecretary of State Dean Acheson, who had been instrumental in advising Truman on his speech on aid to Greece and Turkey, worked with George Kennan and William L. Clayton, the undersecretary of state for economic affairs, in devising a program.

Marshall proposed the European Recovery Program as part of his commencement address at Harvard University on June 5. He proposed a program of major proportions, one that would have to be grounded on European initiative in order to succeed. Truman insisted that the plan should be named for Marshall, since even the "worst Republican" would have a hard time voting against a program named for the highly regarded secretary of state.

The European response was immediate and enthusiastic. France, Britain, and the Soviet Union met in Paris before the month was out to take up Marshall's invitation. The decision to invite the Russians to participate was a carefully considered one; Kennan advised it, but the planners couched the offer in terms the Soviets found unpalatable. Foreign Minister Molotov, the Russian representative at the Paris meeting, walked out and then forbade the Eastern European nations to take part. The Western European nations called another planning session in September, after which Truman went to Congress with a request for the funds to launch the program.

Congress received the proposal less enthusiastically than had the Europeans. Conservative Republicans compared it to the New Deal, which they did not intend to be taken as a compliment. Henry Wallace labeled it a "Martial Plan," a criticism that seemed unjust at the time but less so as more and more American aid became military assistance. Truman and Marshall both fought hard for the plan, and won important support from key Republicans, including John Foster Dulles, the key Republican advisor on foreign policy; Senator Arthur H. Vandenberg from Michigan, an internationalist who had helped develop the proposal for the Marshall Plan; and 80-year-old former Secretary of State Henry L. Stimson, who chaired the Citizens Committee for the Marshall Plan.

Bipartisan support carried the Marshall Plan through Congress; by the time it ended in 1952, it had become a $17 billion program. Sixteen nations participated, and it is not an exaggeration to say that the Marshall Plan financed the recovery of Western Europe. The enormous success of the plan won praise from America's allies. Marshall's own assessment that "no people have ever acted more generously and more unselfishly than the American people in tendering assistance to alleviate distress and suffering" captured this mood. In later years, critics, including many revisionist historians, would argue that the motives behind the plan were more self-interested than altruistic, that the United States needed a strong Western Europe in the interest of its own national security, and robust European economies to provide trading partners for prosperous American businesses. To grant these points negates neither the humanitarian dimensions of the plan nor the genuine idealism behind it.

The Soviet Union responded with programs of its own for Eastern Europe, and indeed a pattern of punch and counterpunch came to characterize the Soviet-American rivalry in the early years of the Cold War. The Russians devised a program for Eastern Europe, the Molotov Plan, but it was a pale imitation since the Russian economy was in worse shape than those the United States was bolstering in the West.

The United States also revamped its national security apparatus. The National Security Act of 1947 created the National Military Establishment, which with revisions two years later became the Department of Defense, replacing the wartime War and Navy Departments, and bringing the Army, Navy, and the newly minted Air Force (the old Army Air Corps, now with independent status on an equal footing with the other services) under one umbrella. At the top stood a civilian secretary of defense, who held cabinet rank. Military officers headed each of the services—Army, Navy, Air Force, and Marines—and together formed the Joint Chiefs of Staff, whose chairmanship rotated among the services.

The Central Intelligence Agency (CIA) was a second creation of the National Security Act. The CIA assumed responsibility for the coordination of intelligence activities, and developed independent capabilities in both the collection of intelligence and the conduct of covert operations. Truman worried about the wide-ranging authority of the CIA, especially the potential for the abuse of its conduct of covert activities, which would indeed become controversial in later years.

The National Security Act also established the National Security Council (NSC). Truman and the other architects of the NSC intended it to be solely an advisory body with no policy-making authority, designed to give the president a source of advice on foreign policy independent of the State Department and the military services. It had no charter to conduct covert operations of the sort under the purview of the CIA. Headed by a national security advisor (originally called an executive secretary), the NSC had its own small staff. Its meetings, however, gathered cabinet-level officials involved in the formulation of foreign policy who gave recommendations both on current crises and on long-range national security planning.

The United States and the Establishment of the State of Israel

The United States would play an increasingly important role in the Middle East in the 1950s, one that developed from its involvement in a signal event in the history of this ancient region, the establishment of the state of Israel in 1948. After the end of World War I, the League of Nations assigned a mandate in Palestine to Britain, making the British responsible for maintaining the security of the region. Early in 1947, Britain determined that it could no longer fulfill this responsibility, and submitted the issue to the United Nations for resolution. The United Nations proposed that Palestine be partitioned into two areas, one for Jews and one for Arabs. The partition plan pleased neither Jews nor Arabs. Arab states in the region refused to accept the notion of designating a portion of Palestine as Jewish territory, and were determined to drive the Jews into the sea before allowing the establishment of a Jewish state, which would be the inevitable outcome of the plan.

As events moved forward, the position of the United States on Israel evolved out of disputes between the White House and the State and Defense Departments. Truman favored partition, but Secretary of Defense James Forrestal vehemently opposed it, as did Loy Henderson, who headed the State Department's Near East division. The State and Defense Departments feared loss of influence with the Arab states, a threat to oil supplies from the region, and opening the region to Soviet influence by isolating the United States from Arab allies. They also feared that a new Jewish state would be a fragile enterprise, and that if it were to be established, it would have to depend on American support for its survival, which would align the United States with the new state and against Arab nations.

The partition plan passed the United Nations General Assembly by only two votes in November, but partition was just the beginning. Jewish militia groups battled Palestinians and their allies from neighboring Arab states through the spring. In Washington, the debate over Israel finally focused on the president and Secretary of State George C. Marshall. Marshall believed it would be a tragic mistake for the United States to favor establishment of a Jewish state, and that Truman's willingness to consider such action was a blatantly political act designed to garner Jewish support in the presidential election that fall. Although Truman admired Marshall and thus found the dispute painful, he was committed to recognition. Reluctantly, Marshall acceded. Zionists declared the establishment of the state of Israel at midnight on the night of May 14. Just minutes later, the United States announced its recognition of the new state.

Many Americans in 1948, and since then, have dismissed Truman's decision as opportunistic politicking, a bid for the Jewish vote. The explanation is too easy, and overlooks the president's deep sympathy for victims of the Holo-caust, his determination to keep his word to Chaim Weizmann, who would become Israel's first president, his resentment at being underestimated by the "striped-pants boys" at the State Department, and his awareness that, in any event, the Jewish vote would not be decisive in 1948. Truman won the elec-tion even though he lost New York, Pennsylvania, and Illinois—the three states with the largest Jewish populations. His decision initiated a close rela-tionship between the United States and Israel that defied the fears of the State Department. And though it would become a more ardent supporter of Israel than anyone could have anticipated in 1948, the United States retained and expanded its influence among Arab states. The American role in the Middle East was never without its hazards, however, and in the 1950s, the United States would experience more of the uncertainties of dealing with the unstable region.

Germany and Containment: The Berlin Airlift

The status of Germany continued to haunt postwar Europe. People who believed that the Versailles Treaty after World War I had fostered the condi-tions that led to World War II argued that German economic recovery was es-sential to the stability of Europe. The prospect of rapid economic recovery for Germany frightened the Soviet Union, however, which twice in thirty years had been drawn into war with a prosperous Germany. Furthermore, by divid-ing Berlin into zones of occupation, the 1945 Potsdam settlement had given Western adversaries a foothold deep within Soviet-occupied territory—a situ-ation the Soviets found intolerable.

Not surprisingly, when a crisis came, it came in Berlin. Cooperation be-tween the four occupying powers had become strained, and by 1948 it was breaking down altogether. In mid-June, the American, British, and French forces issued a new currency that constituted a first step toward economic co-operation, which the Russians feared might lead to political unification. The Soviets responded by severing ground transportation between the West and Berlin on June 24, and then instituted a blockade of the city. Truman received advice that ranged from the bellicose to the timid, and settled for something in between, seeking to avoid direct confrontation with the Soviets. He left no doubt about his ultimate goal, however. "We stay in Berlin, period," he told his advisors. General Lucius Clay, who was in command of the American occupation, began flying supplies into Berlin shortly after the Soviets cut access. Truman decided to expand the effort into a full-scale airlift.

The Berlin Airlift, as it came to be known, was an impressive achievement by any standard. The volume of supplies needed to keep the city functioning was staggering: 2,000 tons of food and 12,000 tons of fuel and other supplies each day. The very idea of flying enough coal to keep a major northern European city operating in winter was audacious. The Americans flew B-29s, the bombers that had been used to drop the atomic bombs on Japan, to London. The Soviets had no way of knowing that the planes were not equipped to carry atomic bombs. American C-47 cargo planes and newer C-54s, aided by British air transports, flew around the clock, landing as often as every four minutes. Over the duration of the airlift, the allies flew 277,000 flights, delivering 2.3 million tons of food, fuel, and supplies into Berlin.

By the spring of 1949, Stalin had to acknowledge that the blockading of Berlin had failed. The city was not dying; instead, its will had only grown stronger. Berliners had helped clear rubble for the construction of new runways in the fall. The allied airlift was a logistical, humanitarian, and strategic triumph that embarrassed the Soviets. On May 12, Stalin lifted the blockade. On the same day, the allies declared the establishment of the Federal Republic of Germany, the foundation for what soon became a self-governing West Germany. The Soviets responded by establishing the German Democratic Republic, or East Germany.

The next year external events forced another reevaluation of American policy toward Germany. The Korean War, which fostered changes in American strategy worldwide, compelled the administration to consider ways to draw Germany into the Western alliance, something that had been inconceivable months earlier. General Omar Bradley warned Truman that the allies would have to rearm Germany or lose it.

From the German dilemma came a reexamination of European policy, and the origins of the short-lived European Defense Community (EDC), which would have incorporated German soldiers into a larger European defense force. The EDC never became a reality, but it did provide the impetus for Germany's full integration into the Western alliance in 1955, a development that took place when Eisenhower was president.

Collective Security: America's First Peacetime Alliances

Until the post–World War II era, the United States had heeded George Washington's warning about the hazards of entangling peacetime alliances. Reflecting its newfound postwar worldview, however, and the increasingly internationalist perspective of lawmakers and public alike, the Truman administration began to reexamine the nation's relations with its allies as another dimension of national security.

The United States looked first to Latin America, where a series of inter-American meetings in the 1930s had prepared the way for a more formal arrangement. World War II had sobered Americans; the penetration of Nazism and Fascism in the region exposed the hazards of ignoring inter-American relations. In 1947, Secretary of State Marshall represented the United States at another inter-American conference, in Rio de Janeiro, which culminated in the Rio Pact, whereby the United States and the nations of Latin American agreed that an attack on any of them would be considered an attack on all.

Because the Rio Pact was strictly a mutual defense agreement, it left unanswered the economic concerns that still trouble Latin Americans. A conference in Bogotá, Colombia, the following spring confronted these issues, and exposed remaining regional differences. The Latin Americans pressed the United States for economic aid. The Truman administration responded that Latin American problems paled beside those of Europe, but offered $500 million in assistance from the Export-Import Bank. As its most significant accomplishment, the Bogotá conference agreed on a charter for a new organization, the Organization of American States (OAS), which would provide a forum for the resolution of inter-American disputes and problems. The organization's charter included a clause that the United States had long resisted in inter-American conferences forbidding intervention in the "internal or external" affairs of other states.

The OAS provided a model for other collective security organizations with other American allies. Key American allies in Western Europe had signed the Brussels Pact, a mutual defense agreement, in March 1948. The Europeans intended to include the United States in a broader arrangement, and a year later achieved that end. Negotiations were difficult; given the distrust between Western European nations, the United States had to play a central role in mobilizing the organization. Yet Americans were divided in their opinion of the wisdom of an organization that defied long-held American traditions. Isolationists and United Nations supporters alike had reservations. During the Berlin Airlift, however, Britain, France, Belgium, the Netherlands, Luxembourg, Denmark, Portugal, and Italy joined the United States, Canada, and Iceland to form the North Atlantic Treaty Organization (NATO). Member nations signed the treaty on April 4, 1949. The collective security approach bound its members in an anti-Soviet treaty and in a defense organization funded largely by American dollars. Member nations agreed to treat an attack on any of them as an attack on all. From the beginning, Americans played a central role in its leadership and decision making.

In coming years, the United States applied the collective security approach in other regions, with Australia and New Zealand in the ANZUS Pact and with Pakistan, Thailand, the Philippines, Australia, New Zealand, Britain, and France in the Southeast Asian Treaty Organization (SEATO). None of the other organizations would occupy NATO's central position in American foreign policy.

A Singular Campaign: Truman Defeats Dewey in '48

In 1948, Truman staged the most dramatic come-from-behind victory in the history of the American presidency. The race appeared so one-sided in its final weeks that national pollsters stopped sampling registered voters. Republicans made plans for the new administration of New York Governor Thomas E. Dewey to set up shop in Washington. Even Truman's own inner circle doubted that their chief could pull off the political miracle that was needed. Yet he did.

Truman's victory in 1948 seemed to be a personal triumph, and indeed it was. Yet Truman had excellent advice, and appears to have taken much of it to heart. In the fall of 1947, his advisors David Rowe and Clark Clifford drew up a blueprint for victory. (Years later, acknowledging that Rowe was the principal author, Clifford said he had taken credit only because Truman distrusted Rowe, and likely would have ignored the plan if it had come to him over Rowe's signature.) The blueprint called for the president to draw on traditional sources of Democratic strength, to somehow reunite the three "misfit groups"—Southern conservatives, Western progressives, and Big City labor—and to hold the other groups of the Democratic coalition in line.

Farmers were the "Number One Priority." Labor would not support the Republicans, but it "could stay home," and thus had to be wooed. The president had to make "new and real efforts" to reach African Americans, or they would desert the party. The Jewish vote was important only in New York—but New York was needed. The president had to establish closer liaison with Catholics. Finally, Henry Wallace, leader of the liberal wing of the Democratic Party, had to be isolated.

As the convention season neared in the late spring of 1948, there was little reason to believe that Truman had a realistic chance to be reelected. Although some of the actions he had taken that spring now appear to be among the greatest achievements of his presidency, that was by no means clear at the time. In February, Truman sent a civil rights message to Congress asking for legislation that would have gone further than had any of his predecessors in guaranteeing the rights of minorities. The president called for the establishment of a permanent Commission on Civil Rights, a Civil Rights Division in the Justice Department, and a permanent Fair Employment Practices Commission. He called for federal action to prevent lynching, protect the right to vote, prohibit discrimination in public transportation, and strengthen existing civil rights statutes. Truman had scant success in gaining approval for his proposals, and by the time the convention neared, it appeared that he had succeeded only in losing the support of the South.

In the spring, Truman signed legislation that would implement the Marshall Plan, the program for the recovery of Western Europe, one of the signal triumphs of the Truman presidency—but one that in 1948 remained to be tested. The recognition of Israel in May and the implementation of the Berlin Airlift late in June likewise would reflect well on Truman's presidency years later. As the convention loomed in 1948, however, the State Department was still brooding over his rejection of its advice not to recognize Israel. The airlift took nearly a year to have its desired effect, and when the convention began it was only three weeks old.

The Republicans met in Philadelphia in June, exultant in their optimism. They nominated New York Governor Thomas E. Dewey, who had been the Republican nominee four years earlier, and named California Governor Earl Warren as his running mate. More liberal than most Republicans, Dewey was determined to stick to the issues. He had lost ground four years earlier when he attacked the Roosevelt administration. This time, his lead seemed so secure that he did not believe he would have to attack.

Long before the Democratic National Convention, it was clear that Truman would have problems holding his party together. White Southerners had warned him of their vehement opposition to his civil rights initiatives. To back off on civil rights, however, risked alienating Northern liberals, who had other reasons for disenchantment with Truman. Many of them believed that Truman was not a worthy successor to President Roosevelt. Old New Dealers considered Truman's domestic policy to be a pale shadow of FDR's program. Early in 1947, liberal Democrats formed the Americans for Democratic Action (ADA), which began searching for someone other than Truman to run. General Eisenhower became their favorite, but by the time Ike declined, it was too late to look elsewhere. Among liberals who faulted Truman's foreign policy, many began to rally behind Henry Wallace, who had been an outspoken critic of the administration's hard line against the Soviet Union. Wallace declared late in 1947 that he would run against Truman as an independent; in February 1948, the Progressive Citizens of America (PCA) nominated Wallace for the presidency.

When the Democrats assembled in Philadelphia on July 12, the party seemed determined to squelch what little chance it had to hold the presidency. Northern liberals and Southern conservatives clashed over civil rights. Although the White House had decided to wait until after the convention to take action on civil rights, the liberal wing of the party, led by Hubert Humphrey of Minnesota, forced through a civil rights plank that was even stronger than the one proposed by the president. Delegates from Alabama and Mississippi stormed out of the convention hall.

On July 15, the convention nominated Truman, but even at this high point, the Democrats seemed unable to put their house in order. First, Southerners refused to extend to Truman the usual courtesy of making the nomination unanimous. Then the evening's activities dragged on into the night, so late that Truman was not able to give his acceptance speech until the next morning at 2:00 A.M., long after most potential listeners had already gone to bed.

What Truman had to say was worth staying up to hear. He exploited the gulf between the Republican platform, which reflected Dewey's more liberal point of view, and congressional Republicans, who voted against programs similar to those offered in the platform. After cataloguing the differences, Truman threw down the gauntlet. "On the 26th day of July, which out in Missouri we call 'Turnip Day,' I am going to call Congress back and ask them to pass laws to halve rising prices, to meet the housing crisis—which they say they are for in their platform." Truman challenged Congress to make good on its platform promises, or tell the American people why it couldn't. When Congress did meet in special session, it lived down to Truman's expectations. On the campaign trail, Truman reveled in attacks on the "do-nothing" 80th Congress.

Southerners took a parting shot at Truman just before the convention ended, declaring formation of the States' Rights Party and nominating Governor Strom Thurmond of South Carolina for president. Although third-party challenges aren't unusual in American politics, the Democratic Party itself had now split into three parties, with Thurmond, Truman, and Wallace all as announced candidates. Seldom had a sitting president faced such a challenge from within his own party.

The campaign was unusual in yet another respect: the incumbent acted like the challenger, and the challenger like the incumbent. Dewey believed that he could only hurt himself by campaigning actively, that Truman couldn't overcome Dewey's apparently insurmountable lead. Few could argue with this strategy until it was too late. Dewey was neither well known nor well liked nationally, and he did have a tendency to hurt his own cause when he campaigned. But Truman had his own campaign liabilities. Not only was his party split; even those who supported him doubted he could win. He was not an effective speaker, although that shortcoming was more apparent when he read from a prepared text than when he spoke extemporaneously, and his advisors charted his campaign accordingly. He had a solid base, the coalition that Franklin Delano Roosevelt had fashioned in the thirties. If he could reach the core of that coalition and hold it, he could win.

In mid-September, Truman embarked on a vigorous campaign that carried him into 28 states. He traveled around the nation by train, stopping at every little whistle-stop—and hence the campaign acquired a theme. Speaking from the back platform of his train, the Ferdinand Magellan, the president seemed to gain strength from the people who turned out in increasing numbers to see him. The pugnacious fighter who wasn't afraid to go to the people was an attractive alternative to the cold, distant Dewey. Speaking extemporaneously, bolstered by a few well-chosen facts of local significance at each stop, Truman connected with his audience. He gained confidence as the campaign went on, giving three or four speeches each day, buoyed by small-town and rural America. Crowds didn't turn out to see has-beens, he reasoned. "Give 'em hell!" someone would invariably yell. "I just tell the truth, and they think it's hell," Truman would reply.

Truman held the key Democratic constituencies—farmers, labor, and African Americans. Truman even held the South; the Thurmond challenge there was weaker than anticipated, carrying only four states. Of the five most populous states, Dewey took only his home state of New York and neighboring Pennsylvania. Truman took California, Texas, and Illinois. He tallied nearly 50 percent of the popular votes, earning more than two million more votes than Dewey, and winning the electoral vote by a surprisingly wide margin of 303 to 189, with Thurmond picking up the remaining 39.

Pollsters failed to detect the late rise in Truman's support, for they had stopped polling. Confident in a Republican victory, the *Chicago Tribune* published an early edition trumpeting: "Dewey Defeats Truman," and setting up one of the most famous photographs in American political history when Truman held it aloft. "The people have put you in your place," cabled one of the president's supporters, the actress Tallulah Bankhead.

Recommended Reading

Readers should begin with the three exceptional biographies of the Truman, Robert H. Ferrell's *Harry S. Truman: A Life* (Columbia: University of Missouri Press, 1994), Alonzo L. Hamby's *Man of the People: A Life of Harry S. Truman* (New York: Oxford University Press, 1995), and David McCullough's Pulitzer Prize–winning *Truman* (New York: Simon and Schuster, 1992). Donald R. McCoy's *The Presidency of Harry S. Truman* (Lawrence: University Press of Kansas, 1984) is a fine one-volume examination of the Truman administration.

Literally dozens of books examine the origins of the Cold War, an area of scholarship that has engendered controversy since the late fifties. Thomas G. Paterson's *On Every Front*, revised edition (New York: Oxford University Press, 1992) is among the most accessible accounts. Two fine books that take a longer perspective on the changing relationship between the superpowers are Walter LaFeber's *American, Russia, and the Cold War*, 9th edition (New York: McGraw-Hill, 2002)and John Lewis Gaddis's *Russia, the Soviet Union, and the United States*, 2nd edition (New York: McGraw-Hill, 1990). Melvyn Leffler's *Preponderance of Power: National Security, the Truman Administration, and the Cold War* (Stanford, Calif.: Stanford University Press, 1992) and

Michael J. Hogan's *Cross of Iron: Harry S. Truman and the Origins of the National Security State* (Cambridge: Cambridge University Press, 1998) are scholarly works that subject Truman foreign policy to scrutiny. Arnold A. Offner's *Another Such Victory: President Truman and the Cold War, 1945–1953* (Stanford, Calif.: Stanford University Press, 2002) is particularly critical of Truman.

2

Fair Deal to Farewell

The Domestic Tribulations of Truman's Second Term

FOR PRESIDENT HARRY S. TRUMAN, the new decade began on January 20, 1949, with his inauguration for a second term. No longer merely the small man from Missouri filling the large shoes of Franklin D. Roosevelt, Truman was now fully president in his own right, reelected, heading his own administration. At the midpoint of the twentieth century, the inaugural united in symbolic ways the old and the new. Truman summoned the "old": the men of Battery D of the 129th Field Artillery Regiment, the unit that Truman commanded during World War I, came to march in the inaugural parade, swinging canes, jauntily marching behind their "Captain Harry." The "new" came unbidden: for the first time in history, an inaugural appeared on television. Politics, the news, and the nation would never be the same.

"The initiative is ours," Truman told the nation in his inaugural address. He had every reason to strike an optimistic note. Rejuvenated by his remarkable election victory the previous fall, the president faced an international situation calmer than at any other time in his presidency. He expected to be able to turn his attention to domestic policy. In his State of the Union address, delivered on January 4, Truman explained: "Our domestic programs are the foundation of our foreign policy." For the first time, he used the name "Fair Deal" to describe his domestic agenda—a name that linked his administration to that of his predecessor, yet also gave it a distinctive identity.

Although the name "Fair Deal" may have been new, the content of the program was not. Truman had first proposed most of his program in September 1945, when he listed twenty-one points he hoped to achieve. Republicans had successfully fended off most of the proposals, but their recalcitrance had backfired. Truman campaigned against the "do-nothing" 80th Congress, and had won the 1948 election by condemning Congress more than he criticized his opponent.

Truman called for a smorgasbord of domestic programs that he claimed would strengthen the economy, bring prosperity to farmers, conserve and develop natural resources, broaden social security coverage, repeal Taft-Hartley labor legislation, improve health care, provide adequate housing, and offer civil rights to all citizens. It was an ambitious agenda, and one that fared little better in Truman's second term than it had in his first. The 1948 victory had been narrow, and Truman could not claim a mandate. Powerful constituencies rallied against portions of his agenda, and he was unable to convert his 1948 electoral success into enacted programs.

Congress itself remained a considerable obstacle. Many in Congress resented Truman's vociferous criticism in 1948. Despite a Democratic majority in the House (263 to 171) and the Senate (54 to 42), the Democratic Party was not united behind its president. The South had bolted the party's convention in 1948 and nominated a "Dixiecrat" for president. The Solid South stood as a bloc against any civil rights bill, and its opposition spilled over into other issues. Southerners chaired key committees in both houses of Congress; leadership positions came to those with the most seniority, and since the South was virtually a one-party region, sitting members seldom had serious opposition in winning reelection.

The second term was difficult, of course, not only because of problems with Congress. As with many other presidents who saw themselves as reformers, foreign policy issues interfered with Truman's domestic plans. Before the end of 1949, the world situation had deteriorated once again with two dramatic developments. First, the Communist Chinese forces led by Mao Tsetung (pinyin: Mao Zedong) defeated the American-supported forces of Chiang Kai-shek (pinyin: Jiang Jieshi), forcing them to flee the mainland for the island of Formosa (Taiwan). Then in September, the Soviet Union successfully tested its first atomic bomb, breaking the American monopoly on the secret of atomic energy. A year later, the United States would be embroiled in another war, this time fighting Communists in Korea. With the emergence of what soon came to be known as "McCarthyism," Communism would also dominate the domestic scene in ways that no one could have anticipated.

The administration had not prepared the American public for Chiang's defeat. To answer Republican charges that the Democrats had "lost" China, the State Department issued a white paper, arguing that the outcome of the civil war was ultimately the product of internal developments in China, not of a failed American policy. Republicans remained unconvinced, and would continue to lambaste the administration until its last day in office. For some months, it appeared that the United States and China could nonetheless establish diplomatic relations. The prospect dimmed when Mao signed a treaty of alliance with the Soviet Union in February 1950, however, and collapsed altogether when China intervened against the United Nations forces in Korea in November.

The other seminal development of 1949 occurred in September, when the Soviet Union successfully tested an atomic bomb. On September 23, President Truman announced the startling development to the American public. For the preceding four years, since the summer of 1945, the United States had enjoyed a monopoly on both atomic energy and the atomic bomb. American military strategists knew that the Soviets would eventually develop a bomb, but most expected it would take them ten to fifteen years to do so, an expectation that had shaped early strategy in the Cold War. And even though sole possession of the bomb had seemed to give the United States a greater sense of security, Soviet policy seemed little affected by "atomic diplomacy."

Cold War Strategy: The H-Bomb and NSC-68

Even before the Soviet test, Truman had begun reevaluation of American atomic strategy, and had appointed a committee to recommend policies to him. The committee consisted of three top-ranking national security advisors, Secretary of State Dean Acheson, Secretary of Defense Louis Johnson, and Chairman of the Atomic Energy Commission David Lilienthal. Johnson was a cantankerous, arrogant, politically ambitious go-getter, whose efforts to push through Truman's proposed cuts in military spending earned him the enmity of many. Acheson and Lilienthal had worked together in the early Truman years on the internationalization of atomic energy.

Several problems related to atomic policy lay before the administration in 1949, some of them predating the Soviet acquisition of the bomb. Britain had begun working on its own bomb, and had been requesting information from the United States. The administration was divided on whether it should share atomic information, even with America's closest ally. The Joint Chiefs of Staff had requested additional funds to build more bombs, a request Truman had granted before. The shift toward reliance on the bomb, usually associated with Eisenhower, thus had its roots in the Truman administration. As diplomatic historian Melvyn Leffler suggested, "Comparatively, atomic weapons were cheap, and Truman accepted plans and approved budgets that made the United States dependent on their use should war erupt." Now, however, worried about budget growth, Truman questioned the policy. The Soviet bomb nudged the committee toward granting the request, with Acheson and Johnson advising in favor. Truman concurred, and between the summer of 1948 and the summer of 1950, the nation increased its atomic arsenal nearly sixfold, from about 50 bombs to nearly 300.

The Russian bomb also thrust another decision on the administration. The atomic bomb dropped on Hiroshima had used nuclear fission, the splitting of the atom, to create its destructive power. Scientists knew that a bomb employing nuclear fusion would be much more powerful, perhaps a hundred times more. Whether to develop a fusion, or hydrogen, bomb was a troublesome question. If the United States developed a hydrogen bomb, or "Super," as it came to be called, surely the Russians would be compelled to follow suit, and the threat of nuclear war would be much more terrifying. On the other hand, if the United States did not develop a hydrogen bomb, but the Soviets did—that was a much more horrifying prospect.

Truman turned to the Acheson-Lilienthal-Johnson committee once again for a recommendation. Some of the scientists involved in the Manhattan Project, which had developed the atomic bomb during World War II, had spoken out both against further expansion of the atomic arsenal and against development of the hydrogen bomb. Those who were willing to consider developing the H-bomb advised a cautious, gradual—rather than a crash—program, believing that if the United States showed restraint, the Russians might do so as well. J. Robert Oppenheimer, the lead scientist on the Manhattan Project, was the best known in this camp. Others, led by Edward Teller, another Manhattan Project veteran, advocated rapid development. The Atomic Energy Commission (AEC) was split, with Lilienthal urging caution, on the one hand, and outspoken commission member Lewis Strauss advocating rapid development, on the other. After an initial vote of 3–2 against, the commission finally voted 4–1 in favor of development.

When Truman's advisory committee came together, Acheson and Johnson urged immediate development, and Lilienthal again found himself in the minority. He decided to support his colleagues, and the committee's report endorsed going forward. When they met with Truman on January 31, the president made clear that his principal consideration was whether the Russians could build an H-bomb. All three committee members agreed that they could. That was enough for Truman. He decreed that the United States would go forward with the Super. Years later, information became available that demonstrated that Soviet physicist Andrei Sakharov was already at work on a Russian H-bomb at the time of Truman's decision.

On the same day that Truman ordered the development of the H-bomb, he directed the State and Defense Departments to undertake a study of American defense strategy in light of the evidence of Soviet atomic capability. Several factors stimulated the president to commission the review, the most immediate of which were the Soviet atomic test and the Communist victory in China. Truman's defense budget was another factor.

The military had subjected Truman's budget goals to intense criticism, and by early 1950, the public was beginning to echo what the Defense Department had been saying for some time. Truman believed in a balanced budget, and in an effort to achieve that goal he had been seeking to trim defense spending. The services requested a $20 billion budget for fiscal year 1951, but the administration trimmed it to $13.5 billion. The military services argued that such a stringent limit would cripple national security. The new military structure, created after World War II, complicated the defense budget, since the establishment of the Air Force meant that defense appropriations now had to be split three ways, between the Army, Navy, and Air Force. The Air Force received the lion's share of the budget, especially because strategists believed that long-range bombers were essential as delivery systems for the atomic bomb, and thus vital to American defense. By early 1950, even members of Truman's inner circle, including Secretary of State Acheson and special counsel Charles Murphy, were beginning to push for larger defense budgets. Another important change was the promotion of Leon Keyserling to the chair of the Council of Economic Advisors. Unlike his predecessor Edwin Nourse, whose conservative economic philosophy was actually closer to Truman's, Keyserling believed that military spending would fuel general economic expansion. And Keyserling was able to win the confidence of the president, as Nourse never had.

Thus the study Truman commissioned early in 1950 gave the administration a chance to take a fresh look at the nation's Cold War strategy. The National Security Council provided a forum for the study, and a means to provide input from both State and Defense. The report, which came to the president's desk in April, became known as "NSC-68," one of a series of consecutively numbered reports. Its principal author was Paul Nitze, who had been working as George Kennan's assistant on the State Department's Policy Planning Staff.

NSC-68 accepted the premise that the Soviet Union posed an extraordinary threat, so serious that within four or five years it might possess the power to inflict massive destruction on the United States in a surprise atomic attack. The document viewed competition with the Soviet Union in apocalyptic terms, claiming that the issues involved "the fulfillment or destruction not only of this Republic but of civilization itself." It described the Soviet Union as "animated by a new fanatic faith, antithetical to our own, [which] seeks to impose its absolute authority over the rest of the world." Given the gravity of the threat, the American defense system was "dangerously inadequate."

To meet the Soviet threat, NSC-68 urged that America embark on a "rapid and sustained build-up of the political, economic, and military strength of the free world." The United States would have to increase its defense spending fourfold, reduce its nondefense spending, and increase taxes to pay for military expansion. Military budgets would have to increase, as would military and economic assistance programs abroad, covert operations, and internal security and civil defense programs.

The president found NSC-68 disturbing, but not convincing. He still expected to hold the line on defense spending. Before long, however, events carried the debate in a new direction. Two-and-a-half months after Truman received NSC-68, North Korea crossed the 38th parallel, initiating the Korean War. Increases in defense spending approximated those recommended in NSC-68.

Foul Weather for the Fair Deal

To its critics, the Fair Deal seemed a faint echo of the New Deal, and Truman's program did have many inherent problems that gave substance to criticism. As the nation entered a period of prolonged prosperity, the social concerns that prompted the Fair Deal seemed less compelling than had New Deal programs during the Great Depression, when the American people were much more tolerant of experimentation. President Roosevelt had been willing to engage in Keynesian economics and the deficit spending that this approach entailed. Truman, however, fervently believed that you could not spend money that you did not have. Leon Keyserling, a member of the Council of Economic Advisors and its chair after the spring of 1950, worked tirelessly to convince Truman that an expanding economy allowed the luxury of increased federal spending. Such spending, Keyserling insisted, would push the economy to continue expanding, making every slice of the economic pie larger. Truman wasn't deaf to Keyserling's entreaties, but he still wanted to balance the budget. A balanced budget, however, left less money to finance Fair Deal programs.

Key Fair Deal programs ran into strong opposition. Much of the attention paid to the Fair Deal focused on civil rights. Truman knew well that his proposals would face the opposition of the white South, but resistance also came from other quarters. Even executive orders, which had the advantage of circumventing Congress, had little impact unless the administration monitored them closely. In July 1948, Truman issued Executive Order no. 9981, which mandated an end to segregation in the armed forces, and appointed a committee chaired by former Solicitor General Charles H. Fahy to oversee its implementation. Opposition rose in all services, but it was especially strong in the Army. General Omar Bradley was one of the most outspoken critics, arguing that the Army should not be used to conduct social experiments. Not until the Korean War, when battlefield casualties made it difficult to maintain racial separation, did the Army begin to make meaningful progress.

Another civil rights proposal, to make the Fair Employment Practices Commission (FEPC) permanent, foundered in Congress. First initiated during World War II, the FEPC had a spotty record. Congressional opponents had weakened it by denying adequate funding. Truman wanted to make it permanent, and ensure the funding necessary to make it effective. Instead, he provided a platform for Southern congressmen to rant and rave, and score points among segregationists back home in the process. The FEPC would not win approval until the sixties, when President Lyndon Johnson shepherded it through Congress.

Another cornerstone of the Fair Deal was its support for health care legislation. Here the administration ran into another non-congressional opponent, the powerful American Medical Association (AMA). Truman called for more medical facilities, both to expand health care and to train new physicians, dentists, and nurses. The most controversial part of his proposal centered on a plan for national health insurance. The AMA attacked the plan as "socialized medicine." Despite a strong counterattack by the administration, spearheaded by Federal Security Administrator Oscar Ewing, Congress defeated the proposal, and granted only a small appropriation for building more hospitals.

Presidential Popularity: Truman's Downward Drift

Truman entitled the second volume of his memoirs *Years of Trial and Hope*. In his second term, trials predominated over hopes. Three issues emerged in 1950 that would plague his administration until its last day. The Republicans would exploit all three as their major campaign themes to great effect in 1952. Two of the issues, McCarthyism and the Korean War, became so large that they merit extended treatment in this book. McCarthyism is usually dated from February 9, when the Wisconsin senator spoke in Wheeling, West Virginia; the Korean War, from June 25, when the North Koreans crossed the 38th parallel and invaded South Korea.

The third issue, a series of scandals infecting several federal agencies and individuals with connections to the president, became known in 1952 as the "mess in Washington." Even his harshest critics never accused President Truman of personal involvement in the scandals, but they did accuse him of failing to respond to the allegations, of misplaced loyalty to undeserving subordinates, of protecting cronies, and of creating an environment in which corruption could flourish.

The first of the scandals began to emerge in 1949. At the center of the controversy was the president's military aide, Major General Harry H. Vaughan. Vaughan had known the president since the early 1920s. Truman kept him around because he enjoyed Vaughan's sense of humor and storytelling ability, but the president never gave him any authority over policy. The general unfortunately had no sense of political propriety, and stumbled into embarrassing situations on more than one occasion. In 1949, the Republicans accused Vaughan of accepting the gift of a deep freezer from individuals seeking favors from the highly placed general. In August, the Senate's Investigations Subcommittee held hearings to determine whether alleged influence peddlers know as "five-percenters" had sold their influence for a 5 percent kickback on government business they arranged. Vaughan, Republicans charged, provided access. His accusers could never prove that Vaughan had done anything illegal, but his name was sullied. Truman suffered because he refused to dismiss a subordinate whose name was under suspicion. The deep freezer became a convenient and memorable symbol of corruption.

In February 1950, a Senate subcommittee chaired by Senator J. William Fulbright (Democrat-Arkansas) opened an investigation of the Reconstruction Finance Corporation (RFC), an agency founded in 1932 to assist railroads, banks, and other businesses in recovering from the Depression. In the postwar period, however, the RFC had been exploited as an irresistible cash cow. According to the subcommittee's provocatively entitled report, "Favoritism and Influence," administration officials pressured RFC directors into making questionable loans to favored companies.

By the fall of 1950, Truman's popularity entered a slide from which it would never recover. As the election neared, attacks came from many quarters. The Republicans had discovered the political effectiveness of the anti-Communism issue, and used it to bludgeon the administration. Campaigning against the president's national health insurance plan, the American Medical Association pointed to the administration's "totalitarian tendencies." Farmers, usually staunch Democrats, found fault with the Brannan Plan, which provided for price supports at 90 percent of parity. When Truman traveled to Wake Island to confer with General MacArthur over developments in Korea, his critics claimed he had made the trip only to enhance his own stature in the reflected glow of the great general.

Less than a week before the election, two Puerto Rican nationalists tried to assassinate Truman. The Trumans were residing in Blair House while the White House underwent renovation. The president was napping on the second floor when he heard a commotion in the street below. He looked out the window, and his guards shooed him back as they suppressed the attackers. One of the potential assassins and a guard died from wounds inflicted in the scuffle, and two other guards and the other attacker also suffered injuries. No shots came close to the president, but he was deeply disturbed that the guard Leslie Coffelt had died defending him.

The election was another political setback. Off-year elections—which is to say elections that fall midway between presidential elections—often exhibit some decline in support for the president's party. Truman experienced a setback that exceeded the norm. Just two years after his stunning 1948 victory, Truman's political capital had slipped to the point that Democrats were reluctant to have the president speak on their behalf. Truman, whose energies were being sapped by the war in Korea in any case, did little campaigning. Three days before the election, he spoke on a national radio and television broadcast, and accused the Republicans of "having been taken over by special interests." Any farmer who voted for the Republicans "ought to have his head examined." Democrats were able to hold on to their majorities in both houses of Congress, but they lost ground. Republicans picked up 5 seats in the Senate, and 28 in the House, and positioned themselves for further gains two years hence.

Truman's popularity continued to slide after the election. In 1951, another scandal emerged, this time in the Bureau of Internal Revenue (BIR), forerunner of the Internal Revenue Service. An investigation revealed corruption that included embezzlement, bribery, and willingness on the part of officials to use their positions to obtain business for private activities. Corruption was widespread, and reached into districts from San Francisco to Saint Louis to New York. The investigation led to the dismissal of several collectors, and forced the firing of an assistant attorney general and the chief counsel for the BIR. To make matters worse for the administration, the Department of Justice bungled its part of the investigation, and Attorney General J. Howard McGrath had to resign.

Seizure of the Steel Mills

A crisis of a different sort loomed in the fall of 1951, as steelworkers and big steel executives headed for a showdown over wages. Steel was the dominant industry in the nation; whatever decision came out of the dispute would affect other industries. A series of wage increases would trigger inflation and threaten the stability of national price controls that had been in effect since the beginning of the year. The war in Korea magnified the importance of the dispute and demanded presidential attention, since the Defense Department claimed that a steel strike would have disastrous implications for national security. With a presidential election less than a year away, the controversy took on political significance. The steel executives were Republicans. The head of the United Steelworkers of America, Philip Murray, had supported Truman in 1948 and remained a political ally. He also presided over the Congress of Industrial Organizations (CIO), and members of his union were firmly in the Democratic camp.

Truman wanted to avoid a strike if it was at all possible. Before the end of the year and the expiration of the contract, Truman asked the Wage Stabilization Board on December 22 to consider the dispute. He directed management and the union to continue work under the existing contract until resolution of the dispute. Three months later, on March 20, the Wage Stabilization Board voted a substantial raise—approximately 26 cents per hour. Management quickly responded by demanding a compensatory increase in the price of steel. Existing law allowed the companies to institute an immediate increase of two to three dollars per ton, and the companies asked for an additional nine or ten dollars per ton.

The president's alternatives were limited. To invoke the Taft-Hartley Act, which would have mandated an 80-day cooling-off period, was politically unacceptable. It would have the appearance and effect of punishing the union, which after all had been working without a contract since the end of the year. Furthermore, the Republicans would have delighted in the prospect of the president who had vetoed Taft-Hartley (only to have the veto overridden) invoking it against a union that had supported him—particularly six months before an election.

Truman decided instead to seize the steel mills. He presented his case to Congress, but Congress refused to concur, thus suggesting that the seizure lacked statutory authority. He had no direct legal authority, but he believed that his powers as president and commander in chief were sufficient to justify the action. He first consulted Chief Justice Fred Vinson, who reassured the president that the Court would likely back him. Then, on April 8, he directed Secretary of Commerce Charles Sawyer to supervise the seizure. In practice, the action was less onerous than it might have been. Sawyer, a conservative, was the cabinet member least likely to seem threatening to the steel companies, and Truman directed him only to keep two duplicate sets of books—one for Sawyer and one for themselves—during the strike. The president ordered that labor and management begin negotiations in Washington.

The companies filed suit, and the case headed toward the Supreme Court's docket. The federal district court ruled against the president, and the administration appealed. The Supreme Court agreed to hear the case immediately. The Court heard arguments on May 12 and 13 in *Youngstown Sheet & Tube Co. v. Sawyer.* Despite Vinson's earlier reassurances, the June 2 decision went against the president by a 6–3 vote. Only Stanley Reed and two Truman appointees, Vinson and Sherman Minton, supported the president's position.

Most disappointing to Truman was Tom Clark's opposition vote, for Clark was also a Truman appointee. The president had earlier indicated that he would accept the Court's ruling, saying, "I have no ambition to be a dictator."

McCarthyism

Anti-Communism has deep roots in the American past. Late in the nineteenth century, opposition to class-based reform flourished, tinged with political activity that was at once antiunion, antiradical, and anti-immigrant. The government and big business staged a concerted effort to rid the nation of such threats as socialism, anarchism, and the radical labor union Industrial Workers of the World (IWW), also known as the "Wobblies." Repressive legislation, particularly the Espionage Act and the Sedition Act, enabled the government to restrict radical activity during World War I.

Russia's Bolshevik Revolution of 1917 made Communism appear even more ominous after the war, when widespread strikes exacerbated the sense of danger, and the Wilson administration took advantage of the mood to attack radicals in a campaign soon to be known simply as the "Red Scare" of 1919–20. Attorney General A. Mitchell Palmer's Big Red Roundup of January 1, 1920, led to the arrest of hundreds of radicals, and the deportation of scores.

The Great Depression revived fears of Communism, and indeed many Americans dabbled in leftist politics during the 1930s, joining the Communist Party or leftist organizations. Critics of the New Deal accused the Roosevelt reform program of encouraging Communistic ideas. The American Federation of Labor (AFL) accused its new rival, the CIO, of being a haven for Communists. Congressman Martin Dies (Democrat-Texas) exploited the allegations of leftist influence in the New Deal when he requested and received support to establish the House Un-American Activities Committee (HUAC) in 1938. Better known by its acronym, the committee developed many of the tactics of witness intimidation later fine-tuned by Senator Joseph R. McCarthy (Democrat-Wisconsin). For its part, the Communist Party of the United States (CPUSA) pressed for support among unskilled workers and minorities; it garnered favorable publicity by championing causes such as that of the Scottsboro Boys, young African Americans charged with raping white women in Alabama.

Events of the late 1930s, particularly the Stalinist purges and the Nonaggression Pact of August 1939 between the Soviet Union and Nazi Germany, disillusioned many CPUSA members and led many more Americans outside the Party to distrust the Soviets, a distrust that persisted even after Hitler invaded the Soviet Union, and the Soviets sided with Britain against Nazi Germany. Many would have agreed with then Senator Harry S. Truman's comment: "If we see that Germany is winning, we should help Russia, and if Russia is winning we ought to help Germany."

The Smith Act, passed in 1940, provided the World War II equivalent of the repressive legislation of the World War I era. It tapped American nativist tendencies, requiring resident aliens to register and have their fingerprints taken. It also provided the legal backing for a new Red Scare, outlawing groups that would teach or advocate the overthrow of the United States government.

By the time that McCarthy began to preach the gospel of anti-Communism, he was not exploring new terrain. Others had preceded him, and many of them were still active. Laws and apparatus were already in place. The atmosphere was already thick with distrust of the Soviet Union and of the international Communist movement. Once McCarthy discovered the issue, he had well-worn paths to follow and plenty of allies to accompany him on his journey.

Background to McCarthyism: The House Un-American Activities Committee and the Hollywood Ten

Long before McCarthy's name became linked with anti-Communist hysteria, Hollywood had been infected with the virus. Hollywood was an attractive target for Washington's anti-Communist crusaders for several reasons. First, Communism had been appealing to intellectuals and people in the arts in the days of the Great Depression, and many had been affiliated either with the Party or groups later condemned as front organizations. One estimate suggested that perhaps 300 directors, actors, writers, and designers had joined the Party, although by the late forties most had long since cut their ties. Most who rejected the Party had been disillusioned either by their personal experiences, or by Stalin's actions—purges of Party members and the nonaggression pact with Hitler—that exposed his regime as something less than a noble experiment. Another reason Hollywood was ideal for an investigation was the high degree of public recognition of the industry, which brought attention to the investigators as well as their subjects. Some historians have suggested that anti-Semitism may have been another motivating factor, since a disproportionate number of the targets of the investigation were Jews.

Washington's most prominent Red hunters in the 1940s sat on the HUAC. The committee, chaired by J. Parnell Thomas, launched its most famous investigation in September 1947, when it summoned forty-one prominent members of the film industry. Of these, nineteen were hostile or "unfriendly" witnesses, and thirteen of those were Jews. The committee eventually called ten of them to testify, and they soon became known as the "Hollywood Ten," or simply the "Ten." Eight of the Ten were screenwriters (Lester Cole, Alvah Bessie, Ring Lardner Jr., John Howard Lawson, Albert Maltz, Samuel Ornitz, Adrian Scott, and Dalton Trumbo), and the other two were directors (Herbert Biberman and Edward Dmytryk). The "friendly" witnesses, who testified on behalf of the committee's investigation, included Ronald Reagan, who was then the president of the Screen Actors Guild, and George Murphy, who later served as a senator from California. The committee's hearings developed into shouting matches, with the Ten refusing to cooperate in any way, and the committee often cutting them off in mid-sentence. The Ten refused to answer questions, invoking the freedom of speech provision of the First Amendment, rather than the protection from self-incrimination provision of the Fifth Amendment, but the tactic failed. Convicted of contempt of Congress, all served from six months to a year in prison.

Many of the prominent names in Hollywood, including directors John Huston and William Wyler and actors Humphrey Bogart, Gene Kelly, and Lauren Bacall, came out in defense of the Ten. They established the Committee for the First Amendment (CFA), and sponsored a series of radio broadcasts entitled *Hollywood Fights Back*. The HUAC had enormous power to intimidate, however, and the counterattack withered as CFA members backed off under intense pressure. Had they not retreated, their careers, too, would likely have suffered.

Studio heads also caved in to the HUAC, establishing a blacklist that prevented individuals singled out by the committee from getting jobs in the industry. The blacklist ruined careers. Some screenwriters were able to evade its terrors by writing under assumed names, and Dalton Trumbo even won a 1957 Academy Award for *The Brave One*, a screenplay he wrote under an assumed name while blacklisted. Actors had no such opportunity—their recognizable faces were their stock-in-trade, and they had no way to circumvent the HUAC's censure.

The HUAC called new witnesses in 1951, and the cycle began once again. The committee developed what critic Victor Navasky called a "Degradation Ceremony," in which those called to testify could escape censure by naming names—offering others in their stead. Some rationalized "naming names" by naming only people who had been named by others, but people who were named frequently became particular targets. Those called before the committee thus had three options, all unattractive: they could claim the protection of the First Amendment, and risk going to jail; they could cite the Fifth Amendment and refuse to testify, and risk losing their jobs; or they could name names. The insidious process destroyed the creative energy of Hollywood for years, as friends turned on friends. Some recanted their earlier refusal to name names. Edward Dmytryk, director of *The Caine Mutiny* and one of the original Hollywood Ten, was one who did so, claiming loyalty to the United States since leaving the Party in 1945. Elia Kazan, who directed *On the Waterfront*, an examination of the fate of a stool pigeon who named the names of corrupt union bosses, himself recanted and named names. He explained his actions in a quarter-page ad in the *New York Times*.

Ultimately, the blacklist claimed some 250 victims. A select few, like Dalton Trumbo, were able to find work in Hollywood anyway, but more commonly victims were unable to work again in the film industry. Blacklisting collapsed in the early sixties, but by then it had spread its impact far beyond Hollywood. It contributed to the sense of paranoia that poisoned American society in the fifties, served as an example to other industries that adopted their own codes, and gave an aura of legitimacy to McCarthy and other Red-baiters.

The Truman Loyalty Program

The Truman administration contributed to the growing fear of a Communist threat at home by establishing a federal loyalty program. At first wanting no part of it, Truman rebuffed recommendations from his attorney general in mid-1946. But the president's own policies had contributed to the atmosphere that led to the program's creation. It was difficult for him to portray the international threat of Communism in dire terms and yet soft-pedal the domestic threat. So, in March 1947, four months after the Republican victory in the congressional elections of the year before, Truman issued Executive Order no. 9835, establishing a Loyalty Review Board empowered to dismiss federal employees suspected on "reasonable grounds" of disloyalty or subversion. Truman tried to ensure that those suspected would have the right to legal representation. After the outbreak of the Korean War, however, the program became more repressive, with the Loyalty Review Board adopting new procedures to enhance its authority, the Federal Bureau of Investigation (FBI) energetically pursuing its investigations, and the administration wanting to demonstrate its own resolve in the fight against Communism at home. Some three million federal employees were cleared; of those suspected, 212 people were dismissed and several hundred others resigned. Not surprisingly, Truman preferred to emphasize the number of people cleared rather than the number dismissed.

The Spy Cases: Alger Hiss and the Rosenbergs

Alger Hiss was a rising star in the State Department when he became the target of charges that he had been a member of the Communist Party. Hiss had earned a law degree at Harvard, clerked for Justice Oliver Wendell Holmes Jr., and practiced law for three years before serving brief stints in the Departments of Agriculture and Justice in the early years of the New Deal. He moved to the State Department in 1936. In 1945, he was a member of President Roosevelt's delegation to the Yalta Conference, and then served as the temporary secretary general of the United Nations during its founding sessions in San Francisco in 1945.

In 1948, Whittaker Chambers, a former editor at *Time* and an admitted former Communist, named Hiss as a member of the Communist Party during the 1930s who had provided copies of State Department documents to be forwarded to the Soviets. When Chambers made his allegations before the HUAC, powerful supporters, including Dean Acheson, spoke out in defense of Hiss. When he testified, Hiss was polished, articulate, and persuasive. Chambers himself was a less-than-convincing witness; for a time, it appeared that the committee would drop its investigation.

But a young congressman from California, Richard Nixon, doggedly pursued the evidence provided by Chambers. Nixon had already acquired a reputation as a staunch anti-Communist. He had defeated five-time Congressman Jerry Voorhis (Democrat-California) in 1946, in part by linking Voorhis to the Political Action Committee of the CIO, which had endorsed the incumbent, and allegedly had Communist ties. Nixon was a member of the HUAC, although he hadn't taken part in the hearings on Communism in Hollywood. The case had moments of melodrama, none more sensational than a trip to a Maryland pumpkin patch to recover microdot copies of documents that Hiss had allegedly passed to the Soviets. Nixon prodded Hiss, and got him to admit that he had known Chambers in the thirties, which seemed to lend credence to Chambers's allegations after all. Because the statute of limitations had expired, Hiss couldn't be tried for espionage. A New York grand jury indicted him for perjury in December 1948. Although his first trial resulted in a hung jury, his second, in 1950, convicted him. After exhausting his appeals, he continued to insist on his innocence until his death more than forty years later. Nixon emerged as a national figure, using the visibility he had acquired from the Hiss case to run successfully for the Senate in 1950.

The most spectacular of the spy cases also emerged in 1950, when the Justice Department leveled charges of espionage against Julius and Ethel Rosenberg for allegedly passing atomic secrets to the Soviet Union. The Rosenberg case emanated from the case of Klaus Fuchs, a British physicist who had worked in Los Alamos, New Mexico, on the Manhattan Project that developed the atomic bomb. Fuchs confessed in a British court that he had given information to the Soviets, and that his messenger had been an American chemist named Harry Gold. When the Fuchs story came out in Britain, a low-level machinist at Los Alamos named David Greenglass fell under suspicion. Greenglass in turn implicated his sister and her husband, Ethel and Julius Rosenberg.

According to the government's case against the Rosenbergs, Julius was part of a spy ring centered in Schenectady, New York, and had recruited Greenglass to help pass information about the bomb to the Soviet Union. The Rosenbergs allegedly believed that if the Soviet Union had the bomb, it would check the American atomic monopoly, ensuring that neither power would use the bomb. According to government prosecutors, Greenglass, who worked in the Los Alamos lab that fabricated lenses used in the bomb, passed to the Rosenbergs a sketch of a cross section of the bomb. The sketch, on the back of a Jello box, became a key piece of evidence. The trial began on March 6, 1951. Late in April, the jury found them guilty of conspiracy to commit espionage. Absent any recommendation from the jury, Judge Irving Kaufman sentenced both defendants to death, and had them transferred to Sing Sing prison in New York to await their fate.

The trial was plagued by irregularities. Although defense attorney Emanuel Bloch was a dedicated and well-meaning defender, who looked after the Rosenberg's two young sons while their parents were incarcerated, he made serious tactical errors. By simply accepting the government's case against Gold and Greenglass, he closed off a possible avenue of defense, for that case was based on a series of questionable actions. The government tried the Rosenbergs under the terms of the Espionage Act of 1917, which applied to dealings with enemies, whereas the Rosenbergs allegedly had passed information to an ally. The evidence against Ethel Rosenberg in particular doesn't seem to have warranted the death penalty, and it appears that the government used the threat of her impending execution to attempt to extract a confession from Julius. Several actions by Judge Irving Kaufman indicate his lack of impartiality; one of the more egregious was his conferring with prosecution lawyers during the trial about seeking the death penalty.

Doubts persisted about the guilt of the Rosenbergs, the conduct of the trial, and the attitude of the judge. The Rosenbergs continued to proclaim their innocence. International protests rose against their sentence. Even Pope Pius XII, an ardent anti-Communist, appealed for clemency. In the United States, people staged demonstrations for and against the condemned couple. Defense attorneys filed appeals, and the Circuit Court upheld the conviction. The Supreme Court twice refused to review the case. Because the time between conviction and execution straddled the terms of Presidents Truman and Eisenhower, both had an opportunity to grant clemency, and both refused. The best evidence indicates that Julius was indeed guilty, but that Ethel, while complicit, did not deserve the death penalty. On the evening of June 19, 1953, Julius Rosenberg went to the electric chair, to be followed a few minutes later by his wife. They became the first civilians in American history executed for espionage committed during wartime.

McCarthy: From Appleton to Wheeling

When the new decade began, Senator Joseph R. McCarthy, a Wisconsin Republican, had a rather undistinguished career. Known by his colleagues more for his brusque manner than for his legislative record, he showed scant regard for the normal courtesies of the Senate. An Irish Catholic from Appleton, he graduated from Marquette University and served as a circuit court judge in Wisconsin's tenth district in the late 1930s. He enlisted in the

Marines and served in the South Pacific during World War II. His military service later generated controversy when he greatly exaggerated his exploits and solicited undeserved commendations. He created the persona of "Tail Gunner Joe," claiming a record for the most ammunition expended by a tail gunner—a performance marred by the absence of any enemy targets in the vicinity at the time. While he was still in the Marines, he ran against Senator Alexander Wiley in the 1944 Republican primary, and lost. Two years later, he challenged Robert LaFollette for the Republican nomination for the Senate. LaFollette was the son of "Fighting Bob" LaFollette, one of the founders of the Progressive Movement and a nationally respected reformer. The younger LaFollette had served in the Senate since 1925. The LaFollette name had lost much of its magic, and many of his former Progressive supporters would not forgive him for joining the Republican Party. McCarthy won the primary, and then the general election.

Before he discovered its impact at the national level, McCarthy showed his willingness to use Red-baiting in his home state of Wisconsin, where his most persistent critic was the editor of the Madison *Capital Times*. Cedric Parker had been involved in Communist front organizations years earlier, but his paper was anti-Communist down the line. Yet McCarthy called him a "known Communist," and compared the paper with the *Daily Worker*. However groundless, the charges undercut Parker's criticism of McCarthy, who learned how effective a little hyperbole could be.

McCarthy stepped into the national spotlight on February 9, 1950, when he addressed a Republican women's club in Wheeling, West Virginia. Alger Hiss's perjury conviction had come just two-and-a-half weeks earlier, and the anti-Communist issue made good copy, although even McCarthy could not have imagined how good. He told his audience that he had a list of 205 Communists in the State Department, people whose names were known to the secretary of state. Not only did McCarthy have no list, but he revised the number of alleged Communists in later weeks to 57, then to 81, and, when pressed, claimed that the number 205 applied only to "bad security risks." The story took time to gather steam, but as McCarthy traveled on, first to Salt Lake City and then to Reno, he repeated his charges—and the press began to pay attention.

On February 20, just eleven days after Wheeling, McCarthy defended his charges on the floor of the Senate. He gave fragmentary information regarding 81 alleged security risks. His "perfectly reckless performance"—in the words of the recognized leader of the Republican Party, Senator Robert Taft—began with only about a dozen senators in the chamber. McCarthy ranted for nearly eight hours. Senators voted down a motion to recess, and the session continued until almost midnight. Observers noted that it was clear that McCarthy was reading some of his notes for the first time. Fumbling through disorganized files, he misrepresented cases and overstated the findings of security investigations. Democrats tried to counter his charges, but with no prior warning and no information before them, there was little they could do. Critics accused McCarthy of taking refuge in the Senate chamber, where he was immune from charges of slander. The senator claimed he would make no charge on the Senate floor he would not make elsewhere, a claim that proved false.

On March 8, a subcommittee of the Senate Foreign Relations Committee chaired by Senator Millard Tydings (Democrat-Maryland) held a hearing on McCarthy's charges. Tydings went on the attack from the moment his gavel came down. Since witnesses usually were given a chance to present their position before being questioned, Republicans cried foul. Ultimately, Tydings denounced McCarthy in the strongest possible terms, but the hearings became bitterly partisan, blunting the edge of Tydings's remarks. That fall, McCarthy played a decisive role in defeating him at the polls.

The "China Hands" and Owen Lattimore

It was no coincidence that McCarthy selected the State Department for his first assault. The State Department came under vicious attacks from Republicans after Communist forces under Mao Tse-tung defeated the Nationalist Chinese forces of Chiang Kai-shek in 1949, and forced him to flee to Formosa. The so-called China Lobby, a group composed principally of Republicans and including Henry Luce, the influential publisher of *Time* magazine, had long advocated strong support of Chiang. They blamed the Truman administration for failing to increase American support when Chiang's regime tottered in its final days, and directed most of their criticism against Secretary of State Dean Acheson and a group of experts on China in the State Department who became known as the "China hands." The China hands had warned of corruption within Chiang's government, and predicted his defeat by Communist forces. Republicans blamed them for contributing to the fall of Chiang by accusing him of corruption and lack of public support and by convincing the administration he was not worth propping up any longer. Acheson, whose Eastern establishment background and imperious manner aggravated Republicans anyway, became a particular target after the publication of a State Department white paper defending the administration's policy at the time of the "loss" of China. The paper argued that Chiang had sown the seeds of his own defeat, and that there was little the United States could have done to salvage a regime that was collapsing from within. The China hands became victims of their own expertise.

Republicans accused six China experts of having Communist leanings. In the course of their careers, all had all been critical of Chiang's regime, and because of the nature of their duties, had come in contact with Communists or organizations that were either sympathetic to the Communists or critical of Chiang. Ambassador-at-Large Philip C. Jessup became one of the first people McCarthy singled out by name; the former Columbia University professor, he asserted, had "an unusual affinity for Communist causes." Jessup had served on the board of directors of the Institute of Pacific Relations (IPR), a research think tank that conservatives alleged had peddled Communist propaganda. The charges against Jessup were tenuous at best, a case of guilt by association and of retribution for criticizing Chiang in the IPR's journal. Both General George C. Marshall and General Eisenhower, then president of Columbia University, gave Jessup glowing character references. Even after the Tydings committee cleared Jessup, McCarthy and other conservative senators kept after him. Truman and Acheson defended him, and Jessup continued in diplomatic positions until late 1952, when he left of his own accord.

Others of the China hands weren't as fortunate. Subjected to five loyalty investigations, John Stuart Service had to resign, as did O. Edmund Clubb, John Paton Davies, and John Carter Vincent, who all suffered damage to their reputations. The case of Owen Lattimore was more complex. Director of the Walter Hines Page School of International Relations at Johns Hopkins University, Lattimore was another veteran of the IPR, and another of the China hands who had criticized Chiang and called for a flexible policy in Asia. McCarthy labeled Lattimore the "top Russian espionage agent in the United States," and upped the ante by declaring, "I am willing to stand or fall on this one." Lattimore appeared before the Tydings committee, where two admitted former Communists testified against him. Lattimore dismissed their allegations as lies, and the committee's final report absolved him of guilt, while acknowledging that he had ties to the political left. In 1951, Senator Patrick

McCarran (Democrat-Nevada) summoned Lattimore before his Senate Internal Security Subcommittee. McCarran, the most conservative non-Southern Democratic senator and a Red-baiter to rival McCarthy, concluded that Lattimore was part of a Soviet conspiracy, and recommended that he be indicted for perjury. A grand jury indicted Lattimore, but after three years of legal maneuvering, a judge dismissed some of the charges; the Justice Department, the rest. Johns Hopkins offered Lattimore his job back. He returned briefly, and later took a position on the faculty of Leeds University in England.

As McCarthy's impact began to register, McCarran was not the only fellow senator to contribute to the growing hysteria. Even Senator Robert Taft, the most influential Republican senator, was torn between despising McCarthy's methods and recognizing his appeal to voters. Taft ridiculed McCarthy's charges, but told McCarthy to keep pushing, and that if one case failed he should try another. Other senators had no reservations, and became allies. Among them, Senate Minority Leader Kenneth Wherry (Republican-Nebraska) was the most prominent. Senators William Jenner, Karl Mundt, and Owen Brewster joined those whose support for McCarthy was unambiguous.

McCarran and the Internal Security Act

Next to McCarthy, however, the most effective practitioner of the politics of anti-Communism was Senator Pat McCarran of Nevada. A Democrat first elected to the Senate in the Roosevelt landslide of 1932, he nevertheless became a conservative opponent of the New Deal. By the fifties, he was a leader of the conservative coalition that included Democrats and Republicans who endeavored to pass anti-Communist bills. McCarthy's allegations and the Korean War made Congress receptive to anti-Communist legislation, and McCarran seized the opportunity. Senators and representatives introduced dozens of such bills in 1950 alone. McCarran's proposal sought to force Communist organizations to register, to strengthen espionage laws, and to restrict immigration and naturalization. It called for the creation of a Subversive Activities Control Board, which would monitor the actions of registered organizations. Liberal Democrats, seeking to limit McCarran's bill, introduced an alternative that outdid McCarran in certain respects, such as allowing for detention camps similar to those used to imprison Japanese Americans during World War II. The attempt failed utterly, for instead of being diverted, McCarran simply added the stiff provisions to his own bill.

The tenor of the times made it risky to oppose McCarran's bill, and on September 20, 1950, it passed overwhelmingly in both houses of Congress, 312 to 20 in the House, and 51 to 7 in the Senate. Two days later, President Truman submitted a long message vetoing the legislation, which he argued would not accomplish its purpose and actually undermine internal security. "We will destroy all that we seek to preserve," he insisted, "if we sacrifice the liberties of our citizens in a misguided attempt to achieve national security." His statement served only to stiffen the backbones of a few legislators. Congress overrode the veto in the House by a vote of 286 to 48, and in the Senate by 57 to 10.

McCarthy at the Polls: The Political Impact of Red-Baiting

The 1950 senatorial and congressional elections provided a test of McCarthy's appeal, albeit an ambiguous one because the electorate was also deeply bothered by the Korean War. McCarthy contributed to Tydings's loss in Maryland, although some historians believe that McCarthy's importance has been exaggerated. A more important case of flagrant Red-baiting occurred in California, where Republican Congressmen Richard Nixon defeated Helen Gahagan Douglas by labeling her the "pink lady," and by peppering the district with flyers and election eve phone calls alleging her ties to Communism.

McCarthy's peak of influence would not occur until after the 1952 elections; after the Republicans gained a majority in the Senate, the Wisconsin senator would chair a committee, giving him a platform from which to carry on his campaign. In the interim, he continued to level charges, relishing opportunities to attack leading figures in the Truman administration, and even the president himself. Truman's dismissal of General MacArthur in April 1951 prompted scores of attacks on the Truman administration, but McCarthy's were particularly intemperate. Over the next two months, he launched his most virulent assaults on Truman and his secretaries of state and defense. Immediately after the MacArthur firing, McCarthy blasted the president, telling reporters, "The son of a bitch should be impeached." Later that evening, he charged that the president must have been under the influence of "bourbon and Benedictine." McCarthy's attacks on Secretary of State Acheson went further than those of his Republican colleagues. He called Acheson the "Red Dean," and ridiculed diplomats as the "lace handkerchief crowd."

Then, in May 1951, speaking from the Senate floor, McCarthy called for Acheson's impeachment.

But even the calls for impeachment paled in comparison to McCarthy's assault on Secretary of Defense George C. Marshall. Like Truman and Acheson, Marshall had long been a target of the Republican right, for they linked him to the administration's China policy and believed he had been soft on Stalin. Eleven senators had opposed his nomination to be secretary of defense in 1950. Marshall's support for the president's decision to dismiss MacArthur opened old wounds. In one of his most scurrilous attacks, McCarthy declared on June 14 that Marshall was part of "a conspiracy so immense and an infamy so black as to dwarf any previous venture in the history of man." Republicans increasingly found it uncomfortable to react to McCarthy's excesses, torn between their disdain for the senator's tactics and their reluctance to criticize him, both out of a desire to reap benefits of his popularity and fear of the consequences of crossing him. After the Marshall remarks, Taft criticized, but backed off when McCarthy's supporters cried out.

Recommended Reading

Donald R. McCoy's *The Presidency of Harry S. Truman* (Lawrence: University Press of Kansas, 1984) is a fine one-volume examination of the Truman administration. Truman's second term is the subject of Robert J. Donovan's *Tumultuous Years: The Presidency of Harry S. Truman, 1949–1953* (New York: Norton, 1982). Among a number of books that provide an overview of the Truman-Eisenhower years are James T. Patterson's *Grand Expectations: The United States, 1945–1974* (New York: Oxford University Press, 1996); John Patrick Diggins's *The Proud Decades: America in War and Peace, 1941–1960* (New York: Norton, 1988); and William Chafe's *The Unfinished Journey: America since World War II,* 5th edition (New York: Oxford University Press, 2002).

David Caute's *The Great Fear: The Anti-Communist Purge under Truman and Eisenhower* (New York: Simon and Schuster, 1978) is an excellent overview of the Second Red Scare that looks at its impact on civil service, labor, education, and the entertainment industry. Richard M. Fried's *Nightmare in Red: The McCarthy Era in Perspective* (New York: Oxford University Press, 1990) is a succinct yet comprehensive review that gives more attention to McCarthy than does Caute.

The two best biographies of the Wisconsin senator are David M. Oshinsky's *A Conspiracy So Immense: The World of Joe McCarthy* (New York: Free Press, 1983) and Thomas Reeves's *The Life and Times of Joe McCarthy: A Biography* (New York: Stein and Day, 1982).

Several excellent books examine specific cases. The case of Alger Hiss receives its most penetrating analysis in Allen Weinstein's *Perjury: The Hiss-Chambers Case* (New York: Knopf, 1978). Ronald Radosh and Joyce Milton provide a similar thorough examination of the Rosenberg case in *The Rosenberg File: A Search for the Truth* (New York: Holt, Rinehart, and Winston, 1983). Victor Navasky's *Naming Names* (New York: Viking Press, 1980) is an impassioned examination of the impact of the HUAC investigations on the film industry and on individuals who were subject to the inquiry. Ellen Schrecker's *No Ivory Tower: McCarthyism and the Universities* (New York: Oxford University Press, 1986) is an excellent treatment of the effect of the anti-Communist hysteria on higher education.

3

The Korean War

ONE OF THE DEFINING EVENTS of the fifties began halfway through the first year of the new decade. The Korean War spanned more than three years, from June 1950 to July 1953. One of the least popular wars in American history, no monument in the nation's capital commemorated the sacrifices of its veterans until the 1990s—and even then, the monument would rest across the Mall from the polished slabs memorializing another Asian war, in Vietnam, that raised similar questions about the nature of America's role in the world. At the Korean War monument, statues of patrolling soldiers in fifties battle gear gaze at passersby with vacant stares. Why were they there? What did they achieve? Most Americans who remember Korea think of the words of General Omar Bradley: "the wrong war, at the wrong place, at the wrong time, and with the wrong enemy." Never mind that Bradley's words meant to criticize possible expansion of the war rather than the fighting in Korea itself—the words are hauntingly appropriate in either case.

Wrong war or not, Korea left a lasting imprint on America's foreign policy, politics, economy, and culture in the fifties and beyond. It provided a test of the fundamental tenets of postwar American foreign policy, containment, and the Truman Doctrine, and in turn shaped the ways in which those concepts might be applied elsewhere. It recast American policy in Asia for a generation, impacting relations not only with China and North Korea, but also with Taiwan (Formosa), the Philippines, Japan, and Vietnam. The Korean War led the United States to increase its military commitments abroad and, in that sense, influenced American policy worldwide. It heightened American concern over Soviet influence in smaller preindustrial Third World nations, and it increased Cold War tensions globally.

The war influenced politics at home, which in turn affected the conduct of the war. Korea shattered the bipartisan consensus on foreign policy. After 1950, politics would no longer end at the water's edge, as President Truman insisted it must. The war and alarm over the domestic threat of Communism became the principal issues in the election of 1952, and the questions raised then echoed through later elections.

Between the Wars: The United States, Korea, and the Soviet Union, 1945–1950

At the end of World War II, Japan had occupied Korea for more than forty years. The United States had no Korean policy other than to prevent the Soviet Union from replacing Japan as the dominant power on the peninsula. The Americans and Soviets divided Korea into zones of occupation along the 38th parallel, a line selected by American negotiators because it placed the capital city of Seoul in the American zone.

The American forces of occupation, led by Lieutenant General John Hodge, arrived in September 1945 amid a chaotic scramble for power by small parties representing leftists, Communists, and nationalists. Hodge lacked the experience, vision, and knowledge of Korean society that might have allowed him to sort out the factions. Worried that the Soviets might exploit the turmoil, Hodge relied on conservative anti-Communist elements, and especially on an American-educated Korean nationalist named Syngman Rhee. Seventy years old in 1945, Rhee had spent the war in the United States lobbying for Korean independence. Proud and stubborn, Rhee was no American puppet, but his anti-Communist credentials were impeccable.

North of the 38th parallel, where the political situation was equally tumultuous, the Soviets fostered the development of the Korean Communist Party. As its leader, they chose Kim Il-sung, a Communist since the 1930s who had led guerillas against Japanese forces in Manchuria. At thirty-three, Kim was less than half the age of his South Korean counterpart, but equally nationalistic.

Although both sides had already taken steps that would prevent its implementation, in December the United States and the Soviet Union agreed on the establishment of joint commission to supervise election of a provisional government and reunification of the peninsula. It was not to be. Over the next four years, as Soviet-American rivalry intensified in Europe and elsewhere in Asia, distrust made cooperation between the two powers impossible in Korea.

The United States supported separate elections in the south in May 1946; Rhee won a convincing victory, and established a new government, the Republic of Korea. The north responded by forming a government under Kim Il-sung.

Korea presented a dilemma to the State Department and to Hodge's occupying army. Syngman Rhee proved an intractable ally, resisting reforms, instituting repressive policies, and proclaiming martial law, but there seemed to be no acceptable alternative to continuing U.S. support. Truman administration policies cut both ways. The president tried to hold the line on defense spending, but his Truman Doctrine pledged the United States to greater responsibilities abroad. Korea, however, seemed marginal to America's vital interests, which remained centered in Europe. Despite signs of an arms buildup in North Korea, the United States was determined to withdraw its forces from the peninsula, but to leave the Rhee government with sufficient arms to defend itself.

The momentous events of 1949, particularly the successful Soviet test of the atomic bomb and the victory by Communist forces in China, prompted the Truman administration to reappraise its Cold War strategy, and in January 1950 the policy adjustments began to emerge. On January 12, Secretary of State Dean Acheson addressed the National Press Club in Washington regarding U.S. strategic objectives in Asia. The speech laid out the American "defensive perimeter" that encompassed Japan and the Philippines, but excluded Korea and Taiwan. The defense of areas outside of the perimeter, Acheson insisted, must rest with the people themselves, and then with "the commitments of the entire civilized world under the Charter of the United Nations." On the last day of the month, Truman announced that the United States would proceed with the development of the hydrogen bomb, dubbed the "Super" because its potential power would dwarf that of the atomic bombs dropped on Hiroshima and Nagasaki. At the same time, Truman directed his secretaries of state and defense to reexamine American strategic plans in light of the shifts in the atomic balance.

Later, after the war began, Acheson's speech and the joint strategic reappraisal both took on new importance. Critics lambasted Acheson for giving the Communists a "green light" to attack South Korea. Acheson intended no abandonment of South Korea, but rather attempted to place the peninsula in the larger context of American Asian policy. As the new decade dawned, the United States sought to conclude a treaty with Japan that would set forth the terms for ending the postwar occupation, a treaty bound to raise the hackles of China and the Soviet Union. To make the treaty more palatable, Acheson wanted to establish that the United States had no desire to seize Asian territory, either in Taiwan (Formosa) or in Korea. In fact, the Truman administration was not alone in hedging U.S. support for Korea; days after Acheson's speech, Republicans in Congress led a vote defeating a Korean aid bill. Congress later voted funds for Korea, but no one could doubt that leaders of both parties were unenthusiastic about America's role on the peninsula.

Moreover, the United States was ill prepared to undertake a new war. World War II was still a recent memory for Americans; because so many veterans had left the service after the war, the U.S. military was understaffed and its personnel inexperienced. The Truman administration had sought to reduce defense expenditures after the war, and divisions were operating at about 70 percent of authorized strength. The Army had fewer than 600,000 soldiers on active duty in June 1950, with more than half of them stationed in the United States.

In April, the National Security Council (NSC) submitted to the president the report he had requested analyzing America's defense strategy. Designated "NSC-68," the report remains one of the classic documents of the Cold War for its rhetoric and its impact on American policy. It warned that "the Kremlin seeks to bring the free world under its dominion," building an "overwhelming military force" to carry out its threat. Only the United States could lead the West to counter this grave threat, and it would have to make sacrifices to launch "a rapid and sustained build-up of the political, economic, and military strength of the free world." Thus the report lent support to criticism by the armed services of Truman's tight defense budgets; when the Korean War began, those same critics would blame the president for leaving the nation ill prepared, giving him little choice but to increase defense spending. Acheson would later suggest that the Korean War took NSC-68 from the realm of theory to reality.

Attack and Response

North Korea achieved the element of surprise in its invasion of South Korea, not through stealth, but because the 38th parallel had become so contentious that neither the South Koreans nor the Americans remaining in Seoul could be sure at first that the new activity wasn't simply a continuation of ongoing skirmishes. Late June marked the start of the monsoon season, an unlikely time to launch a full-scale attack in which North Korea's heavy Soviet T-34 tanks could become mired in mud. South Korea's defenses were inferior to its attackers in numbers, training, and equipment. Furthermore, on the morning of the attack, many of its soldiers had left their units on 15-day leave passes to assist in the fields, and others staffed reserve positions too far behind the front lines to have much effect against the opening thrust. American and South Korean intelligence failures made matters worse—the most glaring error was American confidence in the ability of South Korean forces to defend themselves.

In the early morning hours of Sunday, June 25, 1950, North Korea launched a massive, coordinated attack: 90,000 infantry troops and 150 tanks crossed the border at the 38th parallel and overran South Korean positions. Convinced at last by fragmentary reports from the front lines that a full-scale invasion was in progress, American Ambassador John Muccio cabled Washington. Secretary of State Acheson called the president in Missouri; they agreed to refer the issue to the UN Security Council as soon as possible. Truman returned to Washington, and that evening conferred with his foreign policy and military advisors. He directed General Douglas MacArthur, then head of American occupation forces in Japan, to dispatch forces to ensure the safe evacuation of Americans from the vicinity of Seoul.

The pace of events in Korea forced the Truman administration to react quickly, with far-reaching consequences that few could have anticipated, committing the United States to fight without a congressional declaration of war, and realigning American defense responsibilities in Asia. South Korean defenses around Seoul crumbled. Truman ordered units of the Seventh Fleet to the Taiwan Strait and to Korea, and gave the American air and naval forces already near Seoul a freer hand, insisting only that they not attack north of the 38th parallel.

On June 27, with Seoul in imminent danger of falling, the United Nations considered the American resolution authorizing the use of ground forces against the North Korean invaders. In the Security Council, circumstances played into the hands of the American delegation. China held one of the five permanent seats on the Council; at the founding of the United Nations, that seat was taken by the Nationalist government of Chiang Kai-shek, which retained it still, even though Chiang had lost control of the mainland and fled to Taiwan, and even though the Soviet Union had demanded the seat be given to the new Communist government of Mao Tse-tung. (The People's

1. Foreign policy team gives farewell to Averell Harriman, who is leaving on mission to Iran. From left to right, Secretary of State Dean Acheson, Averell Harriman, President Harry S. Truman, and Secretary of Defense George C. Marshall, July 13, 1951. Photograph by Abbie Rowe. Truman Library Photographs, Harry S. Truman Library, Accession no. 65–2759.

Republic of China would not be admitted to the United Nations until 1971.) The Soviets, who surely would have vetoed the U.S. Korean initiative, had walked out of the Council in protest of the American refusal to allow the Communists to occupy the Chinese seat. The American resolution thus passed without opposition.

The North Korean offensive exposed the inability of the South Korean forces to defend their positions. On June 28, Seoul fell to the North Koreans. The panic that consumed the city became worse when premature destruction of bridges across the Han River stranded people inside the city before the advancing North Korean troops. Two days later, President Truman announced that he had authorized the use of American ground troops. He directed the Navy to blockade the coast, and the Air Force to strike designated targets in the north. The Security Council approved another American resolution giving the United States authority to designate a commander for UN forces in Korea; on July 8, Truman named MacArthur.

Two questions haunt histories of the opening moves of the Korean War. Why did Kim Il-sung initiate the conflict in the first place? And why didn't President Truman seek a congressional declaration of war, or at least a congressional resolution, in support of his actions? At the time, Americans believed that Kim Il-sung was a Soviet puppet, and that Stalin was behind his decision to invade the South. Scholars have since come to agree that even though Stalin gave him the nod, the initiative was all Kim's. Although the United States viewed the attack through Cold War lenses, Korean internal affairs and the North Korean desire to reunify the peninsula better serve to explain the events of late June 1950. Kim had dispatched infiltrators across the 38th parallel while American troops still occupied the South; as early as 1949, he had begun to pressure Stalin to support an invasion. At that time, Stalin demurred, but Kim persisted. In the spring of 1950, the Soviet leader finally approved, contingent on the approval of Chinese Communist leader Mao Tse-tung. When Mao agreed, the deal was sealed.

Truman's response to the invasion was less calculated. The scale of the North Korean onslaught demanded immediate action at a time when Congress was not in session. Insisting that his role as commander in chief was sufficient justification, the president pointed out that he had conferred with congressional leaders and had their support in any case. Indeed, Truman very likely would have received support from Congress had he sought it. Even Republican Senator Robert A. Taft, known popularly as "Mr. Republican," had expressed support for Truman's actions, although he asserted that they lacked constitutional authority. The president's decision not to seek a declaration of war or a resolution of support would have dire political consequences, for when the war dragged on, Republicans felt freer to criticize a president whose actions they had never officially endorsed. On July 19, in a special message to Congress and in an evening radio and television address, Truman called for increases in the military budget, in personnel strength, and in procurement, and in the taxes necessary to support such actions. In effect, he called for actions proposed in NSC-68.

Halting the Invasion: Pusan and Inchon

Appointed as commander of UN forces in Korea on July 8, General MacArthur faced a formidable challenge. South Korean units continued to re-

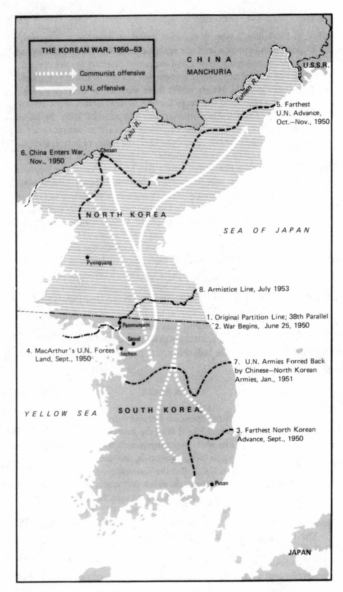

Map 1. The Korean War, 1950–53. "Map: The Korean War, 1950–53," from *U.S. Diplomacy since 1900,* 4th edition, by Robert S. Schulzinger, copyright © 1994 by Oxford University Press, Inc. Used by permission of Oxford University Press, Inc.

treat. The American forces introduced in the first two weeks of the war were outnumbered, undertrained, and poorly supplied, and had to contend with oppressive heat and lack of cover in the Korean interior. It was no secret that the North Koreans' target was Pusan, a city in the southeastern tip of the Korean Peninsula and the country's most important port. Only the fact that the invaders paused after the first week to shore up their logistics gave the Americans opportunity to establish a defensive line around Pusan. The situation remained desperate through the summer as UN forces clung tenuously to the scant territory within the Pusan perimeter.

MacArthur was one of the most complex leaders in American military history. With an ego that matched his undoubted strategic talents, he generated strong reactions: his men either gave him their unswerving loyalty or despised him, as did General Eisenhower, who had served on MacArthur's staff in the Philippines before World War II. Arrogant, headstrong, and one of the most irascible figures in the Army, MacArthur commanded U.S. forces in the Far East, and later served as supreme commander of allied powers in occupied Japan. Truman privately referred to MacArthur as "Mr. Prima Donna, Brass Hat, Five-Star MacArthur," and as a "play actor and a bunco man." But MacArthur had proven his courage during two world wars, and was a brilliant strategist. Now he would face one of his sternest challenges as a commander. He conceived a plan of enormous risk, an amphibious invasion at Inchon, on the west coast of the Korean Peninsula, near Seoul and far behind enemy lines. The area was subject to extreme tides, with as much as 32 feet between high and low tides. Timing was crucial; the landing had to take place at high tide, or the invading force would be stranded on mudflats. The Joint Chiefs of Staff thought the plan was too risky, and nearly vetoed it. MacArthur, whose very self-confidence was one of his most persuasive selling points, argued that the risk was one of the plan's most appealing attributes: the North Koreans would never expect an invasion at such a treacherous location.

MacArthur decided to attack on September 15, one of the days on which tides were most favorable to success. Two days earlier, the Navy bombarded Wolmi Island, which guarded the opening to Inchon harbor, shelling other areas along the coast at the same time to preserve the element of surprise. The assault began at dawn on the 15th, with an invasion force of 70,000 men— Marines, Army infantry, and South Korean recruits. The amphibious invasion succeeded beyond expectations, with only 17 Marines wounded and none killed in the initial assault. North Korean forces mounted a determined defense, however, and UN forces weren't able to recapture Seoul until September 25—three months to the day after the North Korean invasion began. To mark the significance of the date, MacArthur's sense of the dramatic compelled him to announce the seizure of Seoul even before securing its defenses.

The success at Inchon had several consequences. In the short term, it turned the war around. The North Koreans suddenly found their defenses stretched thin. Breaking out of the Pusan perimeter, General Walton H. Walker's Eighth Army drove the North Koreans back across the 38th parallel. Before the end of the month, Syngman Rhee had reestablished his government in Seoul. The long-term consequences of Inchon were equally significant. MacArthur had won an astonishing victory against the advice of the collective wisdom of America's top-echelon military leaders. He assumed an aura of invincibility that made it more difficult for Washington to question his judgment. Finally, Inchon brought the United States to another point of decision: should MacArthur pursue the enemy across the 38th parallel?

Because its stated objective had been to halt aggression, if the UN forces had stopped at the 38th parallel, the United States could have claimed victory. Containment had been achieved, and Syngman Rhee's government restored. Furthermore, to cross the line ran the risk of Chinese or Soviet intervention. China warned the United States through Pakistan (because China and the United States did not have diplomatic relations) of its intention to enter the war if American forces came too close to Chinese territory. Nonetheless, the lure of pursuit was compelling. China's warning bears more weight in retrospect than it did at the time. There had been earlier indications that China would not intervene. No less an authority than MacArthur believed the warning a bluff. MacArthur and congressional Republicans wanted to pursue, and the administration was in a weak position politically to oppose their judgment. Republicans had been lambasting Truman for "losing" China a year earlier, and to halt a popular victorious general on the verge of yet greater achievements would have stirred up a hornet's nest of opposition. Truman's position was made all the more difficult by his having just convinced General George Marshall to replace Secretary of Defense Louis Johnson. A man of unquestioned integrity, Marshall had served as Truman's chief of staff during World War II, and Truman considered him the most admirable American in public life. But as secretary of state in 1949, Marshall was one of the officials the Republicans held most responsible for the "loss" of China. Thus it was that, late in September, Truman authorized MacArthur to cross the 38th parallel; on

2. General Douglas MacArthur (seated), Commander in Chief of UN Forces, observes the shelling of Inchon from the USS *Mt. McKinley*, September 15, 1950. Record Group 111: Records of the Chief Signal Officer, Special Media Archives Services Division (NWCS-S), National Archives at College Park, NAIL Control no. NWDNS-111-SC-348438, War and Conflict no. 1374.

October 7, the UN General Assembly approved an American resolution to that effect. The decision changed the nature of the war; no longer was the United States seeking merely to repel aggression. Now its goal was the reunification of Korea.

From Apogee to Nadir: Wake Island and the Chinese Intervention

Having previously scheduled a trip to San Francisco in mid-October, Truman decided to take the opportunity to confer directly with the general. Because the war was at a critical juncture, Truman's advisors recommended that he not summon MacArthur stateside; instead, the meeting would take place at

3. At dawn on the morning of October 15, 1950, at Wake Island, President Harry S. Truman meets Far East Commander General Douglas MacArthur. Truman Library Photographs, Harry S. Truman Library, Accession no. 67–434.

Wake Island, halfway across the Pacific. Critics suggested that the trip was political. The president had already made the crucial decision to cross the 38th parallel. Why else would a president whose popularity was slipping meet with MacArthur but to bask in the reflected glory of the great general? In point of fact, Truman believed that a face-to-face meeting could clear the air between the two. In August, MacArthur had made statements regarding the possible use of Nationalist Chinese troops in Korea that clearly conflicted with administration policy, and Truman wanted to make sure he would not do so again.

On October 15, Truman and MacArthur met privately for half an hour, then with their advisors for two hours. Contrary to later reports, some of them generated years later in the president's recollections, the meeting was cordial. American spirits were riding high a month after Inchon, and there were no difficult issues to resolve. Optimism prevailed to the point that much of the longer meeting centered on the postwar settlement in the Pacific region. Truman asked MacArthur what the chances were that China would intervene in Korea. The general answered that they were slight, but that if China were to enter the conflict, superior American air power would be decisive. In the days that followed, both Truman and MacArthur issued statements reflecting the new era of good feelings between the old adversaries.

MacArthur's assessment of the unlikelihood of Chinese intervention jibed with the best judgment of most of Truman's advisors, including Secretary of State Acheson and the CIA. Most believed that if China had intended to enter, it would have done so when UN forces crossed the 38th parallel. Moreover, in these early days of the Cold War, most Americans considered China a minion of the Soviet Union, and believed that the Soviets had no stomach for a war in Korea. China continued to send warnings, and journalist Hanson Baldwin reported a quarter million Chinese troops had massed at the Yalu River, with 200,000 more farther behind the lines. The Truman administration believed that any Chinese military action would be restricted to protecting hydroelectric power plants along the Yalu River, which marked the border between Korea and Chinese-controlled territory in Manchuria. The United States responded to these troop movements and warnings with reassurances that it had no intention of spreading the war to China. Meantime, the UN offensive continued. South Korean forces drove northward along the east coast toward Soviet territory in the northeast, while the American Eighth Army approached the Yalu.

On October 24, Chinese units secretly crossed the Yalu. Over the next few days, they clashed with South Korean troops, beating them soundly. By November 1, American intelligence analysts confirmed that China had entered the conflict, although first estimates pegged the number of its invading troops at no more than 20,000. Even on November 4, MacArthur continued to believe that the Chinese intervention did not constitute a major operation.

Two days later, the new reality could no longer be denied. On the eve of off-year elections in the United States, and with Truman back in Independence to vote, China launched an onslaught across the Yalu. MacArthur ordered destruction of the bridges closest to the Manchurian city of Antung. The Air Force prepared to launch a strike from Japan, but first sought to clear the order with the Defense Department. Hurried consultations took place between Defense and State, with B-29s at the ready in Japan. Acheson phoned the president, who ordered delay until the situation could be assessed. MacArthur was outraged, and reported that Chinese troops and matériel were pouring across the river. "I believe your instructions will result in a calamity of major proportion for which I cannot accept responsibility," he warned. Despite the audacious tone of MacArthur's message, Truman believed he had little choice but to back his commander in the field. The bombing mission knocked out two of the bridges, but most of the Chinese troops had already crossed the river.

After the initial thrust across the Yalu, in another astonishing turn of events, the Chinese offensive seemed to melt away. Chinese forces paused to regroup, and the war settled into curious lull. The pause would seem less unusual as the war wore on, for it represented a common Chinese pattern. As China resupplied its forces and Washington weighed its options, MacArthur announced endgame plans. The Joint Chiefs and the Truman administration were hamstrung. Acheson later said that they all "sat around like paralyzed rabbits" while MacArthur pushed beyond Washington's political goals. All yearned to believe MacArthur's promise that the boys would be home by Christmas, and all lacked the political will to force the popular general to accede to administration policy. Even though the Eighth Army had had to retreat, MacArthur still envisioned a counterattack that he believed could end the war. He planned to bomb the Korean side of the remaining bridges across the Yalu since his orders restricted him from initiating action on the Chinese side of the river. He envisioned a vise, with the Eighth Army in the west and the Marine's 10th Corps in the east squeezing the enemy toward the Yalu.

MacArthur's plans proved a great illusion. Between November 25 and November 28, Chinese forces began a great offensive, with some 200,000 troops hammering both wings of the UN advance. By their sheer numbers, the Chinese forces overwhelmed UN forces. Some units suffered extraordinary losses. The American Second Infantry Division recorded 80 percent casualties; survivors had to abandon most of the division's arms as they fled. UN forces reeled in retreat over the same rugged terrain they had taken with such apparent ease just two months earlier. "We face an entirely new war," MacArthur cabled Washington.

As the threat to its forces loomed ever larger, the United States directed all its efforts at saving them. In the west, the Eighth Army retreated quickly: it abandoned the North Korean capital of Pyongyang, midway between Seoul and the Yalu River, and continued south toward the 38th parallel, covering 120 miles in 10 days. In the east, withdrawal was more difficult. Some of the most intense fighting involved 10,000 Marines of the First Marine Division, which sought to link up with the Eighth Army on November 27. As the Marines moved to the west side of the Chosin Reservoir, not far from the Yalu, they fell under attack by a Chinese force three times their size. When the Marines withdrew, other Chinese units numbering about 50,000 attacked along their route. Their embattled retreat inspired their commander, Major General Oliver P. Smith, to exclaim, "Retreat, hell! We're just advancing in another direction." Eventually, the division made its way to Hungnam, on Korea's east coast, preparing for evacuation by sea transport with other American and UN forces that had converged there.

Strategy and Goals: The Bomb and the Great Debate

At a press conference on November 30, reporters asked Truman whether his administration was considering using the atomic bomb in Korea. The president responded, "There has always been active consideration of its use." Given a chance to elaborate, Truman only made matters more confusing. Was its use under active consideration? "It always has been. It's one of our weapons." Did that mean use against military or civilian targets? "It's a matter that the military people will have to decide." That afternoon, the White House tried to clarify. The bomb was only under consideration in the sense that, as part of the American arsenal, it would be considered with all other weapons. Furthermore, the president would personally have to authorize any use.

If Truman's statement was meant to warn China, it also shocked America's close allies. The European press erupted in protest, both over the substance of the policy and over the implied U.S. threat to use atomic weapons without consultation. The British Parliament was in an uproar. Prime Minister Clement Attlee immediately contacted the president, and asked to confer with him directly. The following week Attlee flew to Washington, and he and Truman discussed a wide range of issues regarding the UN effort in Korea. The discussions were productive if strained, and Attlee left reassured by the president's comments about atomic strategy, but without a pledge the United States would not use the bomb in Korea. Truman did promise, however, that he would consult with the allies before ordering its use.

Next to the question of the bomb, the most important item on the agenda for the British-Americans discussions was a reevaluation of goals for the war in Korea. Reuniting Korea, MacArthur's goal since the crossing of the 38th parallel, seemed no longer achievable. Both nations wanted to avoid a larger war with China. The British seemed defeatist—Acheson described Attlee's demeanor during his weeklong discussions as "a long withdrawing, melancholy sigh." Attlee advised a cease-fire, offering China a seat in the United Nations as a carrot to win their support. For his part, Acheson argued that the UN forces were not yet defeated. Yet the Truman administration found itself torn. Even though it feared that a loss in Korea would cripple American efforts elsewhere in the Far East and might even jeopardize the Japanese occupation, it believed that Korea was not the place to fight a major war. MacArthur decried the hand-wringing and asked for reinforcements that might enable him to take the offensive. Truman was not willing to turn the general loose, and in fact informed him on December 6 that he was not to make any public statements without first clearing them with Washington. On December 16, the president proclaimed a national emergency, describing Korean developments as "a grave threat to the peace of the world."

There was another dimension—global in character—implicit in discussions of the fate of Korea. The United States had long centered its international relationships on Europe; indeed, Americans had fought two world wars in the previous half century to preserve that Europe-centered world order. In September, Secretary of State Acheson had advocated introducing four to six American Army divisions into Europe to forestall the possibility the Soviet Union might exploit the Korean War to launch an attack on Europe. Now many Americans had begun to argue that the United States should no longer tie itself so closely to Europe. Some—prominent among them MacArthur, conservative Republicans who blamed Acheson and the Democrats for the "loss" of China, and *Time* magazine magnate Henry Luce—believed that America's future lay in Asia. Others of the anti-Europe crowd chose not to look to Asia, but to turn within. Former President Herbert Hoover, in a late December speech that Truman dismissed as "neo-isolationist," called for the United States to establish a "Western Hemisphere Gibraltar of civilization," protected by American naval and air power. Republican Senator Robert Taft from Ohio blasted Truman's plans to send troops to Europe as a challenge to congressional power; in early January, his colleague, Republican Senator Kenneth Wherry from Nebraska, introduced a resolution requiring the president to obtain congressional approval before sending additional divisions. Wherry's resolution failed, but only after months of debate. The Grand Old Party (GOP) found itself deeply divided. Republicans ranged from isolationists to warmongers who wanted to arm MacArthur with the bomb. What united them was their opposition to the Truman administration, and particularly to Secretary of State Dean Acheson.

Acheson, the Truman administration's foremost Europhile, was—with the president—the key figure on the other side. Korea had prompted Acheson to propose a stiffening of defenses in Europe. Not only did he advise sending more American divisions, but he also raised the possibility of inviting West Germany to join NATO, an idea unthinkable before the beginning of the Korean War, and still unthinkable to many Americans and Europeans. So fundamental was this dispute over policy, which soon became known as the "Great Debate," that it drove a wedge between Republicans and Democrats, destroying the bipartisanship in American foreign policy that had existed since the end of World War II.

The Chinese intervention and the Great Debate forced the Truman administration to recognize new pragmatic realities. Strategic reevaluations that accompanied the Great Debate led the United States to adopt new objectives in Korea. The United States would not abandon Korea, but neither would it seek to reunify the peninsula. The new strategy meant that UN forces would fight a limited war in which absolute victory was no longer the ultimate objective. It was a strategy that bothered many Americans, including many World War II veterans. And it galled MacArthur.

The Truman administration initiated another diplomatic move in January. The United Nations had been pushing for a cease-fire resolution, which the United States had resisted despite the advocacy of some of its closest allies in Korea. The Truman administration walked a tightrope between U.S. allies, who were pushing for a cease-fire, and its domestic critics, who were adamantly opposed. Succumbing to allied pressure, the Truman administration first agreed to support a UN resolution on January 13, and held its breath until China rejected it. It then moved to have the United Nations condemn China as an aggressor nation, an unpopular initiative even among U.S. allies, who feared that such an action might only prolong the war. The U.S. House and Senate both passed resolutions to that effect. The Truman administration presented its own to the UN General Assembly; on February 1, the resolution passed by a 44 to 7 vote, with 9 abstentions.

As the Truman administration debated strategy and goals through the month of December, the military situation in Korea deteriorated. In the west, UN forces continued to be forced back toward the 38th parallel. In the east, the Hungnam evacuation continued to its successful completion just before Christmas. On December 23, General Walton Walker, commander of the Eighth Army, died in a jeep accident on an icy road; his replacement, General Matthew B. Ridgway, flew immediately to Korea to confer with MacArthur. Instructed to halt the retreat and establish a defensive line as soon as possible, Ridgway asked MacArthur whether he could attack if he had an opportunity to do so. "The Eighth Army is yours, Matt," MacArthur told him. "Do what you think best." Ridgway proved to be a masterful division commander. From the time he assumed command, with the Eighth Army having retreated toward the 38th parallel and in places below the line, prospects began to improve. Even though he had to relinquish Seoul and give ground as he sought to establish a defensive line, Ridgway's positive approach, which addressed not only the military situation of his troops but also their well-being, brought about a significant improvement in morale.

By late January, the northern front began to stabilize. If it was clear that Ridgway could not reverse Chinese gains in North Korea, it was equally clear that China could not drive UN forces from the South. The Eighth Army also benefited from the sporadic character of the Chinese offensive. In danger of outrunning their supply lines and hampered by technical deficiencies, the Chinese forces had to halt every few days to regroup, resupply, and consolidate their gains, allowing the Americans to retreat in an orderly fashion, and finally to dig in. Ridgway established a defensive line some 50 miles south of the 38th parallel; by January 25, he was ready to take the offensive. Using tanks and artillery, supported by offshore naval artillery, Ridgway advanced quickly, inflicting heavy casualties on the Chinese and incurring only light losses among his own troops. Although, on February 11, China launched a massive human-wave counterattack, UN forces regrouped and held their ground, inflicting an estimated 33,000 casualties on the Chinese side. From that date until mid-March, Ridgway steadily regained territory and moved north again toward the 38th parallel. His offensive occupied Inchon, and, on March 15, recaptured Seoul. UN forces once again had the initiative.

The Dismissal of MacArthur

Ridgway's advance provided a propitious opportunity for an American overture to end the war. Since December, America's European allies had been advocating a cease-fire as a step toward peace. In the face of the Chinese offensive, such an action would have been tantamount to surrender. But now Ridgway had changed the dynamic of the war and opened prospects for an honorable peace.

Ironically, for this very reason, Ridgway's success was not altogether pleasing to MacArthur. Having long advocated bringing the Chinese Nationalists into the war, General MacArthur now wanted the authority to use air power to strike at Chinese industrial bases in Manchuria. Ridgway's advance undercut these demands; if indeed the UN forces were moving forward on the ground in Korea, there was no need to risk widening the war. MacArthur warned that stopping at the 38th parallel would lead to a stalemate, and would prevent the United Nations from achieving its goal of reuniting Korea. The statement irritated the Truman administration on two counts: first, it violated the restriction on uncleared public statements; and second, it described Korean unification as the UN goal, which was no longer the case—although in MacArthur's defense, he had not been officially informed of a change in policy.

The Truman administration had been under pressure from U.S. allies and from the United Nations to offer a peace initiative. By mid-March, both the State Department and the Defense Department agreed, and the administration prepared a statement offering a cease-fire as a first step toward negotiations to end the war. When the Joint Chiefs of Staff informed MacArthur of the planned peace overture, the general defiantly preempted Washington with a bombshell of his own. On March 24, he issued a statement claiming that China lacked the industrial capacity to fight a modern war, and that only self-defined restrictions had kept the UN forces from expanding operations in a way that would "doom Red China to the risk of imminent military collapse." He offered to meet with the commander of enemy forces at any time.

The reaction in Washington was one of outrage. Truman believed that

MacArthur's statement made it impossible to release the peace overture without giving the appearance that American policy was in disarray. Several presidential advisors recommended that MacArthur be recalled. Although Truman later claimed that MacArthur's March 24 statement had convinced him to fire the general, he held back, settling instead for a pointed reminder of the restrictions on public statements. He had good reason to wait. The debate between those favoring a foreign policy that emphasized ties with Europe and those opposed had reached a crucial stage, and Truman could not risk making MacArthur a martyr. On April 4, the Senate passed a resolution approving the establishment of NATO and the assignment of four additional divisions to Europe. Now Truman could move, but he needed an immediate cause.

The very next day came evidence that MacArthur had crossed the line. In early March, Congressman Joseph Martin, a Republican from Massachusetts and the House minority leader, had written to the general, asking his views on America's policy in the Far East. MacArthur replied that the Chinese intervention suggested that the United States should "follow the conventional pattern of meeting force with maximum counterforce, as we have never failed to do in the past," and agreed with Martin on the wisdom of using Nationalist Chinese forces. He continued that it was apparent that the Communists had chosen to make their stand in Asia, and that "here we fight Europe's war with arms while the diplomats there still fight it with words." He closed with a condemnation of the policy of limited war, saying, "We must win. There is no substitute for victory." Because Martin was no friend of the Truman administration, and because MacArthur had not asked him to keep the letter private, the congressman read it from the floor of the House chamber.

Not only had MacArthur once more proposed to use Nationalist forces, an option long since rejected, he had also challenged established U.S. objectives. Over the next two days, Truman discussed the situation at length with Generals Marshall and Bradley, Ambassador Averell Harriman, and Secretary Acheson, and conferred with congressional leaders and with other members of his administration. After reviewing exchanges of messages over the previous two years, General Marshall concluded that MacArthur should have been fired two years earlier. With the unanimous support of the Joint Chief of Staff, Bradley joined Harriman and Acheson in urging dismissal. Other advisors, concerned about the political firestorm such an action would provoke, expressed reservations.

Truman directed General Bradley to prepare orders relieving MacArthur and appointing General Ridgway to take his place. The president directed that the orders be relayed to MacArthur through Secretary of the Army Frank Pace, who was then in Korea. Pace was at the front, however, and could not receive them. Bradley learned that at least one newspaper intended to publish the MacArthur story in its next edition. Wanting to avoid the embarrassment both of having MacArthur first learn of his dismissal from the press and of having him resign before receiving official word, Truman directed that the orders be transmitted directly. Press Secretary Joseph Short called a press conference for 1:00 A.M. to inform reporters. To no avail. MacArthur learned that he had been dismissed from an aide who heard about it on the radio and telephoned MacArthur's quarters, where he was hosting a lunch. He did not receive the official message until fifteen minutes later, an unfortunate circumstance that would give MacArthur's defenders ammunition to attack Truman for slighting the great general.

Firing MacArthur was the courageous act of an unpopular president. The Truman administration was facing allegations of influence peddling in the Reconstruction Finance Corporation and corruption in the Bureau of Internal Revenue. Republican jibes had taken their toll, as had Senator Joseph McCarthy's charges of Communist influence. In contrast, MacArthur remained popular; many believed his boasts that he could have won the war in Korea if only the Truman administration had unshackled him. Acheson had warned the president that if he fired the general, "you will have the biggest fight of your administration." Truman steadfastly insisted that although the commander in the field must have latitude, ultimately, the American system rested on civilian control, and that policy decisions had to be made in Washington. The unanimous support of the Joint Chiefs of Staff and of respected military leaders such as Generals Bradley and Marshall, along with support of much of the press, enabled the president to weather the storm.

At the time, however, MacArthur came home to one of the most tumultuous public demonstrations in American history. White House mail ran in favor of the general by a ratio of 20 to 1, and the Gallup Poll showed the public supporting MacArthur, 69 percent to 29 percent. Returning to the United States on April 17 for the first time in twenty-five years, he received a hero's welcome in San Francisco. Two days later, he addressed a joint meeting of Congress in a speech viewed on television by 30 million people, the largest audience that had ever seen a telecast. He offered his perspective on the war, and cautioned that Taiwan would have to be defended against Communist encroachment. Attacking the Truman administration's policy of limited war, he insisted: "There is no substitute for victory." He was interrupted by applause thirty times in the course of his address, which ended with a line that tugged at the emotions: "I now close my military career and just fade away, an old soldier who tried to do his duty as God gave him the light to see that duty. Good-bye."

The next day, MacArthur traveled to New York City, which gave him another rousing reception as he rode through Manhattan in an open car. Estimates placed the size of the crowd at 7.5 million, twice as many as greeted General Eisenhower when he returned from leading American forces to victory in World War II. People talked of a possible MacArthur bid for the Republican presidential nomination in 1952.

Seeking to capitalize on MacArthur's remarkable popularity, Republicans called for hearings on America's policy in the Far East. Although the public clamor gave Democrats no choice but to agree, they were able to keep the hearings closed and to release only a transcript, with classified material deleted. Jointly sponsored by the Senate Armed Services and Foreign Relations Committees, the hearings began on May 3 and lasted for seven weeks. MacArthur appeared as the first witness; testifying for a total of twenty-one hours, he answered questions from senators of both parties. The MacArthur charm, self-confidence, and command presence came through from start to finish. His theme of refusing to accept anything less than victory had always resonated with the American public, and continued to do so.

As the hearings progressed, however, the mood began to shift. Democrats probed about the implications of broadening the conflict by bombing Manchuria or bringing in the Nationalist Chinese. Asked what would happen if his actions forced the nation into a larger war, MacArthur responded that his responsibilities were confined to the Pacific, and that others were working on the global problem. That was precisely the point, responded his questioner, Senator Brien McMahon (Democrat-Connecticut): a theater commander must not make judgments that defy the commander in chief and risk global war.

After MacArthur completed his testimony, the Truman administration's witnesses came forward; one by one, they discredited MacArthur's testimony. The two most compelling witnesses were Secretary of Defense Marshall and General Bradley. Marshall insisted there had not been any disagreement between the president, State, Defense, and the Joint Chiefs; the only disagreement had come from MacArthur. Furthermore, MacArthur's March 24 statement had undercut ongoing negotiations that might have led to the end of the war. Bradley underscored the difference between the perspective of a theater commander and that of his senior command. Far from guaranteeing victory in Korea, broadening the conflict with China would have engaged the United States in "the wrong war, at the wrong place, at the wrong time, and with the wrong enemy." Republicans were ready to cut the hearings short, but Democrats insisted that the remaining members of the Joint Chiefs of Staff have their say. One after another, they hammered home the same points: agreement in Washington, and defiance that risked global war from MacArthur. By the end of the hearings, public opinion had begun to swing to the president, and MacArthur's presidential hopes had faded away.

The general himself was not ready to fade, however. After the hearings, he began an extensive speaking tour. At the outset, large crowds lined the streets to see him pass, but, as time went on, the crowds dwindled. Perhaps the biggest disappointment came in Texas, where, despite elaborate preparations, only 20,000 people came to Houston's Rice Stadium, leaving some 50,000 seats empty.

Dying for a Tie: The Beginning of Negotiations

When MacArthur left Korea, General Ridgway assumed his command in Japan; on April 14, General James Van Fleet took command of the Eighth Army. An aggressive commander who had given distinguished service in the Greek civil war, Van Fleet hoped to push the Chinese forces deep into North Korea. Initially, he had some success; on April 22, the UN forces had moved the front some 10 to 15 miles north of the 38th parallel in the eastern sections of the peninsula. Only in the westernmost sector did the Chinese control territory south of the parallel. That night, however, in the largest offensive of the war, the Chinese forces launched a human-wave attack, accompanied by terrifying bugle calls and yells, that drove most of the UN forces south of the parallel within a week. Some of the bitterest fighting occurred in defense of Seoul, where the British 29th Infantry Brigade lost a thousand men in a heroic three-day standoff before being forced to fall back to the capital. Van Fleet fought back with air power and artillery, hoping to preserve his personnel even as they retreated. The tactic worked. Not only were Chinese losses approximately ten times those of the UN forces—70,000 to 7,000—but the retreat had been orderly and well executed. The UN forces gained confidence: the Chinese had mustered an all-out attack, and yet had neither recaptured Seoul nor broken the back of the UN resistance.

On May 16, Chinese forces mounted another, weaker offensive; Van Fleet countered with an offensive of his own a week later, and pushed the demoralized Chinese forces back above the 38th parallel. Van Fleet later insisted that he could have driven the enemy deep into North Korea, but his orders forbade such a pursuit.

For the first time since MacArthur had scuttled a negotiation proposal with his March 24 statement, the United States was in an advantageous position to negotiate. Indeed, America's allies had been pressuring the administration to do so for weeks, and Van Fleet's success made it difficult to ignore the pressure. Since the United States did not have diplomatic relations with China, the administration sought to make contact through the Soviet Union, commissioning America's leading Soviet specialist, George Kennan, to approach Jacob Malik, the Soviet ambassador to the United Nations. The men met twice in late May and early June; Malik had been receptive, but could give no definitive reply. Three weeks later, on June 23, Malik gave a radio address indicating a Soviet desire for peace. Word from China seemed positive, and hopes rose.

Distrust ran deep on both sides, however. Ridgway wanted to continue his offensive until there could be a firm armistice in place. After a diplomatic dance over the time and place for opening negotiations, and the United States accepted Kim Il-sung's proposal to meet on July 10 at Kaesong, which was located in no-man's land, just south of the 38th parallel. The announcement generated an enthusiastic reaction nearly everywhere except South Korea. Syngman Rhee worried that a truce line in the vicinity of the 38th parallel might mean that North Korea would resume hostilities once UN forces departed. The United States had no sympathy for Rhee's objections. Rhee had been a difficult ally, unpopular in his own country because of the brutal measures he took to suppress political opposition in the South. Acheson instructed Ambassador Muccio to remind Rhee that the United Nations had never officially adopted unification as a goal, and that the United States intended to pursue an armistice.

The talks proceeded in fits and starts, sometimes hanging on minor differences of protocol, other times resolving substantive issues with surprising alacrity. For the most part, negotiations proved extraordinarily difficult, with each side looking for slight advantages and viewing concessions from the other side as signs of weakness and reason for tougher demands. At one point during the first month of talks, the Communists said they had nothing further to say, and the Americans responded that, in that case, neither did they; negotiators stared silently at one another across the table for more than two hours. On another occasion, General Ridgway, frustrated by the intransigence of the Communists, would have broken off negotiations if Washington hadn't ordered him to continue.

A protocol issue gave the first indication of how difficult negotiations could be. The North Koreans put harsh restrictions on the UN negotiators, limiting their freedom of movement to a few buildings and refusing permission for reporters to accompany the UN team while allowing North Koreans to take some pictures. Admiral C. Turner Joy, the head of the American negotiating team, broke off discussions on July 12, demanding equal treatment. The North Koreans agreed, and talks resumed five days later.

Fundamental differences surfaced immediately. The Communists insisted on a settlement based on the territory each side occupied before the war, with the 38th parallel as the cease-fire line. Such a settlement would have been a major concession by the Americans, whose forces held territory well north of the parallel along most of its length, as much as 45 miles in some places. When talks resumed on July 17, the North Koreans dropped this demand, but they continued to insist on the withdrawal of foreign troops from Korea. The American team approached the bargaining table with a different agenda, saying that a cease-fire had to be established before other issues could be addressed, and insisting that troop withdrawal was a political issue beyond the scope of the present negotiations.

As the talks moved into late July and early August, they centered on the issue of the line of demarcation. The American negotiators made it clear that the 38th parallel was not acceptable, and for a time it appeared that the Communists were willing to give ground. Then suddenly things fell apart. The North Koreans and Chinese accused the United Nations of violating the neutral zone around Kaesong, and produced debris supposedly caused by the attack. The Americans denied that an attack had occurred. The two sides exchanged charges and countercharges until August 24, when the Communists suspended talks indefinitely.

The Truman administration, which was then preparing a treaty with Japan, welcomed the suspension: the treaty involved issues affecting the Soviet Union and China, and there were good reasons not to be working on the Japan and Korea agreements at the same time. Soviet cooperation in one venue might have encouraged unwarranted concessions in the other. For his part, Ridgway seized on the suspension to insist on a new site for negotiations as a condition for resumption of the peace talks.

From Optimism to Despair: The Resumption and Collapse of Peace Talks

Fighting continued while the peace talks were suspended, although neither side mounted a significant offensive. Military action was particularly heavy in an area on the eastern section of the battlefront that the Americans called the "Punchbowl." There the American 2nd Infantry Division, supported by South Korean forces, captured Bloody Ridge and Heartbreak Ridge, but sustained 5,900 casualties in doing so.

On October 7, the Communists agreed to reopen talks, and to a shift in location to Panmunjom, 5 miles east of Kaesong. When the talks resumed in a tent near Panmunjom on October 25, all signs seemed auspicious for a rapid settlement. The Truman administration felt intense pressure from American citizens and European allies alike to end the war. Having already determined not to push farther north, it saw no reason to prolong the fighting. With winter looming and supplies dwindling, the Chinese and North Koreans had neither the will nor the means to initiate another substantial attack, having launched a major offensive to no avail and lost ground since then.

When the talks resumed, the UN command proposed a demilitarized zone along the line of contact or at a prearranged line agreeable to both sides. Dropping their demand for a settlement along the 38th parallel, the Communists responded positively, although they insisted that Kaesong remain in their hands. The Americans demonstrated their resolve to settle by restraining Ridgway, who along with Van Fleet believed that the Communists were weak and should be driven back. By November 27, negotiators reached agreement both on a 30-day cease-fire and on the line of contact that could form the basis for a settlement. The Americans agreed to the line on condition that all remaining differences could be resolved within the 30-day cease-fire period.

By the end of December, the two sides were at loggerheads again. Talks broke down over the question of the return of prisoners of war. Both sides had earlier agreed to honor the Geneva Convention of 1949 in regard to POWs, which stated that "prisoners of war shall be released and repatriated without delay after the cessation of hostilities." The United States now withdrew its agreement, objecting on several grounds. The Communists had not honored other provisions of the Geneva Convention: they had neither released the names of the POWs they held nor allowed representatives of the International Red Cross to visit their POW camps. More important, the staggering difference in the number of POWs held by each side made a straight exchange of all prisoners completely unacceptable. In the summer of 1951, the United Nations held about 150,000 prisoners—ten times the number held by the Communists. Many on the United Nations side believed the disparity was a clear indication that POWs had been mistreated by the Communists—that many prisoners had been killed after being taken prisoner or had died because of inhumane treatment in Communist POW camps.

Returning all prisoners would give the North Koreans and Chinese the equivalent of another army, an overwhelming advantage in personnel strength should the war resume. On the other hand, exchanging prisoners one for one would leave some 90 percent of Communist POWs in their enemy's hands, an outcome unacceptable to the Communists. After both sides agreed to a 15-day extension of the cease-fire period, the Americans proposed releasing only those prisoners who wished to be repatriated. The Chinese were incensed. Many of the POWs held by the United Nations were Nationalist Chinese forced into military service by the Communists. Because, understandably, these prisoners had no desire to return to China, their release would only embarrass the Chinese. Thus, at the end of the extension, the two sides were even farther apart than they had been at the beginning.

The Making of a Stalemate: Prisoners of War, Airfields, and a Peace Commission

Of all issues at the peace talks, the POW issue was the most complicated, but many others remained unresolved. Most had to do with the postwar settlement. Although both sides had agreed in December to establish a neutral armistice commission to monitor the peace, they had not agreed either on the composition of the group (particularly whether the Soviet Union should be a member) or on how to verify compliance. Nor had they agreed on whether airfields could be reconstructed, how many troops could be rotated, and which ports could be used for troop rotation and resupply.

By mid-January 1952, the Communists' military situation had improved
to the point where they had much less reason to seal a peace agreement. The
ground war had come to a stalemate. The UN forces had ruled out a new offensive, reasoning that any new territory gained would likely have to be surrendered at the time of an agreement anyway, so it would be foolhardy to risk
the lives of their troops for no purpose. The Communists had used the lull to
dig in—and to fortify, resupply, and reinforce their positions. In the air, the
Communists had registered impressive gains. Soviet-built MIG-15s, considered perhaps the best fighter jets in the world (even including American
F-86s), made up nearly half of their 1,400-plane air force. Moreover, the
Communists' antiaircraft defenses were now much improved, allowing them
to send a curtain of flak in the path of oncoming UN aircraft. In January
1952, UN forces lost 44 planes, more than they would lose in any other single
month of the war.

The buildup of Communist forces created another dilemma for the
American negotiators. Even if they were to settle, how could they be sure the
North Koreans would not simply attack again once the United States had
pulled out? Why continue negotiations if the Communists were simply using
the talks as a cover for a substantial entrenchment? Ridgway wanted the UN
team to break off negotiations if the Communists did not bargain in good
faith, whereas the Joint Chiefs believed that if they broke off, the war would
be prolonged indefinitely. The Truman administration was determined to
press on with the negotiations. To deter a post-settlement Communist offensive, Washington announced that if China were to instigate an attack, the
United States would retaliate by attacking China itself. Returned to office in
late 1951, British Prime Minister Winston Churchill gave his government's
backing to such a strategy during a visit to the United States in January 1952.

The POW issue became even more intractable as both sides sought to use
it for propaganda value. For their part, the Communists turned the repatriation issue around, arguing that there should be no forced retention. UN negotiators were severely limited by President Truman's resolve that there be no
forced repatriation. Further complicating the issue, the Communists began a
program of "brainwashing" prisoners they held in the hope that many would
refuse repatriation to the United States and its allies at the end of the war.
They ordered their own soldiers to let themselves be taken prisoner in order to
stir up mutinies in the United Nations POW camps. And they launched a campaign of accusations, charging, for example, that the United Nations had

waged bacteriological warfare—that it had dumped infected rats and insects to spread typhus and smallpox in North Korea and China, and had sent lepers into North Korea.

A series of incidents at Koje-do, an island off the coast of Pusan that the UN command used as a POW camp, inflamed the prisoner-of-war issue and robbed the United States and United Nations of much of their moral leverage on this most sensitive of issues. The island housed most of the POWs held by the U.S./UN command, some 20,000 Chinese and 130,000 North Koreans. Prisoner complaints had merit. The camp was indeed overcrowded and treatment often inhumane. Administrators would turn the other way when Nationalist Chinese guards beat Communist Chinese prisoners. Although there had been disturbances as early as the fall of 1951, a major riot erupted on February 18, 1952. Using homemade weapons, POWs attacked guards; by the time the authorities were able to restore order, 77 prisoners had been killed and 140 wounded. Over the next three months, conditions deteriorated to the point where prisoners were running their own affairs and flying Communist flags. On May 7, they seized the American commander of the camp, and refused to release him until authorities publicly acknowledged inhumane treatment and pledged to improve conditions. Camp authorities issued a statement that satisfied the prisoners, who released the commander, but the camp remained out of control until mid-June, when UN soldiers used flamethrowers and tear gas to restore order in a clash that killed 41 POWs, wounded 274, and killed 1 American. The enemy used these incidents to undermine claims by the United Nations that many prisoners did not want to be repatriated to China or North Korea.

Nevertheless, negotiations continued. Despite the charges and countercharges, both sides wanted to bring the war to an end. Indeed, by early April, negotiators had reached agreement on all but three issues: the return of prisoners of war, reconstruction of airfields, and the question of Soviet membership on the peace commission. Truman's adamancy on "no forced repatriation" gained public support in the early months of 1952, and the UN command became committed to the position. Convinced that no progress on the issue could be expected until hard numbers were available, the United Nations began screening POWs early in April to determine how many might accept repatriation to China or North Korea. In the belief that any figure above 100,000 would probably satisfy China and Korea, before they began the screening, UN authorities had told the Communist negotiators that as many as 116,000 of the 132,000 Chinese and North Korean prisoners might wish to be repatriated. When screening revealed that only 83,000 were willing to return to China or North Korea, the Communists responded that such a figure was absolutely unacceptable.

On April 28, the U.S./UN delegation presented a package proposal to Communist negotiators at Panmunjom offering its position on all three remaining issues: airfields could be rebuilt during the armistice; Poland and Czechoslovakia would be allowed on the peace commission, but not the Soviet Union; and repatriation would be voluntary. After threatening to walk out, on May 7, the Communist negotiators agreed to drop their insistence on Soviet membership on the peace commission in return for compromise settlement of the repatriation issue. Although repatriation was all that remained to be resolved, negotiations on this issue had again reached an impasse.

New Fronts: Military, Diplomatic, and Political

In an effort to break the stalemate, the United States decided to increase pressure on North Korea. Having warned that air attacks would resume if the Communists were not going to negotiate, on May 23, the UN command ordered an attack on a Yalu River power plant and a number of power distribution stations, knocking out electricity in much of North Korea. UN forces struck Pyongyang, the North Korean capital, on July 11 and again on August 29, in the heaviest air attack of the war.

Even as the United Nations increased military pressure on the North, South Korean President Syngman Rhee created more difficulties in the South. Rhee had never been a cooperative ally. His authoritarian leadership rankled American leaders. He had complained bitterly about the abandonment of the goal of reunification, and President Truman had warned him that, if he continued his outspoken criticism, the United States would withdraw its support. In the summer of 1952, Rhee made a bid to solidify his power in the South. By May, it became apparent that the South Korean Assembly would not renew Rhee's claim to the presidency. Rhee responded by declaring martial law in the area around Pusan and by arresting some of his political opponents in the assembly. Confident that he could use the South Korean army and police to ensure victory in a popular election, he planned to have a new assembly elected, which would then declare a popular election for the presidency. Before General Mark Clark, who had relieved General Ridgway, could intervene,

Rhee coerced the assembly both to extend his term and to hold a popular election, which reaffirmed his presidency on August 5. Although opposed to Rhee's dictatorial tactics, the UN command welcomed the end of the political crisis and chose not to take action against him.

Rhee's coerced reelection and the failure of the bombing attacks to move negotiations forward left the Truman administration in a quandary. Late in September, the administration decided to make one last attempt to break the impasse. On September 28, U.S./UN negotiators presented their package proposal at Panmunjom, offering a 10-day period for its consideration. When, on October 8, the Communists rejected the proposal, the United Nations suspended negotiations indefinitely.

The Truman administration entered the last month before the U.S. elections with its foreign policy in shambles and the president's popularity at a low point. When General Clark expressed his regrets that the UN forces had not pressed their military advantage after beating back the Communist offensive in the spring of 1951, his remarks struck a chord with the American public. Democratic presidential nominee Adlai Stevenson, the governor of Illinois, sought to separate himself from the Truman administration and its policies in Korea, but Stevenson faced long odds and a formidable opponent. General Dwight D. Eisenhower, whose heroic feats during World War II made him a popular figure, had defeated Ohio Senator Robert Taft for the Republican nomination. Taft had been explicit in his criticism of the Truman administration's policies in Korea. Eisenhower didn't have to be; moreover, he had said very little about Korea while serving as NATO commander, where his responsibilities centered on Europe in any case. Even after returning to the United States in May 1952 to seek the Republican presidential nomination, the general did not lay out a strategy for ending the war. He had distinguished himself as a moderate in comparison to Taft, who had pledged to name MacArthur as his running mate, and whose combative statements suggested the possibility of a wider war. Although, once nominated, Eisenhower moved to the right, criticizing the administration's "loss" of China as one of the causes of the war in Korea, he continued to avoid specific promises, even to the bellicose right wing of the party. In a major campaign speech on October 24, he simply pledged that, if elected, he would go to Korea, a pledge that, in itself, solidified the general's lead over Stevenson in the polls just days before the election. On November 4, Eisenhower defeated Stevenson decisively, receiving 55 percent of the votes. The president-elect made his promised trip to Korea at the end of the month, but he played down its significance. For security reasons, he didn't even announce the trip until it was nearly over, and turned down an inspection tour prepared by General Clark.

Shortly after the election, Prime Minister Krishna Menon of India proposed that a commission of neutral nations be established to manage the repatriation issue. China and North Korea rejected the proposal, the Soviet ambassador to the United Nations attacked it, and Secretary of State Acheson criticized it. Despite broad opposition among the principal warring states, Menon's proposal had support from Britain, France, and several other nations. Responding to pressure from U.S. allies, Acheson sought modifications to make the proposal acceptable to the Truman administration, the most important of which dealt with the timing of the release of POWs. Menon agreed to the modifications, and the United States accepted the changes. In December, the resolution passed in the UN General Assembly by a vote of 54 to 45.

The Truman administration, however, was now in its twilight. Even a substantial bombing attack on bridges near the mouth of the Yalu early in January 1953 could not compel the Communists to negotiate.

War's End: The Eisenhower Administration and the Completion of Negotiations

In his February 4 State of the Union address, the new president announced that the Seventh Fleet would no longer patrol the Formosa Strait, raising fears that Chiang Kai-shek's Nationalist forces might be unleashed on China. The Chinese responded that the war could be ended quickly on terms already presented at Pamunjon—in other words, no voluntary repatriation. When the Eisenhower administration insisted it would only accept a solution based on voluntary repatriation, it became clear the impasse remained.

With the death of Joseph Stalin on March 6, the equation in Korea suddenly changed. His successor, Georgi Malenkov, announced that there were no differences between the United States and the Soviet Union that could not be resolved by peaceful means. Before the end of the month, the Communists agreed to an earlier proposal by General Clark to exchange sick and wounded prisoners; China proposed that a neutral party might supervise the release of those prisoners who had refused repatriation. Amid these signs of hope, however, were signs that the road to peace would still be bumpy. The Communists offered only about one-tenth the number of sick and wounded prisoners of-

fered by the allies—684 in exchange for 6,670—in what became known as the
"Little Switch." Then, when the exchange took place, they published stories
complaining of the treatment of their prisoners by the UN command. Finally,
on April 16, one of the most celebrated single battles of the war took place, a
heavy but unsuccessful three-day Chinese assault on the American position on
a small mound that the Americans called "Pork Chop Hill."

Nonetheless, negotiations resumed at Panmunjom on April 26, after a
hiatus of more than six months. Hopes for a quick resolution of the repatriation issue soon evaporated. The two sides disagreed over who would supervise
repatriation, over where the exchange would take place, and even over
whether there should be an interim period during which reluctant prisoners
might be persuaded to return.

On May 25, the UN command offered what the Eisenhower administration considered its final proposal on the POW issue. A repatriate screening
center would be established in the demilitarized zone between North and
South Korea under supervision of India. Although the Communists could
employ persuasion—a major concession by the United Nations—after six
months, all remaining prisoners would be released. While considering the
proposal, the Communists initiated several attacks against the UN line, the
most successful of which threatened to break through South Korean defenses.
Reinforcements shored up the line, however, and it held.

With its POW proposal on the table, the Eisenhower administration developed contingency plans in case either the Communists or Syngman Rhee's
government rejected it. It discussed widening the war and even using the
atomic bomb should the Communists not cooperate. Eisenhower refused to
give the Joint Chiefs the authority to use the bomb if the peace proposal fell
apart, but did not foreclose the possibility he might reconsider. When Syngman Rhee made it clear he was not satisfied with the American proposal and
would accept nothing short of reunification, Eisenhower made it equally clear
he wanted to end the war quickly along the lines of terms then in place.

The Communists replied to the U.S./UN proposal on June 4, demanding several insignificant changes. On June 8, negotiators for both sides signed
terms of reference settling the prisoner-of-war issue. Upon conclusion of an
armistice, both sides would turn over all their prisoners to India, which represented the Neutral Nation Repatriation Commission. During the first two
months, all prisoners who wished to return to their homeland could do so.
During the next three months, each side could attempt to persuade its citizens

who chose not to return to reconsider. Ultimately, the Communists exchanged 12,773 prisoners for 75,823. Of the 19,840 Chinese prisoners, 14,200 chose not to return to China (they went to Taiwan instead); of the 55,983 North Korean prisoners, 7,760 chose not to return to North Korea; and of the 3,618 American prisoners, 21 chose not to return to the United States.

With the POW issue resolved, the biggest obstacle to peace was Syngman Rhee. The Eisenhower administration used a combination of threats and persuasion to try to bring its ally into line. The Army drew up contingency plans in an attempt to anticipate South Korean actions, the most extreme of which would have included a declaration of martial law. Rhee welcomed Washington's pledges of economic and military aid, but still refused to accept the peace proposal. Instead, he engineered anti-American protests outside the American embassy in Pusan, and the mass breakout of more than 25,000 North Korean prisoners. Eisenhower responded with a threat to pursue "another arrangement" if the Rhee government continued its intransigence. By the end of the month, Rhee reluctantly agreed that he would no longer to oppose the peace treaty. He exacted a price: increased economic aid from the United States—and a mutual defense pact.

Although all the elements for a peace agreement were now in place, the ground war continued. From July 6 to July 19, the Chinese conducted a final offensive, concentrating on American forces at Porkchop Hill, and assaulting South Korean forces in other locales. In fighting even more intense than it had been three months before, the Communists overran the American position; South Korean forces had to give ground. By July 19, the front stabilized, with UN forces regaining some of the territory they had relinquished. This last battle was costly, with more than 14,000 casualties on the U.S./UN side, and an even greater number on the Communist side. General Clark suggested that the Communists wanted to demonstrate to Syngman Rhee the futility of any attack against North Korea. It was an effective but deadly demonstration.

The negotiators at Panmunjom finally reached an agreement on July 19, stipulating that fighting had to end twelve hours after the signing of an armistice. Each side had to then withdraw 2 kilometers from the front, creating a demilitarized zone, and to freeze the number of non-Korean troops in the country. In the days that followed, the two sides established the cease-fire line. Finally, on the morning of July 27, representatives of North Korea and the U.S./UN command met in a newly constructed wooden building, and formally signed the armistice agreement. Twelve hours later, at 10:00 P.M., the Korean War came to an end without a formal peace treaty. Two later attempts to conclude a treaty—in October 1953, and at Geneva in the spring of 1954—failed. The people of Korea had to settle for an uneasy armistice, indefinitely extended. Nearly half a century after the end of the war, North and South Korea remain bitter adversaries, glaring at one another across the demilitarized zone.

The human costs of the war were staggering, all the more so in light of the meager changes in territory. Some 4 million people, half of them civilians, lost their lives, with American losses totaling 54,246. The war cost the United States approximately $20 billion, and an additional $5 billion in aid after the war.

The Korean War had a lasting impact on American policy around the world. In the Far East, it led to a fundamental realignment of interests. The United States now had a stake in the future of South Korea. As in the case of its support for Chiang Kai-shek, Washington supported an authoritarian leader in Asia who often pursued policies antithetical to American constitutional principles, but who nonetheless represented a bulwark against Communism. No longer would South Korea or Taiwan rest outside the American defense perimeter. Relations with the new Communist government in mainland China had been poisoned by the war, and for the next two decades there would be no move toward reconciliation. China, however, had emerged as the dominant force in Asia, the nation with the most formidable military capability. China had given ample evidence of its independence from the Soviet Union, foreshadowing the Sino-Soviet split that would occur a decade later. Japan also took on new importance in America's Far East equation. No longer a conquered enemy, it offered the prospect of another barrier against Soviet expansionism in the Pacific.

American policy elsewhere also felt the effect of Korea. The fourfold increase in defense spending and the placement of increased numbers American troops, ships, and planes abroad reflect the accuracy of Secretary of State Dean Acheson's comment that the Korean War took NSC-68 from the realm of theory to reality. The United States moved to solidify the NATO alliance, sending two new divisions to Europe and moving to incorporate West Germany into the Western alliance.

The Korean War was America's first major international conflict since the beginning of the atomic age. One of the positive developments of the Korean War thus was something that did *not* happen. The bomb was not used, even though both the Eisenhower and the Truman administrations had considered doing so. A more ominous development was President Truman's decision to proceed with development of the hydrogen bomb, which was many times as powerful as the atomic bomb that had been dropped on Hiroshima. The first successful test of the H-bomb occurred on October 31, 1952.

The presidency gained in power as a result of President Truman's conduct as commander in chief. The dismissal of General MacArthur firmly established the principle of civilian leadership of the American armed forces. That it was carried out with the unanimous backing of the Joint Chiefs of Staff gave the decision additional weight. The means by which the United States entered the war also had enormous consequences. As the first undeclared war in American history, the Korean War strengthened the ability of the president to commit troops abroad without congressional assent.

The war shattered the bipartisanship that had characterized American foreign policy since the end of World War II. President Truman had always insisted that politics must stop as the water's edge, that foreign policy must be bipartisan. That hope died on the snowy battlefields of Korea. The war showed the hazards of fighting a land war in Asia, and demonstrated that technological superiority was not enough to ensure victory. The next generation of American soldiers would have to relearn those lessons in Vietnam.

Recommended Reading

There are many excellent books available on the Korean War. Burton I. Kaufman's *The Korean War: Challenges in Crisis, Credibility, and Command* (Philadelphia: Temple University Press, 1986) stands out as a concise, readable account that gives attention to the prewar situation in Korea and to the diplomatic, political, and military aspects of the war. Other accessible accounts are Richard Whelan's *Drawing the Line: The Korean War, 1950–1953* (Boston: Little, Brown, 1990) and Joseph Goulden's *Korea: The Untold Story of the War* (New York: Times Books, 1982). William Stueck's *The Korean War: An International History* (Princeton, N.J.: Princeton University Press, 1995) places the war in a broad global perspective. Rosemary Foot's *The Wrong War: American Policy and the Dimensions of the Korean Conflict, 1950–1953* (Ithaca, N.Y.: Cornell University Press, 1985) concentrates on the development of U.S. foreign policy, and includes an excellent chronology. The best biography of General MacArthur is D. Clayton James's three-volume study *The Years of MacArthur* (Boston: Houghton Mifflin, 1967–85). Geoffrey Perret's *Old Soldiers Never Die: The Life of Douglas MacArthur* (New York: Random House, 1996) is an excellent recent one-volume biography.

4

Liking Ike

Domestic Politics in Eisenhower's First Term, 1953–1956

REPUBLICANS EAGERLY AWAITED the 1952 election. Democrats had held the presidency for two decades, and Republicans had come tantalizingly close to defeating Truman in 1948. Even after he declared that he would not run in 1952, Republicans wanted to be sure that the Democratic candidate would have to run on Truman's record. The Republican Party had several prospective candidates, but the race changed dramatically when party moderates convinced the World War II hero General Dwight D. Eisenhower, who had commanded Allied forces in the D-Day invasion of France in 1944, to seek the nomination. Although he had been affiliated with neither party, Eisenhower's name was well known and his reputation sterling.

Eisenhower: A Military Man for President

Born in Denison, Texas, on October 14, 1890, Dwight David Eisenhower had spent most of has boyhood in Abilene, Kansas, just 150 miles west of Harry S. Truman's home in Independence, Missouri. Eisenhower grew up in a fundamentalist and pacifist religious tradition, in which regular Bible readings reinforced the moral lessons of daily life. Sports—especially football—were an important part of his youth: he was the best athlete of five competitive brothers. His father worked at a creamery, and the large family crowded into a small house that today stands on the grounds of the Eisenhower Presidential Library and Museum. Appointed to the Military Academy at West Point, he graduated in 1915 in the top third of his class.

During World War I, Eisenhower served Stateside as a tank instructor; in the early 1920s, he served in Panama under General Fox Conner, whose professionalism left a deep impression on him. Conner recommended Eisenhower for an appointment to the Command and General Staff School at Fort Leavenworth, Kansas, the Army's equivalent of graduate school. Eisenhower's performance gained him admission to the Army War College, from which he graduated in 1929. Assigned to the staff of General Douglas A. MacArthur until 1938, he accompanied the general to the Philippines in 1935, serving as MacArthur's assistant and as an advisor to the Philippine government.

When World War II began, Eisenhower served under General George C. Marshall, the Army's chief of staff, where he gained invaluable managerial experience. Marshall assigned him to London, where he took command of the European Theater of Operations. In command of the Allied war effort, Eisenhower coordinated the Allied invasion of North Africa, the invasion of Sicily, and the campaign in Italy. His abilities to organize and to get independent-minded individuals to cooperate won him one of the most important assignments of the war, command of the D-Day Normandy invasion in 1944 and of the war-ending drive to Germany. Opponents who later criticized Eisenhower for his lack of political experience overlooked his years on MacArthur's staff, and his masterful wartime performance in commanding, cajoling, and coordinating egocentric figures such as the strong-willed General Charles de Gaulle, leader of French forces in exile, Britain's prickly Field Marshall Bernard Montgomery, and the American martinet General George S. Patton. President Truman rewarded Eisenhower by naming him Army chief of staff.

After the war, speculation rose about Eisenhower's potential as a presidential candidate. Figures as diverse as President Truman and Generals Marshall and MacArthur suggested that he consider running. Eisenhower expressed no interest, insisting that the American people did not want a military man for president. He resigned from the Army in June 1947 to become president of Columbia University, a position that enabled him to avoid the trials of politics. When, in the fall of 1950, President Truman asked him to take command of North Atlantic Treaty Organization (NATO) forces, he agreed to out of a sense of duty. Like the Columbia presidency, the position as supreme Allied commander in Europe enhanced his prestige, and kept his

4. President Truman shaking hands with General Dwight D. Eisenhower at Washington National Airport, upon Eisenhower's return from Europe, January 31, 1951. Truman Library Photographs, Harry S. Truman Library, Accession no. 73–3497.

hands clean of the dirt of politics, which at the time, thanks to Senator Mc-Carthy's anti-Communist campaign and allegations of corruption in the Truman administration, had become dirty indeed.

In the meantime, friends and supporters began to organize for a presidential run. Most of his Republican supporters were part of the Eastern liberal wing, which believed Eisenhower could wrest control of the party away from Senator Robert Taft, whose base of strength was his home state of Ohio and the Midwest. Among those eager to throw Eisenhower's hat in the ring were Massachusetts Senator Henry Cabot Lodge Jr.; former Republican standard-bearer Thomas E. Dewey, who lost to Truman in the dramatic 1948 election; Wall Street attorney Herbert Brownell, who had worked with Dewey; and the financier-industrialist Paul Hoffman, who had served as administrator of the Marshall Plan. Hoffman chaired a group called the "Advisory Committee of

Citizens for Eisenhower." Governor Sherman Adams of New Hampshire, who would later become Eisenhower's chief of staff, also signed on early and played a key role in the campaign. It fell to them to convince Eisenhower, first, to run for president and, second, to run as a Republican. Neither task was as difficult as Eisenhower made it appear; despite his professed lack of interest, he had been considering running for some time. His background and beliefs predisposed him toward the Republicans. Divisions within the party between moderates and conservatives and between internationalists and isolationists disturbed him. Indeed, more than anything else, it was his commitment to internationalism and his vehement opposition to isolationism that propelled him into the race.

The Republicans in 1952: Eisenhower versus Taft

Eisenhower's opponent in the quest for the Republican nomination was Robert A. Taft, the leading representative of the conservative-isolationist wing of the party. The son of former President and Chief Justice of the Supreme Court William Howard Taft, the younger Taft was the choice of most party regulars for the nomination. Having graduated first in his class at Yale and at Harvard Law School, he had become an accomplished lawyer and a successful politician in his own right. Taft and his supporters believed he should have been nominated in 1948, and believed just as fervently that the man who defeated him, Thomas E. Dewey, had squandered an opportunity to win the general election. Taft was bright, honest, trustworthy, and respected by Senate colleagues in both parties. A senator since 1938, he had developed such influence that contemporaries proclaimed him "Mr. Republican." Unfortunately, when it came to personal appeal, Taft was no match for Eisenhower; as often as reporters used "warm" to describe Eisenhower, they used "cold" for Taft.

Their positions on foreign policy stood in striking contrast. Internationalist Eisenhower supported NATO and vigorous U.S. involvement in Europe. Isolationist Taft had opposed NATO; he had supported Truman's program of aid to Greece and Turkey and the Marshall Plan only because he believed they might help in the battle against Communism. Although a less-determined isolationist when it came to Asia—Taft supported the American role in Korea—he contested the means by which Truman had taken the nation to war, and agreed with other Republican critics of Truman's China policy.

The campaign battle between Eisenhower as "Mr. Outside" and Taft as "Mr. Inside" played out through the early months of 1952 and right into the Republican convention. Eisenhower announced early in January that he was a Republican, and that he would accept a draft for the party's nomination, but that he intended to stay on the job at NATO headquarters for the time being, and thus out of politics. He would return home only in early June. In the meantime, Taft had built up a lead among party regulars, and as the convention neared he believed he had nearly enough votes to clinch the nomination. The battle turned bitter, with Taft supporters criticizing Eisenhower's lack of experience, alleging that he had had an affair with his military driver Kay Summersby, and claiming that Mamie Eisenhower had an alcohol problem, an allegation that Eisenhower denied categorically.

Ironically, at the Republican National Convention in Philadelphia, the political veteran Taft found himself outmaneuvered by the supposedly naïve political amateur, who found a weak spot in Taft's supposed strong suit, his control of the party apparatus. As a concession to the Taft wing of the party, Eisenhower suggested he might choose Richard Nixon for his running mate. When Taft amassed delegates through his ties to officials who dominated the state Republican Party in several states, Eisenhower supporters cried foul. At the center of the dispute was the Texas delegation, whose votes both sides considered crucial. Eisenhower's backers convinced Taft that, Democratic corruption being one of the strongest issues for Republicans, the Republican nomination could not be determined by what appeared to be a rigged system. Taft accepted a "fair play" proposal under which disputed credentials could be examined. The proposal gave Eisenhower the opening he needed, and soon Taft supporters, who decided they would rather win with Eisenhower than lose with Taft, began to switch. On the third ballot, Eisenhower went over the top.

Eisenhower may not have had much experience in the political arena, but he knew better than to alienate the Taft wing of the party. By selecting as his running mate Senator Richard M. Nixon of California, whose 39 years nicely balanced Ike's 61, and whose pursuit of Alger Hiss helped consolidate support from conservative Republicans, Eisenhower showed that he wasn't simply a creature of the Eastern establishment. Morever, in September, the nominee invited Taft to his residence in Morningside Heights, near the Columbia University campus. Eisenhower accepted most of Taft's domestic program, and minimized their differences over foreign policy. Accusing

Eisenhower of selling out his moderate credentials for the support of the Republican Right, Democrats crowed about the "Surrender at Morningside Heights." Ultimately, however, the agreement the two men reached would matter little in terms of policy. After the election, as Senate majority leader, Taft served the administration effectively and loyally, holding together a consensus that won approval for most of Eisenhower's domestic program despite the Republican Party's meager one-vote advantage.

The Democrats in 1952: Adlai Stevenson, the Reluctant Candidate

The Democrats also fought among themselves before accepting Illinois Governor Adlai Stevenson as their standard-bearer. Although Truman had decided not to run for reelection in April 1950, he didn't tell his staff until the spring of 1952, making his decision public on March 29. As Truman surveyed the Democrats' field of prospective nominees, he found that most had serious liabilities. The one candidate aggressively pursuing the nomination was Senator Estes Kefauver of Tennessee, who had gained national attention with an investigation of crime in America in 1950–51. The televised hearings captivated Americans, but angered Truman, who was peeved that Kansas City and Saint Louis in his home state had such a high profile in the investigation. Because Kefauver had also alienated other party regulars, even a strong showing in early primaries made him an unlikely choice. The president dismissed him as "peculiar" and disloyal, referring to him privately as "Cow Fever."

The party had good men, Truman believed, but some of the best were not electable. Senator Richard Russell of Georgia, as a Southerner, could not attract Northern liberals. Vice President Alben Barkley, at 74, was too old. Oklahoma Senator Robert Kerr had ties to oil interests. Averell Harriman, who had held several diplomatic posts, and who might have been the ablest candidate, had never run for election; his reputation as a Northeastern Wall Street tycoon would make him unattractive to other sections of the country. Gradually, the list narrowed to Illinois Governor Adlai Stevenson.

Stevenson's grandfather had been vice president under Cleveland, and his father had been active in state politics in Illinois. He was a sophisticated, witty speaker, whose speeches read like polished essays. Educated at Princeton, Harvard Law School, and the Northwestern University law school, he developed a reputation as an intellectual—a drawback in the give-and-take of

American politics, and one he could never entirely shake, enduring ridicule as an "egghead" throughout the campaign. During World War II, he served as special assistant to the secretary of the Navy. Running as a reformer in 1948, he was elected governor of Illinois, largely on the promise to clean up the mess in state politics. Truman decided to back Stevenson, and told him so—becoming the first president to have told both of the major party presidential candidates he would back them if they ran for his office. A further irony is that, by Election Day, Truman wasn't sure that he wanted either one.

Stevenson refused to commit himself to the race until the convention, a stance that irritated the decisive Truman. But the president, without meaning to do so, had placed Stevenson in a difficult position. Truman's approval rating had plunged, dropping to as low as a 23 percent, lower even than President Nixon would reach during Watergate. Stevenson believed that even though he needed support from the administration, he could not afford to appear to be Truman's handpicked candidate. A breach between the two would have been disastrous, but Stevenson needed to establish his independence. The remaining months of the campaign involved a delicate dance between the two men, with Stevenson executing the most difficult steps, and not always very well. Stevenson acceded to Truman's suggestion of a running mate, Senator John Sparkman of Alabama, but selected his own party chairman, rejecting Truman's handpicked incumbent. Stevenson set up his campaign headquarters in Illinois rather than in Washington, where Truman believed it should be.

Stevenson's biggest problem was to establish that his administration wouldn't simply be an extension of Truman's, as Truman's had been of the Roosevelt administration. Late in August, a reporter asked Stevenson what he would do to clean up the "mess in Washington," referring to the charges of corruption then plaguing the administration. Stevenson replied, "As to whether I can clean up the mess in Washington, I would bespeak the careful scrutiny of what I inherited in Illinois and what has been accomplished in three years." The Democratic nominee had in effect acknowledged that he agreed that there was indeed a mess in Washington. Truman was understandably angry, but nonetheless campaigned vigorously in the late weeks of the campaign. Stevenson believed that Truman's high profile might not help his campaign, but to tell Truman to stay home could have split the party. Truman toured the country in a whistle-stop trip reminiscent of his victorious 1948 journey, perhaps more intent on establishing the record of his administration than on electing Stevenson.

Campaign 1952: Political Chess and Checkers

Stevenson's campaign reflected what friends praised as freewheeling spontaneity, and critics condemned as a lack of organization. He had a talented group of speechwriters, including the historian Arthur Schlesinger Jr., and when their efforts were blended with Stevenson's own wit and eloquence, the result lifted the level of campaign rhetoric to levels it had seldom achieved. Voters and commentators alike often described the Illinois governor as a "statesman." He ran a distinguished race. If the electorate had awarded points for style, the election would have been a much closer contest.

In the end, Stevenson had too much to overcome. He was running against an attractive candidate who had no personal connection to the underside of Republican politics—McCarthyism, conservative isolationism—and whose military service had established him as one of the genuine heroes of the Allied victory in World War II. Meanwhile, against his will, Stevenson had been forced to carry the baggage of the Truman administration. The Democrats had held the White House for twenty years, and many people believed it was time for a change.

The Republicans touted their formula for victory: "K_1C_2," suggesting that Korea, Communism, and Corruption were issues that Truman had bungled so badly that the Republicans could ride them into the White House. Republicans blamed the Democrats for the war, alleging that by placing Korea outside the American defense perimeter, Secretary of State Dean Acheson's January 1950 speech was an invitation to attack. Now, three years later, the war in Korea was stalemated, and many people still resented Truman's dismissal of General MacArthur. Thus, according to the Republican line, Truman had started the war, mismanaged his responsibilities as commander in chief, and now couldn't find a way out. Eisenhower's late-October campaign promise that if elected, "I shall go to Korea," offered little more than hope as a means of ending the war, but that was enough. Many people believed that the World War II general might fare better than the World War I artillery captain had in ending the war.

Even though many Republicans, including the nominee, had begun to feel uncomfortable with Senator McCarthy's demagoguery, anti-Communism was still a winning issue for the Republicans. And Nixon could match anti-Communist rhetoric with anyone. He accused Alger Hiss of being a "graduate of Dean Acheson's spineless school of diplomacy." Eisenhower, who knew as well as anyone the value of consensus, was unwilling to risk splitting his party by attacking the Wisconsin senator directly, but one of the foremost questions about his candidacy was his position on McCarthy. In September, Eisenhower traveled to McCarthy's home state of Wisconsin, prepared to defend General George Marshall against McCarthy, with the senator close by on the speaker's platform. Eisenhower admired Marshall, who had chosen him to lead the Normandy invasion in 1944. As written, the speech would have defended Marshall against McCarthy's charges, but without naming McCarthy as the source of those charges. Coaxed by the governor of Wisconsin and his own staff, Eisenhower agreed to drop the paragraph from his key Wisconsin speech in Milwaukee. Although Eisenhower would criticize McCarthy's techniques elsewhere during the campaign and speak obliquely about differences with the senator, it was mild stuff. An opportunity for a firm denunciation had passed.

McCarthy turned his venom on the Democratic nominee, Adlai Stevenson. Calling the Roosevelt-Truman years "twenty years of treason," he associated the nominee whenever possible with the outgoing Truman administration, and especially the secretary of state. He condemned Stevenson as having a "Ph.D. from Dean Acheson's cowardly college of Communist Containment." In an address in Chicago on October 27, just days before the election, McCarthy labeled the Democratic nominee part of the "Acheson-Hiss-Lattimore group." In a deliberate slip of the tongue, he referred to "Alger—I mean Adlai."

Corruption—the "mess in Washington"—was the third ingredient in the Republican formula for victory. Truman's second term had been plagued by scandals, none of which had implicated the president directly, but which collectively had created the impression of a president who was too tolerant of the misdeeds of subordinates, and of a party too long in power. The most serious of the scandals had touched two federal agencies. After the war, the Reconstruction Finance Corporation loaned federal money to private businesses in large amounts—too large to monitor. Moreover, tax collectors in the Bureau of Internal Revenue, forerunner of the Internal Revenue Service, had abused their positions of trust.

When it came to corruption, however, the Republicans had one anxious moment. Word leaked out that a group of wealthy Californians that contributed to a fund at the disposal of Richard Nixon, the Republican vice presidential nominee. The $18,000 fund threatened to take the corruption issue away from the Republicans. Eisenhower edged away from Nixon, and considered dropping him from the ticket, but decided to wait to see how the public reacted to Nixon's defense of his actions on television.

Nixon's "Checkers Speech," delivered with his wife Pat seated beside him, was a landmark in television history, and showed the power of the new medium to reach into American homes. Nixon disclosed his personal finances, saying that the only gift his family had received was a little dog named Checkers, and that he had no intention of giving him up no matter what people might say. He attacked Democrats as the party that had tolerated corruption, and insisted that he hadn't personally profited from the fund. More important, Nixon, who felt he had been treated as a mere appendage of the Eisenhower team, did two things that assured his own continuation on the Republican ticket and that incurred Eisenhower's abiding distrust. First, he suggested that Stevenson and Sparkman should follow his example and reveal their personal finances. The proposal, which hadn't been cleared with Eisenhower, angered the Republican standard-bearer since it implied that he, too, would have to release his finances to public scrutiny. Second, Nixon asked people to write to the Republican National Committee, which, he said, would have to decide whether he would stay on the ticket. The decision was not the committee's to make, of course. By implying that it was, Nixon made it difficult for Eisenhower to dismiss him if Nixon received substantial public support, which indeed is what happened. When Nixon flew to Wheeling, West Virginia, Eisenhower met him at the airport. Dashing up the stairway to the plane, Ike put his arm around his running mate and said, "You're my boy!" Nixon believed he had been patronized, even humiliated. The incident left scars.

On Election Day, Eisenhower's victory testified to his extraordinary popularity throughout the country: he won 55 percent of the popular vote to Stevenson's 44 percent and 442 electoral votes to his 89. Indeed, Stevenson won only nine states—seven Southern states and the border states of Kentucky and West Virginia. Even in the Solid South, a traditional Democratic stronghold, Eisenhower picked up Virginia, Tennessee, Florida, and Texas. Although Republicans also won control of the House and Senate, they

gained a disappointing 22 seats in the House and held only a one-seat majority in the Senate. Even Henry Cabot Lodge Jr., who had played in important
role in Eisenhower's campaign, lost his Senate seat—to upstart Congressman
John F. Kennedy. In Wisconsin, McCarthy won reelection—though not decisively. Eisenhower carried the state by 357,569 votes; McCarthy, by only
139,042. The senator trailed all other Republicans on the Wisconsin ballot
seeking statewide or national election, and trailed badly in Madison and Milwaukee, where he had won handily before and where the press had attacked
him regularly.

The consensus was that Eisenhower's victory had been personal; the electoral contest had been less between parties than between personalities. Eisenhower seemed much more a man of the people, and had far broader appeal
than his opponent; Stevenson's erudition won him the votes of intellectuals.
Even if Stevenson had successfully distanced himself from Truman's policies,
the Democratic candidate still faced one of the most popular figures in American public life. Former General Eisenhower was a very human hero, not distant or Olympian. Ike's smile dazzled voters, and suggested a warmth that
people who knew him claimed was genuine. It is unlikely that any Democrat
could have defeated him in 1952.

Transition: Preparing for a New Administration

The president-elect now began the ritual of transition and the selection of
a cabinet and staff. General Lucius Clay, who had served as military governor
of the U.S. zone of occupation in Germany, and Herbert Brownell, who
would be appointed attorney general, headed the transition team that
screened candidates for high-ranking positions. They turned to business leaders for advice, and the cabinet they selected, described by critics as "eight millionaires and a plumber," showed it. Union man Martin Durkin, who had
served as president of the United Association of Plumbers and Steamfitters,
lasted only a few months; by the summer, only millionaires came to cabinet
meetings.

The vital position of secretary of state went to John Foster Dulles, who
was more than two years older than the president, and who had over thirty
years of experience in areas related to foreign policy. Dulles's grandfather and
father had been Presbyterian clergymen, and his own views on foreign policy
were influenced by religious and moral considerations. His uncle had been

secretary of state under Wilson, and Dulles himself had served on Wilson's staff at the Versailles Peace Conference in 1919. He had devoted most of his career to international law; although a Republican, he had held diplomatic posts under Roosevelt and Truman, serving as a delegate to the United Nations conference in San Francisco. Thomas Dewey's foreign policy advisor in 1948, Dulles expected to be nominated as secretary of state in the Dewey administration. In 1950 and 1951, he negotiated the peace treaty with Japan that allowed the United States to maintain its defense bases there. By 1952, he had earned a reputation as the Republican Party's most experienced spokesperson on foreign policy issues.

Having left his position as president of General Motors to become Eisenhower's secretary of defense, Charles Wilson got in trouble during his confirmation hearings and never fully recovered. When he was asked to relinquish his stock in GM because of the company's defense contracts, Wilson refused, replying, "For years, I thought what was good for the country was good for General Motors, and vice versa." The statement, often misquoted as "What is good for General Motors is good for the country," haunted him, but gave indication of what was to come. Wilson never fully shed his reputation for arrogance and "foot-in-mouth" disease, suggesting at one point that he might seek to cut back the National Guard, which he claimed was made up of people trying to avoid regular military service. But he was loyal to Eisenhower, and worked hard to get the president's defense budget cuts enacted.

As secretary of the treasury, Cleveland industrialist George M. Humphrey became Eisenhower's most important domestic policy advisor. Humphrey's pro-business perspective and desire to cut federal spending and the budget deficit sat well with the president, with whom he developed as much rapport as any member of the cabinet; his influence extended well beyond the purview of Treasury. Eisenhower placed him on the National Security Council, and sought his advice on other matters as well.

Appointed chief of staff, former New Hampshire Governor Sherman Adams, who had been one of the first governors to endorse Eisenhower a year before the election and later Ike's campaign manager, served as indispensable gatekeeper for the president. Eisenhower's approach to governing, drawn from his military experience, relied on a chain of command that went through Adams, who monitored the president's schedule, controlled access, handled patronage, and often said no to protect Eisenhower from having to do so. Only Secretary of State Dulles could get through to the president directly. Resenting his iron hand, reporters came to refer to Adams as the "Abominable No-Man."

Eisenhower's younger brother Milton became his closest confidant. Former president of Kansas State and Pennsylvania State Universities, Milton had served as a consultant during the Truman administration on agricultural and labor issues. Although he didn't hold an official full-time position, he advised the president on several domestic issues, including agriculture and education, and served as his personal representative to Latin America.

The Truman-Eisenhower transition was not a smooth one. Bitter attacks during the 1952 election campaign had left a chill between the incumbent and the president-elect. When Truman offered the assistance of his staff, he believed that Eisenhower had shown little grace in turning him down. Resentment built over small slights that would not be forgotten for many years. Without consulting Truman, the president-elect chose to wear a homburg instead of the traditional top hat to the Inaugural. Truman went along with Ike's choice rather than make an issue of it. When the Eisenhowers arrived at the North Portico of the White House, the president-elect did not go to the door to greet the president, but waited until Truman walked toward the car.

As Truman rode beside Eisenhower on the way to the Capitol for the inauguration ceremony, their conversation was anything but cordial. When Eisenhower remarked that he had stayed away from the 1948 Inaugural so that he would not draw attention away from the president, Truman remembered replying, "You were not here in 1948 because I did not send for you. If I had sent for you, you would have come." When the conversation turned to who had ordered Ike's son John home from combat in Korea so that he might attend the 1952 Inaugural, Eisenhower recalled Truman replying, "I did." But, as Truman recalled it, he had said, "The President thought it was right and proper for your son to witness the swearing in of his father to the presidency."

The chill of Inauguration Day developed into a "feud" that became the subject of occasional articles in the nation's press. In the eight years of Eisenhower's presidency, Truman and Eisenhower did not see each other once. Only after he retired did Eisenhower meet with Truman, in Kansas City. Later, Truman hosted an Eisenhower visit to the Truman Library in Independence, bringing about a thaw in the presidential Cold War.

A New Course: The "Middle Way"

Eisenhower assumed the presidency at a difficult time, with major crises abroad, where the Korean War continued to rage, and at home, where McCarthyism was still rampant. He made it clear, however, that he was going to seek balance in his personal life. He had been dealing with large issues for years, and had learned to keep a sense of proportion, reserving time for relaxation. His leisure pursuits became the subject of criticism, and led some to believe that he was too passive, devoting insufficient time to affairs of state. He was not well read, and critics began to ridicule him when they learned that his favorite reading material included westerns. Golf, however, was his consuming leisure passion. He set aside Wednesday and Saturday afternoons and Sundays, and often spent them on the links. He frequently vacationed at Augusta National. Golf became the subject of barbs, and contributed to the misperception that Eisenhower was a grandfatherly figure who delegated important responsibilities to subordinates, but was often out of touch with important developments.

The president contributed to this image in press conferences that seemed to expose a leader who was ill informed and spoke in convoluted ramblings. Often, however, the opacity of his press conference statements prevented reporters from pinning him down into positions he did not want to take. Eisenhower's reluctance to develop the kind of give-and-take with reporters that distinguished Truman's press conferences left the press at an arm's distance. Once, Press Secretary James Hagerty came to the president moments before Eisenhower was scheduled to meet with reporters, trying quickly to fill him in on details of a breaking story. "Don't worry, I'll just confuse them," the president told Hagerty. And he did. On the other hand, those who recalled attending administration meetings uniformly praised the president's ability to organize his thoughts, clarify issues of contention, and summarize proceedings. Eisenhower's prose—clear, vigorous, astute, and to the point—belies the image of Ike as an imprecise bumbler. He was neither a fuzzy thinker nor did he tolerate fuzzy thinking in his advisors.

For a leader who could be incisive on paper, direct in one-on-one conversations, and commanding in small groups, Eisenhower appeared awkward and ill at ease when speaking in public. Television offered enormous opportunities for an astute politician to reach the public, but Eisenhower was slow to appreciate its potential. No less than the master television interviewer Edward R. Murrow suggested to the president that he needed to improve his television appearance. Finally, prodded by the prominent Republican Henry Cabot Lodge, Eisenhower accepted coaching from the actor Robert Montgomery. Over time, the president developed more polish, although he was never entirely comfortable with the new medium. But, in a sense, it never mattered, for Eisenhower established a rapport with the American people that few other presidents ever did. His popularity never flagged; it was unusual for his ratings to fall below 65 percent and usually they stayed above 70.

Eisenhower believed that the political extremes threatened American democracy. He sought the "middle way," believing that "pressure groups," interests of the Left or Right, and class-based politics, especially in the context of the pressures of modern society that was increasingly complex, could disrupt and divide American society. Likewise, he distrusted big government, which could undermine individual initiative. Historian Robert Griffith described Eisenhower's vision as that of a "corporate commonwealth" based on "a broad, internally consistent, social philosophy" designed to "fashion a new corporative economy that would avoid both the destructive disorder of unregulated capitalism and the threat to business autonomy posed by socialism." Such a vision required moderation, conciliation, and cooperation. To critics, such sentiments seemed rationalizations for inaction, particularly in Eisenhower's response to some of the most challenging issues of the day, McCarthyism and civil rights.

Fiscal Conservatism and the Legacy of the New Deal

Eisenhower's route down the middle of the road involved a commitment to conservative fiscal policy. But those who expected Eisenhower to dismantle the programs of the New Deal would be disappointed. Although, from the beginning, Eisenhower worked to reduce expenditures and balance the budget, he selectively supported New Deal programs such as Social Security that had broad public support, and demonstrated a pragmatic willingness to commit funds to large-scale public works projects. Clear differences existed between Eisenhower and the Roosevelt-Truman policies on natural resource issues, but rather than scrap many of these programs altogether, the president tried to alter them, limit their growth. Usually, this entailed providing opportunity for private investment or state involvement. In only one major sector of the economy—that of agricultural policy—did the administration try to reverse the legacy of the New Deal.

Welfare was anathema to many Republicans. To many conservatives, Social Security epitomized the evils perpetrated by the New Deal. But, far from killing it, Eisenhower proposed to extend it to an additional ten million citizens. Congress rejected the proposal the first time he brought it up in 1953, but passed it the following year. Furthermore, Eisenhower revived a proposal first presented by Truman, the creation of a new cabinet-level department to deal with social issues, the Department of Health, Education, and Welfare, using the Federal Security Agency as a core foundation, and appointing its administrator, Oveta Culp Hobby, as secretary. Hobby thus became only the second woman to hold a seat in a presidential cabinet, the first having been Frances Perkins, under Franklin D. Roosevelt. Likewise, on health care, Eisenhower also found himself somewhere between leaders of his own party and the Democrats. Truman had proposed a program of national health insurance, which encountered stiff opposition from the American Medical Association (AMA), and failed to pass. Eisenhower had no intention of supporting a national health insurance program, but he did propose a reinsurance program under which the federal government would have authorized payments to private health insurance companies. The AMA dusted off its old "socialized medicine" allegations and turned back Eisenhower's proposal, as they had Truman's.

In an early test of his leadership, Eisenhower clashed with Senate Majority Leader Robert Taft over budgetary issues. Eisenhower hadn't intend to do battle with Taft, considered by many in Congress to be the real leader of the party. Ike recognized that, whatever their differences, he and Taft would be playing into the hands of the Democrats if they weren't able to cooperate. But the issue was a fundamental one of how and when to reduce federal expenditures, and whether to reduce taxes. Despite pressure from congressional Republicans, the president refused to reduce taxes unless the budget could be balanced. Because Eisenhower's proposed $5 billion reduction wouldn't be enough to balance the $80 billion budget Truman had submitted for fiscal year 1953, Ike's revised proposal included no tax cut. Taft, whose feathers had already been ruffled by what he considered insufficient consultation on appointments, and who had helped hold the line against the tax cutters, voiced his opposition in a Republican leadership meeting. He angrily protested that the administration should make deeper cuts in spending, that the first Repub-

lican budget in twenty years had to be balanced. Intervention from Secretary
of the Treasury Humphrey gave a visibly angry president a chance to simmer
down before replying. Defense commitments in Korea and around the world
made a balanced budget impossible, Ike argued calmly but firmly, going on a
verbal tour of the globe to drive home his point. Taft backed down. Eisenhower not only got his budget, but also held Republican leadership together.
He and Taft found ways to cooperate in the majority leader's final months
(Taft would die of cancer on July 31).

The first of the large-scale public works projects to come before the
Eisenhower administration was a joint Canadian-American proposal to build
the Saint Lawrence Seaway. In the face of American foot-dragging, Canada
announced that it would build the seaway alone if the United States wouldn't
participate in a joint venture. Although Eisenhower listened to its chief opponents, U.S. railroad interests, who did not want the competition the seaway
would bring, he agreed with its supporters that the seaway was vital to national defense, giving access to Great Lakes industry. But when the Senate
Foreign Relations Committee slashed the proposed American contribution of
$566 billion by more than 80 percent, Eisenhower backed the revised bill.

The Control of Natural Resources: Oil, Public Power, and Agriculture

Differences between the Roosevelt-Truman and the Eisenhower approach to government emerged most clearly in issues related to natural resources and agriculture. On questions related to the control of offshore oil,
the management of the Tennessee Valley Authority (TVA), and public power,
the Eisenhower administration sought to reverse the policies of its predecessors without dismantling the New Deal agencies. Agricultural policy represented an even more dramatic break with the past, for the administration
sought to introduce an entirely new relationship between farmers and the federal government.

The first test came over control of offshore oil. Florida, Louisiana, Texas,
and California had laid claim to these rich deposits during Truman's presidency, but he had always resisted, claiming that the deposits belonged to the
entire nation, not to individual states. Truman cited the Harding administration scandals over oil deposits at Teapot Dome and Elk Hills as evidence that
the federal government needed to protect the nation's oil reserves. Truman

forced the coastal states to take their case to the Supreme Court, which upheld his position. Aware that Eisenhower's position differed sharply from his own, Truman threw down the gauntlet. Invoking national security, he established offshore oil as a protected naval reserve by executive order, just days before leaving office.

Less than a month later, Eisenhower's attorney general, Herbert Brownell, moved to reverse Truman's order. Over the opposition of liberals and non-oil state Southerners, Congress then passed the Submerged Lands Act, which granted coastal states control over tideland oil to a distance of ten-and-a-half miles from their shores. A companion act granted the federal government control of oil beyond that distance to the Continental Shelf.

The Eisenhower administration was equally aggressive in reversing Democratic policies on public power. Democrats viewed the TVA as the New Deal's showpiece for federally developed public power, whereas Republicans considered it a threat to free enterprise. Few controversies placed the two parties at such loggerheads. Long critical of the TVA, Eisenhower referred to it as "creeping socialism" in the summer of 1953. His administration moved to weaken the agency, to abandon public power projects begun under the Democrats, and to promote private power. In what historian Herbert Parmet called "the most blatant reversal of New Deal policy," it stopped work already begun, or slated to begin, on the Columbia River in Oregon, on the Snake River along the Oregon-Idaho border, and on the Coosa River in Alabama, and it turned the Coosa River project over to the Alabama Power Company.

The administration's most dramatic attack on public power, however, came in response to the TVA's plans to build a steam plant near Memphis. Because of the heated differences between Democrats and Republicans over the larger issue of public power, the Memphis controversy took on symbolic meaning. Ahead of schedule in repaying its bonded indebtedness, the TVA wanted to increase its generating capacity, in large part to supply federal consumers such as the Atomic Energy Commission. The Truman administration had included $4 million in its fiscal year 1953 budget for the steam plant. The incoming Eisenhower administration deleted the line and asked private power companies to supply the needed electricity instead.

Edgar H. Dixon and Eugene Yates, heads of two private utility companies, pooled their resources to form Mississippi Valley Generating Company and made a bid for the project. Dixon and Yates proposed to build a steam plant that would supply power, to be distributed over the TVA network, to meet the needs of the AEC and other consumers in the area. Because the Eisenhower administration was committed to meeting the AEC needs by 1957, negotiators for the AEC and the Bureau of the Budget accepted the proposal, ignoring another bid and a TVA estimate that it could meet system needs for $5 million less than the Dixon-Yates proposal.

Early in 1955, Democratic defenders of the TVA in the Senate learned of an apparent irregularity in the negotiations that led to the federal contract with Dixon-Yates. An officer in the bank that arranged financing for Dixon-Yates, Adolphe Wenzell, had also been a consultant to the Bureau of the Budget at the time of negotiations. In the meantime, the City of Memphis decided to build its own power plant. The decision made the Dixon-Yates plant unnecessary, and enabled the Eisenhower administration to avoid further embarrassment by canceling the Dixon-Yates contract in July. Public-power Democrats and private-power Republicans would ultimately compromise on the fate of TVA in 1959: federal appropriations would be cut, but the agency would be allowed to finance its own expansion by issuing bonds. Thenceforth, the TVA would have to become largely self-sufficient.

The Eisenhower Administration and McCarthy

Eisenhower's critics, in the 1950s and since then, question why he never used the "bully pulpit" of the presidency to publicly rebuke McCarthy. A wave of Eisenhower revisionism, launched by political scientist Fred Greenstein's influential book *The Hidden-Hand Presidency,* applauded Eisenhower for working behind the scenes to undercut the Wisconsin senator. The judgment of historians about the Eisenhower presidency is considered in chapter 11. The president's failure to lead his party in dealing with its most controversial figure is hard to ignore, however. Although he detested McCarthy, Eisenhower was reluctant to confront the senator directly, believing that to do so would only give McCarthy more attention and damage the presidency in the process. "I will not get into the gutter with that guy," Eisenhower said. Yet no one did more to undermine Eisenhower's quest for consensus, and words from the White House might have restored balance to American politics. Eisenhower's caution served neither his administration nor the nation well.

As it happened, by bringing the Republicans a majority in the Senate, along with the chairmanships of key committees, Eisenhower's election strengthened McCarthy's hand. The Republican leadership could not deny one of its more prominent members the right to chair a Senate committee. They tried to minimize McCarthy's impact by giving him the relatively insignificant Government Operations Committee, a body that ordinarily handled noncontroversial issues. Undeterred, McCarthy took control of that committee's Permanent Subcommittee on Investigations, in ordinary times an innocuous body undertaking inquiries into government waste, but with a broad enough charter that, in McCarthy's hands, it became a machete he could swing in any direction. He hired Roy Cohn as the committee's counsel.

With the Republicans in power, McCarthy could operate with impunity. Early in 1953, McCarthy resumed his assault on the State Department, this time going after its International Information Agency (IIA). McCarthy's subcommittee attacked the agency's flagship, Voice of America, which beamed pro-American messages into Eastern Europe and elsewhere around the world, for the content of its broadcasts, and even for mislocating one of its transmitters. The latter charge, though completely without merit, had tragic consequences: one of the engineers who had worked on the transmitter committed suicide as a result. Other members of the IIA staff resigned under pressure, often as a result of allegations made by fellow employees. Subcommittee attorney Roy Cohn and his friend David Schine developed contacts in the agency, intimidating its employees with their power to subpoena them.

In addition to the impact on its personnel, the IIA felt McCarthy's sting in other ways. The State Department issued directives to Voice of America stations ordering them not to quote Communists. The subcommittee attacked the agency's overseas libraries for holding books and other publications sympathetic to Communism. After a wave of self-censorship by worried employees, Cohn and Schine traveled to Europe and terrorized IIA library staffs, rifling through card catalogs and demanding that collections be purged. The list of authors they considered subversive included respected historians, educators, and novelists such as Henry Steele Commager and Bernard De Voto, John Dewey and Robert M. Hutchins, Edna Ferber and Theodore Dreiser; it even included Secretary of State John Foster Dulles's cousin Foster Rhea Dulles. The absurdity of the list was exceeded only by the absurdity of the trip itself.

Charges of High-Level Disloyalty: J. Robert Oppenheimer
and Harry Dexter White

Late in 1953, two high-profile security cases with political shadings came to light. One targeted a former treasury official, and indirectly President Truman; the other, a leading nuclear scientist. Attorney General Herbert Brownell, a key Eisenhower advisor during the 1952 campaign, became one of the administration's most ardent anti-Communists. In November 1953, he sought to embarrass former President Truman by dredging up the case of Harry Dexter White, which still resonated in the red-hot political atmosphere of the early fifties, although White had died in 1949. According to Brownell, Truman had received an FBI file on White in 1946 alleging that the assistant secretary of the treasury was a Soviet spy, but had appointed him executive director of the International Monetary Fund anyway. Truman forcefully rejected the allegations. President Eisenhower said that he did not believe Truman would have knowingly appointed a Communist to office, but that the case was Brownell's to handle. Brownell replied that, though the former president had not been disloyal, he had not been vigilant, either. Acknowledging receipt of the FBI file, Truman claimed its evidence was insufficient for him to act against White; he had therefore done nothing that might tip off White he was being investigated. In an effort to rebut Truman's statements, Brownell and FBI Director J. Edgar Hoover appeared before the Senate Internal Security Subcommittee, and Brownell released the original FBI file on White. The demonstrable inaccuracies in Truman's statements appeared to come more from a faulty memory than from any intent to mislead. In the best account of the case, historian R. Bruce Craig concluded that "Harry Truman did not emerge the victor but, in the end, neither was he the loser." The same could not be said of the Republicans, who suffered from their attempt to embarrass the former president.

Another prominent American came under scrutiny in 1953, and the case cut to the core of the American nuclear arms policy. J. Robert Oppenheimer, who had been the lead scientist on the Manhattan Project, worked as a consultant to the Atomic Energy Commission in addition to his duties at Princeton's Institute for Advanced Study. He had never given any reason for suspicion of disloyalty, but he now ran afoul of powerful constituencies willing to exploit anti-Communism to discredit him. Oppenheimer worried about the escalating nuclear arms race, and his stature as an eminent physicist gave his words weight. In the summer of 1953, he wrote an article in the influential journal *Foreign Affairs,* warning that the United States and the Soviet Union were like "two scorpions in a bottle, each capable of killing the other, but only at the risk of his own life." Oppenheimer opposed Air Force efforts both to monopolize American nuclear weaponry, arguing that the Army should also be allowed to develop tactical nuclear weapons, and to develop an atomic-powered bomber. He also argued against further development of the hydrogen bomb, incurring the wrath of Edward Teller, the physicist who became the known as the "father of the H-bomb." Chairman Lewis Strauss of the Atomic Energy Commission sought to curtail Oppenheimer's crusading by asking the FBI to investigate his activities.

In November, William L. Borden, formerly the executive director of the congressional Joint Committee on Atomic Energy, wrote to J. Edgar Hoover to warn that Oppenheimer "more probably than not" was a Soviet agent. There was plenty of circumstantial evidence in Oppenheimer's background that seemed to lend credence to the charges; his first wife had been a Communist, and he had dabbled in leftist politics himself while a student, joining organizations that the House Un-American Activities Committee later labeled subversive. President Eisenhower ordered that Oppenheimer's security clearance be suspended pending an investigation. Given the choice of resigning his position as a consultant to the AEC or having a hearing, Oppenheimer demanded a hearing. AEC Chairman Strauss named a three-man panel to carry out the investigation. Leading scientists, including Albert Einstein and Linus Pauling, came to Oppenheimer's defense, and only his principal adversary, Teller, spoke against him. The panel concluded unanimously that Oppenheimer was loyal, but curiously, by a 2–1 vote, the same panel ruled that his security clearance should be lifted. The matter then went before the AEC board, which confirmed the panel's recommendation by a 4–1 vote.

McCarthy Versus the Army

Riding high, McCarthy now took on a target that gave him unprecedented exposure and, in so doing, led to his downfall. By alleging Communist influence at the Army's signal station at Fort Monmouth, New Jersey, McCarthy initiated a battle with the Army. But rumors about the station had been circulating since World War II. Julius Rosenberg had visited on several occasions, and charges about breaches in security there had appeared in the

Chicago *Tribune* on a number of occasions. The FBI's general review of security risks included those at Fort Monmouth, and Roy Cohn had obtained a copy of the bureau report. McCarthy chaired his subcommittee's security hearings in hallmark fashion, badgering witnesses and exaggerating revelations to the press. He recycled old charges, but found nothing new. No spy ring existed, and all but two of those suspended won their jobs back.

The next stop in McCarthy's campaign against the Army involved an Army dentist named Irving Peress, who had invoked the Fifth Amendment on the loyalty form he filled out upon receiving his commission. Peress accepted a commission as a captain and, in due course, won promotion to major. When McCarthy learned that a potential security risk had slipped through the screening process and then been awarded a promotion, he screamed, "Who promoted Peress?" The senator berated Peress's commanding officer, General Ralph Zwicker, saying he wasn't fit to wear his uniform. General Zwicker was a highly respected officer, and Secretary of the Army Robert Stevens vowed to come to his defense. But conferring with other members of the subcommittee convinced Stevens he was no match for McCarthy. He signed a memorandum of agreement that amounted to capitulation: he would pursue the Peress investigation in return for a vague promise from McCarthy to treat Army personnel courteously in the future.

When David Schine learned that he might be drafted, Cohn, who had arranged a commission in the inactive reserves, attempted to ease his friend's predicament. Refusing to cooperate, the Army proceeded to draft Schine and sent him to Fort Dix, New Jersey, for basic training. Cohn then pressured the officers at Fort Dix to release Schine from the routine military drudgery all other privates had to endure, and to assign him only light duty.

The Army-McCarthy Hearings

Early in 1954, Army General Counsel John G. Adams compiled a chronology detailing Cohn's actions on Schine's behalf. In March, the Army informed McCarthy about the report, and demanded that he dismiss Cohn. McCarthy refused, and claimed that the Army had been harassing Schine and Cohn in an effort to force McCarthy to drop the Fort Monmouth investigation.

The impasse set the stage for the most dramatic confrontation of the McCarthy years. Both sides agreed that hearings should be held to get to the bottom of the case. McCarthy agreed to step down from the subcommittee in return for the right to participate in the hearings and cross-examine witnesses. Senator Karl Mundt (Republican-South Dakota) took the gavel in McCarthy's place. With Cohn a subject of the inquiry and thus unable to serve as its counsel, the subcommittee hired Tennessee criminal lawyer Ray Howard Jenkins to take his place. The Army hired a patrician Boston trial attorney, Joseph Welch, to argue its case.

Even before the hearings began, another incident foreshadowed what was to come, revealing McCarthy's sudden vulnerability and demonstrating how television could influence the public perception of national events. Edward R. Murrow was the most distinguished investigative reporter on television, mentor to many of the World War II–era reporters who later moved from radio to television. His weekly program *See It Now* on the Columbia Broadcast System (CBS) examined some of the difficult issues of the day in a brusque, analytical style unmatched by any other program in the early years of television. Although he despised the Wisconsin senator, Murrow had yet to devote any time on *See It Now* to McCarthy. He now decided the time was right, and that, if he delayed much longer, he might appear to have waited until it was safe to attack. Murrow's staff assembled film clips of McCarthy that exposed his crude manner, his use of use of his political power to intimidate. In his telecast on March 9, Murrow let McCarthy indict McCarthy, something that could be done more effectively on television than in any other medium. McCarthy had crossed "the line between investigating and persecuting," Murrow said. He had exploited, not created an atmosphere of fear, Murrow went on to say; it was no time for opponents to remain silent. CBS received phone calls and letters overwhelmingly supporting Murrow; telephone calls ran ten to one against McCarthy.

The Army-McCarthy hearings began on April 22. Through television, as millions of people watched, they became a truly national event. McCarthy again was his own worst witness. Both sides were contentious, with Senator Stuart Symington of Missouri, one of the subcommittee Democrats, and McCarthy sniping at one another. McCarthy appeared boorish, overriding other witnesses with frequent interruptions, shouting, "Point of order, Mr. Chairman, point of order!" so often that it became tedious, comic, and discourteous all at once. Senator Mundt, the subcommittee chairman in McCarthy's stead, had difficulty controlling the proceedings, which threatened to slip out of control from their opening moments.

The hearings unearthed no smoking guns, but two moments symbolized

McCarthy's slide to desperation. The first involved a doctored photograph showing Secretary of the Army Robert Stevens and David Schine. The photograph, taken on November 17, 1953, and entered into evidence by McCarthy's team, seemed to show Stevens turning to face Schine, smiling at him. On November 17, the Army and McCarthy were in the middle of the dispute that prompted the hearings, with the Army contending that Cohn had sought preferential treatment for Schine, and Cohn claiming that the Army was using Schine as a hostage to pressure a favorable resolution of the Fort Monmouth case. So why would Stevens be smiling at Schine? It turned out that he was not, as Joseph Welch pointed out in his rebuttal. In fact, there had been a third person in the original photo that had been cropped out, thus altering the context of the picture and the meaning of Stevens's expression. The information was particularly damaging to McCarthy, who had been caught using a composite photo in 1950 that purported to show Senator Tydings with American Communist Party chairman Earl Browder.

The other case involved a young attorney named Fred Fisher, whom Welch brought onto his staff. Before the hearings began, Welch had asked Fisher if there was anything in his past that might be used against them. Fisher conceded that he had earlier belonged to the National Lawyers Guild, which HUAC had listed as a subversive organization. He and a man named Greenberg had organized a chapter of the Guild. Greenberg, as it developed, had been a member of the Communist Party. Fisher insisted that, despite his association with Greenberg, he had never been a member of the Party. Because of the Greenberg connection, Fisher stayed in Boston and did not work on the case. After the hearings were under way, according to Cohn, he and Welch had agreed that neither the Fisher case nor Cohn's military service record would be brought up during the hearings. Cohn in turn told McCarthy about his agreement with Welch.

The climactic moment came on the afternoon of June 9. Welch was questioning Cohn, pressing him about the Fort Monmouth investigation. The intent of his questions was to put Cohn on the defensive—if he knew of a Communist, wouldn't he want to remove him from his position as quickly as possible? McCarthy interrupted, launching into an attack on Fred Fisher, justifying his remarks on the basis of wanting to expose anyone who was doing work for the Communist Party, claiming that Welch had tried to "foist him on this committee." Welch interrupted, asking for a point of personal privilege, which Chairman Mundt granted. McCarthy rudely ignored Welch, conferring with an assistant, but Welch insisted on his full attention. McCarthy continued to go through papers, but the rest of the hearing room was silent as Welch, visibly upset, began, "Until this moment, Senator, I think I never really gauged your cruelty or your recklessness." Welch recounted the background of his discussions with Fisher, and his decision to leave the young lawyer off his team for the hearings, omitting any reference to Greenberg. Fisher was still in Welch's law firm, he acknowledged, and "he shall always bear a scar needlessly inflicted by you. If it were in my power to forgive you for your reckless cruelty, I would do so. I like to think I am a gentleman, but your forgiveness will have to come from someone other than me."

McCarthy bulldozed on, even as Cohn shook his head, passing a note to McCarthy asking him to honor the agreement with Welch. Even Mundt, as loyal to McCarthy as anyone in the Senate, interjected that he didn't believe Welch had recommended Fisher for a position on his staff. Still McCarthy persisted.

Finally, Welch insisted, "Mr. McCarthy, I will not discuss this further with you. You have sat within six feet of me, and could have asked me about Fred Fisher. You have brought it out. If there is a God in heaven, it will do neither you nor your cause any good. I will not discuss it further. I will not ask Mr. Cohn any more questions. You, Mr. Chairman, may, if you will, call the next witness."

The hearing room erupted in applause. Mundt, recognizing the futility of trying to stop it, let it run its course and dismissed the session. McCarthy, apparently not comprehending what had just transpired, turned to people near him, saying, "What did I do?"

The hearings continued for eight more days, until June 17, but McCarthy no longer appeared invincible. Other senators traded barbs with him in defiance of his threats, and in another dramatic episode, several senators trooped out for a roll call on the Senate floor, ignoring McCarthy's demands that they listen to him first, with Symington taunting him on the way out. Although the clash over Fred Fisher was perhaps the most telling incident, no single moment signaled the end of McCarthy's reign. Rather it was the day-by-day exposure on television that showed people the senator's means of operating—his proclivity to badger witnesses, his failure to substantiate reckless charges, and his willingness to damage people's lives seemingly on a whim—that destroyed his credibility.

Censure: The Decline and Fall of Senator McCarthy

After the hearings ended, McCarthy went into a precipitous decline. Even before then, on June 11, Senator Ralph Flanders had introduced a resolution to strip McCarthy of his committee chairmanships. When the resolution received little support, Flanders tried a different approach on July 30, recommending censure for conduct "contrary to Senate traditions" that brought the Senate into disrepute. The censure proposal generated bipartisan support. Many Republicans had wearied of McCarthy's act, and recognized that he could be a severe liability to Republican congressional candidates in the fall.

The Senate leadership designated the members of a special censure committee, naming senators unlikely to generate controversy, avoiding liberals that would have polarized deliberations and presidential contenders who might have used committee membership as a means to get media attention. Chaired by Arthur Watkins (Republican-Utah), the committee deliberately sought to avoid the circus-like atmosphere of the Army-McCarthy hearings. The committee refused to admit television cameras, and prevented McCarthy from interrupting, insisting that he speak through his attorney, Edward Bennett Williams. It narrowed the censure charges from five to two: abuse of General Zwicker and contempt of the Privileges and Elections Subcommittee. The latter charge referred to an investigation of charges made against McCarthy by Senator William Benton in 1951, when Benton had, among other things, called for McCarthy's expulsion from the Senate. Benton's call for expulsion had died with no support, but in the subsequent inquiry, McCarthy had failed to appear before the committee when requested to do so. He had also vilified members of the committee, calling Senator Hendrickson "a living miracle" for living "so long with neither brains nor guts."

The committee's report came out late in September, too late for censure to be considered by the full Senate until after the elections. It was a foregone conclusion that McCarthy would be censured, but McCarthy's supporters and his critics nonetheless engaged in a rancorous debate. The Senate dropped the Zwicker charge before submitting the censure resolution to a vote. When the vote came on December 2, the resolution passed by 67 to 22, with all 44 Democrats, 22 Republicans, and Independent Wayne Morse voting in favor. The Senate had chosen to narrowly consider the violation of its mores, and not to undertake broader issues of anti-Communism, abuse of the constitutional rights of citizens, or any of the other catalog of concerns that had become associated with the umbrella term "McCarthyism."

The censure vote symbolized the end of McCarthy's influence, but by the time it came, the senator had already drifted to the margins of politics. He still issued broadsides against alleged Communist influence, but the press paid scant attention. He remained on the sidelines during the 1954 elections, by which time the McCarthy name had become more of a liability than an asset to other Republicans. His health had begun to erode as well, due in large part to an increasingly serious drinking problem. He had but two-and-a-half years to live after the censure vote, and had little political impact in his remaining days. He died on May 2, 1957, of liver disease exacerbated by alcohol abuse.

McCarthyism after McCarthy

The death of Senator McCarthy did not signify the end of McCarthyism. Zealous anti-Communism faded away, but its less virulent forms continued to influence Americans for years. Groups and institutions that felt the sting of anti-Communist persecutions in the early fifties continued to experience it near the end of the decade, and sometimes beyond. Teachers, labor union leaders, filmmakers, minorities, and immigrants all experienced McCarthyism in one guise or another into the sixties.

Educators, lambasted as "reducators" by Red-baiters, found themselves the targets of inquiries in some states, and of social pressure in most. Textbook publishers succumbed to the pressure, and high school civics textbooks became sermons on patriotism. The New York Teachers Union, long a source of Communist influence, endured a decade of investigations by the Senate Internal Security Subcommittee. Historian David Caute tabulated the toll: 321 schoolteachers and 58 college teachers either resigned under pressure or were fired.

Soon after World War II, leaders of the civil rights movement and other prominent African Americans who criticized American racism became targets of anti-Communist crusaders. Singer Paul Robeson, who spoke out against anti-Soviet policies in the late forties, had his concerts canceled. In 1949, when he tried to give a concert in Peekskill, New York, for the benefit of the Civil Rights Congress, a group labeled subversive by the attorney general, protesters attacked concertgoers. In the mid-fifties, Martin Luther King's

Southern Christian Leadership Conference became the target of an FBI investigation. The FBI also conducted a long-term investigation of King himself, beginning the investigation because of his association with Stanley Levison, a Communist who became one of King's closest associates, and his closest white friend. FBI director J. Edgar Hoover used the Levison connection as justification for continued surveillance of King well into the 1960s, long after FBI pressure had forced King to break off relations with Levison.

Indeed, the FBI became the agency that most fully perpetuated the spirit of McCarthyism. Its counterintelligence program, COINTELPRO, not only gathered information, but also deliberately sought to disrupt organizations and individual activities it deemed threats to the nation. It targeted, in particular, the Communist Party of the United States (CPUSA), which wasn't much of a threat in any sense by the time COINTELPRO launched its probe. COINTELPRO's net spread rapidly; in the 1960s, it carried out activities against various protest organizations, ranging from antiwar groups to women's liberation groups. FBI Director J. Edgar Hoover had accumulated such power that there was no effective check on his activities.

Labor leaders with leftist connections likewise became the subject of lengthy investigations. Best known among leftist labor leaders was Harry Bridges, an Australian immigrant who led the International Longshoremen's and Warehousemen's Union, and who had been subjected to attempts by the Justice Department and Congress from the mid-1930s to deport him because of his avowed Communist views. Bridges denied membership in the Communist Party, however; after twenty years of legal maneuvering, the government finally dropped its campaign against him.

Although Bridges successfully fended off deportation, many others weren't as fortunate. Historian Richard Fried found that an average of 140 people per year—and 302 in 1957 alone—were denied entry into the United States as suspected subversives during the 1950s, compared to a *total* of 29 for the entire decade of the 1940s. Similarly, the average number of deportations reached 24 per year in the 1950s, compared to a *total* of 17 in the 1940s.

The congressional committees that carried out security investigations during the peak of McCarthyism managed to survive into the seventies, albeit with diminished power and soiled reputations. HUAC lost funding in the late sixties, and attempted to reconstitute itself under a new name, the House Internal Security Committee—only to be scrapped in the mid-seventies. Its Senate counterpart held on until 1977, when it, too, folded.

Midterm Setback: The Election of 1954

As is often the case, first-term presidents reach midterm elections with programs launched but not implemented, and such was the case with several of Eisenhower's programs in November 1954. Coming into the elections, the Republican Party controlled both houses of Congress, but by narrow margins. Strains were apparent, with moderates and conservatives wrestling for the control of the soul of the party in the aftermath of Senator McCarthy's rampage. Furthermore, the party faced the historical likelihood of congressional losses in the midterm elections. More troubling was the reluctance of Eisenhower, whose popularity was the best thing the Republicans had going for them, to bear the Republican standard. He considered Truman's campaign activities as president unseemly. Once convinced that the party was in trouble, however, and that the conservative right wing could wrest control of the party from the moderates if the Republicans lost, Ike campaigned at a frenzied pace, logging 10,000 miles and traveling 1,500 miles in one day to speak in Cleveland, Detroit, Louisville, and Wilmington.

Despite Eisenhower's late efforts, the party suffered a devastating loss in the elections. Democrats gained control of both houses of Congress, picking up 19 seats in the House for a 232–203 majority, and gaining 2 seats in the Senate for a one-seat majority. The defeat plunged the Republicans into further acrimony, with conservatives blaming the president for failing to follow their lead.

The Interstate Highway System

Given Eisenhower's opposition to public power, it is ironic that one of his most enduring domestic legacies is the Interstate Highway System, which counts among the most ambitious federal projects in the nation's history. Eisenhower had been impressed by Germany's autobahn system during World War II, and envisioned something comparable at home. A diverse constituency of supporters took shape in the United States, including truckers, the American Automobile Association, bus companies, and automobile manufacturers; during the war, they formed the American Road Builders Association. Diversity gave the group a broad base, but also made it difficult for all to agree on specific plans or financing.

Eisenhower launched his plan in the summer of 1954, commissioning

Vice President Nixon to present it to a conference of governors. The administration's bold proposal sought to augment annual federal highway expenditures of $700 million with an additional $5 billion per year for ten years. The president then assigned General Lucius D. Clay, a member of the board of General Motors, to prepare a report on the nation's highways. Clay's blue-ribbon commission ratified the interstate concept early in 1955, and Congress approved it the following year. To pay for the 42,000-mile system, the federal government pledged to pay 90 percent of the costs, and asked the states to pick up the rest. Money from taxes on gasoline went into a trust designated for highway construction, and virtually guaranteed the success of the program.

No other legislation in the decade had as much impact on American society. The automobile and trucking industries were the most visible beneficiaries. Denied a share of the interstate bonanza, public transit and railroads entered a long decline. The cities felt the impact in unanticipated ways, as the interstate highways allowed people to flee to the suburbs. Historian Kenneth T. Jackson observed that the system "virtually guaranteed that future urban growth would perpetuate a centerless sprawl." Where the interstate highways bypassed small cities and towns, downtown districts declined and business shifted to the periphery. Just as businesses proliferated at railroad junctures in the late nineteenth century, they grew at interstate highway interchanges in the late twentieth.

Farm Policy: Paring Back Parity

If Eisenhower's policies on the Saint Lawrence Seaway and the Interstate Highway System might have been mistaken for Democratic proposals, his farm program was pure Republican. His administration set about dismantling what remained of New Deal agricultural programs. Indeed, as historian Stephen Ambrose noted, "farm policy was the only area in which Eisenhower called for a repudiation of the basic New Deal economic structure." Truman and his secretary of agriculture, Charles Brannan, had developed a system of price supports for basic commodities at a level of 90 percent of parity. Eisenhower, who had grown up in a farming community in Abilene, believed that price supports benefited neither the farmer nor the country, and that paying farmers for not growing crops made no sense at all. Nonetheless, in the 1952 campaign, he had promised that the administration could achieve 90 percent of parity, a promise he later regretted. He worked with his secretary of agriculture, Ezra Taft Benson, in an attempt to shift farming back to a free enter-prise system. One of the twelve apostles who governed the Mormon Church, Benson had long criticized big government, and believed that Democratic farm policies smacked of socialism. Benson's personality—cold, arrogant, and patronizing—didn't help the new program pass, but served to make him a lightning rod for criticism, sparing the president. Both Benson and Eisen-hower believed that the Brannan Plan had been inefficient and counterpro-ductive; commodities bought from farmers and stored in silos led to waste and drove prices down, making it doubly difficult for farmers to escape the debt cycle.

Benson proposed to replace fixed price supports with a flexible system. Farmers were outraged, and small farmers complained that lowering price supports would drive them out of business. Eisenhower never wavered in his public support of Benson, although, privately, he counseled the secretary to be less aggressive in promoting his program. Nonetheless, urban Democrats supported it in sufficient numbers to pass the Agricultural Act of 1954. The law allowed for price supports to drop from 90 percent of parity to as low as 75 percent in the program's second year and for commodities to be sold abroad. In the long run, the administration never achieved its goal: the basic system of agriculture price supports remained in place. More troubling was the fact that farmers did not share in the prosperity enjoyed by other eco-nomic groups throughout the decade.

The President's Heart Attack and the Decision to Run in 1956

In the early morning hours of September 24, 1955, Eisenhower suffered a heart attack while vacationing in Colorado. His personal physician, Howard Snyder, transferred him to an Army hospital in Denver, where the renowned heart surgeon Paul Dudley White joined the group treating the president. Eisenhower remained in an oxygen tent for the first two weeks, and stayed in the hospital until November 11. Press Secretary James Hagerty kept the pub-lic informed of the president's condition with regular press briefings.

The president's health raised questions—both constitutional and prag-matic—about how to keep the administration functioning. With the election just over a year away, most people assumed that Eisenhower wouldn't be able to seek reelection. That assumption put Vice President Nixon in a precarious position. He needed to show leadership, but not to appear too eager to assume presidential responsibilities. Eisenhower's inner circle, suspicious of Nixon, wanted Chief of Staff Sherman Adams to fly to Denver to coordinate administration policy. Nixon agreed, and remained in Washington until Eisenhower summoned him to Denver on October 8. The president made it clear that Dulles would speak for the administration, not only at the upcoming meeting of foreign ministers, but also on other foreign policy matters. Everyone involved had high praise for the way Nixon responded to what was clearly a trying circumstance. As Eisenhower recovered, he kept involved in the affairs of the nation; one after another, cabinet members came to visit him in Denver.

On November 11, the president returned to Washington and then to his farm in Gettysburg, where he considered whether to seek reelection the next fall. In a long conversation with Hagerty in December, he ran down the prospects. As he considered whom the Republicans might run in 1956, the list narrowed. Eisenhower wanted no part of Senator William Knowland (Republican-California), a logical front-runner. Chief Justice Earl Warren would likely want to remain on the Supreme Court. Nixon needed more seasoning. Other members of his administration such as Herbert Brownell, George Humphrey, and Sherman Adams probably could not be elected. Dewey was a possibility, as was Ike's brother Milton, but each had drawbacks. The discussion came to focus on Eisenhower himself, an option Hagerty had promoted from the beginning of the discussion.

Back in Washington early in January, Eisenhower hosted a dinner meeting with key advisors to seek their opinions about whether he should run again. The consensus was that Eisenhower was the only Republican candidate sure to win the election. Worried as he was about both the president's health and the historical reputation of his administration, which seemed secure in the home stretch of his first term, Ike's brother Milton was the most vociferous opponent of a second term.

As Eisenhower ruminated, his health became the issue, both pro and con. On the pro side, his heart attack and the rehabilitation that followed had brought home to him how much he craved political activity, and how desolate retirement might be. He would later admit that the heart attack changed his mind, and that no one knew how close he'd come to deciding to retire before he'd been stricken. On the con side, he worried about whether anxiety over his health might paralyze the nation. Not only had he had the heart attack, but he also suffered from stomach problems and insomnia of late. His family was divided: whereas Milton believed that serving another term would put Ike's health at risk, Mamie believed that retiring now would. When a checkup confirmed that he was physically capable of running again, Eisenhower stopped agonizing and decided to seek reelection; he announced his decision on February 27.

Rematch: The Election of 1956

The only question that remained on the Republican side was whether the president would run again with Nixon. The vice president brought several strengths to the ticket. He was intelligent, loyal to Eisenhower, and a hard worker. He could reach the Republican Right in ways the president never could. He didn't hesitate to dirty his hands with political infighting, allowing the president to be presidential and yet turn back attacks. But the two men had never become close, and when reporters broached the topic, Eisenhower seemed unusually noncommittal, defending the performance of his vice president in ways that left them wondering what Ike really thought about Nixon.

Most of Eisenhower's staff preferred to see the president drop Nixon from the ticket. The president told Dulles that he would like to see Nixon head a large department, commerce perhaps. He told Nixon he could have any position except attorney general or secretary of state, and added, "if you calculate that I won't last five years, of course that is different." Nixon responded that he was willing to do whatever the president wanted him to do. When Eisenhower finally asked his vice president whether he wanted to run again, Nixon said he did. The president concurred, and immediately went with Nixon to inform the press.

The Democrats had three old faces from which to chose: Adlai Stevenson, Senator Estes Kefauver of Tennessee, and New York Governor Averell Harriman. Harriman fell by the wayside early; even support from former President Truman wasn't enough to breathe life into a campaign that sputtered from the start. The contest came down to a battle between Kefauver and Stevenson. Kefauver shocked Stevenson's supporters by winning the Minnesota primary, in the Illinois governor's backyard, but the defeat seemed only to energize Stevenson. No longer the Hamlet-like candidate he had been in 1952, debating whether to run or not to run, Stevenson acted more like a typical self-assured American politician and proceed to run off a string of primary victories. Entering the Democratic convention with a clear lead over Kefauver, he coasted to a first-ballot victory. He then defied precedent by opening the vice presidential nomination to the convention, and Kefauver came away with the consolation prize. Eisenhower was delighted, labeling the Democratic ticket "probably the weakest they could have named." Either Lyndon Johnson or Hubert Humphrey, he believed, would have been a more formidable opponent.

Although Eisenhower's dismissive assessment of the Stevenson candidacy was not shared by most political observers, any Democrat would have had a hard time defeating the popular president in 1956. By the same token, those same observers believed that Stevenson would have defeated any Republican except Eisenhower. Stevenson brought advantages to the rematch that he hadn't had in 1952. In the earlier contest, he had been a one-term governor with no national experience; in 1956, he had earned a national reputation serving as the acknowledged head of his party for four years. The campaign had organizational problems; indeed, Robert Kennedy said he'd never seen one so poorly run—to which Stevenson assistant and later biographer John Bartlow Martin replied, "He should have seen 1952." Stevenson had worked hard to shore up weak spots in his support among Democrats, paying particular attention to the South, and to offset the inroads Eisenhower had made in the Democratic base in 1952.

But even though he had gained much in four years, Stevenson had also lost something: he seemed more tired, his rhetoric less polished, his message less fresh. Stevenson's prospects looked brightest in the fall of 1955, when it appeared that Eisenhower wouldn't be healthy enough to run, and no one could think of another Republican who could defeat Stevenson. As Eisenhower's health improved, however, those prospects began to pale. But the health issue had not yet run its course. On June 7, Eisenhower suffered an attack of ileitis, an inflammation of the small intestine. The president had been plagued by stomach pain for years, and now knew the cause. There was no choice but to operate, despite the recent heart attack. The surgery went well; the next day, it was clear that the president was well on the way to recovery. He never considered pulling out of the race.

Yet Stevenson ran a vigorous campaign. Unlike 1952, when he was forced into defending an administration in which he had no role, in 1956, he could attack the administration of the other party. His intellectual rigor served him well as he questioned the fundamental assumptions of the Eisenhower presidency. "One can identify idea after idea that Stevenson made issues in 1956,"

John Bartlow Martin observed, "and [that] later became law in the Kennedy-Johnson administrations, from nuclear testing to Medicare." He called for an end to the military draft, aid to economically impoverished areas, and aid to education. On September 5, he raised the most controversial issue of his campaign, calling for an end to surface testing of the hydrogen bomb, which he said was contaminating the atmosphere. Both candidates spent much of the last month of the campaign clarifying their positions on the testing of the bomb. On October 15, Stevenson called for unilateral cessation of testing. The president defended his record, claiming that he had sought mutual arms reduction, but that the Soviet Union had not cooperated. Ultimately, the testing issue did little damage to Eisenhower. Stevenson spent much of the last two months debating military policy with one of the nation's greatest military heroes. Despite Stevenson's deeply felt convictions about nuclear testing, the issue made little headway with the electorate, although it did serve to open debate on an important issue.

As if Eisenhower's lead weren't secure enough, events in Europe and the Middle East in the two weeks before the election created a sense of crisis that worked to the advantage of the incumbent. On October 23, Hungary erupted in revolt against Soviet control. On October 29, Israel attacked Egyptian positions in Gaza and the Sinai. Two days later, France and Britain intervened on the side of the Israelis, attacking Egypt along the Suez Canal. On November 4, two days before the American election, the Soviet Union sent tanks into Budapest to crush the Hungarian revolt. As Eisenhower responded to the two unfolding crises, he inevitably rose above the political fray of preelection politics. He properly assumed a presidential pose that left Stevenson in the difficult position of having to choose between backing his opponent's policy or criticizing the president in time of national crisis and risk charges of putting his own election ahead of the welfare of the nation. With the president meeting with the National Security Council, conferring with world leaders, and addressing the nation on television, the job of the challenger became extraordinarily difficult. Stevenson tried to make the best of it, backing Eisenhower's actions, but blaming the administration for policies that created crises in Europe and the Middle East. "Just think, after all the bond drive rallies I've addressed," Stevenson joked about the Israelis, "they couldn't have waited another week."

The election was an Eisenhower landslide: he won nearly 58 percent of the popular vote, and more votes than any president in U.S. history. Stevenson held only seven states, six from the Democrats' stronghold in the Solid South, and Missouri, with Virginia and Louisiana going to the Republicans, Louisiana for the first time since Reconstruction.

Eisenhower's overwhelming personal popularity was not enough to win Congress for the Republicans, however. In the Senate, Democrats picked up a seat when maverick Republican Senator Wayne Morse from Oregon switched to the Democratic Party; they now held a 49–47 majority. In the House, they extended their lead over the Republicans from 29 seats to 33, winning a 234–201 majority.

Recommended Reading

Stephen Ambrose's several books on Eisenhower are a fine place to start an analysis of Eisenhower's long career; the two volumes of Ambrose's *Eisenhower: The President* (New York: Simon and Schuster, 1985) are excellent sources for this and later chapters in this book. Geoffrey Perret's *Eisenhower* (New York: Random House, 1999) is a fine one-volume biography.

Chester J. Pach Jr. and Elmo Richardson's *The Presidency of Dwight D. Eisenhower* (Lawrence: University Press of Kansas, 2000) is a concise reexamination of the Eisenhower presidency. Charles Alexander's *Holding the Line: The Eisenhower Era, 1952–1961* (Bloomington: University of Indiana Press, 1975) and Herbert Parmet's *Eisenhower and the American Crusades* (New York: Macmillan, 1972) are also fine accounts.

The reading list at the end of chapter 2 includes books on McCarthy and McCarthyism. For the specific cases of J. Robert Oppenheimer and Harry Dexter White, see David C. Cassidy's *J. Robert Oppenheimer and the American Dream* (New York: Pi Press, 2004) and R. Bruce Craig's *Treasonable Doubt: The Harry Dexter White Spy Case* (Lawrence: University Press of Kansas, 2004).

5

The Uneasy Mantle
of a Major Power

Foreign Policy, 1953–1956

DWIGHT D. EISENHOWER began his presidency with a worldview closer to that of his Democratic predecessor than to that of the core of his own Republican Party. To be sure, during the campaign, candidate Eisenhower had made clear his differences with Truman, as well as his misgivings about Truman's ability to conduct American foreign policy. But, in fact, it was Eisenhower's internationalism and his aversion to the isolationism of Senator Robert Taft and other conservative Republicans that had motivated him to seek the presidency. Eisenhower had supported most of Truman's international programs in the early years of the Cold War, including the Marshall Plan, the establishment of NATO, and the American entry into Korea. Like Truman, Eisenhower believed America's future was tied to Europe more than to any other region. Perhaps only Eisenhower could have steered the Republican Party in such a direction.

Although as a candidate he had never endorsed the strategy of containment, it was mainly because the term had become inextricably linked to Truman and the Democrats. Republican internationalists such as John Foster Dulles argued that containment was too limited, that Communism ought to be rolled back, not merely contained. Republican isolationists such as Senator Taft believed that containment risked American involvement in the affairs of Europe. Eisenhower found himself at odds even with his party's internationalists; he refused to endorse a plank in the 1952 Republican platform that called for liberation of nations under Communist domination. He had confidence in his ability to manage foreign affairs: he knew many foreign leaders personally and believed that his military experience would serve him well in Washington. Indeed, when he measured his own experience against that of his predecessor, he had every reason to expect success.

On the need to trim military budgets, Eisenhower agreed with Truman. But here he had more leverage than his predecessor, for people were more likely to listen to the advice of the World War II general who directed the Normandy invasion than to a World War I artillery captain. The centerpiece of Eisenhower's approach to defense was his "New Look" program, a media label he disliked even more than its shorthand slogan, "More bang for the buck." The New Look was not new, he insisted. "To call it revolutionary or to act like it is something that just suddenly dropped down on us like a cloud out of the heaven is just not true," he told reporters. The New Look sought to cut defense spending, but to do so responsibly. In a campaign speech on August 25, 1952, candidate Eisenhower called for policies that would make the nation militarily, productively, and economically strong. Eliminating duplication in defense procurement could cut costs and therefore spending. The new constellation of U.S. military force would not be one-dimensional. The bomb allowed the United States flexibility it had not had before. The nation could cut back on conventional forces, although to do so, it would not rely solely on the threat to use atomic weapons. There were other weapons in the American arsenal, including the Air Force, the Central Intelligence Agency (CIA), and psychological warfare; as recently as World War II, none of these resources had been available. The United States would not be caught unprepared. In response to questions about defense at a press conference on March 17, 1954, Eisenhower insisted, "We are not fighting with muzzle-loaders in any of the services." Rather, America's current military posture represented "an attempt by intelligent people to keep abreast of the times."

It did not mean, as critics imagined, that Eisenhower planned to rely on the bomb as a substitute for conventional forces, although media accounts of some of Dulles's later comments would have led people to believe just that. Two phrases in particular, "massive retaliation" and "brinksmanship," became associated with Dulles, and seemed to imply excessive reliance on the threat to use nuclear weapons. Each was misleading, yet each bore a kernel of truth. The first came from an address Secretary of State Dulles delivered to the Council on Foreign Relations in January 1954: rather than settling for the treadmill futility of Democratic strategy in Korea, the Eisenhower administration stood ready to strike anywhere with "massive retaliatory power."

No president since the early years of the Republic had as much experience as Eisenhower in foreign policy and military affairs. Indeed, the new president fully expected to make his greatest contribution in the realm of foreign policy, and his inaugural address underscored this expectation. In what historian Herbert Parmet described as "beyond a doubt . . . the most internationalist speech ever delivered as an Inaugural Address," Eisenhower proclaimed, "We hold it to be the first task of statesmanship to develop the strength that will deter the forces of aggression and promote the conditions of peace." He called for disarmament, an issue that his Democratic opponent Adlai Stevenson had made his own during the campaign. He defended the United Nations, already under attack by isolationists, as "the living sign of all people's hope for peace."

The Eisenhower Foreign Policy Team

Eisenhower's foremost advisor on foreign policy was Secretary of State John Foster Dulles. Few men have come to the office with as impressive credentials. Dulles's grandfather, John W. Foster, had been secretary of state under Benjamin Harrison. His uncle, Robert Lansing, had served as secretary of state under Woodrow Wilson. Dulles graduated from Princeton, earned a law degree at George Washington University, and joined the influential law firm Sullivan & Cromwell. He accompanied President Wilson's delegation to the Versailles Peace Conference after World War I; as a member of the Reparations Committee, he assisted in work on one of the key issues of the conference. Dulles remained involved in diplomacy between the wars, accepting assignments from both Roosevelt and Truman administrations, including service as a member of the U.S. delegation to the United Nations conference in San Francisco. In both 1944 and 1948, he served as an advisor on foreign policy to Republican candidate Thomas E. Dewey.

In an article in *Life* magazine in 1952, Dulles outlined what would prove to be Eisenhower's approach to foreign policy. He argued that the Truman administration had not gone far enough in battling Communism, and that the United States ought to roll back Communism in Eastern Europe and Asia. He also said that it was a mistake for the United States to limit itself to the use of conventional weapons, and suggested that it should not rule out the use of atomic weapons.

By 1952, Foster Dulles, as he was known to colleagues, had become the most experienced Republican in the realm of foreign policy, and the odds-on favorite to be named secretary of state in a Republican administration. It surprised no one when Eisenhower named him to the post. Dulles's proclivity to speak out on issues, along with Eisenhower's willingness to allow his subordinates to do so, led contemporaries to believe that the president had delegated authority to Dulles to run the administration's foreign policy. Revisionist scholars since the early 1980s have demonstrated that the president remained decisively in control, and that Dulles clearly understood his role, seeking, accepting, and acting on recommendations from Eisenhower. Although the president had confidence in his secretary of state, that confidence was not unconditional. Indeed, Eisenhower regretted that Dulles sometimes failed to appreciate the impact his words had on others—that as many supporters as were won by Dulles's wide-ranging experience and his intellect were lost by his pedantry.

Five years younger than his brother Foster, Allen Dulles became the director of the CIA under Eisenhower, a position he held into the early months of the Kennedy administration. He had a résumé almost as impressive as his brother's, having accompanied Foster to the Versailles Peace Conference after World War I, and headed the State Department's division of Near Eastern Affairs in the 1920s. During World War II, he served with the Office of Strategic Services (OSS), forerunner of the CIA, and directed espionage activities against Germany. His close relations with the president and his brother guaranteed that he would have a great deal of latitude as director of the CIA and its covert activities.

Embroiled in controversy from the early months of the administration, Secretary of Defense Charles E. Wilson never became part of Eisenhower's inner circle of advisors and played only a marginal role in policy formulation. His principal responsibility was to administer the spending cuts imposed on the Defense Department by Eisenhower's fiscal conservatism and by the tenets of his New Look defense program.

Although he held no formal position in the administration, Eisenhower's brother Milton was personally closer to the president than anyone, advising him on all manner of domestic and foreign affairs. The president consulted his brother on every issue related to Latin America, about which Ike knew relatively little. Milton made several trips there and worked to encourage U.S. investment, pressing the administration to cultivate its relationship with the region.

Ike's close friend and wartime associate C. D. Jackson helped shape the administration's foreign policy in its critical early months. As special assistant to the president for Cold War planning, Jackson drafted speeches and coordinated efforts to incorporate psychological warfare into the U.S. military arsenal, then left government service after only one year. Ike's wartime chief of staff Walter Bedell Smith advised the president on Vietnam in 1954, the year that the United States began to get involved in Southeast Asian affairs. Harold Stassen, former governor of Minnesota and presidential candidate in 1948 and 1952, chaired the Foreign Operations Administration during the first two years of the Eisenhower administration, assisting in its foreign aid programs. In 1955, Stassen was named special assistant to the president for disarmament, a new cabinet-level position.

The national security advisor played a more important role in the Eisenhower administration that in its predecessors, with the National Security Council (NSC) becoming an independent source of advice rather than an echo of cabinet departments. Under Bobby Cutler, the first of Ike's four national security advisors, the NSC was reorganized along military lines, its staff strengthened, and its role in budgetary planning formalized.

The Bricker Amendment: An Attempt to
Limit Presidential Power

One of the most persistent foreign policy issues to face the Eisenhower administration originated from within the ranks of the Republican Party. Senator John Bricker of Ohio was one of several conservative Republicans outraged at what they considered Truman's usurpation of the role of Congress in shaping foreign policy. Bricker and his allies, who included Southern Democrats, also believed that American participation in international organizations and agreements such as the Universal Declaration of Human Rights and the Genocide Convention might force the United States to alter its domestic social policies and might, in particular, force it to end segregation. To meet this perceived threat, in 1951 Bricker proposed a constitutional amendment to limit American involvement in international organizations, to restrict the effect of treaties and executive agreements within the United States, and to reduce presidential authority in foreign policy. The so-called Bricker amendment became one of the strongest constitutional challenges in the postwar period to the balance of power between the executive and legislative branches, and to presidential prerogatives in foreign policy.

Two weeks before Eisenhower's inauguration, on January 7, 1953, Bricker introduced a modified version of his original amendment, having assembled an impressive cast of sixty-four cosponsors, precisely the required two-thirds majority of the Senate. Eisenhower opposed the Bricker amendment from the beginning, and told his brother Edgar that passage would "cripple the executive power to the point we [would] become helpless in world affairs." But he needed the support of conservative Republicans, and could ill afford to get into a public fray with them in the first weeks of his administration. He made his opposition clear to his staff, but allowed them to lead the fight. When reporters questioned him, the president would begin his answer with "As analyzed for me by the Secretary of State. . ." Although Eisenhower himself submitted no testimony to the Senate hearings, he marked up a draft of Dulles's with detailed rebuttals that demonstrated his mastery of the issues involved.

Faced with the mildest of opposition from the president, Republican Senators felt it would be no breach of loyalty to vote in favor of an amendment with such strong party backing. Bricker himself was uncertain where Eisenhower stood; he continually tried to modify its wording to satisfy the White House. In its final, watered-down form, the amendment required only that international agreements other than treaties be approved by Congress if they were to apply domestically. Put before the full Senate early in 1954, it failed to pass, but only by a single vote, 60–31.

The defeat did not end Bricker's quest for alternative wording that might win administration approval. But he found himself caught on the horns of a dilemma: if he moved too far to satisfy the administration, he risked losing the support of his conservative allies, and if he didn't move far enough, the administration had enough votes to defeat the amendment. Although the full Senate did not take up the Bricker amendment a second time, the issue didn't die until Bricker's defeat in the elections of 1958. Thus Eisenhower defeated the amendment without alienating conservatives, but by concealing his opposition he encouraged proponents to needlessly prolong the debate—which showed both the strengths and weaknesses of what historian Duane Tananbaum calls the "hidden-hand" approach.

In a historical irony, the Eisenhower administration would consult with Congress on major foreign policy undertakings except covert CIA actions in the years that followed. But, instead of asserting its constitutional prerogatives, Congress would consistently acquiesce.

The Cold War Thaws: "Atoms for Peace" and the Hope for Nuclear Disarmament

On March 5, 1953, just seven weeks after Eisenhower's inauguration, Soviet Premier Joseph Stalin died. A power struggle ensued in the Kremlin that cast the rivalry between the Soviet Union and the United States in an entirely new light. Stalin had not provided for a successor, and four possible claimants emerged: Georgi Malenkov, who first moved to seize the reins of power; Lavrenti Beria, feared head of the secret police, who tried to use his control of the secret police to gain power; Nikolai Bulganin, who edged Malenkov aside to become premier; and Nikita Khrushchev, who gained control of the Communist Party apparatus. Malenkov maneuvered to become prime minister, but had to relinquish his position as first secretary of the Communist Party in the bargain. Khrushchev proved the most adept at behind-the-scenes manipulation. He held high positions in the Party and in the government, the only person to sit on the Secretariat and the Presidium of the Central Committee. The power struggle continued until 1955, before it became clear that Khrushchev had emerged on top.

The death of Stalin opened opportunities for improved Soviet-American relations, and both sides indicated a willingness to work toward that end. By now, however, the distrust between the two adversaries had increased to such an extent that neither side believed the other. Ten days after Stalin's death, Malenkov announced that no current problem existed that "cannot be decided by peaceful means." Malenkov indicated a desire to end the war in Korea and to settle European issues. The Soviets followed words with deeds, negotiating for the release of prisoners in Korea, and for a solution to differences over Germany. Dulles, reluctant to trust the Russians, advised caution.

Eisenhower, however, told his staff that he was tired of the constant confrontations with the Soviet Union, and ready to try something different. Before the American Society of Newspaper Editors on April 16, Eisenhower appealed for the Soviets to take specific steps to end the constant state of confrontation the two nations had endured since the end of World War II, to take

the nations out from under "the cloud of threatening war." In a speech entitled "The Chance for Peace," Eisenhower emphasized in particular his hope
for nuclear disarmament. Two days later, Dulles spoke to the newspaper editors in terms that seemed to undercut the president's message. He blasted the
Soviet leaders for failing to accept "guidance from the moral law," and suggested that the United States would have to "act boldly and strongly" for
what it believed to be right.

Despite promising rhetoric on both sides, nothing much came of the
hopeful words of the Soviet and American leaders. Each side thought the
other was playing politics. Dulles believed the Soviet leaders were simply trying to forestall German rearmament. The Soviet leaders resented Eisenhower's failure to meet them halfway and his expectation that they take the
first step.

Late in the afternoon of May 8, three weeks after the "Chance for Peace"
speech, the president met with Dulles and other high-level defense advisors in
the White House solarium to discuss the state of Soviet-American relations.
Dulles worried that the Soviets had put the United States on the defensive,
leaving them with the initiative—a situation that would only deteriorate as the
Soviets developed a nuclear arsenal matching that of the United States. The
meeting gave rise to Project Solarium, one of the most comprehensive reviews
of American national security policy ever conducted.

The administration commissioned three task forces to consider possible
scenarios for dealing with the Soviet threat, and directed each to present the
case for a particular strategy. Task Force A, under the direction of George
Kennan, examined an approach derived from the containment strategy Kennan had helped frame under Truman, using economic and military strength to
maintain Western defenses. Task Force B evaluated a more aggressive variation of containment in which the United States would threaten war if the Soviet Union attempted to expand beyond its current sphere. Task Force C
considered a still more aggressive strategy designed to roll back Soviet influence. The task forces met for the next two months at the National War College, which provided staff and material support. On July 16, all three task
forces submitted their reports in an all-day session. The president then evaluated the day's proceedings in a 45-minute analysis that Kennan later claimed,
"showed his intellectual ascendancy over every man in the room." Eisenhower rejected every approach that would be too costly, too unlikely to win
support of U.S. allies, or too unmindful of the risks of nuclear war. Eisen-

hower believed, and Kennan agreed, that, as the Soviet Union matured into a major power, it would become less belligerent. In the meantime, the United States ought to make clear its vital interests and those nations it was prepared to defend without hesitation; in Eisenhower's view, these should include the nations of Western Europe, Israel, Japan, Formosa (Taiwan), and Korea.

The National Security Council used the analysis as the basis for recommendations for defense, disarmament, and nuclear strategy. The resulting proposal, NSC-162/2, argued that, in the aftermath of Stalin's death, the Soviet Union had not suffered any appreciable reduction in strength or control over its Eastern European satellite states. The threat of nuclear war thus remained undiminished. Disagreements remained within the administration over portions of the new policy, which evolved over the next several months under Eisenhower's direction.

Britain's wartime Prime Minister Winston Churchill called for a summit meeting of the major nations. In what was perceived as a thaw in the Cold War, the new Soviet leaders had signaled they were ready to bargain. For their part, in the midst of McCarthy-inspired anti-Communist hysteria, the Americans weren't sure how to respond, although they'd availed themselves of the thaw to bring the Korean War to an end.

Compelled by the practical need to reduce military spending, Eisenhower had adopted the New Look, which relied on atomic weaponry to slash defense budgets. Now advances in nuclear technology forced the president to move in the opposite direction, toward nuclear disarmament, at the very time it was testing new hydrogen weapons that dwarfed the first generation of atomic bombs. In August 1953, only months after the United States, the Soviet Union detonated its first hydrogen bomb. The nuclear arms race was accelerating at a dangerous rate.

Eisenhower was determined to open another peace initiative. C. D. Jackson, the president's advisor on psychological warfare, had been working since spring with the physicist J. Robert Oppenheimer on a report examining the risks of nuclear war. Their study, soon labeled "Operation Candor," recommended that the administration be frank about the size of the American nuclear arsenal, and Jackson worked on a speech to that end. Others, especially Chairman Lewis Strauss of the Atomic Energy Commission (AEC), disagreed, believing that it would be foolhardy to give away American nuclear secrets.

Eisenhower had been pondering the dilemma, trying to find a means to resolve the contradictory advice of his staff. He proposed that the United

States and the Soviet Union both turn over to the United Nations a specified amount of fissionable material that could be used for peaceful purposes. Operation Candor quickly gave way to the president's new proposal, and to discussions of how to build support for it. After publicizing the concept as widely as possible beforehand, on December 8, Eisenhower presented it to the UN General Assembly. He called for the creation of an International Atomic Energy Agency, and offered fissionable material from the American nuclear stockpile as a first contribution toward the establishment of a worldwide peaceful atomic energy program. He pledged that the United States would "devote its entire heart and mind to find the way by which the miraculous inventiveness of man shall not be dedicated to his death, but consecrated to his life." Eisenhower's conclusion brought the delegates to their feet, with representatives of the Soviet bloc states joining in.

Unfortunately, despite the high ideals of the speech, the Cold War adversaries soon lapsed back into old habits. In response to fears that the Soviet Union had moved ahead of the United States in H-bomb development and engineered "deliverable" bombs, the United States began testing a new series of hydrogen bombs on uninhabited islands in the Pacific in March 1954. The first American test had involved a bomb far too large to be flown to its test site. The administration had intended to keep the tests secret, but that proved impossible, both because of the size of the detonations, and because a shift in wind at the time of one of the tests carried radioactive debris over a Japanese fishing boat. When the fishermen became ill from radiation sickness, the Japanese public was outraged.

In a press conference held on March 24, the president admitted that the test had brought about unanticipated consequences, which only served to heighten international anxiety. After the United States staged another test six days later, the president held a second press conference, accompanied by AEC Chairman Strauss. Although intended to calm fears, Strauss's participation had the opposite result. When the chairman acknowledged that an H-bomb could be built large enough to "take out a city," reporters asked him how large a city. "Any city," Strauss replied. Even New York? "The metropolitan area, yes." A week later, on April 7, still another H-bomb was detonated on schedule in the Pacific. Eisenhower, still trying to allay fears, appeared at another press conference. Asked, at a third press conference, whether the United States intended to create bigger and bigger bombs, the president replied that it did not. He ordered the tests completed as quickly as possible, and the series concluded with explosions on May 5 and May 14.

Elsewhere, the early development of the Cold War would be played out in the Third World.

Iran: Mossadegh, the Shah, and the CIA

Colonial powers that had dominated much of the Third World for decades—Britain and France in particular—emerged from World War II battered and bruised, incapable of administering their vast empires. In the retreat of colonialism, uncertainty replaced certainty. As revolution spread among the former colonies, it became difficult to discern whether revolutionary leaders were straightforward nationalists, or whether they might be Communists. The United States tended to view revolutionary movements with suspicion, at first perhaps only because Americans desired stability, and revolutions are the enemy of stability. The Cold War led the United States to assume that if Communists weren't present at the start of a revolution, they would soon appear to exploit the opportunity. Furthermore, because revolutionary leaders seldom found aid and comfort from the United States, it made sense for them to turn to the Soviet Union, which was likely to provide aid to increase its own influence.

The first Third World revolution to confront the Eisenhower administration occurred in Iran, which had weathered its first postwar crisis in 1946. After the war, British, Soviet, and American troops remained in occupation, but all agreed to withdraw within six months. After the British and American forces pulled out, the Soviets lingered, demanding oil concessions. President Truman warned the Soviet Union to withdraw. They hesitated, but the Iranian government secured an agreement from Stalin, promising oil rights to the Soviets and influence in the northern Iranian province of Azerbaijan to Iran's Communist Tudeh Party in return for Soviet withdrawal. After the Soviets withdrew, Iran reneged on its promises; the Soviet threat seemed neutralized, at least for the moment. For the next several years, the Truman administration supported Britain's colonial presence in Iran, although concerned about appearing supportive of British colonialism.

Iranian politics in the postwar years were dominated by the shah, Mohammad Reza Pahlavi, and the leader of the political opposition, Mohammad

Mossadegh (modern spelling; Mosaddeq). As a member of the Majlis, the Iranian parliament, Mossadegh had battled the current shah's father, Reza Pahlavi, in the years before World War II, accusing him of seeking personal power at the expense of the Majlis. Now he made similar charges against his old adversary's son. Mossadegh was a fascinating figure; diminutive in stature, he could cry or become hysterical with little effort. A compelling orator, he sought to steer an independent course for Iran between the major powers, Britain, the United States, and the Soviet Union. Although he and the shah became bitter enemies, both men worked to reduce foreign influence in Iran.

Under an arrangement that had not been unusual in the colonialist days before World War II, Britain's Anglo-Iranian Oil Company monopolized oil production in Iran, returning 20 percent of its profits to Iran. After the war, the U.S. company Aramco negotiated a deal with Saudi Arabia that returned 50 percent of the profits to the Saudis. Understandably, Iran wanted a similar arrangement. Mohammad Mossadegh, now the Iranian prime minister and long a nationalist critic and political adversary of the shah, demanded that Britain renegotiate its oil contract. When Britain refused, he nationalized Iran's oil. The United States tried to mediate, to no avail. Britain feared continued disintegration of its empire, whereas the United States was concerned about the pragmatic aspects of oil production. When Britain began to assemble a military force to oust Mossadegh in 1951, the United States refused to cooperate.

The Eisenhower administration quickly shifted U.S. priorities in Iran. Once convinced that Mossadegh was moving too close to the Tudeh Party, it cooperated with a British boycott that kept Iranian oil off the world market. By this time, Mossadegh's domestic support had begun to give way. Religious leaders in the holy city of Qom, business leaders, landowners, and even some of the workers turned against him. Cornered, Mossadegh threatened to appeal for Soviet help. He held a plebiscite that gave him 95 percent support.

The CIA, working with British intelligence, planned to oust Mossadegh in a scheme dubbed Operation Ajax. In July 1953, Kermit Roosevelt, the grandson of Theodore Roosevelt, went to Iran with a million dollars to put the plan in motion. On August 16, with the shah out of the country to avoid danger and the appearance of complicity, the plan seemed to misfire. A planned announcement by the shah that he had fired Mossadegh never came,

5. Prime Minister Mohammad Mossadegh of Iran being greeted by Secretary of State Dean Acheson at the Union Station in Washington, D.C., October 1951. Truman Library Photographs, Harry S. Truman Library, Accession no. 66–8005.

and Mossadegh appealed for support, saying that the shah and foreign supporters had tried to get rid of him. The Tudeh backed him, and for three days the matter held in the balance; Washington urged Roosevelt to leave Iran. Then Iranian General Fazlollah Zahedi, with the support of a pro-shah mob raised by Roosevelt and his CIA bankroll, turned the tide. Mossadegh's regime collapsed, and he surrendered. Zahedi, appointed prime minister by the shah, arrested supporters of Mossadegh, and the Shah returned.

Ousting the populist leader Mossadegh and installing the shah served American and British interests in the region. Although, under a new agreement, Iranian oil remained nationalized, in reality, an international consortium would control production. The British Anglo-Iranian Oil Company received a profit share of 40 percent, as did a group of major American oil companies; French companies received 14 percent and Dutch Shell the final 6 percent. By supplanting the Soviets' access to Iranian oil with its own, the

United States was able to counter Soviet influence in Iran. The success of the CIA operation helped cultivate a myth of invincibility for the young agency, still trying to prove itself in the cutthroat world of intelligence and covert action. The price of that success would not become apparent for a generation.

The CIA and the 1954 Coup in Guatemala

Latin Americans had always regarded the United States with ambivalence, envious of its prosperity, but disdainful of the materialism that accompanied it. Despite having much that was admirable, the United States was nonetheless the "Colossus of the North," willing to use its power to exploit weaker nations to the south. Latin Americans long complained that their northern neighbor ignored them, although they preferred being ignored to being invaded.

The Cold War posed new problems for U.S. policy in the Third World. Although born of revolution, as a major power, the United States had become leery of other nation's revolutions, valuing stability over unpredictable change. Latin America posed particular problems: it had a long record of instability, it was nearby, and it had good reason to apprehensive of U.S. interference, which had occurred frequently in the twentieth century. Americans often looked down on Latin Americans with a smug superiority, assuming that the lack of political stability meant that they weren't quite ready to assume the burdens of democratic government. Thus, they rationalized, it was better to entrust government to dictators, who at least provided stability, than to the people of Latin America, who seemed incapable of managing it. So it was that when Guatemala overthrew its dictator toward the end of World War II, alarms sounded in the United States.

The case of Guatemala reveals much about the attitude of the United States toward Communism in Latin America, and throughout the Third World. Jorge Ubico was an almost stereotypical Latin American dictator: he loved the trappings of office and ostentatious displays of his own power, courted U.S. support, and called anyone who opposed him a "Communist." Opposition came from many quarters, however, especially when Guatemala's economy declined during the war. An uprising led by Guatemala's small middle class and intellectuals, soon joined by the church, labor, and the army, forced Ubico to resign in October 1944.

Juan Jose Arevalo, who replaced Ubico, believed in democracy and tried to avoid any actions that could be construed as Communist. But when he severed relations with Caribbean dictators, including U.S. allies, invited the country's large Indian population to participate in Guatemalan society, and introduced labor reforms affecting United Fruit Company, a U.S. company and the largest landowner in Guatemala, the United States became concerned. Encouraged by United Fruit, the U.S. ambassador to Guatemala, Richard J. Patterson, alleged that Communist influence was apparent, and even demanded that the Guatemalan government dismiss seventeen officials he claimed were Communists.

In 1950, after a bitter campaign that included the murder of his strongest opponent, Jacobo Arbenz was elected to succeed Arevalo. Arbenz's actions as president seemed even more threatening to the United States than those of his predecessor. Recognizing that Guatemala was a poor agrarian country whose most important commodity was the land itself, Arbenz instituted a land reform program. The plan stipulated that land should be taken only from large landowners, and although all landowners would be allowed to keep all of the land they had under cultivation, the United Fruit Company believed it was being singled out. With only 15 percent of its 550,000 acres in production, the company stood to lose 400,000 acres—one-seventh of all the arable land in the nation. As rumors of Communists in Guatemala multiplied and accounts sympathetic to United Fruit appeared in the press, the CIA drew up a plan for military intervention. President Truman and Secretary of State Dean Acheson, however, did not approve it.

After President Eisenhower's inauguration, United Fruit Company's prospects in Washington improved. Secretary of State John Foster Dulles had been an attorney for United Fruit in the 1930s, and his brother Allen, director of the CIA, had been a member of the same law firm. Allen Dulles and his wife had frequently vacationed in Guatemala. Moreover, Eisenhower's personal secretary, Ann Whitman, had once been married to one of the directors of United Fruit. Although there is no evidence of any collusion or corruption in these relationships, they suggest that influential members of the Eisenhower administration looked with sympathy upon the plight of United Fruit.

In the first six months of his tenure, President Eisenhower faced Communist threats at home and abroad. The Republican right wing, led by Senator McCarthy, had contributed to the party's strong showing the previous November. As much as Eisenhower despised McCarthy, he could not ignore him. Appeals in the Rosenberg case kept Americans focused on the domestic threat of Communism, while the war in Korea continued unresolved and increasingly unpopular. Against this backdrop, when Eisenhower, the Dulles brothers, and top CIA and State Department officials turned their attention to the situation in Guatemala, they decided it was time to intervene.

The CIA and the State Department coordinated planning. In Honduras, the CIA courted as proxy Carlos Castillo Armas, a son of a wealthy Guatemalan landowner and one of several influential Guatemalans working to try to raise a force to overthrow Arbenz. In Venezuela, at a meeting of the Organization of American States (OAS) in Caracas, Secretary of State John Foster Dulles strong-armed delegates into ratifying a resolution that called for "appropriate action in accordance with existing treaties" to meet the Communist threat. Although the vote was 17–1, with only Guatemala opposed, it did not in fact represent the overwhelming endorsement the U.S. delegation had sought. Two of the most influential Latin American nations—Mexico and Argentina—abstained, and many of the nations that voted with the United States did so reluctantly. The final version of the resolution called for further consultation before any action might be taken, and Dulles failed to convince the conference to sanction intervention in case of the threat of international Communism.

Moving ahead with its plans to oust Arbenz, the CIA used its training centers in Honduras and Nicaragua to create the impression of a large rebel force preparing for a military strike. It also worked with Guatemalan military leaders, Catholic priests, and businessmen, each of whom had their own reasons for opposing Arbenz, and initiated a CIA-backed radio station that began broadcasting to Guatemala under the banner of "The Voice of Liberation." By instituting an arms embargo, which threatened Arbenz's control of the Guatemalan army, the Eisenhower administration forced him to look to Eastern Europe for weapons. When Guatemala received a shipment of arms from Czechoslovakia, the administration had the pretext it needed.

The CIA operation, which began on June 18, 1954, succeeded far beyond the expectations of its planners. Broadcasts fabricated stories of the success of the invading force and the defection of pilots, and accounts of U.S. bombing raids created a sense of panic. Guatemala appealed to the United Nations, but the U.S. ambassador Henry Cabot Lodge was at the time serving his turn as chair of the Security Council, and was able to defer consideration of the appeal, and redirect it to the OAS as the regional organization concerned. There, too, the United States had enough clout to brush aside the appeal. On June 27, Arbenz resigned, and went into exile in Mexico City.

Although the CIA considered the Guatemalan coup to be a textbook case of how to conduct a covert operation, circumstances in Guatemala had been especially favorable for a coup. Opposition to Arbenz had been widespread; anti-Communism had crystallized among wealthy landowners, businessmen, and even among the poorer classes; the country's leading cleric, Archbishop Mariano Rossell y Arellano, had led the church in opposition. Key figures in the military played a crucial role: their complicity had ensured the success of Castillo Armas's small invading force, which on its own could not have defeated the Guatemalan army, and had convinced Arbenz he couldn't hold on. Moreover, leaders of neighboring states, including dictatorships and conservative oligarchies, had cooperated with Arbenz's enemies.

Nevertheless, the 1954 Guatemalan coup fed the CIA's sense of invincibility; seven years later, in another CIA operation, at Cuba's Bay of Pigs, its hubris would be undone. Even in Guatemala, however, success quickly turned sour. Installed as president after the coup, Castillo Armas was assassinated in July 1957, to be followed by a succession of repressive dictators.

The Vietnam Quagmire

During Eisenhower's first year in office, the war in Korea dominated concerns about Asia. By January 1954, a new crisis in Southeast Asia broadened anxiety about the spread of Communism. While Americans led United Nations forces on the Korean peninsula, France pursued its own Asian war in Vietnam. With what in retrospect seems an incremental inevitability, the United States found itself drawn ever closer to the quagmire of Vietnam.

For years, American fortunes in Southeast Asia had been intertwined with those of France. After World War I, the Vietnamese nationalist leader Ho Chi Minh, the son of a French colonial administrator, appealed to the leaders of the victorious Allies at the Versailles Peace Conference in 1919 for independence from French colonialism. Ho used the promise of self-determination extracted from President Wilson's Fourteen Points to seek the attention of the Big Four. Wilson's agenda dealt more with the adjustment of colonial claims than with the demise of imperialism, however, and the Big Four ignored the Vietnamese leader's appeal. Although France continued to rule in Vietnam between the World Wars, in the face of peasant unrest and the rise of nationalism, its ability to manage the colony became ever more precarious.

Japan occupied Vietnam during World War II, and, by happenstance,

Ho's Vietnamese supporters found themselves fighting side by side with American representatives of the OSS against a new imperialist adversary. But when peace brought no change, Ho Chi Minh again appealed for freedom from colonial status, declaring independence with a document modeled after the U.S. Declaration of Independence. The Truman administration had to choose between restoring the colonial regime of its French ally and support-ing a little-known revolutionary leader and alleged Communist—a decidedly easy choice to make in the early months of the Cold War. France reestablished its colonial bureaucracy, and selected a puppet leader named Bao Dai as em-peror. More taken with the attractions of France than with the difficulties in his own country, Bao Dai did little to interfere with France's decisions in the management of Vietnam.

In the early postwar years, at least in Southeast Asia, it seemed the United States could contain Communism painlessly, allowing France to occupy the front lines while having only to contribute its dollars, and relatively few at that. By the time Eisenhower took office, however, the United States was pay-ing 40 percent of the costs of French occupation.

The new administration felt America now had a vested interest in the fate of France's colonial mandarins. Much was at stake; as the weeks passed, the prospects for defeating the nationalist guerillas dimmed. French military con-trol in Vietnam shrank to defensive islands around the cities of Hanoi, Haiphong, and Saigon. Worse, it seemed that France suffered from a lack of will: politicians at home began to call for a withdrawal. American military leaders, brimming with confidence born of recent success in Korea, believed that the French forces in Vietnam had made crucial errors, the most serious of which had been their unwillingness to deploy Vietnamese soldiers, as the United Nations forces had South Korean.

Thus, in early 1954, through no fault of its own, the Eisenhower admin-istration found two of the fundamental tenets of its newly announced defense policy challenged. First, under its New Look defense posture, it had pledged to reduce military expenditures and ground forces. Second, in the pro-nouncements of its secretary of state, it had pledged not merely to contain but to roll back Communism. It was faced with the imminent threat of Commu-nist takeover in Vietnam and of the possible spread of Communism to Laos and Thailand, where pro-Western governments confronted pro-Communist adversaries. The new administration now encountered the prospect of setting aside its first pledge and honoring its second.

During 1953, under direction of General Henri Navarre, French forces had attempted to restructure their defenses. Admitting that it was no longer possible to win the war, Navarre proposed to centralize his forces and to take the initiative, conceding that even this conservative strategy could only be implemented with an infusion of $400 million from the United States. The Eisenhower administration had no alternative but to back the plan: it approved allocation of $385 million, bringing its share of the costs of the fighting to 80 percent, and found itself playing for a tie in Vietnam, the very strategy Republicans had ridiculed in Korea a few months earlier.

Seeking to reclaim French control, General Navarre established a base in northwestern Vietnam at Dien Bien Phu. The locale seemed ideal. A flat basin large enough to contain an airstrip, but ringed by high hills and thus deemed impregnable to artillery attack, the outpost gave France time to regroup even in the face of a two-to-one disadvantage in troop strength. Reports coming out of Vietnam at the start of 1954 were highly optimistic, but General Vo Nguyen Giap, the commander of Vietnamese forces, soon demonstrated that French optimism had been misplaced. In defiance of French military assessments, his forces hauled artillery pieces over the 1,000-foot hills ringing the French base and began to fire on the French troops below. Before long, French defenses began to crumble, and withdrawal seemed the only option.

If France hadn't the will to prevail, should the United States intervene? When Eisenhower and his advisors debated this painful question in January, Admiral Arthur W. Radford, chairman of the Joint Chiefs of Staff and a naval aviator, believed that the United States could rescue France with air strikes alone. General Matthew Ridgway, the Army chief of staff and former commander of U.S. forces in Korea, who knew firsthand the vagaries of a land war in Asia, advised against intervention. Eisenhower chose not to send American forces, and held his ground as the French military situation grew worse that winter.

By this time, France was looking for a diplomatic means to end the war, and agreed to place Vietnam on the agenda of an international conference scheduled for Geneva in April. The Eisenhower administration acceded to the proposal, even though it didn't share France's enthusiasm for an international settlement. The opposing sides looked at the prospect with contrasting goals. War-weary France saw a chance to salvage at the conference table what it had lost on the battlefield. The Vietminh saw an opportunity to strengthen their hand at the bargaining table with a decisive victory on the battlefield. Giap's forces continued to fire at French positions from the circle of hills around Dien Bien Phu, and began to tunnel toward the French airstrip. French soldiers later reported hearing picks and shovels as the Vietminh burrowed ever closer. On March 13, Giap launched a conventional attack that would soon spell the end of French resistance. Agonizingly, day by day, the French held on to their precarious toehold in Dien Bien Phu until April 26 and the opening of the Geneva meetings.

The most critical period during the protracted denouement took place during the first week in April. Douglas Dillon, the U.S. ambassador to France, cabled Dulles, explaining that Premier Joseph Laniel had urgently requested U.S. assistance to France's besieged forces at Dien Bien Phu from carrier-based aircraft. Eisenhower gave the request serious consideration, but insisted that any American intervention would have to be accompanied by multinational forces, including Asian troops, and would have to include a commitment on the part of France to keep troops in Vietnam and to move Vietnam toward independence. For the United States to intervene alone would invite charges of imperialism. Dulles and Radford urged an American bombing attack, but Congress had no stomach for another Asian war. Congress refused to support intervention without British support. Britain had no interest in joining; Churchill refused to lend support despite an impassioned personal plea from Eisenhower. The president nonetheless worried about the consequences of a possible French defeat, however; in a press conference on April 7, he elaborated what he called the "falling domino" principle. The loss of Indochina might lead to the spread of Communism to Burma, Thailand, and Malaya. "You have a row of dominos set up," the president explained. "You knock over the first one, and what will happen to the last one is the certainty that it will go over very quickly."

Eisenhower sought throughout his handling of U.S. involvement in Vietnam to preserve flexibility. Historians recently have praised Eisenhower for his restraint, for his refusal to commit American troops. The story is more complex, however, for Eisenhower's position was not a flat refusal, but rather a statement of conditions under which the United States would intervene. As historian David Anderson argues, "Eisenhower charted the course that President Lyndon Johnson followed to the fateful decisions of 1964 and 1965 to drop the bombs and land the Marines."

The Geneva conference on Southeast Asia commenced April 26, with France clinging to its Dien Bien Phu outpost but on the verge of defeat. The meeting was a summit of the major powers, with representatives of the Soviet Union, China, France, Great Britain, the United States, and the Southeast Asian nations of Vietnam, Cambodia, and Laos. Dulles was present for the opening sessions, but had no confidence that anything good could come out of negotiation with Communists. His biographer Townsend Hoopes wrote that he acted as if he was a "puritan in a house of ill repute." Disdaining to shake hands with China's Chou En-lai, Dulles departed even before delegates began discussing Vietnam. He left the U.S. delegation in the hands of Walter Bedell Smith, Eisenhower's wartime chief of staff, who was close to both Dulles and the president, with instructions to avoid personal involvement in the negotiations and not to accept any settlement turning land over to the Communists.

On May 7, after fifty-five days of siege, Dien Bien Phu fell, and with it, the last bastion of French colonialism in Southeast Asia. Premier Laniel had lobbied for U.S. intervention until the end, and Eisenhower had kept the option open just as long, even after he was convinced that France had no desire to hold out any longer.

Although no consensus on the fate of Vietnam had been reached at the Geneva conference, the option that seemed to have the greatest chance for acceptance was some form of partition. The Democratic Republic of Vietnam—Ho Chi Minh's revolutionary government, the political arm of the Vietminh—stood to lose much of what it had won on the battlefield. France had perhaps had the most to gain from partition, but Laniel had promised Bao Dai he would oppose it. Although recognizing that partition was tantamount to conceding territory to the Communists, during the course of the meetings, the Eisenhower administration came to realize the United States would have to settle for middle ground between the two extremes, one of which was "unattainable, the other unacceptable," in the words of the president. By late June, the administration accepted the prospect of partition, and changed its goals for the conference. The unpalatable but unavoidable solution of a partition would allow the United States to regroup, and to prevent the spread of Communism to the rest of Southeast Asia. China and the Soviet Union pressured Ho Chi Minh to accept partition. To do otherwise, they reasoned, might provide an excuse for the Americans to intervene. When the government of Pierre Mendés-France replaced that of Premier Laniel on June 12, it did not feel bound by Laniel's promises to Bao Dai. The emperor in any case wasn't present at the conference and had little chance of swaying the delegates

Map 2. Southeast Asia. Cartographic Research Laboratory, University of Alabama, Tuscaloosa.

in any direction, though he worked behind the scenes with his allies in Vietnam, seeking to shuffle his cabinet in order to survive the conference.

The final accord on Southeast Asia agreed to a partition of Vietnam at the seventeenth parallel, and prohibited the introduction of foreign troops into the country. No foreign nation would be allowed to establish a military base either north or south of the dividing line. The participants agreed that elections to reunify Vietnam would be held in July 1956 under the supervision of Canada, Poland, and India.

Eisenhower and Dulles responded to the Geneva accords in characteristic fashion. The United States, while officially noting the accords' conclusions and agreeing not to use force to disrupt the agreement (the president wishing to preserve flexibility in foreign affairs), refused to sign them (Dulles having announced at the outset he would not be a signatory to any agreement with Communists). Although the National Security Council considered the accords a disaster, by diminishing France's role and providing a two-year window before elections, they had at least given the United States time and room to maneuver.

Dulles meanwhile moved to shore up a regional alliance, the Southeast Asian Treaty Organization (SEATO). The new organization, formed as part of the Manila Treaty of September 8, 1954, between Pakistan, Thailand, the Philippines, Australia, New Zealand, the United States, Britain, and France. Perhaps as significant as the list of members was the exclusion of Formosa (Taiwan) from the organization. The NATO-like title of the organization was misleading, for SEATO was a much looser organization that did not commit member nations to come to the aid of other members who came under attack. Although it failed to attract major regional neutral nations and never had more than symbolic importance, Dulles never acknowledged its shortcomings.

Weighing the situation from his resort in Cannes, Emperor Bao Dai recognized that France was no longer a factor in shaping the future of Vietnam. Late in May, while the Geneva conference was still in its early stages, he contacted U.S. officials in a bid for their support. Apparently at least in part to curry favor with the Americans, Bao Dai facilitated the emergence of one of his erstwhile opponents in Vietnamese politics, Ngo Dinh Diem, whose fortunes would become linked to those of the United States for the next several years.

Diem came from a powerful family. His father had been an official in the imperial court at Hue. Diem's large family—he had five brothers and three sisters—assisted in his political climb. Most influential were his older brother, one of the leading figures in the Catholic clergy in Vietnam, and Ngo Dinh Nhu, who served as Diem's protector and whose flamboyant, ambitious wife, known as Madame Nhu in the Western press, became one of the best known of the Vietnamese people to the West. Diem spent time in the United States in the early fifties, and met several prominent Americans, including Senator Mike Mansfield. Although, as a Catholic, Diem also sought out leading American Catholics such as Francis Cardinal Spellman and Senator John F. Kennedy, there is no evidence that any of these men contributed to his rise to power. More likely, Bao Dai and Diem realized they could use each other. Bao Dai used Diem to establish credibility with the Americans, and Diem used Bao Dai to gain personal influence.

Although Diem proved adept at winning American allies and American material support, his standing among his own people was questionable. A Catholic in a country that was 90 percent Buddhist, Diem had support principally from the cities and from among Vietnam's Europeanized elites. Emerging from a fractious political battle to win appointment as prime minister, Diem won praise from Americans as a staunch anti-Communist. Being an outspoken critic of the French didn't hurt his stock among Americans either. As the Eisenhower administration surveyed the situation in the South, no one believed that Bao Dai, the pro-French emperor, had the will, energy, or support to fend off Communist assaults. Diem, who had long sought influence in the South Vietnamese government, emerged as the only viable alternative, although, distrusting him, Bao Dai had not supported his bid for power. Now, however, Diem's high-level support in the United States, his indisputable anti-Communism, and his family connections led Bao Dai to set aside his reservations. The emperor, who was enjoying the good life in France and had no intention of returning to Southeast Asia himself, named Diem as prime minister on June 18, 1954.

Eisenhower dispatched Colonel Edward Lansdale, a specialist in covert action, to Vietnam to assist in the anti-Communist campaign. Fresh from a successful mission to assist Philippine President Ramon Magsaysay in suppressing a rebellion by the pro-Communist Hukbalahap rebels, Lansdale was a notorious independent operator whose exploits were dramatic enough to help shape two novels. Graham Greene's *The Quiet American* (1955) used a character based on Lansdale to show American naïveté in trying to establish an American-style democracy in the jungles of Southeast Asia. In their fictional critique of American foreign policy, *The Ugly American* (1958), William Burdick and Eugene Lederer celebrated Lansdale as their protagonist Colonel Hillendale, a man who went into the countryside and worked directly with the people rather than frequent the bars of the capital. Exploiting his close ties to Allen Dulles, Lansdale influenced the Eisenhower administration in its decision to support Diem. He became a confidant of Diem; he assisted the flight of Catholics from the north to the south after the French defeat at Dien Bien Phu; he encouraged Diem to develop reform programs to secure support in the countryside; and he defended Diem against critics who wanted to remove him from office.

Diem's support was far from universal among the Americans, however. General J. Lawton Collins, for one, who had traveled to Saigon as Eisenhower's emissary, recommended that Diem be removed. Moreover, Diem also had enemies among South Vietnamese elites. To Washington, however, there seemed to be no alternative—a refrain that would characterize Diem's relations with the Americans from this point forward.

The American dilemma was complex. It was easy but misleading to draw parallels to Iran or Guatemala, where the threat of Communism defined the issue. Ho Chi Minh's Communism made the comparison attractive, but the rise of nationalism and the defeat of France complicated matters. Pondering nationalism in Vietnam and elsewhere in the Third World, Eisenhower could not come to terms with the forces that inspired it. Historian David Anderson lamented "the profound absence of a positive U.S. response not only to nationalism but to the full spectrum of social, cultural, economic, and historical factors in the Third World." If any Westerners understood the role these forces played in Vietnam, it was the French, but neither Dulles nor Eisenhower put much faith in their judgment. General Collins also weighed in against Diem. Despite Diem's American connections, the Eisenhower administration knew his personal weaknesses and the limits of his support in Vietnam. French contacts who knew Diem considered him unfit to govern, even "mad" in one assessment. Nonetheless, there seemed to be no one else to support. Senator Mansfield said as much when he returned from a fact-finding mission to Vietnam. Dulles agreed, and his State Department became one of Diem's most ardent supporters.

With resignation rather than enthusiasm, the United States moved to strengthen Diem's regime. Colonel Lansdale brought his freewheeling tactics to bear on Diem's behalf, making full use of propaganda, subterfuge, and direct contacts with the Vietnamese people to win their "hearts and minds." In the two-year interim between Geneva and the date of scheduled elections, Diem faced internal challenges that nearly toppled him, even as he tried to contain the Vietminh. He had been unable to unify rival factions in the South, and it was unclear whether he would be able to hold on to his office. Lansdale helped him win the factional struggle. Diem suppressed the Binh Xuyen, a powerful group that used drug smuggling, control of vice, and political expediency to maintain influence, and who posed the gravest threat to Diem's leadership after the Vietminh. By late 1955, Diem had consolidated his control. He defeated Bao Dai in a referendum that Stanley Karnow, who served as a reporter in Vietnam in the mid-fifties, claimed was "a test of authority rather than an exercise in democracy." Lansdale and Diem's lieutenants did all they could to take the element of risk out of the election. In several polling places, ballots for Diem were red (which signified good luck in Vietnamese culture) and those for Bao Dai were green (which stood for misfortune). Diem's poll monitors counted the red ballots, threw away the green ballots, and roughed up those who'd had the temerity to cast green ballots. Assisted by strong-arm tactics, Bao Dai's continued absence, and Lansdale's ability to manipulate elections, Diem secured over 98 percent of the vote, and became de facto chief of state in the South.

In defiance of the Geneva accords, Diem refused to hold the elections scheduled to take place in the summer of 1956. The United States agreed to back his decision, citing violations of the accords by the North as justification for the decision. There was little doubt that Ho Chi Minh, who was popular throughout the country, would have won a decisive victory in a fair election. By 1956, Ho had consolidated his power in the north. He had been ruthless in doing so, and a stream of refugees had fled to the South.

Early in 1956, by assuming the formidable responsibility for training and outfitting the South Vietnamese army, the United States risked sinking into the Vietnamese quagmire. France had never put much faith the Vietnamese troops, so the Americans had little to work with. The Geneva accords limited the number of American advisors who could serve in Vietnam, although the United States found ways to augment its contingent of advisors beyond those limits to nearly 700. The U.S. Military Assistance and Advisory Group (MAAG), based in Saigon, directed the training mission. Later criticized for failing to train their soldiers for the guerilla warfare that became the North Vietnamese pattern in the years that followed, MAAG understandably trained what it knew. The United States poured millions of dollars in military aid and commercial credits into Vietnam, bolstering Diem's regime.

Diem proved a difficult client. U.S. pressure for reform generated little response. Diem knew as well as his American advisors that the United States had no alternative but to back him, so he determined how American money would be spent, giving scant attention to American pleas for reform. The situation in the South was chaotic. The influx of thousands of intensely anti-Communist Catholic refugees from the North stretched resources to their limit. Diem operated with impunity, unleashing his brother Nhu to suppress opposition in the countryside, waging a violent campaign against alleged Vietminh sympathizers, and striking at factional enemies.

The situation in the North was no more stable. The flight of Catholics to the South eased one burden, but the economy was prostrate after long years of fighting France. Ho Chi Minh used violence to purge his domain of former French sympathizers even as Diem struck at the Vietminh in the South.

In two years, the United States had moved from being the banker for a failing French colonial enterprise to being the patron of an undisciplined client. The Eisenhower administration had accepted the logic that there was no viable alternative to Diem, and once it had made that judgment, it became ever more difficult for an alternative to emerge. By 1956, the United States had spent more than a billion dollars in Vietnam, first in support of France, which had now departed, and then in support of Diem, whose priorities didn't always match those of the Americans.

Quemoy and Matsu: The Chinese Island Crisis of 1954

After its defeat at the hands of the Chinese Communist government of Mao Tse-tung in 1949, the Nationalist Chinese government of Chiang Kai-shek fled to the island of Formosa (Taiwan). Chiang also claimed possession of small islands situated off the coast of China, the Tachen Islands to the north, the Matsu Islands between northern Formosa and the mainland, and the Pescadores between southern Formosa and the mainland. The small islands, some merely rockpiles, were important because of their strategic locations. Quemoy, 100 miles northwest of Formosa and 15 miles off the Chinese coast, and Matsu, 120 miles west of Formosa but less than 10 miles off the Chinese coast, twice became the center of controversy in the fifties.

The People's Republic of China never recognized Chiang's right to the islands, which it claimed should belong to mainland China under the terms of agreements reached at the wartime conferences at Cairo, Yalta, and Potsdam promising to return all territory occupied by Japan to China. The question that hovered over the islands was the same one that influenced all postwar Chinese issues: which government was the legitimate ruler of China? During the Truman presidency, the U.S. relationship with Chiang's government on Formosa (Taiwan) changed as the administration reevaluated its Asian policy after the Korean War. Although Formosa (Taiwan) did not lie within the U.S. defense perimeter defined by Secretary of State Acheson in January 1950, during the Korean War, Truman dispatched units of the Seventh Fleet to protect Formosa, and warned Chiang not to attempt an invasion of the mainland.

Between 1950 and 1954, both Chinese governments engaged in hostile posturing. Chiang promised to return to the mainland, a threat that had little value beyond maintaining his regime's mythology. Nonetheless, the offshore islands were essential to that mythology, and also provided a base for commando raids. Chiang kept the islands, particularly Quemoy, well fortified. Mao's government issued its own threats, usually laden with anti-American invective, and promising to absorb the offshore islands, including Formosa. This threat was credible, and brought the United States perilously close to intervention twice during the Eisenhower presidency.

In August 1954, Communist China began shelling Quemoy and Matsu, calling for the liberation of the islands and of Formosa. The action posed a particular problem for President Eisenhower since the status of China was central to the ideology of the Old Guard of the Republican Party, for whom the "loss" of China was the great betrayal of the Truman-Acheson-Marshall clique. Here was a chance to rectify one of the most egregious wrongs of the Truman years.

The United States had no treaty with the Formosa (Taiwan) government, so Eisenhower's options were open. His first step into the murky waters of the Formosa Strait was to warn that if the Communist Chinese government intended to invade Formosa, they would have to "run over the Seventh Fleet." Secretary of State Dulles conferred with Chiang on the way home after discussions related to the establishment of the Southeast Asian Treaty Organization (SEATO), and agreed to terms of a mutual defense pact.

In September, Eisenhower met with the Joint Chiefs of Staff. With its chairman, Admiral Arthur Radford, leading the charge, the Joint Chiefs urged the president by a three-to-one vote to allow Chiang to bomb the mainland,

and to intervene with American forces if the Communists retaliated. Only General Ridgway dissented, arguing that bombing, though unlikely to resolve the issue, was likely to draw American troops into action. Eisenhower agreed with Ridgway, and refused to be pushed into hasty action. Even as the shelling continued into its third month in November, and even when the Communists announced prison terms for Americans held illegally after the Korean armistice, he refused to take precipitous or irrevocable action, but he also refused to back down.

In December, the president signed the mutual defense pact that Dulles had brought back from Formosa, but still kept his options open by limiting the pact to Formosa and the Pescadores, omitting Quemoy and Matsu. Communist activity increased early in January, with an air attack on the Tachen Islands and a raid on an island 7 miles further north. Eisenhower decided to submit a statement to Congress to clarify his position, bolster the Nationalists, and make clear that he had authority to act. He conferred with Dulles and congressional leaders of both parties before submitting a resolution on January 24. It requested authority for the president "to employ the armed forces of this nation promptly and effectively for the purposes indicated if in his judgment it became necessary." Still retaining his options, the president did not clarify whether the resolution applied to Quemoy and Matsu. The resolution offered Eisenhower a blank check. Congress endorsed the resolution by overwhelming majorities, 410–3 in the House and 83–3 in the Senate. The Formosa Doctrine had the force of law.

But even as Eisenhower committed the nation to the defense of Formosa, he persuaded Chiang to withdraw from the Tachens, and offered him the protection of the Seventh Fleet to monitor the evacuation. The threat of war still loomed, however; in March, Dulles told the president that he believed there was a fifty-fifty chance that the United States would have to go to war over China. Dulles suggested to the press that if there were to be war, the United States would employ tactical atomic weapons. At the president's March 16 press conference, reporters asked him about Dulles's statement, and Eisenhower responded, "I see no reason why they shouldn't be used just exactly as you would use a bullet or anything else." The statement set off alarms, just as a similar statement by President Truman had during the Korean War. Eisenhower still refused to give Chiang what he wanted most, however: an irrevocable American commitment to defend Quemoy.

The crisis now entered a crucial phase, for American intelligence expected that if there were to be a Communist attempt to take the islands, it would occur before April 15. The reasoning reflected a belief that Mao would want the islands as a prize heading into the conference of African and Asian non-aligned nations scheduled for in Bandung, Indonesia, later in the month. By early April, Chiang's reinforcements had made the island's defenses formidable; Eisenhower believed that the most critical period had passed.

Tensions did appear to have eased. When the Bandung conference began, instead of bellicose rhetoric, as expected, the Communists issued peace feelers, offering to negotiate, asserting that they would seek to win Formosa by peaceful means rather than by force. The shelling of Quemoy and Matsu tailed off; by the middle of May, it ended. The crisis was over, although the status of the offshore islands remained unresolved, and trouble would erupt again in 1958.

Eisenhower had weathered a perilous storm, and had handled it masterfully. It was, in the words of historian Stephen Ambrose, "a *tour de force,* one of the great triumphs of his long career." By keeping his options open throughout, the president had kept both sides guessing. The threat to use the bomb came as the crisis entered its most critical juncture, and may have influenced Mao's decision to hold back. Neither Chiang nor Mao ever knew whether the Americans would intervene if the Communists did seek to take the islands by force. By exercising restraint when others, including his own advisors, urged him to use force, Eisenhower was able to keep his options open, preserve the *status quo ante-bellum,* and avoid intervention.

In a more sobering assessment of the crisis, by granting Eisenhower the authority spelled out in the Formosa Doctrine, Congress had set a dangerous precedent, ceding its war-making powers to the president. This action stands beside Truman's entry into the Korean War as one of the two most dramatic shifts of power from the Congress to the president in the 1950s, fostering the growth of what the historian Arthur Schlesinger Jr. would later call the "imperial presidency." The crisis also brought the United States closer to Chiang, and made it clear that in certain circumstances the Americans would defend his regime. Furthermore, the United States, which had twice used the atomic bomb against Asians (both times in Japan), had threatened to do so again. Moreover, it had discussed using nuclear weapons at the highest levels three times in the early fifties—in Korea, in Vietnam, and now in China. An opportunity for improved relations with China after the offer to pursue negotiations had passed without significant contact.

Open Skies and Aerial Spies: Geneva and the U-2

Early in 1955 Eisenhower began to consider the possibility of holding a summit conference with the leaders of the Soviet Union, Premier Bulganin and Party leader Nikita Khrushchev. It had been ten years since the leaders of the Cold War adversaries had sat together at a conference table. That meeting, in Potsdam in the summer of 1945, had served to crystallize issues that led to the breach between the two nations that weeks earlier had been Allies against Nazi Germany. Both sides had been chastened by the events that followed Potsdam, and neither had suggested a summit conference since. Now the former Allies—or their clients—stood across from one another beside hostile borders in Korea, Germany, China, and Southeast Asia. Indeed, Eisenhower saw little reason to believe that a summit conference would solve any of these problems. Secretary Dulles was leery of a summit, and advised against it; he had little confidence that this meeting with Communist leaders would be any more productive than the Geneva conference on Vietnam had been. Moreover, treating the Soviet Union as an equal to the United States would give the Soviets stature they wouldn't otherwise have and a platform from which to disseminate propaganda.

Several factors convinced Eisenhower to go to Geneva despite his own doubts and the strong reservations of his secretary of state. Both France and Britain pushed for the summit, as did many Americans supported it, with Walter Reuther of the United Auto Workers being perhaps the strongest advocate, and conservative Republicans the most vocal opponents. Overriding his serious doubts, Eisenhower finally concluded it was worth the effort to confer: regional issues might be irresolvable, but the threat of thermonuclear war transcended all other concerns.

Anticipating that the Soviets would likely want to talk about disarmament, Eisenhower formed a committee to evaluate possible U.S. responses. The Quantico Panel, which held its first sessions at the Marine base in Virginia, included Nelson Rockefeller, Harold Stassen, Deputy Secretary of Defense Robert B. Anderson, and other prominent national security experts. From the panel's meetings and Eisenhower's own contributions came a proposal Eisenhower called "Open Skies."

By the time Eisenhower addressed the summit conference in Geneva on July 21, Bulganin had already presented a Soviet proposal on the elimination of nuclear weapons. With a storm raging outside the conference hall, Eisenhower laid out his plan. He proposed that the United States and the Soviet Union would exchange blueprints of each other's defense establishments, and allow flights over each other's territory to conduct aerial photography, thus building trust and guaranteeing compliance with international agreements on disarmament. As he reached a key point in his address, there was a brilliant flash of lightning and the hall went dark. "Gentlemen," the president exclaimed after a pause, "I did not intend to turn out the lights."

After the address, as the conferees talked informally, Eisenhower spoke to Bulganin, who refused to take a position on the proposal. A short time later, Khrushchev approached Eisenhower and told him that the plan was unacceptable, a subterfuge for using aerial observation to spy on the Soviet Union. For the Americans, who had been trying to sort out the power struggle in the Soviet Union since Stalin's death, there was no longer any doubt who was in charge.

Open Skies was dead. It was an imaginative proposal, but Eisenhower knew that there was little chance the Soviets would accept it, and admitted as much in an interview years later. Khrushchev had no intention of giving his Cold War adversaries easy access to information about Soviet military readiness. Moreover, one of the advantages the Soviets had in the Cold War was that secrecy shrouded their research. In contrast, the character of American society made it far easier for the Soviet Union to gather information about American arms programs than it was for the United States to learn about Soviet military development. For nearly three decades following Geneva, it became a Russian article of faith to prohibit inspections by the West. Many proposals for disarmament foundered on the shoals of inadequate verification that both sides were complying with agreements.

The end of Open Skies did not signal the end of hopes for aerial reconnaissance of the Soviet Union, however. Early in 1955, months before the Geneva conference, the CIA had begun development of a high-altitude aircraft designed for such a role. Under the direction of Richard Bissell, the CIA architect of the successful coup in Guatemala, development proceeded at Lockheed's vast plant in Burbank, California. Bissell convinced CIA Director Allen Dulles to support the project, and to draw on agency research funds to finance it. For technological expertise, Bissell relied on creative innovators such as Edwin Land, developer of the Polaroid Land camera, and Kelly Johnson, an accomplished aircraft designer. For added secrecy, the CIA avoided the usual "R" designation for experimental aircraft and code-named the plane U-2, with "U" standing for "Utility."

The U-2 specifications were extraordinarily demanding, and seemed almost contradictory. The craft had to be light and able to perform at altitudes that would strain the performance of jet engines, forcing them to consume fuel more rapidly than normal. Yet it had to be able to fly for ten hours or more, which meant that it had to carry fuel in quantities that would strain its carrying capacity. Johnson solved the dilemma by designing an aircraft that was a cross between a jet and a glider, constructed of ultralight materials such as titanium, with a wingspan twice the length of its fuselage. Meanwhile Land's team developed camera lenses and film that would allow top-performance photography at high altitudes.

After the refusal of the Russian leaders to accept Open Skies, Eisenhower gave the CIA the green light to proceed with the U-2. Although the U-2 was a remarkable technological breakthrough, its development wasn't trouble-free. Two pilots died in test flights of the fragile, lightweight craft. Bissell protected the U-2 from usurpation by the Air Force. He protected its secrecy by convincing the National Advisory Committee on Aeronautics (NACA), forerunner of the National Aeronautics and Space Administration (NASA), to announce that it had developed a high-altitude weather plane, the Lockheed U-2.

Within a year of the Geneva summit, the U-2 was ready for its maiden mission over Soviet airspace. The first such mission took place on July 4, 1956. The plane flew at such a high altitude that it was impervious to Soviet antiaircraft fire. The president nonetheless insisted that because of the potential impact on foreign relations if a plane were to be shot down, he had to approve each flight. The Soviets, who weren't eager to let the world know they didn't have the ability to shoot down the U-2, refused to lodge a protest against the flights and instead set about improving their air defenses.

The Hungarian Uprising of 1956

In February 1956, Soviet Premier Nikita Khrushchev delivered an astounding speech to the Communist Party's Twentieth Congress. Speaking at length of the brutality of the Stalin years, he denounced Stalin's crimes against the Russian people. His address initiated a program of de-Stalinization, under which people tore down statues of Stalin, renamed sites that had been named after him, and began to reexamine the recent past. The reaction in Eastern Europe shocked Soviet leaders, and presented them with a dilemma of unintended consequences. First in Poland and then in Hungary, people used de-Stalinization as a rationale to push for liberalization from oppressive Soviet domination.

The resulting crisis challenged Soviet leaders, but also provided a test for the Eisenhower administration. Since 1952, Republican leaders had been crowing that they would not settle for a Trumanesque containment of Communism, but would instead assist in the liberation of Soviet satellite states from Communism. Eisenhower knew better, and did not employ the rhetoric of liberation. But Eisenhower was in the hot seat when the liberation rhetoric of his party's leaders was put to its first test in Eastern Europe in the fall of 1956.

In Poland, protests in reaction to Khrushchev's speech forced the pro-Soviet government out of power. Wladyslaw Gomulka took power, supporting Poland's own de-Stalinization program, which soon went further than Khrushchev could tolerate. He flew to Warsaw, and attempted to compel Gomulka to back down, moving troops into position near the Polish border. Gomulka refused to be intimidated, and threatened to unleash a revolt of the Polish people. Khrushchev backed down.

The success of anti-Soviet protests in Poland inspired a similar reaction in Hungary. A crisis erupted on October 22. Demonstrators demanded that Imre Nagy, who had been forced out by the Kremlin the previous year, be restored to power. The following day, with Soviet acquiescence, the Hungarian government reinstated Nagy. The protests took on a life of their own, however. In Budapest, protestors toppled a statue of Stalin and threw Molotov cocktails at Soviet tanks. Although Khrushchev appeared willing to accept a settlement modeled after the accommodation reached in Poland, the protestors had tasted success and now demanded the removal of Soviet troops and the creation of a new political party to challenge the Communist Party.

In the frenetic two weeks before the U.S. elections, the Hungarian uprising competed for attention with the homestretch of political campaigning and an emerging crisis in the Middle East. Eisenhower responded cautiously to events in Budapest. He wanted neither to intervene nor to alarm the Soviets. Khrushchev withdrew Soviet tanks from Budapest, and the level of tension seemed to ease in Hungary.

Then events spun out of control, as developments from the two crises cascaded atop one another. The Israelis attacked Egypt on October 29 with support from France and Britain, and without prior warning to Washington. Hungary announced that it would withdraw from the Warsaw Pact, taking a step beyond what Poland had done. On November 4 and 5, England and France moved into Egyptian territory near the Suez Canal. The joint British-French-Israeli action diverted international attention from Hungary, and altered events there. Khrushchev faced humiliation on two fronts. He was in no position to come to the aid of Egypt, and could not afford to be seen as backing down in Hungary, as he had in Poland. He thus seized the opportunity, and moved to crush the Hungarian uprising. Russian tanks moved into Budapest. The Russians seized Nagy, took him back to the Soviet Union, and executed him the following year. Thirty thousand people died when the Hungarian revolt was crushed by the Russian invaders.

The Eisenhower administration could do little but track events in Budapest. Despite conservative Republican saber-rattling pledges to roll back Communism, Eisenhower would not—could not—respond with military force. To do so would risk war with the Soviet Union. Eisenhower had never made rollback promises, but neither had he refuted them. In what historian Piers Brendon labeled a "disingenuous conversation," Dulles, who had made substantial contributions to the liberation rhetoric, reassured the president that the administration had never actually sanctioned or encouraged rebellion.

The Suez Crisis

In the Middle East, the United States found itself in a quandary. After the establishment of the state of Israel in 1948, an event in which prompt American recognition of the new state contributed to its success, the United States had backed Israel in the face of Arab threats. At the same time, it sought to maintain good relations with the Arab states in the region, an effort rooted in a desire to minimize Soviet influence and to foster peace in the region in order to preserve Israeli security and to maintain the flow of oil to the West.

The American dilemma developed with the rise of Arab nationalism, and particularly Egyptian nationalism, which altered the strategic balance in the region. In July 1952, a group of young officers in the Egyptian army forced King Farouk to abdicate and to flee the country. The Truman administration refused to get involved in the revolution, and recommended that Britain refrain from sending troops. When the king requested assistance in leaving the country, the United States refused. Control of the new Egyptian government fell to Mohammed Naguib, one of the leaders of the coup.

After the coup, the United States sought to maintain regional stability and prevent Soviet access by both placating Egyptian nationalism and accommodating the British colonial presence in the Middle East—a course that in the long run proved impossible. For some time after the coup, however, the balancing act worked. Naguib wanted American aid, and proved willing to cooperate with the Americans. When disputes arose between the Egyptians and the British, the United States served as an intermediary. Secretary of State Dean Acheson even advocated giving military aid to Naguib, but U.S. ties to Israel precluded it. Even in late 1952, the issue of control of the Suez Canal had begun to emerge as divisive, and on this issue the United States strongly supported continued British management of the canal. When violence erupted in the Canal Zone over an Anglo-Egyptian dispute, the United States mediated a settlement. Here in retrospect, however, it is clear that the American balancing act was already in trouble, for establishing Egyptian control of the canal was perhaps the one concession that might have satisfied Egyptian nationalism.

After the Eisenhower administration took office in January 1953, Secretary of State John Foster Dulles took a particular interest in the Middle East. He continued to mediate between the British and the Egyptians, often pressuring Britain to make concessions to mollify Naguib. In April 1954, Gamal Abdul Nasser and a group of cavalry officers forced Naguib from power. The subsequent rise in Egyptian nationalism had an immediate impact on British and American policy, and caused a strain between the two allies. Americans found balancing Egyptian and British interests increasingly difficult. As the historian Peter Hahn concluded, "Americans retreated from their objective of satisfying Egyptian nationalism when it conflicted with their more vital objective of preserving Anglo-American harmony."

Although the United States considered peace between Egypt and Israel as the key to peace in the Middle East, a National Security Council study in 1953 argued that if Israel attacked Egypt, the United States should aid Egypt to avoid Arab enmity and Soviet advantage in the region. The Eisenhower administration cooperated with Britain in devising a plan called "Alpha" to improve prospects for peace by delineating permanent boundaries and assisting in the resettlement of Palestinian refugees. The plan died in the wake of Israeli-Egyptian clashes on the Israeli-Egyptian border in the spring and summer of 1955.

Nasser was among the first of the Third World leaders to recognize the advantages of playing the great powers off against one another. He requested arms from the United States, strongly implying he would go to the Soviets if the Americans did not deliver. When the Eisenhower administration turned him down, Nasser negotiated a deal in September 1955 to procure Soviet arms through Czechoslovakia. The arms deal persuaded the Americans and British to agree to finance construction of a high dam at Aswan on the upper Nile in southern Egypt, for fear the Soviets would if they did not. Working through the World Bank, the two allies agreed to underwrite the first stage of construction of the $1.3 billion dam, with United States providing $56.4 million and Britain $13.6 million, and to sympathetically consider requests for further assistance in later stages.

Nasser's diplomatic style gained support and international stature at a meeting of nonaligned nations at Bandung, Indonesia, in April 1955. Arranged by Indonesian President Sukarno, the meeting attracted leaders like India's Jawaharlal Nehru, China's Chou En-lai, and Nasser. They discussed means by which Third World leaders could take control of their own destinies, develop a common power base among nonaligned nations, and deny domination to either the United States or the Soviet Union. The meeting gave impetus to Nasser's plans to reshape the Middle East, a notion that ultimately took the form of the United Arab Republic, an Egyptian-dominated anti-Israeli partnership of Syria and Egypt.

Early in 1956, the Eisenhower administration dispatched Under Secretary of State Robert Anderson to the Middle East to try to broker an agreement between Nasser and Israel's Prime Minister David Ben-Gurion. Anderson's shuttle diplomacy—traveling back and forth between Cairo and Tel Aviv—settled only minor points, encountering intransigence on both sides on crucial issues such as the fate of Palestinian refugees, the status of the Negev as a connecting artery between Egypt and Jordan, and the format of the Israeli-Egyptian peace talks.

Nasser continued to steer an independent course, moving beyond nationalism to neutralism. He became more outspoken in his criticism of Britain. He accepted the assistance of Soviet nuclear experts, recognized the People's Republic of China and began to trade with it, continued to accept Soviet weapons, and criticized the Baghdad Pact between Iraq, Iran, Turkey, Pakistan, and Britain. For its part, Britain began to explore ways to get rid of Nasser, and broached the subject with the United States.

Although not interested in British attempts to oust Nasser, the Eisenhower administration began to reconsider its pledge of assistance on the Aswan High Dam. Dulles and representatives in both the House and Senate Appropriations Committees spoke out against Nasser's neutralism. U.S. allies in the Third World, including Turkey, Iran, and Iraq, questioned why the United States was rewarding Nasser's neutralism more so than their own pro-American positions. France wondered why the United States was aiding Nasser while he was aiding Algeria in its uprising against France.

The United States and Britain decided to withdraw their offer of aid for the building of the Aswan High Dam, agreeing to delay any announcement in order to prevent Nasser from going to the Soviet Union for assistance. Nasser learned of Anglo-American intentions in July, and forced Dulles's hand by instructing his ambassador to accept outright all terms, including U.S. reservations. Dulles chose not to maintain the ruse, and announced abruptly, in terms that the Egyptians rightly considered insulting, that the United States was withdrawing its offer. When Britain did so as well, the World Bank had no choice but to follow suit.

Days later, on July 26, Nasser retaliated. He announced nationalization of the Suez Canal Company, and his intention to use revenues from the canal to build the Aswan High Dam. The action boosted Nasser's prestige in the Arab world. Although Nasser's nationalization of the Suez Canal challenged all Western powers, it posed a greater threat to British than to American interests. Britain immediately began planning for an invasion of Egypt. When British Prime Minister Anthony Eden informed Eisenhower that Britain was considering using force against Egypt, he objected strenuously. Eisenhower believed that an invasion would be counterproductive, inviting Soviet intervention and intensifying Egyptian nationalism. Eden was determined to proceed with his plans, even over U.S. objections. To prevent military action, Dulles and Eisenhower attempted to call an international conference of canal users, to form a Suez Canal Users Association, and to take the issue to the United Nations—all to no avail. Personal dislike between Dulles and Eden made resolution of British-American differences more difficult, and when Dulles in a press conference contrasted the United States with the "colonial powers," France and Britain, he only strengthened Eden's resolve.

Enlisting the help of France, Britain went forward with plans for an inva-

6. Secretary of State John Foster Dulles and President Eisenhower confer. Contemporaries believed that Eisenhower deferred to Dulles; Eisenhower's papers show that not to be the case. National Park Service photograph, Eisenhower Library Audio-Visual Collection, Dwight D. Eisenhower Library, Accession no. 72–1827–2.

sion, believing (without grounds for doing so) that the United States would join once the operation started. Concerned that Eisenhower would try to prevent the invasion, Eden cut off communications with the United States. Eisenhower believed that if Britain or France intended to initiate military action, they would wait until after the American presidential election.

On October 29, Israel attacked Egyptian territory at Mitla Pass in the Sinai, some 40 miles east of the Suez Canal. Britain and France issued an ultimatum to Israel and Egypt, demanding that each nation withdraw its forces 10 miles from the canal on either side. Israel accepted and Egypt refused, as expected.

Eisenhower was enraged, both because the two allies had taken such a provocative action without consulting the United States, and because he believed the invasion foolhardy, likely to stir Arab resentment of the West and to

give the Soviet Union an opportunity to gain influence in the region. Furthermore, by shifting world attention from Soviet military intervention in
Hungary to the joint French-British-Israeli action in Egypt, the timing of the
invasion couldn't have been worse. When the United States introduced a
cease-fire resolution in the United Nations General Assembly on October 30,
it received the acclaim of Third World nations, who were astonished that it
would side with one of their brethren against invasion by one of America's
staunchest allies. The Soviet Union also introduced two cease-fire resolutions,
and the Eisenhower administration found itself aligned with the Soviet
Union, facing down Britain and France. Britain and France responded by vetoing all three cease-fire resolutions in the Security Council.

On October 30, the situation became more complex. Britain bombed
Cairo, and Nasser retaliated by sinking ships to block passage through the
Suez Canal. On the following Monday, November 5, the day before the U.S.
elections, British and French troops landed in the Canal Zone. The Soviet
Union threatened to send in troops unless the British and French withdrew,
and suggested to Eisenhower that the United States and the Soviet Union
march in together. The White House greeted the proposal with appropriate
derision, but the crisis lingered. The following day, Eden announced British
acceptance of a cease-fire, and the French followed suit.

The cease-fire did not end the debacle, however: the British and French
troops remained in place, and the British believed they had secured the canal.
Under pressure from the United States, Britain and France agreed to withdraw in favor of a United Nations Emergency Force, which was to occupy the
area immediately around the canal; by the end of November, the force was
nearly in place, and France and Britain were completing their withdrawal.

The Suez Crisis left a bitter taste among the Western alliance. Britain and
France resented that the United States had not supported their joint action,
and the United States resented the breach in cooperation among its allies, a
breach that created divisions in NATO that would never totally heal. France,
particularly under the leadership of General Charles de Gaulle, came to resent
U.S. domination of the Western alliance, and steered an increasingly independent course. The United States and Britain both took steps to restore a cooperative relationship at the next NATO ministers meeting, and in the end,
the Suez Crisis did no lasting damage to Anglo-American relations.

Ironically, the U.S. role in forcing a withdrawal of British, French, and Israeli troops did little to strengthen ties between the United States and Egypt. In the short term, it appeared that relations might improve, but ultimately the crisis served to strengthen Nasser's nationalism, which was at odds with U.S. interests. Nasser's defiance of the West enhanced his stature as a leader of the Third World and, in particular, of a growing and increasingly influential non-aligned bloc. Nasser delayed clearing the Suez Canal until March 1957. The next year, he established the United Arab Republic. The crisis also gave the Soviet Union opportunity to enlarge its role in the Middle East. The Soviets assisted in the construction of the Aswan High Dam, and sent advisors, who would stay in Egypt until after Nasser's death in 1970. The principal U.S. goal in the Middle East had always been to foster stability, and the Suez Crisis proved that its policy of accommodation to achieve that goal was a failure. Egypt entered a period that the historian Peter Hahn described as one of "rampant instability" that left the anchor of the Arab World adrift.

The three aggressor nations in the Suez Crisis all found their position in the Middle East diminished after the war. The French role in the Middle East was of only marginal significance before the 1956 war, and its stature in the Arab world declined as it attempted to quash a revolutionary movement in Algeria. Having lost virtually all of its political influence in the Middle East, Britain found itself pushed out of Egypt and Jordan. Israel withdrew from the Sinai, which it had occupied during the war. Israel's security felt the impact of the British withdrawal from Jordan to the east, and the gathering of hostile forces of the United Arab Republic to the north and south.

The diminished role of America's allies in the region affected the United States in contradictory ways. On the one hand, U.S. policy in the Middle East had long operated in tandem with British policy, and the departure of Britain altered that chemistry. On the other hand, the United States now was the dominant Western power in the region, its relationship with Israel undisturbed, its respect among Arab nations enhanced, and its regional role large and destined to increase. In the aftermath of the crisis, President Eisenhower proposed what soon became known as the "Eisenhower Doctrine." He asked that Congress grant the president the authority to intervene in the Middle East with economic or military aid to assist any country threatened by "international Communism" that requested U.S. aid. Congress initially refused, but, in March 1957, it granted him the authority he wanted, subject to congressional approval of the necessary funds.

Recommended Reading

A rich literature has developed on U.S. foreign policy of the 1950s. Previously cited biographies of Eisenhower have excellent coverage of foreign policy. Much of the recent literature on the Eisenhower presidency has sought to test revisionist interpretations that praised Eisenhower's leadership by examining his policy in foreign affairs.

Several fine studies examine the war in Vietnam in its entirety, including Stanley Karnow's *Vietnam: A History* (New York: Viking, 1983) and George C. Herring's *America's Longest War: The United States and Vietnam, 1950–1975,* 2nd edition (New York: Knopf, 1986). Lloyd C. Gardner's *Approaching Vietnam: From World War II through Dien Bien Phu* (New York: Norton, 1988) examines American involvement through 1954. David L. Anderson's *Trapped by Success: The Eisenhower Administration and Vietnam, 1953–1961* (New York: Columbia University Press, 1991) carries the story beyond Gardner, and considers diplomatic aspects of American involvement.

U.S. intervention in the Third World is treated both in studies of the Cold War and in case studies of U.S. relations with specific countries. Zachary Karabell's *Architects of Intervention: The United States in the Third World and the Cold War, 1946–1962* (Baton Rouge: Louisiana State University Press, 1999) examines U.S. intervention in both Iran and Guatemala. The 1954 intervention in Guatemala also receives analysis in Richard H. Immerman's *The CIA in Guatemala* (Austin: University of Texas Press, 1982) and Stephen Schlesinger and Stephen Kinzer's *Bitter Fruit* (New York: Anchor Books, 1983). Stephen G. Rabe's *Eisenhower and Latin America* (Chapel Hill: University of North Carolina Press, 1988) provides a broad context and examines other aspects of Latin American policy. For Central America, see Walter LaFeber's *Inevitable Revolutions,* 2nd edition (New York: W. W. Norton, 1993).

Peter L. Hahn's *The United States, Great Britain, and Egypt, 1945–1956* (Chapel Hill: University of North Carolina Press, 1991) is an excellent study of the Suez crisis and its background.

Two fine surveys of Soviet-American relations, by historians with differing points of view, are good places to begin an examination of the Cold War in the fifties. Walter LaFeber's *America, Russia and the Cold War, 1945–2002,* 9th edition (New York: McGraw-Hill, 2002), and John Lewis Gaddis's *Russia, the Soviet Union, and the United States,* 2nd edition (New York: Knopf, 1990), both provide background and analysis.

6

People of Plenty

The Transformation of American Society

IF EVER PEOPLE LIVING in the United States had reason to believe that theirs was the American century, it was during the fifties. The United States came out of World War II, not only one of the most powerful nations in human history, but also one of the most affluent. The postwar expansion triggered a quarter-century economic boom that eclipsed any similar period in the nation's history. In the fifties alone, the gross national product nearly doubled, from $285 billion to $500 billion, and most other economic indicators experienced similar growth. By mid-decade, historian David Potter observed the pervasive effect this newfound prosperity was having on the American character.

The forces that drove the prosperity of the fifties had their roots in the late forties, when Americans still bore the scars of Depression and war, and the nation seemed beset by economic uncertainty. Many people feared that, without the wartime spending that had fueled recovery from the Great Depression, the economy might slip into a postwar recession. By 1950, however, such fears had begun to recede, with only the Korean War clouding prospects for economic expansion.

With the money they had saved during World War II, returning veterans invested in housing, automobiles, clothing, furniture, and other household goods to provide for themselves, their wives, and their children, whose births were so numerous that demographers began speaking of a "baby boom." Manufacturers responded to this ever-expanding market by producing goods to satisfy not just the needs but also the wants of consumers. Thus, alongside laborsaving appliances and devices to help homeowners maintain their houses, there appeared a whole range of new products for recreation and entertainment.

Whereas European and Asian nations struggled to recover from the ravages of World War II, the United States, aided by inexpensive energy from abundant fossil fuels and equally abundant hydroelectric power provided by federally funded projects such as the Tennessee Valley Authority in the Southeast and the newly built dams in the West, moved smoothly from a wartime military to a peacetime consumer economy. American heavy industry converted from producing ships and submarines, military aircraft and tanks to producing commercial aircraft and automobiles, and to building a peacetime infrastructure that would keep foreign competitors at bay throughout the decade.

The United States had, in abundance, the natural resources required for the postwar industrial boom—petroleum, minerals, and rivers; it had the wealth to purchase the resources it lacked from nonindustrial nations abroad, and to do so under favorable trade agreements. And it also had ample room for industrial expansion, particularly in the Pacific Coast states, where new industries, such as the commercial aircraft industry, found attractive locations for their new factories, stimulating a boom in cities such as Seattle, Los Angeles, and San Diego.

Having gone to college under the GI bill in the late forties, in the early fifties World War II veterans moved into the professions, providing an educated workforce that formed the basis of the expansion of U.S.-based multinational corporations. American technological experts, often supplemented by talented refugees who had fled war-torn countries in Europe and Asia to seek opportunities in North America, created new industries and revitalized old ones. Government spending provided contracts and research dollars to private corporations, further stimulating the expansion of the economy. Despite the best efforts of the Truman and Eisenhower administrations to hold the line on defense spending, crisis-driven military procurement contracts continued to be a major source of business for private industry. Military pensions provided an infusion of money into the economy, even as veterans moved into other professions.

Car Culture: The Automobile as an Agent of Change

Like the baby boom, the "automobile boom" had a profound effect on the nation, one that rippled down the decades. It affected not only how Americans traveled, but also where they lived, where they shopped, where they ate, and how they spent their leisure time. The automobile industry drove the general economy, and the prosperity of the fifties reflected a robust consumption of cars.

The "Big Three" American car manufacturers—General Motors, Ford, and Chrysler—dominated the automobile industry at the beginning of the decade, and their dominance would remain unchallenged until 1960, when foreign car manufacturers began to enter the U.S. market. In 1950, however, only 1 percent of the automobiles sold in the United States came from outside of the United States. Americans bought only 300 Volkswagens in 1950, and the notion of a Japanese automobile was indeed a foreign concept, for the term "made in Japan" suggested something that was cheap and flimsy. Americans wanted "big, roomy boxes," noted historian Ronald Oakley: the typical popularly priced models were 8-cylinder, 100-horsepower vehicles with manual transmissions that sold for around $1,800. At the lower end, Fords and Chevys cost $1,329; at the upper end, Cadillacs and Chryslers cost $4,959 and $5,384, respectively. In 1949, automobile sales surpassed the previous record high of 4.5 million set in 1929, signaling the beginning of the automobile boom. In the first year of the fifties, sales reached 6.7 million, on their way to a peak of 7.6 million in 1955. Whereas, in 1950, three out of five American families (60 percent) owned an automobile, by 1960, almost four out of five (more than 78 percent) did; there were more cars in the United States than in the rest of the world put together.

Detroit knew its market. The Big Three stimulated demand by introducing significant changes in the appearance of cars each model year, and launching the new line with expensive advertising campaigns. By mid-decade, the pricier models had sprouted fins that grew to outlandish proportions, the essence of conspicuous consumption. Models from the mid- to late fifties became "classics" in later years: the Ford Thunderbird, which represented sporty power, and the '57 Chevy, which symbolized the Golden Age of American automobile manufacturing, found their way into classic car shows, and into folk and country songs that evoked the era.

Not all was golden for the automobile industry, however. Ford's Edsel, introduced on the heels of its great success with the Thunderbird in the fall of 1957, when visions of catching General Motors danced before the eyes of Ford executives, turned out to be one of the century's greatest marketing disasters. Indeed, to many, the Edsel became synonymous with the hubris afflicting the American automobile industry in an era when little seemed to go wrong. Ford had awarded the Edsel advertising campaign to FCB (Foote, Cone, and Belding), one of the most successful marketing firms of the fifties and the firm that had devised Hallmark's phenomenally successful slogan: "When you care enough to send the very best." After shrouding the new model line in unusual secrecy, Ford unveiled the Edsel with great fanfare. Unlike the most successful cars of the day, the Edsel lacked dramatic tailfins and sported a prominent "nose," with its name displayed vertically on a protruding panel in front of the grille. The public immediately pronounced the nose ugly and the rest of the car's design ordinary. Although FCB took the heat for a marketing disaster, Ford contributed to the failure in at least two major ways. To meet anticipated demand, it rushed its production schedule, and the haste resulted in sloppy production and ill-fitting parts. And Ford delayed release the Edsel until late in the production year, forcing it to compete with the now lower-priced cars from the preceding model year, and at a time when demand for medium-priced cars had begun to wane. Worse, and something Ford could not have anticipated, the Edsel appeared within days of the Soviet launch of Sputnik, an earthshaking event that left fewer Americans looking for new cars of any sort. Bowing to consistently poor sales, Ford finally buried the Edsel line in 1959. As Edsel chronicler James Baughman noted, Madison Avenue "did not acknowledge the extent to which incessant product promotion reflected rather than fashioned the new consumer culture."

The Edsel was the exception, however; the automobile industry continued to prosper throughout the decade and, with it, ancillary industries. Most directly affected were those producing raw and processed materials needed to manufacture cars: steel, of course, but also fabric for upholstery, plastic for interior accessories, and even paint, as well as those producing components that went directly into automobile production itself: tires, windows, engine parts. In response to increasing demand for gasoline and lubricants, the growth of the petroleum industry proceeded apace. Having explored Texas and California for new wells since the twenties, in the fifties it expanded into the offshore environs of the Gulf and Pacific coasts, and into the Middle East, where oil began to impact American foreign policy. Highway construction underwent its own boom in the fifties, most significantly abetted by the federally funded construction of the Interstate Highway System—more than 40,000 miles of controlled-access roads—authorized by Congress in 1956. Counties, municipalities, and burgeoning suburbs benefited as well when roads were extended to connect them to the new interstate arteries.

By redirecting traffic off well-traveled roads, especially in the West, the new interstate network initiated a decline in the older federal highway system. Towns and cities along these highways experienced an immediate drop in transport-related business, often their major source of revenue. Highways such as the famous Route 66 that crossed New Mexico and Arizona into California were used almost exclusively for local traffic and all but abandoned by interstate motorists. Gradually, over the next few decades, businesses serving travelers shifted from Main Street of the small towns to interstate interchanges.

The automobile permeated the daily lives of Americans in ways few could have anticipated, enabling people to shop, eat, and even worship from their automobiles. Basic facilities adapted to the automobile, allowing ample parking or delivering services to customers who remained in their cars. Among the prototypes of this new kind of service was the shopping mall. Although the concentration of stores that culminated in the mall dated back to the 1920s, with Kansas City's Country Club Plaza billing itself as the first shopping center, these earlier shopping centers encompassed traditional streets and storefronts. By the fifties, however, shopping centers had evolved into islands of stores surrounded by vast parking lots, physically removed from downtown shopping districts. Early shopping centers preserved traditional storefronts, although they fronted on parking lots some distance from streets rather than on the streets themselves. Downtown shopping, accessible via public transportation, served pedestrians; suburban shopping centers served automobile drivers. In the suburbs, covered malls, which began to appear by the end of the decade, turned within, away from the streets.

The automobile affected American eating habits even more dramatically than its shopping patterns. "Fast food," the car culture's mode of dining, though culturally rooted in the fifties, like shopping centers, dates back to the 1920s and the first drive-in in Dallas. The best-known, largest, and most successful such operation was a product of the entrepreneurial enterprise and mass marketing typical of the fifties, although it, too, had its origins earlier. The McDonald brothers, Dick and Maurice, began their first drive-in restaurant in San Bernardino, California, in 1940. Recognizing that Americans wanted to eat quickly, they began to streamline their operation to meet that demand. They cut their menu to nine items, concentrating on hamburgers, cheeseburgers, fries, and shakes. They developed machines to prepare these items in identical portions. They trimmed the size of their hamburgers, squeezing ten out of a pound of ground beef instead of the traditional eight. They dispensed condiments in premeasured doses, saving space, time, and cleanup over competitors whose customers spread their own mustard.

The long lines outside their San Bernardino restaurant testified to the success of the McDonald brothers' formula in serving mid-twentieth-century American tastes and yearning for speed. In 1954, when Ray Kroc joined them as a franchising agent, they had franchised nine stores. Kroc was "the classic American boomer," as author David Halberstam observed, "a self-made man [who] boasted, with good reason, of his ability to anticipate mass taste." He had ideas that capitalized on the basic concept pioneered by the McDonald brothers. Kroc developed a "Multimixer" that could mix five shakes at once. Recognizing that his principal market was the family, Kroc sought to keep his hamburgers affordable; the price of a burger was kept at fifteen cents for more than a decade. Targeting young suburban families, he discouraged franchisees from installing juke boxes or other attractions that might lure congregating teenagers. To the McDonald formula, Kroc added consistency, conformity, and quality control. By 1959, Kroc opened the one-hundredth franchise McDonald's restaurant. Two years later, he bought out the McDonald brothers, who had no desire to build a hamburger empire, and accelerated his pace of expansion. He envisioned as many as a thousand McDonald's around the country—a figure that would prove too conservative by a factor of more than twenty.

Although the McDonald's restaurants inspired plenty of imitators and even innovators, some of whom offered broader product lines, none could match the success of the McDonald-Kroc formula for fast food. Nevertheless, the drive-in restaurant, with or without Golden Arches, became an institution. Drive-ins with "carhops," the car culture's term for waitresses, proliferated in American suburbs. Trays attached to car windows enabled customers to eat without ever leaving their cars; at some drive-ins, the carhops raced from car to car on roller skates, so that diner and server alike were equipped with wheels.

Other industries also experimented with the drive-in concept. Hollywood found the car and the movie to be a perfect match in the fifties, when television was still in its infancy. The first drive-in theater appeared in the early thirties; by 1949, there were 1,100 drive-ins around the country. During 1950 alone, the number of drive-in theaters nearly tripled, to more than 3,000. By the end of 1959, the number had topped 4,000, a fourfold increase from start to finish of the decade. Young parents of baby-boomer children found the drive-in theater an inexpensive way to entertain the family. Newly mobile dating teenagers found that drive-ins gave a modicum of privacy not available in conventional movie theaters. Americans could go out for an evening, have dinner, and see a movie, and never leave their cars.

A uniquely American melding of religion and the automobile, drive-in church services emerged in 1955, not surprisingly in the uniquely American environment of Southern California. The Reverend Robert Schuller of the Reformed Church in America held services in a drive-in theater in Garden Grove, California, preaching from the roof of the concession stand to worshippers who remained seated in their automobiles. As Schuller's congregation grew in succeeding years, he continued to hold drive-in services, even as he accumulated enough capital to build the enormous Crystal Cathedral a quarter century later.

Motels, whose name derives from "motor hotels," had been around nearly as long as cars, but, because the motel industry was also ancillary to the automobile industry, it experienced phenomenal growth in the fifties, as several trends converged. More "car friendly" than hotels by virtue of their location along major highways and their ample parking, motels grew in popularity as Americans came to prefer travel by automobile for business and for vacations. And as Americans began to flee the cities for the suburbs, the downtown locations of hotels began to deteriorate, making outlying motels seem more attractive. The 1956 Interstate Highway Act guaranteed the growth and success of motels. Interstate interchanges at the outskirts of major cities became attractive sites for new hotels, which in effect became motels as well.

The Ray Kroc of the motel industry was a Memphis builder named Kemmons Wilson. While on a 1951 family trip to Washington, D.C., Wilson was struck by the inconsistency of motel offerings along the way. He thought of applying franchise techniques to motels and, specifically, of standardizing both their construction and their operation. When he founded the Holiday Inn chain, whose first motel was built in Memphis, Wilson envisioned a thousand Holiday Inns around the country; the chain would comprise many times that number. Wilson had an instinct for picking ideal locations; as word of his success spread, imitators built nearby to capitalize on his instincts. Like Kroc, Wilson sought to appeal to the family market. He kept room prices affordable by employing the same construction methods he had used for houses. And he offered a number of attractive features as well. Each Holiday Inn had a swimming pool and a restaurant on the premises; whereas others charged a nightly fee for television, Holiday Inns offered it at no charge.

The Baby Boom and What It Wrought

Seldom has a generation transformed society while still in its infancy, but it is no exaggeration to suggest that the generation born in the period from 1946 to 1964 did so. The impact of the baby boom would reverberate through the fifties and the decades that followed; as the baby boomers aged, the unparalleled magnitude of their numbers would have an equally unparalleled effect on patterns of consumption, residence, and employment, as well as on government policy. Although its statistics are surprising, it is even more surprising that few people expected the baby boom in the first place. Because the boomers' parents, born in the twenties and thirties, were relatively few in number, demographers had predicted only a brief, relatively small increase in numbers of births as veterans returned home after the war. They would prove to be sorely mistaken.

The 3.4 million babies born in 1946 represented a 20 percent increase over the previous year. Rather than the temporary blip predicted by demographers, it was but the beginning of a decades long trend. The birthrate had never exceeded 20 per 1,000 between 1932 and 1940; it would never drop below 24 from 1947 to 1959. The number of babies born per year continued to increase until it topped 4 million in 1952, and it never dropped below that number until 1965.

Explanations for the baby boom must begin with the obvious: the return of veterans from the war and their establishment of families—a pent-up demand that demographers anticipated, and that helps to explain at least the start of the boom. Many couples delayed marriage until after the war, and young married couples delayed having children, either because of their own decision or because of separation imposed by the war. The decision to have children after the war pertains not only to young adults returning from the war or waiting on the home front, but to their older siblings, who had been constrained by the Depression as well as the war from having families. Trends in marriage and in divorce also help explain the boom. Not only were women more likely to marry than their mothers had been; they also married younger and were more likely to have children. Moreover, they had their first child earlier, and they had more children. Finally, the modest divorce rate reinforced these trends: having increased dramatically immediately after the war, it dropped in 1947 and remained relatively low throughout the fifties.

Social scientists have offered several explanations for why statistical trends combined to produce the baby boom. The most persuasive of these explanations center around the sense of security postwar couples experienced in comparison to the uncertainties that confronted their parents. The Great Depression and World War II made Americans, especially young couples, feel profoundly insecure about their future. In contrast, young couples after the war had many reasons to be hopeful. New government programs provided them with substantial assistance in housing, education, and jobs. Loans offered by the Veterans Administration (VA) and the Federal Housing Administration (FHA) enabled young families to purchase their first homes. By giving them the chance to receive a college education, the GI Bill made it likely veterans would qualify for better-paying, more secure jobs than those of their parents. As the economy continued to expand, fear of an economic depression receded. Consumer confidence reflected this sense of security.

The baby boom contributed to the economic boom of the fifties and, by doing so, reinforced itself. Consumer goods related to child care—clothing, toys, baby furniture such as high chairs and cribs, larger automobiles to transport growing families, and books on how to care for babies, most notably, the surprising best seller, Dr. Benjamin Spock's *The Common Sense Book of Baby and Child Care*—all reflected the boom. As the babies grew into children, they continued to influence the economy, becoming consumers themselves; businesses that served the new market in music, sporting goods, and toys profited.

The baby boom influenced school districts across the country, which had to adjust to a sudden increase in class size that moved through the grades. By 1960, there were 3.5 million 13-year-olds in the nation, most of whom were then eighth graders. No older age cohort numbered more than 2.9 million, and every class that followed the 1960 eighth graders was larger yet. There was a boom in teacher education programs, fueled by the baby boom and the Cold War fear that the United States was falling behind the Soviet Union in the aftermath of the 1957 launch of Sputnik, the first earth satellite. The demand for new schools provided jobs for the construction industry.

On the Move: American Demography in the Fifties

Demographic trends in the fifties demonstrated a continuation of long-term developments, but the postwar era also demonstrated that other new trends were surfacing. Two trends dominated most of the demographic statistics of the 1950s: increased growth and increased mobility. With the baby boom influencing increases on one extreme of the age ledger and with increased longevity doing the same on the other, the United States experienced a significant overall increase in population during the fifties, from 151,325,798 in 1950 to 179,323,175 in 1960, an increase of 28 million, or more than 18 percent. This was the largest numerical increase in a single decade by a wide margin—no previous decade had increased by more than 20 million—even though the rates of population increase in the nineteenth century routinely topped 30 percent and never dipped below 20 percent.

Whereas the automobile culture demonstrated that Americans were a mobile people in their daily lives, demographic trends demonstrated that they were mobile in the long term as well. Americans were on the move. They were moving from rural areas to the cities, as they had been doing for a century, but they were also moving from the cities to the suburbs, from the North and East to the South and West.

The proportion of Americans living in cities with a population of more than 2,500 increased from 60 percent to 63 percent during the decade. African Americans, in particular, left farms in the South to move to cities in the Northeast and Great Lakes area where industrial jobs offered a way out of the poverty of sharecropping. This pattern began after World War I, and continued in significant numbers in the fifties. White farmers, too, joined the migration, as small family farms gave way to corporate operations. People also fled from the hilly, impoverished areas of Appalachia and the Ozarks, where subsistence farms had never done well, and where there were no alternative jobs.

The pattern of this movement differed significantly from what it had been in the past, however; once again, the increasing reliance on the automobile bore much of the responsibility for this difference. Automobiles brought about dramatic changes in the more populous areas of the country, where people left the downtown areas of cities to move to outlying suburbs. This trend became so pervasive in the fifties that many of the nation's largest cities—New York, Chicago, Philadelphia, Detroit, Baltimore, Cleveland, Washington, Saint Louis, and several others—actually lost population. Even as smaller cities grew, the proportion of Americans living in cities with more than 1 million residents dropped from 12 percent to 10 percent.

People were leaving the big cities, but not the urban areas. They were moving to the outskirts of cities, where a new suburban lifestyle emerged, dependent on the automobile and the city. Historian Kenneth T. Jackson called the suburbs the "crabgrass frontier." Americans continued to work in the cities, but now they were less obliged, thus also less likely, to live there. They moved to suburbs, where less expensive land aided in the construction of new, more affordable housing. Jackson shows that, although the move to the suburbs began in the nineteenth century, the mid-twentieth-century phenomenon was different in motivation and scale.

The model for the modern suburb was the postwar creation of Abraham Levitt and his sons, William and Alfred. The Levitts began developing their formula before and during World War II. By the end of the war, they had refined their production techniques in ways that put them far ahead of the competition. Returning veterans gave them a ready market, and federal VA and FHA loan programs provided prospective buyers with the financing they needed. The Levitts employed mass production technology to home construction. In their first Levittown, built in Hempstead, Long Island, after the war, they divided the process of home construction into twenty-seven steps. Crews laid out materials in formulaic patterns at 60-foot intervals across the 4,000-acre plot. Crews followed along, completing each of the steps, from laying the concrete slab, to framing, plumbing, wall construction, painting, and roofing. At the peak of activity, the crews could complete 30 houses per day. The completed development provided 17,400 homes for 82,000 people, most of whom were young couples buying their first house.

The second Levittown, located near Bucks County, Pennsylvania, occupied the brothers through much of the decade of the fifties. Located near a United States Steel Corporation plant, the new Levitt development provided homes mainly for employees. The Levittowns followed prescribed formulas in every detail. The lots were identical in size and shape: 60 feet by 100 feet. The brothers boasted that they had planned every tree, color, and shrub.

Critics found the formulaic patterns stultifying, but the residents got exactly what they wanted: affordable, well-built, single-family houses. New houses ranged in price from $7,990 to $9,500, and mass production allowed the Levitts to make a greater profit than competitors who had to charge more for each house they sold. On sale days, long lines of people waited to have a chance at buying one of the houses. The fact that most of the residents in each Levittown were young couples starting families provided the added benefit of social cohesion.

Typically, suburbs were homogeneous with respect not only to age and marital status but also to race, and restrictive covenants ensured that they would stay that way. Jackson noted that none of the 82,000 residents in Levittown on Long Island were black at the end of the fifties. William Levitt justified discrimination by asserting, "We can solve a housing problem, or we can try to solve a racial problem. But we cannot combine the two." Nor was Levittown an exception. By 1960, only 8 percent of African Americans lived in the suburbs, whereas more than 50 percent lived in central cities. In contrast, 23 percent of white Americans lived in the suburbs, and 30 percent in central cities.

Homogeneity in the suburbs extended to measures other than race. The 1960 census revealed that suburbanites were not only younger, but also better educated, and more likely to have children than city dwellers. By most statistical measures, people who lived in the suburbs were better off than their urban neighbors. They were more likely to be employed and to own their own homes. Those homes were newer, and had more rooms and more bathrooms than urban homes. Suburbanites earned more money, with average incomes of $7,114 compared to $5,940 for city dwellers and $3,228 for those living on farms. By the end of the decade, a suburban "pattern" had emerged. Suburbs had detached single-family homes—split-level and ranch houses. The suburbs remained linked to the nearby city certainly by new roads (and often by superhighways of multiple lanes), and often by public transportation. Suburbanites had services close to home: shopping centers or malls, schools, and political structures independent of the city.

Although most houses in the suburbs were larger than those in the cities, there was an alternative form of housing that allowed many people to flee cities, often as a temporary way station on the way to larger houses. Mobile homes, which originated early in the century, underwent a transformation in the fifties. Ironically, unlike most everything else in America in the decade, they became *less* mobile. More accurately, the market for mobile homes split during the fifties into two submarkets: manufactured homes, which seldom moved from their original sites, and trailers, which preserved the original vacation-oriented mobility of vehicle-drawn shells. An inexpensive form of housing born of American mobility, throughout the fifties, manufactured homes were increasingly located in trailer parks. Before the end of the decade, the FHA recognized these homes as eligible for federal financing; when the 10-foot limitation on width was relaxed in later years, double-wide construction allowed manufactured homes to grow to the size of smaller permanent houses.

The move to the suburbs had a profound impact on cities. The decline in the population of large cities led to a decrease in their tax revenues and a corresponding decline in city services. Since the people leaving for the suburbs were generally more affluent than those left behind, merchants soon followed them. When large department stores built new stores in shopping centers or malls outside of the downtown area, they often closed their downtown outlets. Although people continued to commute to the cities to work, the quality of life there deteriorated.

The process of suburbanization often had racial consequences for the cities. The suburbs were predominantly white, and the proportion of African Americans in the cities began to increase. This had both positive and negative implications for black Americans. It gave them more political clout. Although it was not until 1967 that an African-American candidate won election as mayor of a major American city (Carl Stokes in Cleveland), African Americans won seats on city councils, school boards, and other municipal institutions. But the constricted tax base left them with less money, and the cities continued to decline.

Cities responded in various ways to the emerging crisis. Some sought to maintain their tax base by annexing additional land on their peripheries. Of fourteen cities with a population of over a quarter million whose population doubled during the fifties, eleven attributed more than 50 percent of that increase—and nine more than 80 percent—to annexation. Between 1950 and 1970, Houston, Dallas, San Diego, San Antonio, Memphis, and Columbus all more than doubled their geographic territory. Indianapolis and San Jose grew seven times larger in area, Phoenix almost fifteen times larger, and Jacksonville almost twenty-eight times.

Responding to the urban crisis, Congress passed legislation in 1949 to assist the cities in funding urban redevelopment projects; it appropriated $500 million to seed the program, aimed mainly at slum clearance and subsequent redevelopment. Legal uncertainties—especially those related to property condemnation and the relocation of people whose houses were to be razed—hampered the program from the beginning. Private contractors had little incentive to risk building on cleared slums. Four years after the program started, only 21 percent of the appropriated money had been committed, and only a small fraction of that amount had been spent.

The Eisenhower administration supported a new, more comprehensive approach that became known as "urban renewal," a program that allowed the expenditure of federal funds on much more than just slum clearance, extending its interests to education, police and fire protection, and recreational facilities. Urban renewal projects took various forms, but usually included the extension of the Interstate Highway System into downtown areas, the razing of "blighted" neighborhoods, and the construction of new housing. Often, however, these efforts only served to accelerate the decline of cities they were supposed to regenerate. Blocks of residences were razed to make way for complicated interstate interchanges, and civil rights activists complained that "urban renewal" was just another name for "negro removal." When new development took place, it seldom served to provide housing for those who had been displaced, often replacing residential housing with civic centers or government buildings. Developers still hesitated to start new projects in areas where the population had been declining, and where signs of urban renaissance seemed to be the airy talk of politicians. Blocks were left undeveloped and soon became overgrown with weeds, standing as signs of decay rather than of renewal.

First approved in the late forties as a solution to the postwar housing shortage, public housing, subsidized by the federal government, seemed a partial solution to the urban problem of the fifties. Unfortunately, it never fulfilled its promise. The number of units built fell far short of expectations: by 1955, there were only 200,000, less than a quarter of the 810,000 planned. The completed units were often poorly constructed high-rises, and residents, who often had previously lived in flats or duplexes, sensed that they were being warehoused. Builders were more attracted to the suburbs, where construction was more lucrative. Those who took contracts for public housing projects cut corners.

It did not become apparent until the sixties how far short of its optimistic goals public housing had fallen. In a notorious example, the Pruitt-Igoe project in Saint Louis, touted as a great success only a few years before, had become little more than a high-rise slum by the mid-sixties. Apartments and common spaces alike had been trashed; the grounds, intended to provide residents of the project's thirty-three eleven-story buildings parklike open spaces, were strewn with litter and barren of grass. By the mid-seventies, city authorities acknowledged that the project had failed and demolished its buildings.

Americans not only moved from city to suburb, they also moved from region to region, and especially to the West and South. All regions experienced growth during the fifties, and only three states—Arkansas, West Virginia, and Mississippi—lost population. Of the ten fastest growing states, which together gained 2.1 million people, Florida was in first place, with an increase of 79 percent, and seven were Western states. California's population increased by 5.1 million people, or 49 percent, a growth rate almost as large as what it had experienced in the forties, when wartime industries attracted laborers from all over the country. Drawn by Southern California's Mediterranean climate, available jobs (particularly in the defense industry), and excellent education system, people headed from the nation's midsection to the West Coast. California was gaining on New York, still the nation's most populous state at the end of the fifties, and would surpass it by the mid-sixties.

The South and West both benefited from having safe congressional districts whose representatives, reelected time after time, were able to accumulate seniority and thus gain influential committee chairmanships. With the result that these regions received the lion's share of defense appropriations and, after the establishment of NASA in 1958, of aerospace money as well.

Revival: The Resurgence of American Religion

In the fifties, church membership and the proportion of Americans claiming religious affiliation reached the highest levels they would achieve in the century. As the nation's population grew by 45 percent over the previous thirty years, church membership grew by more than twice that rate, or 92 percent. It began the decade at 49 percent of the adult population (which was higher than the average of 43 percent early in the century), and rose to 69 percent by 1960. Of those who claimed religious affiliation in a 1957 survey, Protestants constituted nearly 66 percent, Roman Catholics 25 percent, and Jews slightly more than 3 percent; Americans claiming no religious affiliation at all constituted less than 3 percent of the adult population. Regional differences were significant: Protestants constituted 83 percent of those claiming religious affiliation in the South, but only 42 percent in the Northeast.

Why the dramatic increase? Sociologists offered several plausible explanations. The anxiety of the Cold War and the ever-present nuclear threat contributed. Some suggested that the depersonalizing influences of modern society pushed people to seek connections with others, that people were yearning more for attachment, for the security of belonging to a group, than for religion as such. Others argued that church membership provided a connection that ethnic identity had offered earlier generations; as time weakened the connection to their country of origin, immigrants beyond the second generation looked to other sources of identity.

The popularity of religion showed in ways other than church membership. The Bible continued its long reign as the best-selling book in the nation, selling an incredible total of 26.5 million copies in 1953, the year after publication of the Revised Standard Version. Novels and nonfiction works with religious themes also sold well. Henry Morton Robinson's *The Cardinal* (1950) and Thomas B. Costain's *The Silver Chalice* (1952) were both best sellers, and Jim Bishop's *The Day Christ Died* (1957) fared well in the nonfiction category. Movies also capitalized on the popularity of religion. *The Robe* (1953) told the story of a Roman centurion who converted to Christianity after receiving Christ's robe. Although Hollywood risked money on epic films only when producers believed the theme gave them a likelihood of profit, two of the biggest blockbusters of the fifties had religious themes. *The Ten Commandments* (1956), which ran for more than three-and-a-half hours, starred Charlton Heston as Moses. *Ben-Hur,* nearly as long as *The Ten Commandments* and also starring Charlton Heston, depicted the Romans as the exploiters of early Christians.

Religion made its mark on television, too. Bishop Fulton J. Sheen's show *Life Is Worth Living* went up against the king of prime-time television in the early fifties, Milton Berle, and won the ratings battle. Sheen, who appeared on screen in full liturgical regalia, told biblical stories and modern parables, and mixed them with moral observations. He published a book with the same title as his show in 1953, and the book also became a best seller. Sheen's show finally succumbed, not to Milton Berle or any other television mortal, but rather to religious factionalism. Boston's Francis Cardinal Spellman resented Sheen's popularity, and forced the show's cancellation.

The Reverend Norman Vincent Peale, whose *Guide to Confident Living* was a best seller in the late forties, wrote the most popular nonfiction book of the fifties: *The Power of Positive Thinking,* a straightforward self-help book that urged its readers to rely on a "Higher Power" to achieve success. Central to

Peale's approach was a positive outlook on life, which would rid an individual of negative thoughts and build confidence and optimism.

The best known of the religious leaders in the fifties was the evangelist Billy Graham, who brought old-fashioned revivalism into the media age. A Southern Baptist preacher, Graham became a national figure in the late forties as a preacher for the Youth for Christ movement; then and in the years to come, his "crusades"—extended campaigns in a given city, region, or country—would reach hundreds of thousands. His 1949 crusade in Los Angeles, for example, drew 350,000 people during its two-month run. The Reverend Graham's style and message may have been reminiscent of stump preachers like Billy Sunday, but his operation was streamlined and up to date, with advance work, careful planning, and ample publicity and media relations. Whereas earlier evangelists were lucky to draw a crowd in the thousands, Graham spoke to athletic stadiums packed with crowds numbering into the tens of thousands.

Graham's renown grew in the fifties. He preached weekly on his radio program *The Hour of Decision,* and moved to television in 1952. He wrote a syndicated newspaper column, and formed a film company to document and publicize his crusades. Starting in 1952, he traveled abroad, appearing before American troops in Korea and Japan and hosting crusades in Germany, Scandinavia, Britain, India, Australia, Latin America, and Africa. One of the most political of the prominent preachers, Graham spoke out on the moral dimensions of public issues, seldom straying far from official administration policy, always as patriotic as he was religious. An ardent anti-Communist, he used the pulpit as a Cold War rostrum, claiming that Communism was "master-minded by Satan himself." One of his most eloquent statements on public policy, however, was nonverbal; even before the Supreme Court's *Brown v. Board of Education* desegregation decision in 1954, Graham had begun insisting that his public appearances in the South must be before biracial audiences.

Graham proved adept at cultivating relationships with presidents; Eisenhower solicited his assistance in writing a prayer for his first inauguration, and afterward Graham became a frequent visitor to the White House. Although the president had never attended church regularly and had not belonged to a church before his election, acting on Graham's advice, he became a Presbyterian, delaying the announcement until after the election to avoid the appearance of election-eve conversion. Eisenhower's connection with Graham served both men well, giving Graham access to the visibility of the White House, and giving the president a religious identification that suited the public. Graham influenced the administration's public posture on religious issues.

Oral Roberts and other evangelists, following the path to public ministry paved by Graham, soon began to use television even more successfully. Roberts, a Pentecostal Holiness preacher, used modern marketing strategies, television, and direct mailing to raise millions of dollars; by the mid-fifties, his income was reported to be in the neighborhood of $50 million a year. He founded a university that bore his name and at which he preached his message. Following in Roberts's footsteps, the "televangelists" would use the new medium to reach millions of potential donors instantly.

One of the most highly regarded American theologians of the twentieth century, Reinhold Niebuhr eschewed the emotionalism of Graham and Roberts. Although he served for many years on the faculty of Union Theological Seminary in New York, it was his lecture tours and his comments on issues of moment, widely reported in the press, that brought him to the public's attention. Niebuhr's major contribution to American Protestantism was his ability to apply his erudition in biblical studies and theology to the great issues of the day. His thoughtful reflections on the moral and theological implications of dominant political systems, particularly Nazism during World War II and Communism after, stirred people who didn't necessarily share his Protestant faith. He spoke, not as a moral crusader, but rather as a Christian rationalist, realist, and pragmatist. Politically active throughout his life, he had been an advocate of socialism as a young man; he later rejected socialism, headed the pacifist Fellowship of Reconciliation, and was a founder of the liberal Democratic organization Americans for Democratic Action. He had a profound impact on influential people of the day, including his fellow theologian Billy Graham, historian and presidential advisor Arthur Schlesinger Jr., and civil rights leader Martin Luther King Jr. He was an early leader in dawning ecumenical movement, often sharing platforms with Jewish and Catholic leaders.

With Niebuhr's assistance, Paul Tillich, another highly regarded Protestant theologian of the fifties, had come to the United States in 1933 as a refugee from his native Germany. Tillich sought to develop a theological response to the crosscurrents that were buffeting Western culture in the postwar era, and particularly to existentialism, a philosophy that gained prominence in the United States after the war largely through the writings of the French

philosopher Jean-Paul Sartre. Existentialism suggested that the human condition could not be explained, that the attempt to attach meaning was bound to
lead to frustration, and that individuals needed to accept responsibility for
their actions. Drawing on his familiarity with art, literature, and European
philosophical currents, Tillich's response was that spirituality can counter the
threat of meaninglessness—a theme he expressed perhaps most powerfully in
The Courage to Be (1952).

The most popular and accessible theologian of the fifties, after Billy Graham, was a Trappist monk named Thomas Merton. Something of a rabble-
rouser as a young man, Merton converted to Catholicism and, at age 26, took
the vows of the Trappist order, the most ascetic of all the Catholic monastic
orders. He lived in a monastery in Kentucky for the next twenty-seven years.
His autobiography, *The Seven Storey Mountain* (1948), was a best seller in the
fifties, and continued to sell well long after Merton's death in 1968. He wrote
many articles and books on contemporary issues such as nuclear disarmament,
becoming an ardent support of nonviolence in the civil rights movement. His
humble spirituality, his interest in Eastern religions, and his ability to convey
his own personal religious experiences appealed to a disparate audience, and
reached fifties conservatives and sixties radicals alike.

In an age of religious resurgence, people looked to the president for
moral and even religious leadership. Ironically, President Eisenhower came to
his religion late in life, and to his credit never made an ostentatious display of
it. Indeed, he was embarrassed when others did so in his name. When the pastor of a church he was thinking of joining made too much of a fuss over him,
Eisenhower told press secretary James Hagerty, "You go and tell that goddamn minister that if he gives out one more story about my religious faith I
won't join his goddamn church!" Even though Eisenhower's commitment to
religion was not a profound one, the president nonetheless believed that he
must be a moral exemplar, and joined the church for that reason—in his view,
the denomination was less important that the fact of membership. In one
of the more broadly nonsectarian statements ever uttered by a president about
the role of religion in American life, Eisenhower insisted: "Our government
makes no sense unless it is founded on a deeply felt religious faith—and I
don't care what it is."

Eisenhower's nondenominational sense of religion and his belief that religion had a role in American life fit the temper of the times. Display of faith was
politically popular; Congress and the executive branch looked for ways to link

God to national symbols, formulating a superficial religious practice that official Washington believed did not violate the separation of church and state. Eisenhower decreed that Cabinet meetings would open with a prayer. In 1954, Congress added the phrase "under God" to the Pledge of Allegiance. On Flag Day—June 14—sponsors gathered on the steps to the Capitol and recited the modified pledge as the national media looked on. Two years later, Congress established the phrase "In God We Trust" as the national motto; introduced earlier on some coins, it appeared on all U.S. coins and currency thereafter. The Post Office promptly issued a new stamp bearing the motto. Congress added a nonsectarian prayer room.

Only the Supreme Court seemed to have reservations about the rush to manifest faith. An Italian film entitled *The Miracle* portrayed a woman who believed she had been seduced and impregnated by Saint Joseph, and who began to see herself as the Virgin Mary. The Vatican hated the film, but did nothing to suppress it when it was shown in Italy. The reaction in the United States was less restrained; in 1951, the New York State Board of Regents charged that the film was sacrilegious. Ultimately, the case went to the Supreme Court, which ruled in *Burstyn v. Wilson* that a film could not be banned on the basis of sacrilege.

A Mid-Century American Sexual Revolution

One of the curious juxtapositions of the fifties was that in the same decade Americans rediscovered religion, they also rediscovered sex. The United States has rediscovered sex as often as it has rediscovered religion, of course, and the notion of "revival" seems to apply equally well to each. In the popular memory, the 1920s and the 1960s stand out as the twentieth century's decades of sexual revolution. As was the case with other social trends, however, the seeming excesses of the sixties had roots in the allegedly conservative fifties.

The herald of the sexual revolution was an unlikely revolutionary—a Harvard-trained professor of zoology at Indiana University and the author of *Edible Wild Plants of North America*. Responding to a petition from the university's Association of Women Students in 1938, Alfred Kinsey started a course on sexuality and marriage, and soon had students clamoring to enroll. His research into American sexual practices began with the students in that class. He interviewed students about their sexual histories. When complaints came in from parents, the university administration—which was not unsympathetic to Kinsey—asked him to choose between the course and his research, expecting him to jettison the research rather than a course that he obviously enjoyed teaching.

Faced with the choice, however, he dropped the course and expanded plans for his research. Anyone who knew him, Kinsey later commented, would have known what his decision would be. He received research grants, modest ones at first, and then a substantial grant from the Rockefeller Foundation. He hired assistants and broadened his research base. Interviews were in depth; drawing from 521 possible questions, interviewers asked, on average, some 300 questions in a given interview. Although all his subjects—both male and female—were white, Kinsey sought variation in class, level of education, marital status, age, religion, and geographic location (including region and rural versus urban). In 1947, he established the Institute of Sex Research at Indiana University, and continued his research there through 1963. His work was all-consuming. When asked about it, his wife responded, "I hardly see him at night since he took up sex." In 1948, he published *Sexual Behavior of the Human Male,* essentially a report on the findings of 5,300 interviews. The book's initial press run of 25,000 sold out immediately. Five years later, Kinsey published the companion volume, *Sexual Behavior of the Human Female,* based on a research base of 5,940 women.

Never before had American sexuality been subjected to an empirical research study of this depth, and the results were surprising. Kinsey found that sexual behavior in the United States was more varied than most Americans would have been willing to believe. According to his research, 12 percent of males, but only 6 percent of females, had sex by the age of sixteen. He estimated that 50 percent of males had extramarital sex, and that 26 percent of females had extramarital sex by their forties. Among his respondents, 37 percent of males and 13 percent of females reported having at least one homosexual experience; 10 percent of males and between 2 and 6 percent of females described themselves as predominantly homosexual.

Both volumes of the Kinsey Report, as people soon began to call his two-volume study, received favorable comment immediately after their release. Before long, however, Kinsey's work came under attack, particularly after the release of the volume on female sexuality, which critics considered a slur against the virtue of American women. Kinsey was sensitive to the barbs of critics, but even more sensitive to threats to withdraw financial support that had sustained the research since its early days. At the head of Rockefeller Foundation was former Assistant Secretary of State (and future Secretary of State) Dean Rusk. Despite pleas from Kinsey's supporters and colleagues, Rusk wasn't willing to risk the foundation's reputation by funding research as controversial as any conducted in the fifties. The withdrawal of Rockefeller Foundation funding was a heavy blow, but Kinsey found ways to continue his work. By the time Kinsey himself died in August 1956, he had personally conducted 7,985 interviews. Ultimately, interviews conducted by Kinsey and his associates totaled more than 18,000.

Kinsey's impact would outlive him. The institute continued Kinsey's research project into the early sixties, and then undertook other investigations relating to human sexuality, eventually under the name "The Kinsey Institute for Sex Research, Inc." Kinsey's research was the forerunner of other studies of human sexuality, the best known of which was conducted by William Masters and Virginia Johnson. Depending on their point of view, commentators considered Kinsey's work to have been responsible either for a more open attitude toward sex or for sexual permissiveness.

Whatever good or ill Kinsey's work may have achieved, a principal beneficiary of the new openness about sex was Hugh Hefner, whose magazine *Playboy* came out the same year as Kinsey's report on female sexuality. Hefner acknowledged his admiration of Kinsey, who, in his view, had exposed the hypocrisy of Americans about sex. Willing to gamble, Hefner launched his magazine with a meager budget, an instinct for the prurient interests of the American male, and a nude photo of Marilyn Monroe that he had purchased for $500 as the first of the magazine's trademark centerfolds. The gamble paid off; his first issue sold 53,000 copies, and he was on his way. Within a year, circulation had topped 100,000; two years later, it had increased to 600,000, and by the end of the decade to more than 1 million. *Playboy* peddled a philosophy of gratification and material consumption. Hefner practiced what he preached, cultivating an image of himself as a paragon of hedonism; he was the host of and center of attention at endless parties, seldom appearing in public without a beautiful woman. He expanded beyond his publishing empire to establish Playboy Clubs in large cities, where cocktail waitresses, dubbed "Bunnies," dressed in skimpy skintight apparel with a bunny tail as an accessory. By design, *Playboy* challenged conventional mores, provoking those advocating equality for women, on the one hand, and the importance of family life, on the other.

Redefining American Identity: Conformity and the Fate of the Individual

Americans had long considered their national experience to be unique. From its formative years, the United States was an experiment in government founded on the value of the individual; Americans considered their nation a "city on a hill," an example to the rest of the world, unburdened by class privilege and tradition-bound institutions. By the 1950s, however, several forces seemed to conspire to undermine the primacy of the individual. In the first fifty years of the twentieth century, industrialization had forged an economically successful nation that had surpassed all others in terms of productivity, but mass production methods, the assembly line, and the principles of scientific management had devalued the individual in the workplace. Americans prided themselves on their mechanical ingenuity, and the romantic image of the solitary inventor in his workshop epitomized the nation's confidence in its creative abilities. At mid-century, Americans continued to be innovators, but new inventions were more likely to be the product of research teams working for large corporations, often under government contract. Pressures brought to bear by the Cold War, its attendant superpatriotism, and the rise of McCarthyism made Americans reluctant to take risks that might make them stand out. Individualism—the most basic of core American values—seemed at a crossroads.

Several writers examined this phenomenon, and three in particular—David Riesman, William H. Whyte Jr., and C. Wright Mills—found disturbing trends in American society. Their analyses of social trends sold surprisingly well, indicating that they had touched concerns that other Americans shared. An early entry into the debate on conformity, David Riesman's *The Lonely Crowd* (1950), was one sociologist's attempt to assess the changes that seemed to characterize American society in the fifties. Riesman took on an ambitious task, nothing less than a reassessment of the American character. Society by its nature, he suggested, exerts pressure to conform, and individuals respond to those pressures. The crucial question, to Riesman, was the source of the cues that guide members of a society. He defined three stages through which societies pass: tradition-direction, inner-direction, and other-direction. In tradition-directed societies, such as those of medieval Europe, individuals are governed by social relationships whose character is determined by tradition (religion, ritual, routine). In inner-directed societies, such as those of Renaissance Europe, individuals accept direction from within, reacting to pressures implanted by parents and elders early in life. Finally, in other-directed societies, such as that of mid-twentieth-century America, individuals respond to conformist pressures from contemporary influences, including friends, acquaintances, and the mass media. Barring an unexpected change, "the hegemony of other-direction lies not far off." Such a prospect offered the likelihood of an America in decline. Whereas inner-directed people channel their energies into production, other-directed people apply theirs to consumption; inner-directed people are job-minded, other directed people are people-minded; inner-directed people see groups to which they belonged in terms of what the groups can do, other-directed people worry more about relations within the group. Riesman foresaw the United States in transition from a productive nation to one bent on enjoying the fruits of its elders' labors. The vaunted individualism upon which Americans prided themselves was at stake, Riesman argued, for people are born free, but "lose their social freedom and their individual autonomy in seeking to become like each other."

Riesman believed that America no longer had a ruling class; the industrial barons of late-nineteenth-century America no longer roamed the halls of power. As Riesman's ideas won broad acceptance, another sociologist, C. Wright Mills, offered a very different analysis, insisting that a "power elite" ruled America. Mills was unconventional, even by the standards of academe. A transplanted Texan who did his graduate work at the University of Wisconsin, Mills joined the faculty at Columbia University, and rode his motorcycle around New York City long before it was fashionable to do so. Mills was also unconventional in his scholarly methodology. Whereas most of his sociologist peers were producing statistical studies, or at least bolstering their ideas with statistics, Mills's style was impressionistic, qualitative, and argumentative. Although Mills was a prolific writer, two of the books he published in the fifties established his reputation. In *White Collar* (1951), he argued that the middle class, even though it lacked heroes and the freedom of the farmers who had been the core of American society in the nineteenth century, and even though its social role was prescribed by others, was defining the twentieth century.

Those in power, Mills went on to explain in *The Power Elite* (1956), were "men whose positions enable them to transcend the ordinary environments of ordinary men and women; they are in positions to make decisions having major consequences." Directly opposing the predominant thesis of his sociologist peers—Riesman and others—that there no longer was an elite in American society, Mills found elites in business, in government, and in the military. He foreshadowed President Eisenhower's farewell warning about the concentration of power in the military-industrial complex and the danger posed by the abuse of that power.

People with money, power, and prestige—the "power elite"—were well positioned to make key decisions that would influence the lives of millions of others. They had risen to power, not by their virtue or merit, but rather because of structural developments that had accelerated in the twentieth century. An interrelationship developed between the higher echelons of political, military, and economic power. Corporate leaders moved into government, and with the growth of the executive branch came to dominate its bureaus and agencies; in the fifties, they came to direct the economy, leaving traditional politicians in the "middle levels." Military leaders, the "warlords," rose in influence as the Cold War created a sense of a permanent military threat, which "places a premium on the military and upon their control of men, matériel, money, and power." In the postwar period, the interests of the corporate elites and the military elites coincided, creating an unprecedented concentration of power and an ability to set national policy. Members of this "higher circle" shared a common social background: they were overwhelmingly Easterners, Protestants, and graduates of Ivy League colleges; they shared common perceptions of policy goals. Not representative of the people at large, they held power in a system of "organized irresponsibility," an amoral system that failed to hold them accountable for their actions.

In *The Organization Man* (1956), former editor of *Fortune* magazine William H. Whyte Jr. examined the impact of modern corporations and bureaucracies on mid-level managers. Whyte defined the new social ethos he saw emerging from the corporate culture. Not only did bureaucracies demand conformity; they also fostered a cooperative atmosphere, shunning conflict, and seeking "belongingness" and "togetherness," the same impulses that drove Riesman's other-directed man. If individuals found something in the group that troubled them, it was up to the individual to adapt rather than to try to change the group: this ethos dictated "what's good for the group is good for the individual." The group, not the individual, was to be the source of ideas and innovation. The values that defined the Organization Man on the job also prescribed his behavior at home, where belonging to the group was just as important as it was on the job. Suburbia was as effective a force in shaping society as the workplace; it became a "melting pot" that created a "classless society." Other-directed man had moved to the suburbs, and taken his yearning for acceptance with him. Churches became agents of social connection, and their social role became a more important factor than denomination in determining what church people would join. Whyte thus provided a plausible explanation for the rise in church membership. Pressures to belong—to conform to group values—even affected purchasing decisions, as people sought to live "down" to the Joneses, not to stand out from the crowd.

The historian David Potter offered another perspective on American character in *People of Plenty* (1954), which critics compared favorably with the most famous such interpretation, Frederick Jackson Turner's *The Frontier in American History* (originally presented in 1893). Potter saw economic abundance as the decisive element in shaping the American character. That America was a land of abundance was indisputable, and particularly apparent in the fifties. Using figures for 1949, Potter demonstrated that the United States far exceeded other nations in quantifiable measures of affluence. The United States had a per capita income of $1,453, whereas no other nation exceeded $900. Home to only 7 percent of the world's population, the United States generated 42 percent of the world's income. Americans consumed an average of 3,186 calories a day, whereas even comparatively prosperous Europeans consumed between 2,000 and 2,700.

Potter underscored that it was not merely a question of an abundance of natural resources, but also of a "social abundance," which allowed those resources to be efficiently distributed. Potter argued that abundance sustained American myths of social equality and social mobility, and that the exclusion of African Americans from participation in the abundance did not deny its general application.

Democracy depended on an economic surplus: if people are to believe in a promise of opportunity, there must be some hope that the promise will be rewarded. Whereas in the United States—especially in the fifties—this promise indeed held forth a prospect of fulfillment, such was not the case in other nations. Thus came the great American foreign policy failure, the inability to export an American-style democracy to the rest of the world. More disappointing still was the foreign reaction to the American effort to export democracy; in foreign nations, the effort seemed hypocritical at best, and led to a quandary. As Potter summarized it, "our message to the world has become involved in a dilemma: to other peoples, our democracy has seemed attainable but not especially desirable; our abundance has seemed infinitely desirable but quite unattainable."

Women's Place: The Origins of "The Problem with No Name"

Women at the end of World War II America faced much the same situation their mothers faced at the end of World War I. They had made significant contributions to the war effort, and had proven themselves capable of performing well in traditionally male occupations. The wartime poster girl "Rosie the Riveter" urged women to take factory jobs. When the war ended and veterans returned home, however, society exerted pressure on women to return to their customary roles as housewives and mothers.

The pressure on women to leave wartime employment came from many directions. Many employers treated women simply as stand-ins for men until they could resume their rightful roles in the workplace. Indeed, there was a pervasive sentiment that veterans deserved, at the very least, to have jobs, whether their former jobs or comparable ones. Most women preferred to return to their traditional roles, or at least accepted the social pressure to do so. As the baby boom turned Rosie the Riveter into Mom, women moved out of the workforce and began to establish families. Convention held that even if a woman chose to work for a few years, the birth of her first child signified the end of a career and the beginning of overriding maternal responsibilities. Child care, unusual even during the war when employers sought women workers, became rare indeed.

The "back to the home" movement received a boost with the publication of *Modern Woman: The Lost Sex* (1947), an influential antifeminist book by psychiatrist Marynia Farnham and sociologist Ferdinand Lundberg. Marriage and procreation, Farnham and Lundberg argued, are the biologically determined functions of men and women; to resist these functions is to invite psychological and social problems. Men, by their nature, are meant to provide for their families; women, to be mothers and housewives. Feminism, a product of industrial society and the women's rights movement, threatened the fabric of American society by encouraging women to pursue nontraditional roles and to compete with men. Most Americans in the late forties and early fifties had little quarrel with Farnham and Lundberg's sociopsychological argument.

Women's magazines reinforced the American cult of domesticity. *Ladies'*

Home Journal and *McCall's* celebrated women's roles as wives and mothers. Articles and advertisements touted cooking, beauty aids, household appliances, homemaking tips, and motherhood. *McCall's* coined the word "togetherness" for its vision of the ideal family relationship, but, by whatever name, the magazines prescribed second-class status for women in their own homes. The husband headed the family; the wife occupied a permanent supporting role. His achievements defined her success; only by assisting him could she experience fulfillment. Readers received instruction in how to welcome home tired husbands at the end of their workday, and how to suppress their own frustrations, which, by implication, were less significant. Critic Betty Friedan attacked the magazines for treating women as if they had no identity apart from men, had no interests beyond material things, and had no interest in ideas. *"McCall's* frankly assumes women are brainless, fluffy kittens," she wrote. "The very size of their print is raised until it looks like a first grade primer."

Yet it should be noted that, early in the twentieth century, women's magazines had sometimes included articles on larger issues such as suffrage and other political rights for women among the usual recipes and patterns, a practice that persisted into the fifties. Newer, less "slick," and less expensive women's magazines such as *Women's Day* and *Family Circle,* which accepted the role of women as homemakers, offered straightforward, practical advice on the everyday issues of household management. Media critics John Tebble and Mary Ellen Zuckerman suggested that "one of the most remarkable things that women's magazines did was to give their female readers the idea, often subtly, that they were sisters, democratically bonded together, no matter what their economic or social circumstances might be." Even as women's magazines celebrated motherhood, they often did so at the expense of men, portraying fathers as rather inept creatures who had to be manipulated by women in order to keep the household on a true course. The bumbling male stereotype was used with considerable success in the popular media: on television, by *I Love Lucy* and *Ozzie and Harriet;* in the newspapers, by the popular comic strip *Blondie,* whose lead male character, Dagwood Bumstead, was forever demonstrating his incompetence.

Most educators believed women ought to use their years in school to prepare for their roles as mothers and moral trainers of the next generation. Presidential candidate Adlai Stevenson, in a commencement address to the women of Smith College in 1955, perceptively captured the frustration of college-educated American women, even if, in his conclusion, he urged them to accept their place in the home. "Once they read Baudelaire," he began. "Now it is the *Consumers' Guide*. Once they wrote poetry. Now it's the laundry list. Once they discussed art and philosophy until late in the night. Now they are so tired they fall asleep as soon as the dishes are finished." He acknowledged their sense of "closing horizons and lost opportunities," but encouraged them to make homes where values of Western society could flourish.

The most widely selling book of the fifties, Dr. Benjamin Spock's *Common Sense Book of Baby and Child Care*, perpetuated this traditional role for women. First published in 1947, the book sold more than a million copies every year of the following decade. Spock prescribed a child-centered home in which mothers created a loving environment for their offspring. Underlying Spock's commonsense approach to raising children was a social ethic that demanded that women abandon their own interests, jobs, and hobbies for the sake of their children. Already subordinated to their husbands by the dominant social conventions of the day, women found in Spock that they must also subordinate their interests to those of their offspring. Critics later blamed Spock for encouraging permissiveness, and unfairly laid the social problems of the sixties and the attitudes of the "me generation" of the seventies at his feet.

The most effective indictment of society's treatment of women in the fifties came from a veteran of the cult of domesticity. Betty Friedan, a 1942 summa cum laude graduate of Smith College, who married in 1947 and had her first child in 1949. She and her husband followed the well-trod path from city to suburb. She raised her three children during the fifties in the suburbs of New York City, writing for the same women's magazines she would later criticize. A 1957 assignment for *McCall's* awakened her to feelings common among the women of her generation, feelings she herself had felt but never articulated. It led her to contact her Smith College classmates and query them about their likes and dislikes, their satisfactions and frustrations. She found a widespread dissatisfaction with domesticity. Of the two hundred women who responded to her questionnaire, 89 percent had married. The overwhelming majority of these had found their housewifely duties unfulfilling.

In 1959, Friedan returned to Smith, and after talking to students and faculty, she concluded that the problem had only worsened since her own undergraduate days. The young women seemed passive, and feared to appear too interested in intellectual matters: they were even less likely than their mothers to seek anything other than a husband and a house in the suburbs. "The one lesson a girl could hardly avoid learning," Friedan wrote, "if she went to college between 1945 and 1960, was *not* to get in interested, seriously interested, in anything besides getting married and having children, if she wanted to be normal, happy, adjusted, feminine, have a successful husband, successful children, and a normal, feminine, adjusted, successful sex life."

Lack of fulfillment characterized the suburban refrain, "Is this all there is?" In her 1963 book *The Feminine Mystique,* Friedan called this malaise of middle-class American women in the postwar years "the problem with no name." Only education offered a solution, it seemed, and many regretted not making better use of their own education.

Despite the media's re-creation of a cult of domesticity, a quiet revolution was already under way in the workplace. Women were not universally returning to the home. They had been occupying an ever-increasing percentage of the total American workforce in each decade since World War I, and the trend continued in the fifties. Women now constituted 32 percent of the workforce, up from 27 percent at the start of the decade. The 1960 census revealed that women entered the workforce in impressive numbers during the fifties, and increased their presence in jobs that had previously been the preserve of men. The number of women in the experienced civilian labor force increased by more than 35 percent in the decade, whereas the number of men increased by less than 7 percent. Moreover, the number of women in professional and technical positions increased by more than 41 percent. Some fields began to open up to women (certain categories of engineering, for example), showing astounding percentage increases during the fifties, although the numbers remained small in comparison to men holding similar jobs. The number of women working in public relations and as publicity writers increased by 263 percent, from 1950 to 1960, when they accounted for more than 23 percent of those holding such jobs (compared to less than 11 percent in 1950), even though the census continued to list the category as "public relations men and publicity writers." Some jobs became more predominantly "women's jobs." In 1950, less than 45 percent of the bank tellers were women; by 1960, the number of women working as bank tellers had more than doubled, and women now made up nearly 70 percent of the total. Some signs indicated that attitudes toward women in the workplace were beginning to change. *Womanpower,* a 1957 study conducted under the auspices of the National Manpower Council and funded by the Ford Foundation, referred to women as "essential" workers, and underscored the importance of training them for the vital needs of the U.S. economy.

Despite the dramatic move of women into the workplace, however, their fundamental attitude toward work, the range of work open to them, and their opportunities for advancement had changed very little. Most women who entered the workforce did so out of necessity. As historian Carl Degler has observed: they took jobs to improve the circumstances of their families—not to enhance their own careers or to increase "autonomy within the family." As another indicator of the primacy of family, women over 45 constituted the largest age-group entering the workforce—women who had already raised their families. The percentage of married women in the workforce increased from less than 25 percent to more than 31 percent during the fifties.

Enormous inequities existed in opportunities for advancement for women versus men. Three-quarters of the men working for the federal government were in ranks never reached by three-quarters of the women. More than 50 percent of the women held jobs in the lowest grades of federal service (grades 1–4 of 18)—but less than 20 percent of the men. When advertising for new employees, federal officials were allowed to express a preference for men or women regardless of the official job description or expected responsibilities.

In the private sector, most women continued to enter professions considered traditional "women's" jobs. In the mid-fifties, 60 percent of women entering the workforce who didn't have college degrees took clerical jobs, and a similar percentage of college graduates took teaching jobs. Others became nurses, telephone operators, social workers, and garment workers. The inequities in compensation for women versus men were also enormous. Not only did women receive substantially less pay than men for comparable work, the gap between men's and women's salaries grew larger in the fifties. In 1957, women earned on average 36 percent less than men; by 1960, they earned 39 percent less.

The situation for African American women was much worse on almost any basis of comparison; they were, as historian William Chafe has described their predicament, in double jeopardy, suffering discrimination both as women *and* as blacks. The gap between black and white women left African American women on the margins of any feminist reform. Women's organizations such as the National Women's Party remained overwhelmingly the province of white middle-class women.

7. Women members of U.S. Congress: Seated: Senator Maurine Neuberger, Oregon;
Representative Frances Bolton, Ohio; Senator Margaret Chase Smith, Maine;
Standing, Representatives, Florence Dwyer, New Jersey; Martha Griffiths, Michigan;
Edith Green, Oregon; Patsy Mink, Hawaii; Leonor Sullivan, Missouri; Julia Hansen,
Washington; Catherine May, Washington; Edna Kelly, New York; Charlotte Reid,
Illinois, ca. 1965–67. Of those pictured, only Patsy Mink took office after 1961.
Record Group 306: Records of the U.S. Information Agency, 1900–1988, Special
Media Archives Services Division (NWCS-S), National Archives at College Park,
NAIL Control no. NWDNS-306-PS-D65(1940).

Although the Eisenhower administration increased opportunities for
women at the upper levels of government over what they had been under both
Roosevelt and Truman, the numbers remained small. Eisenhower appointed
28 women to positions that required Senate confirmation, as compared to 18
appointed by Truman and 17 appointed by Roosevelt. Improvement in the
number of women in Congress was similarly modest. In 1950, there was 1
woman in the Senate, and there were 11 women in the House of Representatives; in 1960, there continued to be only 1 woman senator, whereas the number of congresswomen had increased to 16. Even women who were active in
politics recognized the limits a male-dominated political system placed on

them. India Edwards, who had headed the Women's Division of the Democratic National Committee (DNC) and who was instrumental in getting significant positions for women in the Truman administration, received an offer from President Truman in 1951 to chair the DNC. She rejected the offer because she believed that men would be unwilling to work with her—a decision she came to regret. Edwards nonetheless did succeed in gaining high-level appointments for women, and Truman paid her, as she explained, "what men have always considered the ultimate compliment to a female: that I operated like a man." Bertha Adkins, Edwards's counterpart in the Eisenhower administration, never had a relationship as close to her president as Edwards did to Truman, but she benefited from the structure of White House organization, which gave the Republican National Committee (RNC) more latitude than the DNC in making appointments.

Women began to lobby on behalf of women's issues, including the Equal Rights Amendment (ERA), equal pay, women in policy positions, and women's history. The movement on behalf of women's rights suffered from internal divisions and external indifference. The National Women's Party (NWP), the organization that Alice Paul used when she proposed the ERA in 1923, suffered an internal split in 1947 that seemed to typify the problems within the women's movement. The split led to the formation of more organizations, which made cooperation even more problematic, at a time when cooperation was crucial. External indifference proved as difficult an obstacle as any internal divisions. After the war, most people believed that women ought to return to the home, and women's issues were assigned a very low priority. By the late fifties, even as women began to establish their value to the economy, businessmen opposed reform on equal pay, conservative members of Congress had no hesitancy in speaking out in opposition, and women failed to develop coherent leadership on behalf of their proposals.

The crusade to ratify the Equal Rights Amendment, begun by Alice Paul in 1923, continued in the fifties, and was the centerpiece of women's activism. The women's movement of the fifties was a loose coalition of groups that—despite remaining divisions from the split in the NWP—were in general agreement on goals. Despite efforts to attract broader participation, however, it remained an elite movement; those involved tended to be older professional women, well-educated, white, middle-class reformers dedicated to improving society in general and to increasing the political impact of women. In addition to promoting passage of the ERA, they sought to increase awareness of women's history, and to place more women in responsible positions in the workplace and in government. It was not a broad-based movement, and because of its small membership the media generally ignored it or ridiculed it.

The Senate debated the ERA in January 1950, during which time Senator Carl Hayden (Democrat-Arizona) added a rider that became known as the "Hayden amendment." Raising once more the old issue of protective legislation that had long divided the women's movement, the rider declared that the ERA "shall not be construed to impair any rights, benefits, or exemptions conferred by law upon persons of the female sex." Protective legislation offered safeguards for women in the workplace that took into account the physical differences between men and women. Although many women found such laws desirable, most women's rights advocates considered them impediments to women's free access to the workplace. Thus Hayden's proviso pleased no one; it didn't go far enough to satisfy ERA opponents, and it supported a principle that alienated ERA supporters, who believed that it undercut their commitment to equality. The amendment gave senators the chance to vote for the ERA and for protective legislation at the same time, which they did in 1950 and 1953. In the meantime, the proposed amendment did not make it out of committee in the House. Proponents continued to lobby for the ERA throughout the decade. Nonetheless, although both parties kept the ERA in their platforms, it never came any closer to passage than it had in the earlier fifties.

Women's rights activists, losing confidence in their ability to secure passage of the ERA, tried another approach. Instead of seeking support for a broad, all-encompassing umbrella like the ERA, they went after specific legislation aimed at specific problems, particularly differences in pay. A proposal to guarantee equal pay for women performing the same tasks as men had gone down to defeat in 1945, but proponents revived it in the late fifties. It gained momentum when the American Federation of Labor (AFL) and the Congress of Industrial Organizations (CIO) merged in 1956. The AFL had opposed equal pay legislation, but the newly merged AFL-CIO adopted the CIO position in support of the proposal. Strongly opposed by conservative members of Congress, however, it fared no better there than it had in 1945.

Another sign of the glacial pace of change for women in American politics was that the most visible and influential political woman in the fifties was Eleanor Roosevelt, just as she had been in the thirties and forties. She turned sixty-six in 1950, but gave no indication of wanting to retire from her active political life, in which she had always been an outspoken advocate for the disadvantaged in American society. Her visibility was enhanced by the fact that her successors as first lady, Bess Truman and Mamie Eisenhower, had never adopted public causes. She continued to serve as a delegate to the United Nations, a position she held until 1953. She maintained a busy schedule of public appearances in which she lobbied on behalf of the United Nations, and especially its Universal Declaration of Human Rights, passed by the UN General Assembly in 1948, but not ratified by the United States. She traveled widely, and never hesitated to criticize the foreign policy of the Eisenhower administration. She supported domestic policies advocated by liberal Democrats, particularly civil rights and social programs for minorities and the underprivileged. In both 1952 and 1956, she supported Governor Adlai Stevenson for the presidency, praising in particular his expertise on foreign policy.

The Fifties and the Roots of Reform

The discontents of the fifties laid the foundation for reform movements of the sixties and seventies. This became abundantly clear in the campaigns for the rights of women and African Americans (see chapter 7), but also in the reform movements addressing poverty, gay rights, and nuclear policy, issues that would public causes only in the decades that followed.

The Harvard economist John Kenneth Galbraith's influential 1958 book *The Affluent Society* pointed out the disparity between highly visible prosperity and far less visible poverty in American society. He decried what he called "a remarkable attack on the notion of expanding and improving public services" in the postwar years. The great wealth in the private sector had created unprecedented opulence, Galbraith argued, but it had also widened the gap between the rich and the poor. The nation benefited from prosperity, but there were places in the United States where people did not share in the fruits of American capitalism. In rural areas in the South, particularly in Appalachia, and in the center of industrial cities, people lived on the edge, victims of poverty. Only by increasing public sector spending could the nation begin to close this gap, Galbraith asserted, touching off a debate that would echo through the succeeding decades. If Galbraith provided an intellectual justification for the war on poverty launched by the Democratic presidents of the sixties, he also offered a target for conservative opponents of higher taxes and big government.

The gay rights movement could also trace its origins to the fifties, although severe sanctions against homosexuality kept the public expressions of the movement to a low murmur. The FBI monitored the Mattachine Society, founded in 1951 to represent the interests of gays and lesbians, and infiltrated its ranks. Public hostility and revelations some of its founders had previously belonged to the Communist Party compelled the group to keep a low profile. The lesbian organization Daughters of Bilitis also became a target of FBI surveillance.

As a reaction to fears of radioactive fallout from atmospheric nuclear testing by the United States and the Soviet Union, the antinuclear movement had a more public debut late in the decade. In 1957, the Committee for a Sane Nuclear Policy (SANE) began its campaign against atmospheric testing and the nuclear arms race, but soon broadened its mission, calling for nuclear disarmament. Among its members were some of the most prominent liberals of the fifties, including Eleanor Roosevelt, Dr. Benjamin Spock, civil rights leader A. Philip Randolph, and labor leader Walter Reuther. SANE's contributions to the public debate on nuclear arms were significant in achieving the Limited Test Ban Treaty of 1963, in which the United States and the Soviet Union agreed to prohibit atmospheric tests.

Recommended Reading

James T. Patterson's volume in the *Oxford History of the United States, Grand Expectations: The United States, 1945–1974* (New York: Oxford University Press, 1996) provides an informed survey of American society in the fifties. A fine survey that focuses solely on the fifties is J. Ronald Oakley's *God's Country: America in the Fifties* (New York: Dembner Books, 1986). David Halberstam's sweeping *The Fifties* (New York: Villard Books, 1993) captures influential people and examines issues of the day in chapter-length studies. Kenneth T. Jackson's *Crabgrass Frontier: The Suburbanization of the United States* (New York: Oxford University Press, 1985) is the classic study of the move of city dwellers to the suburbs. An older book, but one that is particularly useful, is Ben J. Wattenberg and Richard Scammon's study of demographic change throughout the fifties, *This U.S.A.: An Unexpected Family Portrait of 194,067,296 Americans Drawn from the Census* (Garden City, N.Y.: Doubleday, 1965), the source for many of the statistics used in this book.

Influential books from the fifties discussed in this chapter include David Riesman's *The Lonely Crowd: A Study of the Changing American Character* (New Haven: Yale University Press, 1961, 1989); David M. Potter's *People of Plenty: Economic Abundance and the American Character* (Chicago: University of Chicago Press, 1958); William H. Whyte's *The Organization Man* (New York: Doubleday Anchor, 1956); and C. Wright Mills's *The Power Elite* (New York: Oxford University Press, 2000), which was originally published in 1956.

Stephen J. Whitfield's *The Culture of the Cold War* (Baltimore: Johns Hopkins University Press, 1991) ironically analyzes several aspects of American social development, including religion and anti-Communism. Paul A. Carter's *Another Part of the Fifties* (New York: Columbia University Press, 1983) has insightful essays on politics and intellectual life. Another collection of essays, *The Other Fifties: Interrogating Midcentury American Icons* (Chicago: University of Illinois Press, 1997), edited by Joel Foreman, documents the impact of popular culture on American society, including such icons as the Edsel.

Interest in women's role in society has fostered a broad literature. Betty Friedan's *The Feminine Mystique* (New York: Norton, 1963) started it all, and remains essential reading. Cynthia Harrison's *On Account of Sex: The Politics of Women's Issues, 1945–1968* (Berkeley: University of California Press, 1988), and Leila J. Rupp and Verta Taylor's *Survival in the Doldrums: The American Women's Rights Movement, 1945 to the 1960s* (New York: Oxford University Press, 1987), examine the oft-overlooked feminist political activism of the fifties. William Chafe's *The Paradox of Change: American Women in the 20th Century* (New York, 1992) remains a highly regarded survey. On women's magazines (as well as men's and other magazines), see John Tebbel and Mary Ellen Zuckerman's *The Magazine in America, 1741–1990* (New York: Oxford University Press, 1990).

7

Other Americans

The Rights and Plights of Citizens

NO POSTWAR DEVELOPMENT stimulated more fundamental changes in American society than the civil rights movement. It altered the legal, social, and economic status of African Americans, prompting other disadvantaged groups, most notably, Mexican Americans, Native Americans, and women, to demand changes in their relationship to other Americans. It served as a training ground for the young Americans who would lead campus demonstrations and antiwar protests in the 1960s. It provided a model for movements to protect the environment and to guarantee the rights of consumers. And it brought about changes in electoral politics, as members of groups previously excluded or relegated to the margins moved toward fuller participation in the political process.

Although many of the major achievements of the civil rights movement took place in the 1960s, the contours of the movement were clear well before 1960. African-American communities had long before established networks for communication, organization, and leadership; these readily served the movement. Most of the major civil rights organizations were active, and some already for decades. The Congress of Racial Equality (CORE) had committed itself to nonviolent protest since 1942. The National Urban League, founded in 1910, had concentrated its efforts in Northern industrial cities. And the National Association for the Advancement of Colored People (NAACP), the most active of the three major civil rights organizations in the South, had emphasized the legal rights of African Americans since its inception in 1909.

Martin Luther King Jr. had already led one of his major protests, had emerged as an important leader of the movement, and had formed a new organization, the Southern Christian Leadership Council (SCLC), in 1957. Several other individuals who would play key roles in the sixties had already made an impact, including attorney Thurgood Marshall, labor leader A. Philip Randolph, and activist Ralph Abernathy. The tactic of nonviolence had already been tested and proved its value. The Supreme Court had made its most important civil rights decision, and the other two branches of government had shown what they were, and were not, prepared to do for the movement. The tactics of resistance to advances in civil rights had also emerged. And so, too, had the urban upheavals usually associated with civil rights in the sixties— there had been major race riots in both Harlem and Detroit during World War II.

The United States emerged from the war a segregated society. The Southern states had laws mandating segregation in public facilities, transportation, education, housing, and other facets of social life. Residential patterns elsewhere in the country had established norms of segregation that were equally rigid. By the end of the 1950s, however, revolutionary changes that would permeate and transform American society were well under way.

The civil rights movement can be readily examined from many different perspectives. Calling it the "second Reconstruction," the historian C. Vann Woodward views the movement from the perspective of the roles played by the three branches of the federal government. During the first Reconstruction, he points out, Congress took the lead, passing civil rights laws that were later been overturned by an ultraconservative Supreme Court, while the executive remained at the margins. During the second Reconstruction, however, the judicial branch took the lead, actively assisted by the executive, while Congress dragged its feet. Other perspectives focus on the roles played by leaders such as Martin Luther King Jr. and Thurgood Marshall or on institutions such as labor. More recent perspectives examine the critical role played by the African-American community itself, arguing that, without the support of a grassroots social structure already in place, change would have been more difficult to achieve and longer in coming.

To Secure These Rights: The Truman Administration and Civil Rights

President Truman, whose Missouri border-state background left him imbued with conservative racial views, seemed an unlikely candidate to take aggressive action on behalf of black Americans. Never an advocate of social equality, Truman would become an advocate of political equality, even at the risk of losing the support of the Democratic stronghold in the Solid South. Critics claimed that Truman used civil rights to undermine the progressive wing of the Democratic Party led by Henry Wallace, and that he recognized the growing voting potential of African Americans, especially in Northern cities. Although politics did indeed influence his actions, the fact remains that Truman did more than any president since Lincoln to protect the rights of African Americans, and that he was far ahead of the American public in the civil rights proposals he supported.

Troubled by violence against black veterans returning home from the war, and prodded by the NAACP, in December 1946, Truman established the President's Committee on Civil Rights to investigate means of protecting the rights of black Americans. Issued in October 1947, the report "To Secure These Rights" went beyond the committee's mandate, calling for the virtual elimination of segregation from American society. Among its thirty-five recommendations were proposals for eliminating the poll tax, adopting federal antilynching legislation, establishing a permanent Fair Employment Practices Commission, and desegregating the military, housing, and public transportation.

Truman's staff judged that civil rights could work for him in the coming election despite the opposition it would arouse in the South. Acting from a combination of political calculation and personal commitment, Truman declared his support for many of the measures proposed by his civil rights committee in a special message to Congress on February 2, 1948. When the Democratic Party adopted a strong civil rights plank at its national convention—stronger indeed than Truman himself wanted—several Southern delegates followed South Carolina's Strom Thurmond, who bolted the party. Thurmond and other Southern segregationists formed a new party they called the "Dixiecrats," which ultimately carried only four Southern states in the 1948 election (Alabama, Mississippi, Louisiana, and Thurmond's own South Carolina). In July, Truman released two executive orders, directing the desegregation of the armed forces and mandating equality of treatment in federal employment.

Truman's actions on behalf of African Americans and his narrow victory in 1948 vindicated his strategy and demonstrated the importance of black support for the Democratic Party, but it also marked the high-water mark of his administration's actions on civil rights. During Truman's second term, the administration needed the support of Southern Democrats, particularly in the realm of foreign policy, and especially after the beginning of the Korean War. Since he couldn't afford to alienate key senators and representatives of his own party, Truman was less aggressive in advancing new civil rights proposals; when he did, the South more often than not successfully blocked them. Thus, although the integration of the military was a major milestone, the Truman civil rights legacy was more a matter of bringing the issue to the nation's attention than of achieving specific advances.

The Supreme Court and the Second Reconstruction: The *Brown* Decision

The Supreme Court made few bold moves during the Truman years, but it laid a foundation for groundbreaking decisions later in the 1950s. Chief Justice Fred M. Vinson, one of four Truman appointees, presided over a series of decisions that ruled against segregation in higher education. In *Sweatt v. Painter* (1950), the Court ruled that states could not exclude blacks from graduate schools and professional schools on the basis of race. The decision stemmed from a case in which Texas attempted to establish a "separate but equal" law school for blacks only, and the Court overruled it on the grounds that separate facilities could not be equal, a forerunner of the momentous *Brown v. Board of Education* case of a few years later. *McLaurin v. Oklahoma State Regents* (1950) found unconstitutional an Oklahoma system that admitted a black student to the university's law school, but imposed restrictions on the student that kept him segregated from other students. Although the two unanimous decisions were narrowly framed so as not to require a wholesale elimination of segregation in public schools, they left no question of where the Court was headed on education cases.

The *Sweatt* and *McLaurin* decisions themselves tell only part of the story; the process by which the Court reached these decisions also represented a clear break with the past. Before the late 1930s, even the NAACP used white attorneys, believing they would get a fairer hearing before white judges. In the late 1930s, a group of talented black attorneys affiliated with Howard University Law School, including Thurgood Marshall, began challenging discrimination on several fronts. In *Smith v. Allwright* (1944), they successfully contested the infamous white primary, in which Southern states prohibited African Americans from voting in primary elections. This was tantamount to excluding them from voting at all since the winner of the Democratic primary seldom had a serious challenge in the general election. With the support of the NAACP, Marshall continued to file antidiscrimination suits, and it was he who took the education cases to the Supreme Court. Rather than sticking to judicial precedents that often dated back to the late nineteenth century when a conservative court consistently ruled against the rights of black Americans, Marshall and his colleagues began making sociological arguments to buttress their cases.

In the early 1950s, the NAACP decided to challenge one of the oldest precedents used to justify discrimination. In *Plessy v. Ferguson* (1896), a case involving streetcars in New Orleans, the Court had decreed that separate facilities for blacks and whites were acceptable as long as they were equal. The NAACP decided to test this "separate but equal" principle by invoking the Fourteenth Amendment, which promised equal protection under the laws to all citizens, and which had been the most effective weapon in the battle against discrimination.

Marshall and his associates filed several cases involving segregation in public schools, and those cases began working their way through the appeals process. One of them was filed on behalf Oliver Brown of Topeka, Kansas, whose daughter had to pass by a white elementary school on her way to a black school a mile from their home. *Brown v. the Board of Education of Topeka, Kansas,* became the test case for segregation in public schools. Marshall asked for a sweeping decision that would apply the *Sweatt* principle of qualitative difference to all elementary and secondary schools and abolish "separate but equal."

The case first reached the Court in December 1952; after preliminary briefs, it won a place on the docket for the following year. Chief Justice Vinson died in September 1953, before debate on *Brown* commenced. Vinson's legacy as chief justice was modest. Justice Felix Frankfurter's cruel remark upon his death—"This is the first indication I have ever had that there is a God"—speaks to the lack of esteem from his colleagues. President Eisenhower named former California Governor Earl Warren, a Republican liberal, as Vinson's successor. Warren had come to believe that supporting the internment of Japanese Americans during World War II had been a grave error. His role on the Court would not be the defense of a particular judicial philosophy, but rather the promotion of social justice. Although Warren wasn't a great legal scholar, judicial philosopher, or stylist, no one in the twentieth century was a more able chief justice. He used his talents at persuasion to form consensus on intractable issues, giving decisions a stature they wouldn't have had if issued by a divided Court. As his own stature on the Supreme Court grew, his brethren came to call him "Super Chief."

Warren joined a Court with five Roosevelt appointees (Hugo L. Black, William O. Douglas, Felix Frankfurter, Robert H. Jackson, and Stanley F. Reed) and three Truman appointees (Harold Burton, Tom Clark, and Sherman Minton). The Roosevelt carryovers were in general more liberal, more distinguished, and more assertive than the Truman appointees. When arguments began, only Reed opposed overturning *Plessy*, but each justice used different reasoning to come to his conclusion, making it difficult to frame a decision in which all could concur. Black, an Alabama native with a record of balancing the public interest and individual rights, declared early that he would vote to overturn *Plessy*. Clark, a Texan, wanted to hold off, as did Frankfurter, who, though liberal in his social philosophy, was reluctant to tamper with judicial precedent. Jackson wanted to overturn *Plessy*, but, like Frankfurter, was a believer in judicial restraint. To this maelstrom, the new chief justice brought the talents of a shrewd politician, talents he would need to forge the unanimous decision he believed was necessary to prevent critics from taking comfort in dissenting opinions.

That unanimous decision came down on May 17, 1954. Reading the opinion, Warren declared that "in the field of public education the doctrine of 'separate but equal' has no place. Separate educational facilities are inherently unequal." The decision left unanswered how the decision would be implemented. Should classrooms be integrated immediately? Who would design plans for ending segregation? How would such plans be enforced? A year later, on May 31, 1954, the Court announced another unanimous decision, often called simply *Brown II*, which left the process for implementation deliberately vague. Integration of public schools would have to proceed "with all deliberate speed." As resistance mounted in the years that followed, some critics would complain that emphasis appeared to rest entirely on deliberation rather than on speed. Other critics would accuse the Warren Court of abandoning impartiality and legislating. They blamed Warren more than anyone, and soon "Impeach Earl Warren" bumper stickers began to appear. Eisenhower would later claim that naming Warren as chief justice was the worst appointment he made.

Southern Intransigence: The Reaction to
Brown v. Board of Education

The *Brown* decision marked, not the end of the battle over integration of public schools, but rather its beginning. Opposition mounted immediately, with opponents ranging from normally apolitical citizens to the most influential governors, senators, and members of Congress. Reaction varied from state to state; some, like Virginia, launched vigorous, open campaigns against the decision. Others, like North Carolina, embarked on campaigns of passive resistance. Mississippi employed the threat of violence, and when that failed, resorted to violence itself. Many school districts did nothing, forcing local individuals or civil rights organizations such as the NAACP to file suit to get action. Southerners made clear their resentment, insisting that education, of all things, ought to remain in the hands of local authorities and free from federal interference. Parents withdrew their children from public schools and helped to establish private schools beyond the reach of *Brown*. Some districts went even further, withholding funding from public schools. Virginia announced that it was reviving a doctrine called "interposition," which dated back more than a century to the days of John Calhoun. It claimed that the states had a right to interpose their authority between their citizens and the authority of the federal government when federal action exceeded constitutional limits. The Ku Klux Klan experienced a resurgence, and cross burnings and violence against blacks became common. White Citizens' Councils formed throughout the South, and found means other than violence to pursue the same ends as the Klan. Members often included some of the most prominent citizens, people who used their positions of authority to pressure blacks who sought the protection of *Brown*: bankers would refuse them credit and mortgages; employers would deny them jobs.

Because it involved so many prominent Southerners, the "Southern Manifesto" was perhaps the most dramatic anti-*Brown* gesture. This declaration by 101 Southern senators and members of Congress condemned *Brown* and praised the states that had decreed their intention to resist "forced integration." Among the signers were some of the most prominent Southern political leaders, including constitutional scholar Senator Sam Ervin of North Carolina, Senator Richard Russell of Georgia, and Senator J. William Fulbright of Arkansas. The manifesto would later haunt some of its signers; Fulbright probably would have been secretary of state years later under President

Kennedy had he not signed. At the time, however, defending segregation was an effective political stand, and Southern governors soon recognized the potential appeal to voters of standing up to the federal government. Governors Orval Faubus of Arkansas and Ross Barnett of Mississippi capitalized on public discontent with *Brown* to shore up their own base.

Resistance by political leaders emboldened others. The aftermath of *Brown* saw a dramatic rise in violence against African Americans across the South, with some of the most heinous cases occurring in the months immediately after the announcement of *Brown II*. Lynchings had declined in frequency in the 1940s and early 1950s, but in 1955 alone there were eight reported cases.

Mississippi endured a horrifying epidemic of white-on-black violence in 1955. On May 7, in Belzoni, the Reverend George W. Lee died from a gunshot wound inflicted after he refused to have his name stricken from the voter registration list. On August 13, in Brookhaven, 63-year-old Lamar Smith, a volunteer working on a voter registration drive, was shot front of the courthouse. In these cases, as in many others, the murderers of blacks went unpunished: all-white juries refused to convict white men even in the face of overwhelming evidence. Most disturbing of all the cases in Mississippi's bloody summer was that of 14-year-old Emmett Till, who was on a trip from his home in Chicago to visit relatives in the Delta. Till allegedly whistled at a white woman in a grocery store. Searchers found Till's mutilated body in the Tallahatchie River on August 28. Two local white men, J. W. Milam and Roy Bryant, admitted beating Till to death. An all-white, all-male jury found them not guilty.

Schoolhouse Doors: The Slow Pace of Desegregation

Some of the bitterest battles of the civil rights era centered on integration of the public schools. The *Brown* decision passed responsibility to the executive branch to see how Court's mandate might be enforced. President Eisenhower refused to use the presidential bully pulpit to defend *Brown,* and provided no moral leadership on civil rights. When he did take action, it was with reluctance, and only in the face of an egregious violation of the Court's authority. Eisenhower recognized his responsibility to defend the Constitution, but, in the case of civil rights, it wasn't a responsibility he relished. He believed that it was wrong to try to force morality on people. He was not opposed to civil rights, but he believed that people had to work out their own means in their own time to achieve that goal. Activists condemned him as a "gradualist."

In the fall of 1955, in response to a suit filed by Thurgood Marshall for the NAACP, the Supreme Court directed the University of Alabama to desegregate. The university admitted Autherine Lucy for the 1956 spring term, and, in February, she became the first African American to try to enroll. Although Lucy attended classes for two days without incident, over the following weekend, anti-integrationists from Birmingham and elsewhere in Alabama and Mississippi flocked to Tuscaloosa. A mob gathered on the following Monday morning, February 6, and screamed at her as university officials attempted to escort her from one class to the next; the mob attacked the vehicle in which they were riding, breaking the windshield and back window. Later, police were able to get Lucy off campus but only by hiding her on the floor of a police car. Giving in to the mob, the university ruled that Lucy would have to stay off campus to prevent another riot. When Lucy appealed their ruling and laid some of the blame on the university, the administration expelled her. The hostility surrounding Autherine Lucy's attempt to enter the university was fueled in part by a protest then under way in Montgomery, Alabama's capital, some 80 miles south of Birmingham, where one of the pivotal events of the civil rights movement was then moving into its third month.

Nonviolence: Martin Luther King Jr.
and the Montgomery Bus Boycott

The civil rights movement became a "movement," not because the Supreme Court made certain rulings or because leading politicians freely agreed to abide by those rulings, but because people demanded their rights as citizens. One such incident occurred in Montgomery, Alabama in December 1955. Montgomery, the first capital of the Confederacy, was the heart of Dixie and the center of the segregated South. Blacks, who constituted more than 40 percent of the city's 120,000 residents, faced segregation in schools, public facilities, and public transportation. Montgomery's buses were typical of the way in which segregation forced people to endure indignities on a daily basis. Black passengers would have to enter at the front of the bus, pay their fare, exit the bus, reenter at the rear, and take a seat at the back. If all seats were filled when new white passengers boarded, black passengers would have to relin-

8. The University of Alabama admitted Autherine Lucy (on left) in response to a Supreme Court order that directed the university to desegregate, and she began attending classes early in February 1956. W. S. Hoole Special Collections Library, University of Alabama.

quish their seats. Drivers could tell black passengers to give up their seats, and routinely addressed them as "niggers" when they did so.

Rosa Parks, a middle-aged seamstress, had no plans to launch a protest movement when she refused to give up her seat on December 1, 1955. She was exhausted from a day of shopping, just too tired to stand. The bus driver summoned police, and they arrested Parks on a charge of disorderly conduct. E. D. Nixon, a labor leader with the Brotherhood of Sleeping Car Porters and former head of the Alabama chapter of the NAACP, bailed her out of jail.

The community network of African Americans in Montgomery, which centered on the city's black churches, but also included the local chapter of the NAACP and faculty members of the historically black Alabama State College, rapidly organized a protest against the segregated bus system. Rosa Parks had worked as secretary in Montgomery's NAACP chapter, where Nixon had

9. On February 6, 1956, a mob gathered on the campus of the University of Alabama to protest the admission of Autherine Lucy, the first African American to attend the university. The mob attacked the car in which university officials were transporting her. The university later capitulated to the mob and asked her to stay away from the campus for her own safety. W. S. Hoole Special Collections Library, University of Alabama.

presided. Widely respected, active in the church and in volunteer activities, Parks was an ideal person to serve as a rallying point for a protest. Nixon recognized that immediately; he and some of his colleagues had long considered a protest, and he saw this as their opportunity. Once Parks agreed to support the idea, Nixon began making phone calls.

As the word spread, things began to fall into place. Fred Gray agreed to give Parks legal council. Jo Ann Robinson, an English professor at Alabama State and a member of the Women's Political Council, called her friends on the council to draft a protest letter. They put together a leaflet calling for a boycott of the buses, and began distributing it, mainly through the churches. Nixon called the Reverend Ralph Abernathy, pastor of the First Baptist

Church, and Dr. Martin Luther King Jr., who'd recently accepted a position as pastor of the Dexter Avenue Baptist Church.

Although King was only twenty-six and had little experience, he'd already impressed Abernathy, Nixon, and other leaders of the African-American community with his oratorical ability. He came from a distinguished family in Atlanta, where his father served as pastor of Ebenezer Baptist Church. After graduating from the historically black Morehouse College in Atlanta in 1948, King earned a bachelor of divinity degree from Crozer Theological Seminary in Chester, Pennsylvania, near Philadelphia, in 1951. He received his doctorate in systematic theology from Boston College in 1955, shortly before accepting the call to come to Dexter Avenue Baptist Church. He'd been deeply influenced by the theology of the liberal Protestant philosopher Reinhold Niebuhr, whose *Moral Man and Immoral Society* appeared in 1950 when King was studying at Crozer. Niebuhr's criticism of pacifism and idealism as unrealistic tools to combat social evil stirred King. When coupled with Thoreau's concept of civil disobedience in a just cause, and Gandhi's campaign of nonviolent protest, they formed the theoretical base of his commitment to nonviolent direct action. When it came to organizing a boycott, the elders of Montgomery's black community used their connections to gather a crowd, but they relied on King's ability to express complex ideas in a straightforward manner and on oratorical skills to mobilize those who came forward.

Summoned by Nixon to King's church that evening, the leaders of Montgomery's black community agreed to a one-day boycott of the city's buses on the following Monday, December 5. Through the community network, they organized alternative transportation for people who worked downtown, using any vehicles available to form a car pool. The one-day protest was a resounding success. The leaders met again, formed a new organization that they called the "Montgomery Improvement Association" (MIA), and chose King to be its president.

That night, at a community meeting at Holt Street Baptist Church, Martin Luther King demonstrated the leadership, oratorical gifts, and sense of justice that would make him the most effective leader of the movement, and one of the most revered leaders in American history. His task was to convince people not only to lend their complete support to a protest that would cause many of them daily hardship, but to suppress their anger in a campaign committed to nonviolence. "There comes a time when people get tired of being trampled over by the iron feet of oppression," he told the crowd. But "we are a Christian people," he continued. "There will be no crosses burned at any bus stops in Montgomery," and no people dragged out of their houses and murdered. "If we are wrong—justice is a lie." They agreed to continue their protest until city leaders and the bus company would meet three simple, direct demands: courteous treatment on the buses, black bus drivers on routes that served the black community, and first-come, first-served seating on the bus. In the making last demand, they also agreed that African Americans would first take seats in the back of the bus, and move forward as the bus filled.

The boycott continued, with a level of support from the black community that surprised organizers and city officials alike. Expecting perhaps 60 percent compliance, the boycott leaders were gratified to see no black riders as they watched buses pass the first morning. By the end of the first week, city commissioners began negotiating with MIA leaders. The commissioners expected the boycott to collapse, and refused to offer meaningful concessions. Instead, the city began pressuring black citizens, arresting them on vagrancy and other spurious charges. They arrested King for driving 30 in a 25-mile-an-hour zone. Downtown merchants suffered a decline in Christmas business, but still the city refused to give in. In January, the city coerced three county pastors to sign an agreement, and then claimed that the boycott was over; the ploy might have worked had it not been for the communications network that linked the black community. Then, on January 30, a bomb exploded on the porch of King's house. Fortunately, it did little damage. King, who wasn't home at the time, returned quickly to find his wife and daughter uninjured. Two days later, another bomb went off, this time in the yard of E. D. Nixon. Rather than intimidating the community, however, the two blasts only strengthened its resolve.

By spring, the boycott was taking its toll on downtown businesses, which had lost some three million dollars in business in the first three months. City officials took their case to court, and won an indictment against the leaders of the boycott for violating an old law against conspiring to hinder the operation of business. The court issued indictments against 115 people. Police arrested 90 of them, including King, who was freed on bond. The mass arrests proved to be a blunder: they focused national attention on the boycott and drew sorely needed financial support. King began to emerge as a national figure, and experienced for the first time the benefits and burdens of his new role. His visibility increased support for the boycott—Bayard Rustin, one of the most respected of black activists in the country, came to Montgomery—but it also created tensions with other civil rights leaders, and led to charges of misappropriation of the funds pouring into the MIA coffers. Roy Wilkins, national head of the NAACP, insisted that funds be channeled through his organization. This rankled King, who believed the NAACP had given the MIA too little support to deserve a portion of the donations. The NAACP position became even more complicated when Alabama Governor John Patterson moved to outlaw the NAACP in his state.

Although reaction against it spread beyond Alabama, by summer, the boycott had elicited national support, most dramatically expressed in a New York City rally that included among its participants A. Philip Randolph, Eleanor Roosevelt, Harlem Congressman Adam Clayton Powell, and the performer Tallulah Bankhead, an Alabama native. As contributions poured in, organizers purchased station wagons to supplement their car pool fleet. City officials went after the MIA for operating an illegal, unauthorized taxi service. A local judge issued first a restraining order and then a permanent injunction against the car pool arrangement. The new legal maneuver put the boycott in jeopardy, but the crisis was short-lived. The Supreme Court affirmed a lower court decision declaring unconstitutional state and local laws in Alabama mandating segregation on buses.

The Supreme Court order ended the legal dispute, but it didn't end the ill will that still existed between the white and black communities of Montgomery. Incidents of sniper fire at buses marred the initiation of integrated bus service. Someone fired a shotgun at the door of King's home. A bomb exploded at the Reverend Ralph Abernathy's house in January 1957; on the same night, another bomb inflicted major damage at First Baptist Church, one of the most historic buildings in Montgomery's black community, where Abernathy served as pastor. But the battle was won. In the weeks that followed, some twenty-five other Southern cities ended segregation on their buses, either because of protests or out of recognition that their systems would also fall to legal challenges.

The victory on the streets of Montgomery and in the chambers of the Supreme Court was an important symbolic triumph, but it was limited in scope. It dealt only with buses, and left other public facilities, private businesses, and public schools that hadn't responded to *Brown* remained segregated. Montgomery remained a segregated city. Squabbling within the fledgling movement became apparent, not only in the brief spat between the

MIA and the NAACP, but within the MIA. E. D. Nixon resigned, and the MIA fell apart after the Court decision. But the movements's shortcomings paled in comparison to its achievements. African Americans had won a major victory. The tactic of nonviolent protest had proven itself. And a new leader, Martin Luther King Jr., had emerged. He and Ralph Abernathy, his partner in Montgomery and his lieutenant in the battles that lay ahead, were among those that helped found a new organization, the Southern Christian Leadership Conference (SCLC), which would be at the forefront of nonviolent protests for the next several years.

Congress and Civil Rights: The Civil Rights Act of 1957

Of the three branches of government, Congress was the least likely to take action on civil rights. Southern Democrats, who rarely faced challenges for re-election outside of their own party, amassed seniority that enabled them to chair most of the important committees and, in doing so, to control the flow of legislation. They used this power to prevent civil rights legislation from even reaching the floor. The South had such control that no civil rights legislation had passed in eighty-two years, until 1957.

That the Civil Rights Act of 1957 passed at all was thanks largely to the legislative talents of Senator Lyndon Johnson (Democrat-Texas), the Senate majority leader. Johnson's colleagues held his legislative skills in high regard, and his handling of this bill showed both the strengths and shortcomings of his extraordinary talent. Without Johnson's efforts, it is likely that no civil rights bill would have passed; but in the process, he compromised away most of its meaningful provisions, leaving critics wondering whether the struggle had been worth it. The Act was a pack of concessions, so weak that Southerners didn't bother to defeat it, so inconsequential that the president supported it without knowing all of its provisions. One compromise was an amendment that entitled anyone cited for contempt of court in a civil rights case to demand a jury trial, which in the South nearly guaranteed acquittal before sympathetic jury that was either all white or nearly so.

The Act did establish a Civil Rights Commission, but its record for enforcing voting rights and investigating violations was abysmal. Two years later, in its own report, the commission acknowledged that civil rights enforcement by the Justice Department was no more vigorous after passage of the bill than it had been before. To Martin Luther King, the message of the

Civil Rights Act was clear: African Americans could not depend on whites to defend their rights; they would have to take that responsibility themselves.

Little Rock: Eisenhower and the Continuing School Desegregation Crisis

The integration of public schools proceeded at a glacial pace in the aftermath of the *Brown* decision; much of the blame lay at the door to the Oval Office. President Eisenhower continued to distance himself and his administration from the crisis. As the school year began in the fall of 1957, however, defiance of the Court became so blatant that the president could no longer ignore it. The test of the administration's resolve came in Little Rock, Arkansas.

After a federal court order mandated the integration of Little Rock Central High School, Governor Orval Faubus called out the Arkansas National Guard to prevent nine black students from enrolling. On September 4, the first day of school, a mob gathered outside and watched as eight students arrived together, only to be turned away by the Guard. The ninth student, a young girl, missed the arranged group arrival. When she showed up alone, white women in the mob moved in on her unimpeded by the Guard, screaming at her until a reporter was able to get her aboard a bus. The Guard returned to its post at the start of each school day.

President Eisenhower tried to avoid direct White House involvement. Faubus, who knew that Eisenhower was sympathetic to the white South, requested a meeting with the president, claiming he wanted to find a way out of the crisis. On September 14, he flew to Newport, Rhode Island, where the Eisenhowers were vacationing. Believing he and Faubus had reached an agreement to keep the National Guard at the school, but to admit the black students, Eisenhower praised the Arkansas governor for his constructive approach. On arriving back in Arkansas, however, Faubus continued to use the Guard to block entry of the black students; he changed the wording in Eisenhower's statement to make it appear that he had the president's backing.

A week later, the court cited Faubus for contempt. Faubus consulted with Washington, and seemed to have agreed to admit the black students and use the National Guard to protect them. The contempt citation brought the crisis to a head. On September 23, Faubus dismissed the Guard, in effect unleashing the mob. On that morning, school officials cooperated in helping the nine students to enter by a side door, avoiding the wrath of the mob. When people found out that the students were inside, their threat became so serious that school officials canceled classes and closed the school. The mob swelled, and the next morning appeared even more menacing. Still, Eisenhower hesitated. Later that day, when the mayor of Little Rock cabled Washington asking for assistance, Eisenhower federalized the Arkansas National Guard; he ordered that a thousand troops of the 101st Airborne Division trained in riot control be immediately dispatched to Little Rock; they were on the scene before the end of the day. The next morning integration proceeded peacefully.

Eisenhower justified his actions to the American people, explaining that he took action reluctantly and only in the face of defiance of the federal government. Nationwide, two-thirds of Americans backed his actions, whereas in the South only one-third did. As moderate as Eisenhower's response had been, the South was outraged by the specter of federal intervention in its affairs. Nonetheless, the public crisis was over. Private battles continued for the students who had integrated Central High: they were the target of the taunts of their classmates for the rest of the school year. Nonetheless, integration took effect and was not again challenged at Little Rock Central. Faubus assumed the pose of a martyr, and won reelection. Other Southern governors learned the political benefits of race-baiting.

Resistance Gives Way to Tokenism

The integration of Little Rock Central High School dramatically displayed a process that was under way throughout the South despite persistent resistance. Integration proceeded, though the pace was slow, uneven, and often characterized by tokenism. The *Brown* decision and especially *Brown II* shifted authority to the courts. Federal district courts were on the front line, and, above them, the Circuit Courts of Appeal, of which the Fourth and Fifth Circuits had jurisdiction in the South. Although there were exceptions, most judges reflected the racist—or at least racially conservative—views of their fellow citizens. Federal judges, after all, received their appointments only after they passed muster with the state's senators or representatives, who by tradition gave their nod to acceptable candidates. Although judges in these courts varied in their interpretations of *Brown*'s "all deliberate speed," many began to push districts toward adopting desegregation plans. As legal scholar J. Harvie Wilkinson III, himself a district court judge, explained, "many federal judges sought only to move the South from the first, impermissible stage of absolute defiance to the second stage of token compliance."

The means of resistance began to unravel. Forming private schools to replace public schools may have served students in wealthy communities, but those in poorer areas were ill served by underfunded ad hoc arrangements staffed by parents with no training as teachers. Parents who supported closing the public schools initially had second thoughts when they realized the impact on their children. Pupil placement plans adopted immediately after *Brown* met a varied fate. The courts struck down some plans that were obviously designed to circumvent the law. Others, however, were more difficult to categorize since they allowed for the minimum legally mandated integration and no more. Such plans resulted only in token integration. Following the vague mandate of *Brown,* the courts allowed them to stand; in doing so they implicitly endorsed the policies of Southern gradualists, which only fueled impatience among the civil rights activists of the sixties.

Standing Up by Sitting Down: The Sit-Ins of 1960

On February 1, 1960, as President Eisenhower began his last year in office, the civil rights movement set off in a new direction. In Greensboro, four freshmen at the historically black North Carolina Agricultural and Technical State University (North Carolina A&T) staged the first "sit-in" protest in the South (CORE had staged the very first sit-ins, in Chicago during World War II). Wondering when blacks would ever act to secure their rights, Ezell Blair, Franklin McCain, Joseph McNeil, and David Richmond decided to take matters into their own hands. They sat down at a "whites only" lunch counter in the downtown Woolworth's, only to be told by the black waitress behind the counter that they were embarrassing their race. Undeterred, they held out until closing time, and vowed to return the next morning. Others soon heard about the protest; the next day, there were nineteen protestors, and, by the third day, eighty-five. White students from Greensboro College joined them, and soon the protestors had organized shifts.

News of the protest spread quickly, by word of mouth and in the press, and long before the Greensboro protest came to resolution, it sparked similar protests in Durham, Raleigh, and Winston-Salem. Protests spread to South Carolina, and then to Georgia and Tennessee (Atlanta and Nashville) and, before the end of the month, to cities throughout the South. Dedicated to nonviolence, the student protestors dressed well and behaved with a dignity that often made police officers appear overbearing and boorish in contrast. Authorities clamped down, staging mass arrests to try to weaken the will of protestors. King quickly endorsed the sit-ins, but the NAACP and many older veterans of civil rights battles, including Thurgood Marshall, criticized them as impractical.

Circumstances made the Nashville sit-in one of the most significant. Four black colleges in the city—Fisk University, American Baptist Theological Seminary, Tennessee State, and Meharry Medical School—provided a core of willing recruits. The students who participated were older than Greensboro's freshmen, and more prepared for the challenge they faced. A 31-year-old minister named James Lawson, a Korean War conscientious objector, emerged as a leader of Nashville's movement. Two years earlier, he'd led a seminar in nonviolent resistance sponsored by the pacifist Fellowship of Reconciliation. Students who would leave a lasting mark on the civil rights movement soon joined him: John Lewis, a student at the seminary and later a congressman from Georgia; Marion Barry from Fisk, later mayor of Washington, D.C.; and Diane Nash, one of the most prominent, dynamic, and articulate young women in the movement.

Among the legacies of the sit-ins was the establishment of a new organization for younger activists, many of whom found the NAACP too staid and controlling, CORE too cautious, and the SCLC too much King's organization. Ella Baker, the executive director of King's SCLC, called for a meeting of students involved in the protests. At fifty-five, she was a generation older than the representatives from several of the Southern black colleges who answered her call to the meeting in Raleigh in April. Lawson came from Nashville to give the keynote address, and his criticism of the NAACP's overly cautious approach to civil rights galvanized the crowd and signaled the emerging rift within the movement. The three hundred delegates in Raleigh established the Student Non-Violent Coordinating Committee (SNCC), popularly known as "Snick," and destined to be one of the frontline civil rights organizations in the turbulent sixties. Unlike the older civil rights organizations, SNCC didn't seek large numbers of members; instead, as its name suggests, it concentrated on coordinating protest activities. By the early 1960s, the burgeoning civil rights movement had broadened its base, established organizations to serve as a foundation, and demonstrated a commitment to nonviolence.

Native Americans: Separation, Assimilation, or Termination?

The Indian wars of the late nineteenth century left deep scars on Native American culture and identity and had a devastating effect on their economic well-being. Even after Native Americans were no longer a threat, many people continued to exploit them, and as a result Native Americans viewed both government policy and private actions with suspicion. Reformers who genuinely wanted to improve the conditions of Native Americans found it difficult to overcome their deep-seated distrust—and with good reason since the most well-intended prescriptions often had unanticipated negative consequences. Two conflicting approaches had competed for Washington's support since the late nineteenth century. One held that federal policy ought to be aimed at improving the quality of life on the reservations, that Indian culture could survive only if it remained separate from the rest of society. Critics argued persuasively that this approach had demonstrably failed because Native Americans living on reservations remained among the poorest of all categories of Americans. The other approach held that the federal government ought to promote education and assimilation of Native Americans, that only among other Americans, not isolated on reservations, would their conditions improve. Critics of this approach were equally persuasive, arguing that it only created a brain drain from the reservations, robbing those who stayed behind of their best and brightest youths.

When President Eisenhower took office, it was abundantly clear that previous approaches hadn't worked. By most measures—health, wealth, education—Native Americans continued to rate among the lowest ranking Americans. Even the highly regarded John Collier, commissioner of Indian affairs from 1934 to 1945, had been unable to change the lot of Native Americans significantly. An advocate of the first approach—aid to the reservations—Collier had sought a "New Deal for Indians." Although many Native Americans considered Collier paternalistic, few could dispute his sincerity. Nonetheless, when Collier retired in 1945, anti-Communist critics accused him of having attempted to create Communist enclaves on the reservations. The accusations were without merit, but Collier's limited achievements led officials in Washington to conclude that the problem lay with the reservation system itself.

Initiated during Truman's presidency and enacted during Eisenhower's, the unfortunately named "termination policy" took an entirely new approach. Its goal was to work with Native Americans to devise a plan to terminate reservations, and thus to pursue once again the assimilation strategy. Soon after Collier's resignation, critics of the reservation system called for an end to the policies of federal paternalism. The reaction among Native Americans varied. Many younger people agreed with the assimilationists that their best chance for success was in the cities; even those who didn't want to end all federal protection believed that federal restrictions had prevented them from managing their own affairs.

As early as 1947, the Bureau of Indian Affairs (BIA) tried to forestall reservation critics by pointing out that all Native American peoples could not be treated alike. Although some might be able to operate immediately without federal protection, others needed a transition period of at least ten years, and others needed even longer. As historian Peter Iverson observed, the BIA had unwittingly played into the hands of reservation opponents, who argued that those who no longer needed federal support should immediately be granted independent status. Beginning in 1950, the last two commissioners of Indian affairs under Truman moved to implement the withdrawal of federal protection.

When Eisenhower moved into the White House and the Republicans took control of both houses of Congress in 1953, the pace of termination quickened. In August, Congress passed legislation that slated certain reservations for termination, including those of the Klamath in Oregon, the Menominee in Wisconsin, and the Potawotamie in Kansas and Nebraska. The Eisenhower administration moved not only to eliminate reservations, but also to reduce the authority of the BIA, to relocate Native Americans in cities, and to transfer from the federal government to the states responsibility for other services to Native Americans. In several cases, the states either failed to assume these responsibilities, or funded them at a lower level than the federal government had. Nebraska initially refused to fund law enforcement on former reservation lands, and tried to force the counties to do so. The federal government also relinquished responsibility for Native American education and health care, turning these over to the states and the Public Health Service, respectively.

Several Native American peoples, the two largest of which were the Menominee of Wisconsin and the Klamath of Oregon, agreed in 1954 to accept termination of their reservations and thus also of their protected status as tribes. Ironically, the Menominee agreed to terminate their reservation largely because they had been relatively successful, drawing income from the forestry industry in Northern Wisconsin, and because termination would allow them to distribute their tribal trust fund among individual members. Things did not go as planned, however. When, after termination, a private company took over forestry operations, income among the Menominee plunged. The newly created Menominee County soon had the lowest per capita income and the highest unemployment in the state. In 1973, a referendum restored the Menominee's tribal status. Termination was also devastating to the Klamath. One observer, writing a decade later, claimed that as a result of termination, the Klamath had become "virtually extinct" as a people.

Migration from reservations to cities, mainly by younger Native Americans, prompted by declining economies in Indian communities, prodded by the federal government, and lured by the prosperity in American cites, had a devastating impact on those left behind. The process wasn't new, but it accelerated in the 1950s, and left the economies of Native American home communities in a rapid decline.

As with the civil rights movement, the movement for Native American rights, though born in the fifties, would not mature until the next decade. Historian Peter Iverson traced the roots of several Native American organizations that would later work for political rights and economic opportunities. The Southwest Association on Indian Affairs, which began holding conferences in 1956, formed the core that became the National Indian Youth Council five years later. The Chicago Indian Center, founded in 1953, provided opportunity for joint action that overcame prior tribal allegiances, and generated the important American Indian Chicago Conference held in 1961. Tribes hired attorneys to defend their legal interests. The Navaho even established its own court system.

Changes in federal laws, the migration of young people to the cities, and increasing legal activity and political involvement worked to transform Native American life in vital ways. Most Native Americans of the postwar generation led lives very different than those of their parents. Even on reservation and former reservation lands, social isolation had diminished, if not the poverty that had been characteristic of Indian life since the late nineteenth century.

10. Native American family standing near a trailer with entry lean-to, 1952. Department of the Interior, Bureau of Indian Affairs, Aberdeen Area Office, Fort Bertholt Agency, Records from Record Group 75: Records of the Bureau of Indian Affairs, 1793–1989, NARA Central Plains Region (Kansas City), NAIL Control no. NRE-75-FB(PHO)-489.

Mexican Americans: Between Two Cultures

For years, Mexican immigration to the United States provided a source of cheap labor for American businesses in border towns and for commercial farmers in the Southwestern states. Farmers would alternately encourage and discourage movement across the border, depending on the state of the U.S. economy. In the 1920s, growers in Southern California had welcomed Mexican workers, only to support their deportation when the Great Depression brought Anglo-Americans to the Southwest willing to work the fields. Once World War II began, military service and war industries drew these workers out of the fields, and farmers once again sought Mexicans as a source of cheap labor. In 1942, the federal government cooperated with farmers to create the bracero program, under which Mexican workers could come to the United States under contract to growers for a specified period of time. Work in the fields was backbreaking stoop labor at meager wages; the short-handled hoes they were forced to use made workers more efficient, but left them with chronic back problems. The program was ideal from the standpoint of the farmers since it enabled them to obtain as much cheap labor as they wanted, and yet allowed them to dispose of the workers easily when they were no longer needed.

The plight of the braceros was but one dimension of a complicated situation for Mexican immigrants. Some Mexicans came to the United States illegally rather than under the bracero program because they found the bracero contract too restrictive. In the early 1950s, the U.S. government instituted the crudely named "Operation Wetback" to round up illegal immigrants for deportation. Between 1950 and 1955, the United States deported 3.8 million people of Mexican descent, many of them U.S. citizens. Children born in the United States became U.S. citizens whether their parents were legal or illegal immigrants. When these children grew to adulthood, they resented the bracero program because it brought Mexican citizens to the United States to take jobs that might otherwise have gone to Americans, and because it allowed farmers to keep agricultural wages low.

Cesar Chavez was one of the Mexican Americans caught in this quandary. Born in Yuma, Arizona in 1927, Chavez knew the plight of migratory laborers from family experience. The Chavezes lost their land in Yuma after a Depression-era drought in 1933 left them indebted beyond their ability to repay. Like other Depression-era farm workers, Chavez's family fled to California, where Cesar grew up following his father from one migratory labor camp to another. His childhood memories included the personal experience of discrimination. He remembered the racist remarks of his classmates and being forced to wear a sign around his neck in school that read: "I am a clown; I speak Spanish." He remembered losing the family farm in Yuma to a big agricultural corporation. He remembered living in a tent through a winter in Oxnard, California. He remembered having to attend at least thirty-six different schools as a boy.

Chavez served briefly in the Navy during World War II, and returned to California to marry and to resume the life as migrant farm laborer he'd known since childhood. In 1952, Chavez and his wife were living in the San Jose barrio known as "Sal Si Puedes," or "Get out if you can." Fred Ross, an organizer for the Community Service Organization (CSO), had heard about Chavez, and came to talk to him. Formed in Los Angeles with assistance from the prominent labor organizer Saul Alinsky, the CSO had helped to elect the

Mexican American Ed Roybal to the Los Angeles City Council, and had since become a political force in the Mexican-American community. Ross, who was an Anglo and twice Chavez's age, was one of the people most responsible for the success of the CSO. Although Chavez was at first suspicious of him, Ross was able to overcome Chavez's suspicions by showing him how familiar he was with the common problems in barrios across California. He then convinced Chavez to join him as a staff member with a newly formed San Jose chapter of the CSO, and to assist on a voter registration drive.

The San Jose voter registration drive gave Chavez his first experience with confronting well-connected political opponents. The local Republican Party feared that Chavez's campaign would strengthen the Democratic Party, threatening its own political position. Republicans alleged that Chavez had Communist connections, hassled him at his job in a lumberyard, harassed voters he had registered, and persuaded the FBI to investigate him. When Chavez convinced the agents he was doing nothing illegal, they helped him convince the Republicans to back off as well. The FBI did not abandon its investigation of Chavez, however; it would continue into the sixties as Chavez's career as an activist developed.

Ross became a mentor to Chavez, and the two men worked together in organizing Mexican-American communities around the state. After establishing an office in Sal Si Puedes, Chavez worked on his own to set up an office in Oakland, and another in Madera in the San Joaquin Valley, where he encountered divisions among his own supporters: between Mexican-American and black CSO workers, and between Catholics and Protestants. He learned that one of the most difficult challenges facing any labor organizer was keeping his own forces united.

In 1958, at Alinsky's request, Chavez organized a CSO chapter in Oxnard, where his father had worked in the lemon orchards and vegetable fields years earlier. His work in Oxnard brought Chavez to the cause that would occupy most of his energies in the years that followed: the organization of Mexican-American agricultural workers. The biggest problem facing these workers was regular abuse of the bracero program. Oxnard's growers found ways to circumvent the requirement that they use Mexican Americans who were U.S. citizens, if they were available. Employers could hire braceros, who of course weren't American citizens, only after they exhausted the pool of Mexican Americans. Instead, the growers used braceros with impunity, forcing wages down for Mexican Americans when they were fortunate enough to get work. Chavez soon learned that growers were able to meet bracero regulations by manipulating the system. When local workers showed up in the morning looking for work, the growers would demand referral cards or applications, long forms which had to be filled out daily at an employment office in Ventura, some eight to ten miles away. In the meantime, the growers would hire workers for the day from among the braceros, and by the time the others returned, the growers could technically claim that when they had actually hired workers for the day, there had been no local workers there. The system was especially insidious because it pitted Mexicans against Mexican Americans, diverting attention from the growers, who were exploiting both groups.

Chavez began to gather evidence of the ways in which growers had abused the bracero system. He took workers to the employment office to fill out their employment cards, and kept copies. He filed complaints with state officials, Democratic Party representatives, and federal labor inspectors. Officials forced the growers to hire local workers, but the growers charged them with incompetence and fired them as soon as the glare of official scrutiny dimmed. Chavez came to appreciate the value of publicity, and convinced the local press to cover an organized protest against a tomato grower who had hired braceros. Publicity generated protests to the local placement service. The state of California also responded, and dismissed the regional director of the placement service. The growers finally relented, and agreed to eliminate the daily application cards, hire local workers before braceros, conduct daily hiring outside the CSO office, and increase wages. The CSO promoted Chavez to the position of executive director.

Chavez's fame would grow in the sixties and seventies, when he would found the United Farm Workers and become the most effective Mexican-American leader of his generation. By 1960, Chavez had already laid the foundation for his successful campaign to organize farm workers in California. Voter registration drives, community organization work with the CSO, and the protests against abuses of the bracero program by Oxnard growers all gave Chavez visibility in the Mexican-American community. He met other activists, none more important than Dolores Huerta, another Fred Ross recruit to the CSO in Stockton, and later one of Chavez's most important allies. He learned tactics that he would later apply with great effect in grape and lettuce boycotts. He learned organizing strategies that he would use in forming the United Farm Workers.

Historians often conclude that the African-American civil rights movement paved the way for the protests of others, including those of Native Americans and Mexican Americans. As with most generalizations, there is truth to this one, but it should not blind us to the very real differences between the movements, differences that defy generalization. The American Indian Movement (AIM) of the late sixties and early seventies drew lessons from the Black Power movement, but the complexities of reservation life, the regional particularities of Native American peoples, and the intricacies of many decades of relations with the federal government dictated that Native Americans would have to develop their own strategies. Moreover, the federal policies of the fifties—especially the termination policy—set the stage for AIM's later actions. Similar conclusions can be drawn from the Mexican-American example. The Chicano Power movement of the seventies intentionally echoed the Black Power movement. But as the career of Cesar Chavez clearly shows, Mexican Americans faced a different set of circumstances from those faced by African Americans; in terms of both tactics and allies, Chavez drew more from the labor movement than he did from the civil rights movement, and this pattern was clearly established during the fifties.

Recommended Reading

The civil rights movement has a rich literature. Many excellent works focus on leadership, particularly on the activities of Martin Luther King Jr., and King's own *Stride Toward Freedom: The Montgomery Story* (New York: Harper and Row, 1959) provides a first-person account of the Montgomery bus boycott. The best biographies of King are David L. Lewis's *King: A Critical Biography* (New York: Praeger, 1970) and Taylor Branch's *Parting the Waters: America in the King Years, 1954–1963* (New York: Simon and Schuster, 1988), the first volume of his three-volume study, which covers the development of the movement in the fifties. Robert Brisbane's *The Black Vanguard: Origins of the Negro Social Revolution, 1900–1960* (Valley Forge, Pa.: Judson Press, 1970) and *Black Activism: Racial Revolution in the United States, 1954–1970* (Valley Forge, Pa.: Judson Press, 1974) are briefer accounts that span the fifties. Robert Weisbrot's *Freedom Bound: A History of America's Civil Rights Movement* (New York: Penguin Books, 1991) is a good recent overview. Other participants in the movement, including Ralph Abernathy *(And the Walls Came Tumbling Down: An Autobiography* [New York: HarperCollins, 1991]) and John Lewis *(Walking with the Wind: A Memoir of the Movement* [New York: Simon and Schuster, 1998]), have written memoirs of their participation. William Chafe's *Civilities and Civil Rights: Greensboro, North Carolina, and the Black Struggle for Freedom* (New York: Oxford University Press, 1980) examines the roots of the sit-in movement. J. Harvie Wilkinson III traces the legal case behind school integration and the role the courts in *From Brown to Bakke: The Supreme Court and School Integration, 1954–1978* (New York: Oxford University Press, 1979). Recent literature, including books by Charles Payne *(I've Got the Light of Freedom: The Organizing Tradition and the Mississippi Freedom Struggle* [Berkeley: University of California Press, 1995]) and John Dittmer *(Local People: The Struggle for Civil Rights in Mississippi* [Urbana: University of Illinois Press, 1995]), have begun to examine communities in which the movement made an impact, showing that leadership was able to build on organizations and networks already established in African-American communities.

Peter Iverson's *"We Are Still Here": American Indians in the Twentieth Century* (Wheeling, Ill.: Harlan Davidson, 1998) is a brief, but fine survey. For Mexican Americans, Susan Ferriss and Ricardo Sandoval's *A Fight in the Fields: Cesar Chavez and the Farmworkers Movement* (New York: Harcourt Brace, 1997), a companion book to a PBS documentary, is a concise account that gives balanced attention to Chavez and Mexican-American activism in the fifties.

The Tube and the Big Screen

Television and Movies

AS THE WORLD BECAME COMPLEX and often troubling in the late twentieth century, Americans often looked back with nostalgia to earlier times that seemed to have been simpler, less terrifying, and more stable. Reminiscing about the fifties—its musicals, its Westerns, its televised situation comedies, its cars with large tail fins, the gyrations of a young Elvis Presley—often seemed to provide a nostalgic respite from the difficulties that plagued the nation as it headed toward the end of the millennium. The black-and-white images of fifties television seemed to reinforce mental images of placid simplicity, providing a link not available for retrospectives of seemingly similar decades, like the twenties. All seemed well in this earlier time, when families had two parents, values were rock solid, musical lyrics were inoffensive and comprehensible, and schools were quiet places of learning where student misbehavior was seldom more flagrant than talking out of turn.

Beyond television situation comedies, however, the culture of the fifties was at once richer, darker, and more complex than the comedies or nostalgic reminiscences suggest. Although, in some respects, Americans in the fifties were indeed conformist, in others, they rebelled against conformity. The bomb, the Soviet threat, McCarthyism, the war in Korea, and the emerging divisions in American society—black versus white, rich versus poor, educated versus uneducated—powerfully affected the arts and the entertainment industry. The supporters of McCarthyism made every effort to stifle dissent, which was riskier in the fifties than during most other periods in American history. Yet indications of their failure to do so abound in movies, literature, the theater, and art.

Those who look to the sixties as the decade when American culture and popular arts made a radical break with the past would do well to examine the clear indications that the counterculture, sexual revolution, and virtually every idiom of popular music in the sixties, from folk to rock to jazz and country, were deeply rooted in the formative soil of the fifties.

This chapter examines how television and film developed during the fifties. Chapter 9 will examine the parallel development of art, literature, music, and the theater.

Movies had reigned as the most popular form of mass entertainment since the 1920s. When television became widely accessible in the 1950s, the movie industry shuddered, for fear that it might be supplanted by the small screen. Such fear, though exaggerated, was understandable. Amid the winds of political and cultural change, competition with the new medium would drive the rapid evolution of motion pictures in the 1950s.

The Television Boom

Although Americans have always been fascinated with new technology, television was perhaps unrivaled in its impact on twentieth-century American society. "No other invention," historian J. Ronald Oakley has argued, "not even the motion pictures, automobiles, or radio, brought so much change to so many people in so short a time." For the first time, Americans across the country would be watching and listening to the same shows at the same time. The result made the United States a smaller place. It hastened the decline of regionalism, diminishing differences in accent, attitudes, entertainment, cultural tastes, and preferences in food, clothing, and other consumer goods. Television altered the way Americans used their time, absorbing hours previously spent pursuing other activities. Social critics noted that people spent more time indoors in front of the television and less time on front porches talking to their neighbors. More time watching television meant less time reading. Television seemed even to alter perception and to shorten attention spans.

With the success of experimental telecasts a few years before, communications executives such as David Sarnoff were set to promote the new medium on a national scale in the late thirties. But World War II delayed their plans; limits on frequencies extended the delay after the war. Thus, even though both the technology and the marketing vision were in place earlier, the emergence of television is rightly considered a phenomenon of the fifties.

The impact of television was immediate. Even in 1950, when the federal government continued to constrain its dissemination by limiting available frequencies, television threatened to push aside competing mass media. The motion picture industry, already under assault on the ideological front in Washington because of allegations of Communist influence paraded before sessions of the House Un-American Activities Committee (HUAC), now found its economic position under siege. Movie theaters began to close in cities having even one television channel. In New York City alone, fifty-five movie theaters closed during the first three years of telecasts, 1948–51. Attendance also dropped in the theaters on Broadway. Radio lost many of its biggest stars to television; many others attempting to make the switch failed to meet the far different demands television placed on its performers.

People bought an average of a quarter of a million new television sets each month between 1949 and 1952. The real boom began in 1952, when the Federal Communications Commission (FCC) ended the freeze on new station licenses. By authorizing use of the ultrahigh frequency, or UHF, band of frequencies (300–3,000 MHz) and by expanding the permissible use of the very high frequency, or VHF, band (30–300 MHz), the FCC made possible a dramatic rise in the number of television stations. By the end of the decade, the number of stations more than quintupled, rising from 108 to 562. In 1950, television was still a novelty; only 12 percent of American homes had a set. By 1960, television had become nearly as common as radio. More than 46 million American homes—more than 87 percent—had their own television set, compared to 48.5 million homes with radios, or almost 92 percent.

Comedy became a mainstay on television schedules from the beginning. Production costs were low for comedy shows. Short segments allowed ample time for advertising, and sight gags and skits gave performers countless opportunities to free themselves from the limits of radio. Milton Berle, who began hosting the *Texaco Star Theater* in 1948, became the first television superstar, dominating the airwaves for the eight-year run of his show. Berle's early career had been on the Vaudeville stage, which was a common source of television talent in the early years. His television show departed little from the Vaudeville formula, relying on slapstick and humor that pushed the limits of fifties-era propriety.

Berle's early success spawned many imitators. The comedy show became one of the most popular formats in the early fifties. Sid Caesar and Imogene Coca, who were also Vaudeville veterans, matched Berle's popularity on *Your Show of Shows*. Blessed with phenomenal writers such as Neil Simon and Mel Brooks, the show dominated Saturday-night television from 1950 to 1954.

Almost as popular were television variety shows, with their comedy skits, animal acts, music, dancers, and circus performers. Arthur Godfrey's variety show was among the first, but his tempestuous outbursts attracted as much attention as his guests—several of whom he ordered off the show. Ed Sullivan's *Toast of the Town*, later renamed *The Ed Sullivan Show* (1948–71), became the most venerable show of the genre. Although many of acts on Sullivan's show were amateurish, an appearance there became crucial to success for emerging young talent. The comedy team of Dean Martin and Jerry Lewis first came to national attention on the show. Singer Elvis Presley's appearance, during which cameras focused above his waist to avoid displaying his scandalously gyrating hips, was among the most widely viewed single programs of the decade.

Television quickly latched on to other formulas that soon became staples, most of which adapted successful radio formulas to the visual medium. The "episodic series," as television historian Erik Barnouw labeled it, employed a stock cast of characters, but told a complete story in each appearance. Crime stories were among the most successful of these series. Barnouw recounts that early television dramas were live; to ensure that the story fit within the allotted time, Ralph Bellamy, the hero of the popular show *Man Against Crime*, would expand or contract his quest for clues in a search scene inserted near the end of each show.

Production pressures and the risk of irretrievable error led producers to move away from live production, especially for episodic series. The immediate success in 1951 of *I Love Lucy*, one of the first series to be filmed for television, prompted others to use film. Crime shows found film more versatile. When *Dragnet*, which appeared on film shortly after *Lucy*, became one of the top shows on television, Bellamy's *Man Against Crime* soon followed suit.

Lucille Ball's zany *I Love Lucy*, which aired from 1951 to 1957, became the greatest television hit of the fifties. Ball starred as Lucy with her husband, the Cuban bandleader Desi Arnaz. The improbable couple matched Lucy's madcap antics against Desi's astonished responses, making *Lucy* "a show starring not just one wacko but *two*," as David Halberstam described it. Lucy and Desi's instincts for what would work on the show were unerring, although often contrary to the desires of advertisers and television executives. Ball's demand that Arnaz play her husband on the show, and the couple's insistence that Lucy's pregnancy be treated openly, both met warm responses from audiences, despite the doubts of sponsors and producers. The birth of Desi Arnaz Jr. in January 1953 was one of the major television events of the year.

Ironically, two of the most popular and successful television shows of the fifties portrayed families diametrically opposed in character. If *Lucy* offered daffiness and slapstick, *Ozzie and Harriet*, which debuted in 1952, made a virtue of wholesomeness. The life of the Nelsons centered in the family, and the fact that Ozzie, Harriet, and their sons, David and Ricky, were a "real life" family lent substance to otherwise thin plots. Harriet served as a model wife and mother, always home, usually in the kitchen, offering stability and common sense. Ozzie, a well meaning but naïve and often ineffectual father, seemed to offer reassurance to fathers of baby boomers who could take comfort in Ozzie's bumbling. Ozzie apparently held a job, but what it might have been remained vague. What was clear was that it did not require him to leave home very often. Their sons—rock solid if square David and mischievous but cute Rick—completed the idealized family package. The formula succeeded, and kept the show running for fourteen years.

Other very popular family shows deviated only slightly from the *Ozzie and Harriet* format. *Leave It to Beaver* had more complex and interesting characters, and *Father Knows Best* added the problems of teenage daughters to the mix, but all idealized family life in similar ways. Although television family shows have come to epitomize fifties-era nostalgia, historian Ronald Oakley notes that they actually hark back to earlier years before women began to work outside the home, before their husbands became organization men, and before the complexities of the atomic age descended on the American family.

Westerns provided another popular genre on television, as they did on radio and in motion picture theaters. *The Lone Ranger, Hopalong Cassidy*, Roy Rogers, and Gene Autry offered half-hour morality plays for kids. By the mid-fifties, producers realized, almost by accident, that Westerns would also appeal to older audiences. Jack Warner of Warner Brothers contracted with the National Broadcasting Company (NBC) to provide three short series for its 1955–56 season. *Cheyenne* was the third and least well known of the three. The public reaction surprised Warner and the network. The program soon became a fixture, and ran for seven years. Television success bred imitation, and soon all three networks had weekly Westerns. *Wyatt Earp* and *Gunsmoke* followed the next season. By the end of the decade, Westerns dominated television ratings. The top three shows and five of the top ten were Westerns.

If television made instant stars, it also showed no mercy to those whose careers were in decline. The long run of *I Love Lucy* was the exception, and some of the biggest stars of the early fifties had long since faded away by the end of the decade. By that time, Milton Berle hosted a bowling show. Sid Caesar and Imogene Coca, who together hosted one of the most popular comedy shows of the mid-fifties, faded into obscurity, with only occasional roles, after their split.

The advent of the television age also transformed advertising. In 1950, expenditures for television advertising totaled only $170 million, which accounted for slightly more than 3 percent of total advertising expenditures, placing television far behind newspapers, direct mail, radio, and magazines. By 1960, newspaper advertising remained far in the lead, more than doubling the value of direct mail. But television advertising reached $1.53 billion, nearly 14 percent of the total, nearly as much as direct mail, and surpassing radio and magazines. Stars pitched for their sponsors, as they had done on radio, almost blurring the distinction between content and advertising. Among the most familiar ads on television were Arthur Godfrey's plugs for Lipton Tea, which seemed more like neighbor-to-neighbor conversations over the back fence, Dinah Shore's upbeat warble, "See the U.S.A. in your Chevrolet," and newscaster John Cameron Swayze's reassurance, after subjecting Timex watches to various punishments: "It takes a licking and keeps on ticking."

As advertising revenues soared, television executives soon began to spend more on producing commercials than on regular programming. Barnouw reported that the discrepancy widened; by 1960, television budgets allotted about $2,000 per minute for programming, and $10,000 to $20,000 per minute for ads. The American Broadcasting Company (ABC) became the first network to extend commercial breaks from 30 to 40 seconds, and justified the change by saying it was reducing the number of ads: two 20-second spots would replace three 10-second advertisements. Television industry profits rose accordingly, increasing nearly sixfold during the decade, from $41.6 million in 1951 to $244.1 million in 1960, according to Oakley. Advertisers began to demand influence commensurate with their expenditures, and inevitably some intruded on programming. Usually, advertisers sought to protect the name of their product from any aspersion, actual or implied.

From the beginning, people worried about the influence that television might wield. In 1950, *Reader's Digest* had warned of "hypnosis in your living room." In 1961, after commending television for its production of *Peter Pan*, for *The Twilight Zone*, and for its coverage of the Army-McCarthy hearings and the 1960 presidential campaign debates, recently appointed FCC Chairman Newton Minow challenged viewers to sit before their sets for an entire day: "I can assure you that you will observe a vast wasteland." He criticized situation comedies for portraying "totally unbelievable families," other genre shows including Westerns, gangster shows, and game shows, and he drew especial attention to the "blood and thunder, mayhem, violence, sadism, murder," and commercials that characterized television in the fifties.

Live Television Drama: The Potential of the New Medium

An intriguing alternative to the situation comedies and game shows emerged in the mid-fifties. From 1953 to 1955, television experimented with a genre completely unlike those which would come to dominate its programming. With live theater slumping in New York, and motion pictures scrambling to contend with both McCarthyism and the advent of television, some of the most talented writers, producers, directors, and actors of the era were free to lend their skills to televised dramas.

Starting in 1953 with *Philco Television Playhouse*, *Goodyear Television Playhouse*, and *Kraft Television Theater*, viewers had the opportunity to watch live performances of a caliber never before been seen by most Americans. Other series, most notably *Playhouse 90* and the *U.S. Steel Hour*, joined the lineup the following year, and eventually a dozen theater productions occupied prime-time hours. Paddy Chayefsky and other leading writers of Hollywood and Broadway produced scripts designed for the time and space limitations of television theater. The acting was often superb, by newcomers such as Paul Newman, Sidney Poitier, Rod Steiger, and Joanne Woodward, whose names would grace movie marquees in later years. Leading movie directors such as Arthur Penn and Sidney Lumet had only a week to prepare their casts for the live performances. The results were often dazzling, and some of the dramas, such as the jury-room drama *12 Angry Men*, later found their way to the big screen. Chayefsky's *Marty*, considered one of the best of the genre, also later became a motion picture.

The live performances had an immediacy that could not be duplicated after taped programming became commonplace. Whereas motion pictures could awe their audiences with vast outdoor settings, television's restricted production budgets and the state of its technology demanded that television dramas be staged in small studios. The dramas thus showcased writing and acting in ways that movies did not. Nor were themes necessarily restricted by space limitations. The sinking of the *Titanic* found its way to the small screen in an adaption of Walter Lord's best-selling book *A Night to Remember*. The most successful single entertainment show of the decade was NBC's production of *Peter Pan*. Broadcast in 1955, with Mary Martin starring as Peter Pan and Cyril Ritchard as Captain Hook, the show attracted 65 million viewers.

Television and the News

Although television would transform the way Americans got their news, by the end of the fifties, the transformation had only begun. Radio news had matured during World War II, when its foreign correspondents developed their craft in European capitals under siege. Early television could barely compete. Filmed location shots had to be developed and shipped back to the States, a process that took nearly a day under the best of conditions, whereas radio could broadcast instantly from major cities around the world. The closest parallel to television news was the movie-theater newsreel, which took even longer than televised news to reach its audience, and which consequently was the first to succumb to the onslaught of television.

The earliest televised newscasts were short—only 15 minutes long—and featured mainly "talking heads." But the heads belonged to talented men, seasoned by the demands of radio news. John Cameron Swayze, Douglas Edwards, and Edward R. Murrow headlined the network newscasts. Between news segments, they unabashedly hawked their sponsor's products, from cigarettes to Timex watches.

Murrow, the most influential television newsman of his generation, had earned his credentials broadcasting from Berlin and London during the late thirties and early forties. At CBS in 1951, Murrow and television executive Fred W. Friendly pioneered the feature news program *See It Now*, which explored some difficult issues but, for the first two years, skirted the dominant question of the day, that of McCarthyism. Nevertheless, Murrow used the program to probe the potential of television to engage public issues in ways that no one else did. One such way was his handling of the case of Air Force

Lieutenant Milo Radulovich, who'd been asked to resign from the Air Force because of the alleged radical activities of his father and sister. Murrow agreed that the Air Force ought not to dismiss Radulovich on the dubious grounds of associating with his father and sister, against whom the charges were unspecified in any case. When the Air Force turned down Murrow's invitation to present its position, Murrow decided to go ahead anyway. Otherwise, he reasoned, anyone could veto a show simply by refusing to speak. The show embarrassed the Air Force, which withdrew its demand for Radulovich's resignation.

In 1953, Murrow created another show, *Person to Person,* on which he visited the homes of celebrities in order, he claimed, to do what he really wanted to do on *See It Now.* Beginning in 1953, Murrow initiated a series of programs attacking Senator Joseph McCarthy (see chapter 3). By letting McCarthy speak for himself, by letting the American public see him firsthand, the series helped to diminish McCarthy. The programs demonstrated both the immediate impact that television could have on public affairs and the level of pressure that sponsors and politicians could exert on producers of such shows. Both of Murrow's feature news shows became prototypes for news programming for decades. Other networks produced excellent documentaries, such as NBC's *Victory at Sea,* a review of the naval war of World War II with a stirring score by composer Richard Rogers. But perhaps only someone of Murrow's stature could have consistently engaged such controversial issues. He was there first.

Murrow's attack on McCarthy was but one of the milestones in television news during the fifties. Most dramatically television showed its potential to influence politics. It could promote political careers or savage them. Vice President Nixon, the central figure in several of television's most important broadcasts of the fifties, felt both the kiss and the sting of the new medium. His 1952 "Checkers speech," which salvaged his place on the 1952 Republican ticket, and his "kitchen debate" with Soviet Premier Nikita Khrushchev in 1959, which assisted his bid to win the Republican presidential nomination in 1960, bolstered him at key points in his career. His televised debates with John F. Kennedy in 1960 may have cost him the presidency.

For a medium that seemed best suited to small-scale studio productions, television fared remarkably well in its coverage of large-scale events. The major political parties' political conventions in 1952 provided high-stakes drama, with the battle between Robert Taft and Dwight D. Eisenhower, on the Republican side, and Adlai Stevenson's "draft," on the Democratic.

Thanks to television, John F. Kennedy emerged as a national figure with his stirring nomination speech for Adlai Stevenson. Network coverage was expensive, television equipment cumbersome. Erik Barnouw claimed that CBS brought a hundred television cameras to the 1956 conventions, that NBC had ten thousand pounds of equipment, and that television cables ran everywhere: in the convention halls, down the aisles, and through the halls in the hotels where contenders stayed.

By the end of the decade, the impact of television advertising on the print media begun to be felt. Plagued by declining advertising revenues as corporations shifted to television commercials, newspapers and magazines declined in number. Although circulation climbed during the decade, a trend toward consolidation (which would accelerate in the 1960s) resulted in the demise of venerable newspapers in Brooklyn, Boston, and Los Angeles. Major chains such as Scripps-Howard began to absorb competitors. Several popular magazines also closed down. The publisher Crowell-Collier was especially hard hit, and eventually stopped publishing *Collier's, The American Mercury,* and *Woman's Home Companion.* Television did not lead to the demise of photojournalism, however, as some had feared—at least not in the fifties. *Life* and *Look,* in particular, fared well in the decade. Readers of these magazines reported that the images from the magazines were more indelible than those they'd seen on television.

Overall, however, magazines survived the onslaught of television more successfully than newspapers, at least at first. Advertising revenue for specialty magazines increased dramatically at the dawn of the age of television: in 1955, it was double what it had been in 1946. Americans in the fifties were better educated, and had more leisure time than they had immediately after the end of World War II. New magazines reflected their changing tastes. *TV Guide,* launched in 1952, and *Sports Illustrated,* inaugurated two years later, were the most successful magazine publishing ventures of the decade. Indeed, the dominant trend in magazines from the late forties through the fifties was toward specialization.

The move from cities to suburbs had a negative impact on profits from magazine sales. It forced magazines to find sales venues other than newsstands—drugstores and commercial outlets, for example—where distribution were higher. Sales by subscription increased, but profits were lower than for single-copy sales, and processing fees were higher. Postage costs began to increase, further cutting into profits. And television did eventually make inroads into readership.

By the early sixties, specialization and proliferation of titles, some with narrow audiences, would give rise to another boom in the magazine business. On the other hand, the sixties would also be a bust for some of the standards that had been in existence for decades, leading even the most successful of magazines, such as *Life* and *Look,* to radically reformat themselves or to cease publication altogether.

Spectator Sports: New Empires

Professional sports underwent a surge in popularity in the fifties. Spectators who watched the three major professional sports in fifties America—baseball, football, and basketball—caught a glimpse of the future in three important developments. First, African-American athletes began to demonstrate their crucial, and eventually dominant, role in the games. Second, television made sporting events accessible, marketable, and profitable. Third, sports franchises began to operate more like businesses, moving to other cities when they say the chance to maximize profits.

During the fifties, a core of incredibly talented African-American athletes showed off their skills in baseball, football, and basketball, performing at such a high level that by decade's end there was no longer a question of turning back to the days of segregated major league sports. Integration came to major league baseball in 1947, when Jackie Robinson joined the Brooklyn Dodgers. Later in the year, Larry Doby played his first game for the Cleveland Indians, thus becoming the first African American to play on an American League team. Although Robinson and Doby had broken the color barrier, discrimination remained a routine part of the game in the fifties. Black athletes still had to be more talented than their white teammates to make it to the big leagues; those who followed the two pioneers still had to endure the racist taunts of spectators and hotels on road trips that refused to admit African Americans.

Despite the continuing hostility they encountered, African American athletes began to transform the game of baseball in the fifties. Robinson's grace and speed made him one of the two or three most exciting players of his era, and his ability to withstand racism enabled other black athletes to transfer from the old Negro League. The Dodgers brought catcher Roy Campanella and pitcher Don Newcombe to join Robinson, and the trio thrust the Dodgers into the pennant race each year in the fifties. Across town, the New York Giants introduced Willie Mays, whose speed was a match for Robinson's, and whose ability to hit home runs placed him beside Mickey Mantle. Mays's fielding ability astounded longtime observers of the game. In the 1954 World Series against Cleveland, racing toward the center field wall with his back to the infield, Mays caught a ball off the bat of Cleveland's Vic Wertz on a dead run, when it seemed that the ball would easily fall for extra bases. Mays then wheeled in one motion and threw the ball back to the infield, holding the runners and preserving a tie that the Giants would break in extra innings; for years, it was remembered simply as "The Catch." It was one of the indelible baseball moments of the fifties, matched perhaps only by Bobby Thompson's grand slam home run to win the National League pennant for the Giants over the Dodgers in a one-game playoff in 1951, and Yankee Don Larsen's first-ever World Series perfect game in 1956. Ernie Banks of the Chicago Cubs and Henry Aaron of the Milwaukee Braves were other African-American players whose superstar abilities earned them Most Valuable Player Awards, and whose demeanor won the respect of fans.

It was New York, though, that dominated major league baseball in the fifties. From 1948 through 1956, the Dodgers, Giants, or (usually) the Yankees won the World Series. Each team had a spectacular center fielder: Mays for the Giants, Duke Snyder for the Dodgers, and Mickey Mantle for the Yankees (who'd replaced Joe DiMaggio in 1951). Between 1950 and 1960, the Yankees won six World Series, the Giants and the Dodgers one each. When the Milwaukee Braves broke through to win in 1957, New Yorkers acted as if a pretender had usurped their rightful title.

New York's domination of the world of professional baseball came to a surprising end when Dodger owner Walter O'Malley announced that he would move the team to Los Angeles for the 1958 season. The Giants followed suit, and announced that they would move to San Francisco. At the time, there were no major league baseball teams west of Kansas City; the move echoed demographic changes that had swelled the population of the West Coast in the postwar period. The Dodgers and Giants weren't the first teams to move in the fifties: the Braves had moved from Boston to Milwaukee, the Athletics from Philadelphia to Kansas City, and the Browns from Saint Louis to Baltimore. But the transcontinental moves by the Dodgers and Giants left New York City with no National League franchise, and transformed the intracity rivalry into a rivalry between California's two largest cities. New Yorkers protested the moves as soon as O'Malley's plans leaked out, but to no avail. The era truly came to an end with the demolition in 1960 of Ebbets Field, where the Dodgers had played since 1913. Although the Giants' Polo Grounds saw action briefly in 1962 and 1963, when an expansion team, the Mets, began operations, it, too, was demolished in 1964—by the same wrecking ball that had demolished Ebbets Field.

Franchise shifts reflected demographic trends. The downtown districts of old cities in the northeast were in decline, and the Sunbelt was booming. Boston couldn't support two teams. There was limited parking around some of the old ball parks: Ebbets Field, the Polo Grounds, and Braves Field in Boston all dated to the second decade of the century, when the automobile was still a novelty. Attendance declined at the old stadiums, and California beckoned, a market open for development.

Professional football also began to sign African-American players, although it lagged behind baseball by a decade. Jim Brown, an all-American fullback at Syracuse University, joined the Cleveland Browns in 1957. Although he played for only nine years, he was the league's leading rusher for eight years, and for many years held the record for the most yards gained by a running back. He made the Pro-Bowl, the pro football equivalent of an all-star game, every year he played.

Television contributed immeasurably to the increased popularity of professional sports. The championship game of 1958 marked football's coming of age as a marketable television entity that might rival baseball, which, to this point, had dominated television sports coverage. The game, played in Yankee Stadium before 64,185 fans and a national television audience, pitted the Baltimore Colts, led by quarterback Johnny Unitas and his favorite receiver, Raymond Berry, and the New York Giants, who featured running back Frank Gifford and kicker Pat Summerall. The Colts tied the game with a field goal as time was running out; at the end of regulation play, the game was tied at 17. Professional football entered the first overtime game in its history. Running back Alan Ameche's touchdown won the professional football "game of the century" for the Colts, 23–17.

Professional basketball underwent the most complete transformation of all the professional sports as a result of the advent of African-American athletes. The agents of change, the counterparts of baseball's Branch Rickey and Jackie Robinson, were the Boston Celtic's Red Auerbach and Bill Russell. Russell had led the University of San Francisco to two national championships in 1954 and 1955, and Auerbach already had a reputation as a crafty coach. Auerbach traded away a popular player to get the rights to draft Russell, and as

David Halberstam observed, "with that trade, Auerbach went from being very smart to being a genius." Russell became the dominant defensive player of his era, celebrated for his willingness to put the team ahead of individual records, in which respect contemporaries contrasted him to the other dominant player of the fifties and sixties, Wilt Chamberlain. Chamberlain ran up scoring records, and once scored a hundred points in a single game, but Russell and the Celtics captured the championships, winning eight in nine years. Russell and Chamberlain transformed professional basketball from a game in which perimeter shooters and ball-handling guards controlled the game to one in which no team could expect to win consistently without a mobile, quick, durable big man.

The Disney Phenomenon: The Magic Kingdom and Disney's Entertainment Empire

Few success stories of the postwar era can approach that of Walt Disney. A son of the American Midwest, Disney was born in Chicago in 1901, and grew up in Kansas City, Missouri. By the dawn of the fifties, he'd already established a reputation as one of the pioneering innovators in Hollywood, having built an animation studio and produced popular full-length cartoon features. *Snow White and the Seven Dwarfs*, his first full-length cartoon, appeared in 1937. His hallmark cartoon figure, Mickey Mouse, was already widely recognized.

That was all prologue to the expansion of his entertainment empire in the fifties, which by the end of the decade included television, feature films, documentaries, educational programs, and an amusement park that became a prototype for theme parks across the nation. Disney made his first foray into television in 1950 with a special on NBC. After resisting appeals from the networks to develop a weekly program, he finally agreed in 1954, signing a seven-year contract with ABC, which pledged support for the building of Disneyland, the theme park he planned to build in Anaheim, California.

The *Disneyland* show, which first aired in the fall of 1954, quickly became one of the most successful weekly shows on television. Hosted by Disney himself, the show proved an effective vehicle for promoting other Disney products, from nature documentaries to television specials, and especially for generating interest in the Disneyland amusement park then under construction. Disney divided the television show into segments that paralleled the areas in his park: "Fantasyland," "Frontierland," "Adventureland," and "Tomorrowland."

The show did very well, but one feature moved beyond mere popularity to become an icon of American popular culture. Starring Fess Parker, the three-part series *Davy Crockett* mythologized the life of the American frontiersman, and his heroic death at the Alamo in the war with Mexico in the 1840s. *Davy Crockett* inspired one of the more conspicuous fads of the fifties, the wearing of coonskin caps, complete with trailing tail. Even Estes Kefauver, who came from Crockett's home state of Tennessee, sported one occasionally when he made his bid for the Democratic nomination for president in 1956. But everything about the show, from its ballad theme song to anything with the name Davy Crockett stamped on it, became marketable. Disney biographer Steven Watts quoted a storekeeper who remarked, "Anything with hair on it moved." *Time* magazine claimed, "Davy Crockett is bigger even than Mickey Mouse."

The mouse struck back that fall. Disney started a show for kids, *The Mickey Mouse Club,* and soon had another hit. Airing in the early evening every weekday, and featuring a regular cast of energetic all-American kids called the "Mouseketeers," who wore large felt mouse ears, the show and its catchy theme song had kids around the country chanting, "Who's the leader of the club that's made for you and me? M-I-C . . . See you real soon! K-E-Y . . . Why? Because we like you! M-O-U-S-E." The show's young stars, the Mouseketeers, became role models; well groomed, bouncy, respectful, endlessly cheerful, they cemented the Disney connection to American family life. The most popular member of the cast, Annette Funicello, received hundreds of letters from fans each week. The show featured variety-show types of entertainment aimed at preteen kids, including cartoons, music, comedy, and serialized stories. It proved to be another successful marketing vehicle as well, and mouse ears became as popular as coonskin caps as the Magic Kingdom became a financial empire.

Disney also contributed to the popularization of science, and used television and movies to help make scientific breakthroughs more accessible. The nature documentary films of the early and mid-fifties, including *The Living Desert* (1953) and *The Vanishing Prairie* (1954) ran as feature films in theaters across the country. He took science education to the small screen in the late fifties, most significantly in a series of *Man in Space* specials, in which Disney appeared with rocket expert Wernher von Braun. Disney leavened serious science with comedy, making the shows as entertaining as they were educational.

The Disneyland theme park, in Anaheim, was the capstone of Disney's entertainment empire, and succeeded at many levels. Never had an attraction been so effectively promoted even while still under construction. Fans of Disney's television shows came to the park predisposed to like it. The park was a model of planning, relying on psychology to engage peoples' interest, move them efficiently through the park grounds, and convey a consistent set of values. By the late fifties, it was one of the premier tourist attractions in the nation, even making international headlines when, for security reasons, the State Department refused to allow Soviet Premier Nikita Khrushchev to visit there during his trip to the United States.

From the time they parked their cars, visitors to Disneyland encountered an efficient organization that kept them moving without making them feel rushed. Trams transported them from their cars to the gate, and by the early sixties an elevated monorail brought people from the Disneyland Hotel (another enterprise of the Disney empire) to the entrance. Once inside, people walked down Main Street, U.S.A., a turn-of-the-century main street meant to make people feel comfortable rather than leave them awestruck. Even the scale was reduced: to nine-tenths scale on the first floors of the façades, and to eight-tenths on the second floors. Young employees, scrubbed clean, wearing conservative clothes and short haircuts, drilled in the skills of making guests feel welcome, spread out through the park. Every surface looked clean, new, and freshly painted. At the end of Main Street, the park avoided congestion by having people fan out into the "lands": Fantasyland, Adventureland, Frontierland, Tomorrowland. Disney's engineers designed the waiting lines in front of major attractions to make it seem that the lines moved constantly, reducing visitor frustration. Some five million people visited each year, and most expressed high satisfaction with their visit.

Disneyland celebrated Americana, technology, and capitalism. As people strolled down Main Street, U.S.A., they could stop and see a robotic Abraham Lincoln rise and address his audience. Rides and exhibits highlighted the American past, the state-of-the-art technology of its present, and promise of a future that emphasized technological achievement. Corporate sponsors enjoyed visibility; many had shops in the park, and others sponsored rides.

Disneyland was not without its critics. An article in *The Nation* in 1958 condemned the Magic Kingdom as "a sickening blend of cheap formulas packaged to sell." Writer Julian Halevy blasted the park for appealing to a conformist society, providing it with "tranquilizers for social anxiety." Critics might find fault, but the pervasive philosophy of Disney's many enterprises struck a responsive chord among Americans in the fifties and beyond. As Steven Watts noted, Disney "defined American traditions, built a cultural embankment around them, and assumed a defensive position." Although other entertainment conglomerates would seek to form multimedia networks through merger late in the century, Disney's was uniquely successful not only in exploiting the economic potential of new technology and family entertainment, but also in linking the growth of an entertainment empire to basic American values.

Quiz Shows: Television's First Scandal

In the mid-fifties, the quiz show leapfrogged over other genres: quiz shows became the most popular shows on television. Most popular of all was *The $64,000 Question,* which debuted in June 1955 and within five weeks became the number-one show on television. $64,000 was a staggering figure in the fifties, and the fact that contestants could win it only by risking double or nothing after reaching the $32,000 level created scintillating tension, heightened by confinement in an onstage "isolation booth" for the final, most lucrative questions.

The show's incredible success spawned a slew of imitators; by 1956, the new genre moved toward dominating television's prime hours. *Tic Tac Dough, Twenty-One,* and *Beat the Jackpot* joined the lineup. *The $64,000 Question* even produced a clone, *The $64,000 Challenge,* and at one point the two shows were first and second in the ratings. In the summer of 1957, five of the top eight television shows were quiz shows. CBS led the rankings on the strength of its quiz shows.

Ratings were so strong and advertising revenues so high that television producers could not refrain from trying to improve the their golden goose. The quiz shows sustained viewer interest from week to week by requiring successful contestants to return several weeks in a row to maximize their winnings, thus creating stars with substantial public followings. The temptation to ensure that the most attractive contestants would be sure to return proved irresistible. Producers rationalized that they were providing entertainment, not pure contests. Soon, the fix was on. Methods varied, from selecting easier questions for desirable contestants to asking them "practice" questions that were later used during the actual show. Before long, cheating became more overt. Managers coached contestants in facial expressions and body language that heightened suspense, and fed them answers. Ultimately, when their popularity began to wane, contestants had to deliberately miss answers at dramatic moments. It was great theater, and the quiz shows dominated their time slots. But it was fraudulent.

NBC's *Twenty-One* soon became, in the words of David Halberstam, "the prototype of the completely crooked show." It was also where the scam began to unravel. The most dramatic showdown pitted Herb Stempel, a student at the City College of New York who'd won $49,000, against Charles Van Doren, an instructor at Columbia University whose father, mother, aunt, and uncle were all well-known intellectuals. Stempel's popularity had run its course, and NBC executives ordained that he had to take a dive against the attractive and popular Van Doren on a show in December 1956. Stempel was particularly chagrined about the question he had to miss—What movie won the Academy Award for best picture of 1955? Stempel had seen *Marty,* the winning film, three times.

Stempel decided to tell his story to the press. A Grand Jury in New York and the FCC's congressional oversight committee launched probes. Although, for a time, Van Doren protested his innocence, he finally confessed. He explained how he had rationalized that his victories were helping education. Ultimately, although the public sympathized with him, Van Doren lost his job at Columbia and received a suspended sentence.

The floodgates opened: the investigation revealed that cheating permeated game shows. Many contestants suffered the taint of the scandal for many years, but a few survived with their reputations intact and went on to successful careers. Dr. Joyce Brothers, one of those cleared of charges, became a media psychologist. Patty Duke, too young at the time of her appearance to retain the stigma, became a successful actress.

To many Americans, the quiz show scandal symbolized a betrayal of public trust on a grand scale, the end of an age of innocence. Details revealing the depth of the scandal came out as Americans were reeling from the Soviets' successful launch of the Sputnik satellite in October 1957. To make matters worse, another scandal shocked the entertainment industry during the quiz show investigation. The burgeoning record business depended on radio to publicize new music. In a scandal soon dubbed "payola," record companies paid disc jockeys kickbacks in order to ensure their records would receive airtime.

Motion Pictures: The Course of a Beleaguered Medium

The movie industry began the fifties under siege. The politics of Mc-
Carthyism posed the most serious political threat in the history of the industry. Falling attendance and the growing popularity of television offered little
hope that movies would ever return to the popularity they'd achieved during
the Depression. The studio system, foundation of film production for
decades, was in decline.

The most publicized assault, and the most difficult to counter because it
set workers within the industry against one another, came from allegations of
Communist influence in the industry. The investigations of the Hollywood
Ten and subsequent congressional inquiries ate at the core of the industry,
prompting an orgy of "naming names" that destroyed careers and fostered
distrust. By 1951, major film executives had come to accept blacklisting of
some of its best talent as a means to avoid further congressional scrutiny; caution led them to approve production only of "safe" movies, which were for
the most part uninspired.

A precipitous decline in attendance rightly frightened executives. Revenues plunged by nearly a third during the decade, from $1.4 billion to $951
million. Television and politics were the largest threats, but many attractions
other than movies were now competing for the leisure dollars of Americans.
Spectator and participatory sports were growing in popularity, as was travel.

By the end of the decade, films produced by independents outnumbered
those produced by studios. The total number of films released dropped by
more than 40 percent during the decade to about 250 in 1960. Producers
began filming on location rather than in Hollywood studios. Studios in Los
Angeles, originally located at the edge of the city but, with urban sprawl, now
sitting on choice land, found that they could make more money by selling off
property than by holding on to it.

The industry's response was multifaceted. One solution was to innovate,
not with what films showed, but with *how* they showed it. The most unusual
technical innovation was 3-D, a spectacular, but short-lived gimmick that attracted people back to the theaters out of curiosity—but not much more: 3-D
films tended to have little by way of a story line, and the audience was obliged
to wear specially designed viewing glasses. It lasted only three years, from
1952 to 1954. Another mid-fifties cinematographic experiment, Cinerama,
used a three-projector system to create the exciting illusion of movement. The

audience could experience roller coaster rides, airplane flights, and train rides from the comfort of their theater seats. Unveiled with considerable fanfare, Cinerama was done in by high installation costs, imperfect technology, and an inability to sustain viewer interest. CinemaScope, introduced in 1953 by Twentieth Century Fox as "the modern miracle you can see without glasses," fared better, lasting into the sixties. Its wide-screen (twice as wide as those before), Technicolor images were genuine improvements on television's small, black-and-white ones. Perhaps the most bizarre technical innovation was Smell-O-Vision, which pumped smells through openings at each seat of a Chicago movie theater. It was soon joined by Aroma-Rama, which used a theater's ventilation system to spread odors. Mercifully, difficulties in synchronizing smells with sights and sounds and in clearing out old smells to make way for new quickly spelled an end to both.

Another Hollywood response to declining attendance was to produce big-budget films, soon dubbed "blockbusters." The most expensive of all was *Ben-Hur* (1959), produced in Rome at a cost of $15 million. Close behind was *The Ten Commandments* (1956), which cost $13 million to produce. Charlton Heston had the distinction of starring in both these blockbusters. Classical and biblical themes lent themselves well to big-screen, big-budget epics, as attested by the $7 million *Quo Vadis?* (1951) and by *The Robe* (1953), the first feature film to be shown in CinemaScope. Other blockbusters included *War and Peace, The King and I, Around the World in 80 Days,* and *Moby Dick* (all 1956), each of which cost $5 million or more.

To sell movies, Hollywood fell back on formula pictures and looked to the theater and even to television for inspiration. The Western, popular since the thirties, continued to be a tried-and-true genre. Some of the Westerns of the fifties, more complex than their predecessors, became classics of the genre, such as George Stevens's *Shane* (1952) and John Ford's *The Searchers* (1956). The musical was another genre that continued to have broad appeal, as attested by the popularity of *Singin' in the Rain* (1952), *White Christmas* (1954), *Guys and Dolls* (1955), *The King and I* (1956), and *Gigi* (1958). To combat declining attendance, Hollywood even turned to television as a source for ideas. Two of the best dramatic films of the decade, Delbert Mann's *Marty* (1955) and Sidney Lumet's *12 Angry Men* (1957), came to the big screen via television—as did directors Mann and Lumet.

Hollywood had always recognized that sex sold, and became bolder in its exploitation in the fifties. Ever mindful of limits imposed by production codes and social mores, the industry pushed those limits ever further. Since the epics of the silent film era, Hollywood had learned that it could evade restrictions and dress its leading ladies in revealing clothing so long as the films they appeared in were biblical or classical epics, a tradition that remained alive in the fifties. The openly sexual performance of European actresses such as Brigitte Bardot, Sophia Loren, and Anita Ekberg in foreign films made possible American films that took greater latitude with sex and that expressed frankly sexual themes. *From Here to Eternity* (1953) centered on the issue of marital infidelity, and *Compulsion* (1958) had homosexuality as its theme. Hollywood adapted best-selling books with sexual themes to the screen, most notably, *Lady Chatterley's Lover* (1956) and *Peyton Place* (1959).

American films in the fifties generally took contrasting approaches to sex. Doris Day consistently played the "girl next door," cute, wholesome, and refusing to consider sex outside of marriage, in decorous films where she usually enticed, cajoled, and trapped her men into marriage. At the other extreme, two other American actresses starred in films that used the open display of sexuality to sell themselves. Having entered the movie business as a child actor, Elizabeth Taylor had several roles in the fifties that cast her as a temptress. Ads for Tennessee Williams's *Cat on a Hot Tin Roof* (1958) showed Taylor in a seductive pose beside the tag, "This is Maggie the Cat." Her offscreen affairs and multiple marriages only served to heighten public interest in her. The most widely recognized sex symbol of the fifties, however, was Marilyn Monroe. Monroe radiated sex on the screen. With an attractive figure, appealing face, and a voice and walk that exuded sex, she had multiple roles that typecast her as the dumb blond, whose innocent remarks were loaded with innuendo. Her tight-fitting clothes and sultry voice completed the image. In *The Seven Year Itch* (1955), Monroe stood on a subway grate as the air from below lifted her dress in what became one of the most memorable film moments of the decade. Like Taylor, her offscreen life only added to her mystique. Marriages to playwright Arthur Miller and New York Yankee star Joe DiMaggio both ended in divorce. Between 1950 and her death in 1962 from an overdose of sleeping pills, Monroe would act in twenty-three films. Those who worked with her claimed that she had acting talents that her stock roles never allowed her to develop.

The issue of McCarthyism had to be handled more gingerly than the attendance problem. The most direct response was the anti-Communist film, and the studios ground out a number of them, more as a means of proving

11. Marilyn Monroe, appearing in Korea with the USO Camp Show "Anything Goes," poses after a performance at the 3rd U.S. Infantry Division area, February 17, 1954. War and Conflict no. 1466, Record Group 111: Records of the Office of the Chief Signal Officer, 1860–1982, Special Media Archives Services Division (NWCS-S), National Archives at College Park, NAIL Control no. NWDNS-111-SC-452342.

their patriotism than of producing anything of quality. Indeed, most such movies were low-budget and embarrassingly thin on plot. Communists in these films were easily recognizable. In the words of critic Stephen J. Whitfield: they "treat[ed] the Stars and Stripes with contempt. [They were] rude, humorless, and cruel to animals." *I Was a Communist for the FBI* (1951) and *Red Snow* (1952) were typical of the genre, but perhaps none fit the mold as well as *My Son John* (1952), in which a mother realizes that her son has turned Communist. The son eventually confesses, only to be murdered by Communists on the steps of the Lincoln Memorial. Although not of the genre, *The Caine Mutiny* (1954), based on Herman Wouk's Pulitzer Prize–winning novel, nodded in the direction of authority, and also reflected the high regard accorded the military during the fifties. Junior officers on the USS *Caine* mutiny against a captain who has lost control of his sense of judgment, but in the final scenes the film delivers the message that obedience to authority supersedes independent judgment.

Perhaps the most significant film of the decade, *On the Waterfront* (1954), reflected director Elia Kazan's own experience in the maelstrom of McCarthyism. Kazan had joined the Communist Party in 1934 and left it in 1936. He went on to an illustrious career as a director, winning a Tony Award (for best director in the theater) and an Academy Award for best director in a motion picture (for *Gentleman's Agreement* in 1947). In 1952, HUAC summoned him to appear. He agonized over his testimony, but decided that he would cooperate with the committee and name names. His public statements, in an ad in the *New York Times* and in his autobiography written years later, explained his actions, presenting one of the most articulate defenses of cooperation with HUAC. He based his decision on the corruption of the system he'd supported twenty years earlier, and claimed that to refuse to cooperate would undermine the system that had made his career possible. Not to cooperate, he realized and candidly admitted, would also destroy his career.

Kazan approached his former friend, the playwright Arthur Miller, and asked him to write the screenplay for *Waterfront.*. Miller, who had offered his own reading of McCarthyism in his play *The Crucible,* refused; he could not abide Kazan's decision to cooperate with HUAC. Kazan and Miller's was only one of many friendships shattered by the McCarthy purge. Kazan then approached Budd Schulberg, who had also named names before HUAC, and Schulberg accepted. Kazan enlisted a talented cast, including Marlon Brando, Lee J. Cobb, Karl Malden, Eva Marie Saint, and Rod Steiger. Brando and Saint won Academy Awards for their performances, Brando as best actor and Saint as best supporting actress.

On the Waterfront casts Brando as a dockworker and former boxer who turns informer against a corrupt labor boss. The film overlays moral dilemma with religious symbolism, wrapping the informer in the mantle of self-redemption. Thus despite the film's undoubted power, by favoring the informer Kazan minimizes his own excruciating moral dilemma.

Fifties films also warned of the threat of nuclear war, and science fiction was the preferred genre to convey the message. Movies with plots suggesting threats from outer space, from earthbound mutations, or from the depths of the sea played on the pervasive fear of uncontrollable forces. *The Day the Earth Stood Still* (1951), *Them* (1954), *Godzilla: King of the Monsters* (1956), and *The Blob* (1958) were typical; most used a contrived plot to sustain the ever-present threat as long as possible. *Forbidden Planet* and *The Invasion of the Body Snatchers* (both 1956) had more thoughtful plots that introduced psychological elements into the story line. By most assessments, the best film to confront the nuclear threat was *On the Beach* (1959), set in Australia and based on Nevil Shute's novel. The film depicted people confronting the inevitable end of the human race in the aftermath of a nuclear war, as a cloud of lethal radiation drifted closer.

The Hollywood of the fifties took cautious steps in addressing social issues. *Broken Arrow* (1950) opened the decade with an unusually sympathetic treatment of Indians, and *The Defiant Ones* (1958) closed it with its critical treatment of racial intolerance. Juvenile delinquency emerged as a serious social issue in the fifties, and *Blackboard Jungle* (1955), a film better known for its theme song ("Rock Around the Clock") than its content, explored it in the context of an inner city high school. The "rebellious youth" theme received its most prominent showing, however, in *Rebel Without a Cause* (1955), the film that made actor James Dean into a cult figure. Dean had played in bit parts early in the fifties, but in 1954 and 1955, he earned feature roles in *Rebel* and two other films, *East of Eden* (1955), which was based on a John Steinbeck novel, and *Giant* (1956), in which he appeared with Elizabeth Taylor and Rock Hudson. In late September 1955, a month before the release of *Rebel,* Dean's fatal crash in his Porsche Spider secured his cult status. He became the symbol of disenchanted youth, a role he played brilliantly on the screen in his clothes, demeanor, and sneer.

One fifties film stood out for defying the pressures of genre, conformity, patriotism, and box office. *The Salt of the Earth* (1954) told the story of a strike by Mexican-American miners based on a strike by zinc miners in 1951–52. Using the strike as a theme enraged HUAC and other anti-Communist crusaders since it had been conducted by a union that had been expelled from the CIO because of allegations that it was under the control of Communists. Director Herbert Biberman was one of the Hollywood Ten, and many of the key individuals involved in the production had been accused of Communist associations, so perhaps theirs was the courage of those with nothing to lose. The film encountered strong opposition during production. Mainstream Hollywood unions prohibited their members from participating. The Immigration and Naturalization Service barred a Mexican actress from entering the country, and thugs attacked the cars of people involved in production, and even some of the people themselves. *The Salt of the Earth* showed briefly in several cities, but pressure convinced most theaters to turn it down.

Recommended Reading

In addition to books that examine particular media, there are good overviews of the culture of the fifties. Stephen J. Whitfield's *The Culture of the Cold War* (Baltimore: Johns Hopkins University Press, 1991) includes excellent analytical chapters on television and film. *The Other Fifties: Interrogating Midcentury American Icons* (Urbana: University of Illinois Press, 1997), edited by Joel Forman, offers interpretive essays about icons in society, popular media, and print.

Erik Barnouw's *Tube of Plenty: The Evolution of American Television,* 2nd, revised edition (New York: Oxford University Press, 1990) is an abridgment of Barnouw's classic three-volume study, widely regarded as the best work on the history of television. See also Karal Marling's *As Seen on TV: The Visual Culture of Everyday Life in the 1950s* (Cambridge, Mass.: Harvard University Press, 1994). On film, see Nora Sayre, *Running Time: Films of the Cold War* (New York: Doubleday, 1982).

The development of the multiple components of the Disney entertainment empire is explored in Steven Watts's *The Magic Kingdom: Walt Disney and the American Way of Life* (Boston: Houghton Mifflin, 1997).

9

The Nonconformist Fifties

The Arts and Popular Culture
During the Cold War

RUNNING COUNTER TO THE CONFORMITY of the fifties, a powerful nonconformist current prepared the way for the counterculture of the sixties. Artists have always refused to accept society's norms, whether in America or in Europe, and those of the conformist fifties were no exception. In painting, literature, theater, and music, men and women defied convention, sometimes in dramatic fashion.

Black Mountain College: Early Counterculture

One of the signal moments in the creative reaction against society's pressure to conform occurred in 1952. Gathering at Black Mountain College in North Carolina, a magnet for some of the most creative artists of the early postwar period, composer John Cage and several of his friends, including dancer Merce Cunningham and painter Robert Rauschenberg, staged "Theater Piece #1," a performance art event that presaged the "happenings" of the sixties.

Cage, who would become one of the most influential composers of the twentieth century, experimented with noise as a compositional element, employing everyday objects like radios and buzzers, and modifying pianos to alter their sounds. "In the 1952 'event,' " writes art historian Jonathan Fineberg, "M. C. Richards and the poet Charles Olson read poetry from ladders; Rauschenberg's *White Paintings* hung overhead while he played Edith

Piaf records on an old phonograph; David Tudor performed on the piano; Merce Cunningham danced in and around the audience (chased by a barking dog); coffee was served by four boys dressed in white; and Cage sat on a step-ladder for two hours—sometimes reading a lecture on the relation of music to Zen Buddhism, sometimes silently listening."

New Themes in American Painting

Few decades demonstrated the struggle between traditional and avant-garde art more clearly, and with a wider variety at the extremes, than the fifties. Traditionalists such as Norman Rockwell and Andrew Wyeth painted realistic works that looked backward, hearkening to traditional American values. Rockwell's paintings celebrated American themes, glorified small-town rites of passage, and honored the family, themes rejected by the abstract expressionists. In painting, as elsewhere in the culture of the fifties, the traditional dominated the public consciousness, but the avant-garde left the most enduring legacy for future generations.

Beyond a doubt, Norman Rockwell was America's most recognizable artist in the fifties. As art critic Robert Hughes observed: Rockwell "shared with Walt Disney the astonishing distinction of being one of the two American visual artists familiar to nearly everyone in the United States, rich or poor, black or white, illiterate or Ph.D." Rockwell's paintings of family gatherings, holiday celebrations, children playing, and people working, which had graced the covers of the *Saturday Evening Post* for decades, portrayed an America that was already fading into memory, which of course was the source of their appeal. His artwork was comfortable: neither in its themes nor in its method did it challenge observers or other artists. Yet, being a shrewd observer of American middle-class values and prejudices, he occasionally used humor to challenge racial and gender stereotypes.

The most influential movement in mid-twentieth-century American art, abstract expressionism represented the antithesis of Norman Rockwell: abstract rather than literal, innovative rather than reflective, improvised rather than stylized. Emerging as new forces in American painting in the late forties, the "action painters" among the abstract expressionists—Jackson Pollock, Franz Kline, and Willem de Kooning—emphasized process over image and had the most significant impact. Centered in New York, they fostered the city's reputation as an international cultural capital.

Pollock, the best known of the three, first worked under Thomas Hart Benton. A veteran of the Federal Arts Project of the Great Depression era, he parted ways with traditional forms in the 1940s, and became a bold innovator who rejected not only traditional content, but also traditional methods. He abandoned the easel and began working from above on mural-size canvases spread on the floor. Splashing and pouring paint from buckets, and dripping and slinging it from sticks, he created abstract designs that covered the entire surface. Unlike Pollock, Kline continued to use a traditional paintbrush, conveying a strong sense of movement with bold, thick strokes. Form and motion were central to his canvases, painted in black and white until late in his career. Coming to the United States from the Netherlands, de Kooning employed the methods of the action painters, but maintained a sense of identifiable figures in his work, which is therefore referred to as "symbolic abstract expressionism."

In the mid-fifties, another group of New York artists took art in a new direction, reintroducing elements of realism into their painting. Led by Robert Rauschenberg and Jasper Johns, they began incorporating everyday objects into their work in a collage-like technique they called "assemblage," a term coined in 1953 by Jean Dubuffet. Rauschenberg used the most common of objects—kitchen utensils, bottles, signs, and even stuffed animals—and blended them into compositions that transformed the original identity of the commonplace. The list of materials used in his 1959 "combine" painting *Canyon* included oil, pencil, paper, metal, fabric, wood on canvas, blue buttons, a photograph, a mirror, a cardboard box, a pillow, a paint tube, and a stuffed eagle.

Johns adopted common symbols—targets, letters, numbers, and flags—and employed them in ways that defied conventional interpretation. The American flag became his most recognizable symbol, always appearing flat, sometimes on a background of other American flags, sometimes in unconventional color combinations. Viewers were forced to consider the tactile surface, color, and composition of his flags, to see this most political of symbols as they'd never seen it before—devoid of political context or patriotic association, distilled of emotion, its meaning ambiguous.

Other artists experimented with different means of applying color to their canvases. Inspired by Pollock's work, Helen Frankenthaler painted mural-like canvases, but, instead of dripping her paint from above, she thinned it with turpentine, applied it onto the canvas in light washes, and let it soak into the surface. The new technique, soon called "color-field painting" or "stain paint-ing," created a more luminous design, almost decorative in quality. Her *Mountains and the Sea* (1952), ten feet across, is a composition of large forms, virtually without texture.

Another abstract expressionist influenced by Pollock was his wife, Lee Krasner. Always in the shadow of her more famous spouse while he lived, Krasner came into her own after Pollock's death. Although some of her can-vases echoed Pollock's action paintings, they were always more contained. She experimented with different styles, and especially with color, using large, bold, colorful forms in her later works.

The use of the commonplace appealed to sculptors as well as to painters. In the early fifties, even before Jasper Johns adopted the flag as a motif and be-fore Robert Rauschenberg put his first stuffed bird on a canvas, David Smith and Richard Stankiewicz began creating "junk sculpture," which fashioned sculptural works out of discarded urban trash, mainly metal. Automobile parts and pieces of steel, especially I-beams, were popular materials. Near the end of the decade, George Segal took another approach to the commonplace. He began fashioning life-size human figures out of wire, plaster, and burlap, and seating them in conventional settings—in subways, in kitchens, on park benches.

American Fiction: Rise of a New Generation

The fifties were an extraordinarily rich decade in the development of American literature. American minorities examined their relationship to American society in novels praised for their evocations of universal themes. The South expanded its long-established diverse regional literature. The "beats" emerged as a new voice in fiction and poetry that deliberately chal-lenged convention.

The best-known American writers of the early fifties, well known for years, William Faulkner, Ernest Hemingway, and John Steinbeck, were now receiving recognition and praise for their earlier works. (Faulkner had received the Nobel Prize for Literature in 1949; he would be joined by Hemingway in 1954 and by Steinbeck in 1962.) In the fifties, all three published novels that added luster to their reputations. Faulkner continued to explore the decline of the Old South in stories set in fictional Yoknapatawpha County, Mississippi. With *The Town* (1957) and *The Mansion* (1959), he concluded a trilogy about the Snopes family begun with *The Hamlet* (1940). Hemingway, whose sparse, powerful narrative style served to underscore the masculine values he admired, published the short—and his last—novel *The Old Man and the Sea* in 1952. Hemingway's career declined toward the end of the decade, and in 1961 he committed suicide. Steinbeck's *East of Eden* (1952) was a Cain-and-Abel saga of Western America.

The war novel *The Naked and the Dead* (1948) established Norman Mailer as a writer of great promise. Mailer, whose combative personality led him into frequent conflicts, both literary and physical, went on to publish a novel, *The Deer Park* (1955); an extended essay, "The White Negro" (1957); and a collection of assorted writings, *Advertisements for Myself* (1959). "The White Negro" examined the "hipster," an emerging American type who defied social norms, and in doing so, challenged the persistence of the values that defined American conventions.

Having already published two novels in the forties, Saul Bellow would emerge in the fifties as one of America's leading writers with three major novels: *The Adventures of Augie March* (1953), *Seize the Day* (1956), and *Henderson, the Rain King* (1959). Bellow's eccentric protagonists found themselves in positions that challenged their own inadequacies, particularly their ability to deal with others. Other Jewish writers—J. D. Salinger and Bernard Malamud—joined Mailer and Bellow in the front rank of American novelists.

Stepping out of Faulkner's shadow, writers such as Eudora Welty, Flannery O'Connor, Carson McCullers, and William Styron further enriched the South's regional literature with stories that focused on people struggling to find an identity, if not a place, amid the turmoil of mid-century American society. Georgians O'Connor and McCullers both suffered from physical problems that influenced their work: McCullers from alcoholism and a series of strokes that eventually killed her in 1967, and O'Connor from lupus, which killed her at age 39 in 1964. McCullers's novels examined the lives of people struggling with physical or psychological limitations. Best known for *The Heart Is a Lonely Hunter* (1940), McCullers went on to write the critically acclaimed *The Ballad of the Sad Café* (1951). In *Wise Blood* (1952) and *The Violent Bear It Away* (1960) and many short stories, O'Connor created characters who bore scars of their own—misfits who sank into hopelessness, violence, and despair. In *Lie Down in Darkness* (1951), William Styron probed the suicide of a Southern woman living in New York.

Other popular writers who would help shape American fiction to the end of the century came to public attention in the fifties. Kurt Vonnegut, who began the decade writing short stories for popular magazines, attacked automation in his novel *Player Piano* (1952). In his short stories of the forties and fifties, John Cheever explored the juxtaposition of material comfort and spiritual suffering in American society, a theme that would dominate his fiction. Having published poetry and short stories in the fifties, John Updike would close out the decade with his critically acclaimed first novel *The Poorhouse Fair* in 1959. But not until *Rabbit, Run* (1960), the first of his four-volume examination of white middle-class Harry Angstrom's struggle to come to terms with the changes in postwar American society, would Updike's novels enjoy a wider readership.

The best-selling novel of the fifties—indeed, the best-selling novel of all time until then—was *Peyton Place* (1956), which explored in frank and explicit terms the sexual affairs of the people of a small town in New England. First novel of New Hampshire housewife Grace Metalious, its sales soon passed the 10 million mark, overtaking those of Erskine Caldwell's *God's Little Acre,* which had provided a similar service in the thirties. A more literary bestseller that employed an explicitly sexual theme was Vladimir Nabokov's *Lolita* (American edition, 1958), in which a pedophile professor seduces and becomes obsessed with a sexually precocious 12-year-old girl. *Lolita* outsold Nabokov's other highly regarded novels, achieving more than 3 million sales in paperback. Another of the publishing successes that capitalized on the rising interest in sex was the release of the first American complete version of D. H. Lawrence's *Lady Chatterley's Lover* by Grove Press in 1958.

Voices of Discontent: African-American Writers

Among the sources of inspiration for the civil rights movement of the sixties, African-American writers of the fifties figure prominently. Richard Wright and Ralph Ellison pointed to the isolation of African Americans in American society, creating powerful characters at odds with the society that they sought to join and yet rejected. Wright's own sense of alienation led him to join the Communist party in the thirties and to flee from the United States in the forties. His novel *Native Son* (1940) with protagonist Bigger Thomas established a mid-century model for the expression of black alienation. Wright remained a respected voice of black America in the fifties, although he spent the decade in exile, traveling in Africa, Asia, and Europe, and ultimately dying in Paris in 1960. His work in the fifties carried his concerns to the world stage. In his essay collection *White Man, Listen!* (1957), he wrote about the anti-colonialist reaction to discrimination and abuse sweeping the Third World.

Ellison, who became acquainted with Wright when the two men worked on the New Deal's Federal Writers Project, foreshadowed some of the themes of the civil rights movement. Ellison's powerful *Invisible Man* (1952), which won the National Book award, portrays the quest of a man to establish an identity in the midst of a society that ignores him. Critics praised the universal theme of the novel, which appeared at a time when all people, regardless of race, risked losing their individual identity in an industrial and increasingly impersonal society. The hero of the novel is a young African American who left the South as an idealistic young man, and traveled to New York to prove himself. Bit by bit throughout the novel, as his former identity is stripped from him, he becomes aware of his invisibility. The unnamed protagonist becomes so invisible that he is able to leech power off the local electric company (Monopolated Light & Power) without paying for it. He carries out a private rebellion by lighting his hidden basement abode with 1,369 lights. The novel is all the more remarkable in that it appeared years before the civil rights movement hit its stride. "Do not go too fast," the hero is warned, years before the pace of the movement itself became an issue of controversy. If the book has a universal theme, its particular significance for black Americans in the early fifties gave the story additional power.

James Baldwin was still a teenager when Wright and Ellison were working for the Federal Writers Project. Like Ellison, Baldwin explored the issue of individual identity. His first novel, *Go Tell It on a Mountain* (1953), written while living in exile in Paris, explores the religious conversion of a young boy in Harlem; his second, *Giovanni's Room* (1956), examines homosexuality and identity. Both drew on autobiographical reflections. Baldwin's role as eloquent commentator on race came to the fore in his most powerful writing, essays that probed the racial issue in America, most notably *The Fire Next Time* (1963), written as the civil rights movement developed.

Rebellion of the Beats: Foundations of a Counterculture

Flowering at the start of the fifties, a literature of nonconformist discontent spanned the entire decade, coming to public awareness only in its closing years. In Holden Caulfield, the protagonist of *Catcher in the Rye* (1951), J. D. Salinger created a character that would influence a generation. Often compared with Mark Twain's Huckleberry Finn, Caulfield was a teenager at odds with the middle-class adult world, rejecting the regimentation and pretense of the "phony bastards," yet also seeking recognition from them. He spoke in a street language that resonated among young readers, who found his rebellious demeanor attractive.

Salinger's rejection of middle-class values found its loudest echo in the Beat culture, broadly acclaimed only in the late fifties. The term "Beat," said by some to derive from "beatific," is dismissed by others as simply meaning "tired." Setting themselves at odds with American society in both word and action, the Beats first came together in the mid-forties, but didn't gain their public voice until the fifties. Jack Kerouac and Allen Ginsberg emerged as the most prominent of a group of eight Beats that included author William S. Burroughs, poet and publisher Lawrence Ferlinghetti, poet and playwright Michael McClure, poets Gregory Corso and Gary Snyder, and inspirer and would-be writer Neal Cassady. The Beats defied the values of middle-class society, refusing to measure success by a material standard, engaging in all manner of unconventional behavior including homosexuality, and honoring Eastern religions. Although heirs of an American literary tradition of defiance that included the "Lost Generation" of the twenties and the bohemians who followed them, the Beats were original in how they chose to flaunt American conventions. Centered in New York and San Francisco, the Beat lifestyle seemed especially aberrant amid the conformist pressures of the 1950s. In the sixties, they became cult figures, admired for their refusal to accept the mores of middle-class America.

As the Beats became legendary figures who transcended their poetry and fiction, one defining moment seemed to capture their spirit and rebelliousness. On October 13, 1955, leading figures of what became known as the "San Francisco poetry renaissance" gathered at a place known as "Six Gallery" to read their work. About one hundred people, including Kerouac, Ferlinghetti, and Snyder, crowded into a room converted from two automobile repair bays. Kenneth Rexroth and Michael McClure read from their work, but the highlight was Allen Ginsberg's first reading of his poem "Howl," a jeremiad on the excesses of American society. With Kerouac seated on the platform, beating a rhythm on a wine jug, Ginsberg found himself propelled by wine and the enthusiasm of the audience into a performance that did full justice not only to the poem's despair and resignation, but also to its exhilaration.

Dealing frankly with his homosexuality in public for the first time, Ginsberg attacked the constraints of American society, though in less political terms than he would in later poems. Those present and critics since praised the reading as pivotal, signaling the public emergence of the Beats. "Howl" gained in notoriety when copies of *Howl and Other Poems* (1956), published by Ferlinghetti's City Lights Bookstore, were seized on grounds of obscenity. The court ultimately ruled in favor of Ferlinghetti and Ginsberg in a trial that gave the Beats still more publicity.

Kerouac was the best known of the group of eight. A football star in high school in Lowell, Massachusetts, Kerouac won an athletic scholarship to Columbia University in New York, but dropped out in 1942 before graduating. In the mid-forties, he met Ginsberg and Burroughs, who were among a group that hung out together around Columbia. Neal Cassady, who became the model for Dean Moriarity in Kerouac's *On the Road* (1957), joined the group late in 1946. Kerouac later claimed that he wrote *On the Road* on a continuous scroll of paper in a three-week period in 1951. The book, which would become the anthem of the Beat Generation, wasn't published for another six years. Largely autobiographical, it relates the spontaneous cross-country journeys of Sal Paradise (Kerouac), and his interaction with Dean Moriarity (Neal Cassady). Rather than celebrating the rootless lifestyle, as early critics claimed, the novel treats life on the road as a means to cope with otherwise unshakable depression by seeking out new experiences. Like *Catcher in the Rye*, *On the Road* appealed to readers because of its unwillingness to accept ordinary life on society's terms. Kerouac would write many novels, although, like Salinger, he would never again reach the heights he attained with his first. In the sixties, he became disillusioned with what he considered a misinterpretation of his work; bitter and dissipated by alcoholism, he died in 1969.

Older than the other members of the group of eight, William S. Burroughs wrote the darkest fiction of the Beat writers. *Naked Lunch* (1959), the first and best-known of a series of four books that, in exploring the world of junkies and addicts, attacked conventional middle-class values, used heroin as a vehicle to criticize the oppressive character of American society.

Theater: The World's Stage

The American theater in the fifties seemed at a crossroads. In quantitative terms, it seemed in decline. New York had fewer than half the number of live

theaters that it'd had a quarter century before, a decline from 75 to 31 between 1929 and 1955. Worse, during the same period, the number of plays
produced per year had dropped by two-thirds, from 224 in 1929 to fewer
than 70 on average in the fifties. Broadway appeared to lose ground to Hollywood and television.

In qualitative terms, however, the American theater enjoyed a rich
decade. Although Eugene O'Neill died in 1953, several of his plays were first
produced after his death. Arthur Miller and Tennessee Williams were at the
peaks of their abilities; by the end of the decade, Edward Albee completed the
first of several one-act plays that signaled his rise in the American theater. Carson McCullers and Lillian Hellman, two of the most significant American
women playwrights of the century, produced major works: McCullers's *The
Member of the Wedding* (1950) and Hellman's *Toys in the Attic* (1960).

Having graced the American stage with the broad dramatic range of his
play since the 1920s, O'Neill had come to the end of his career in the late forties, when Parkinson's disease prevented him from working any more. Among
the plays that remained in manuscript form at the time of his death in 1953 were
two that drew on his family experiences, *Long Day's Journey into Night* (1956),
which won a Tony Award in 1957, and *A Moon for the Misbegotten* (1957).

Arthur Miller's long career spanned several decades, but two of his most
memorable plays, *Death of a Salesman* (1949) and *The Crucible* (1953), are
associated with postwar social concerns of the fifties. *Salesman* brought to the
stage Willy Loman, perhaps the most memorable figures in twentieth-century
American drama. Falling from the heights of his superficial success and forced
to confront his own lies and betrayals, Loman descends to utter despair. To
leave an insurance payoff to his son, he seeks redemption in suicide. Based on
the Salem witch trials of 1692, Miller's *Crucible* is an allegory of McCarthyism. Young girls accused of witchcraft spread terror through the town, and ultimately the morally upright protagonist John Proctor must confess to an
early act of adultery in an attempt to save his wife, only to find that his wife had
lied to try to save him. Required to "name names" in order to salvage his reputation, Proctor refuses to do so. Evil resides not in Proctor's transgression,
but in those who accuse him, and in the hysteria that surrounds the witchcraft
trials. Produced regularly since its debut in the early fifties, *Crucible* would
rank among the most popular of American plays. In the latter fifties, Miller's
considerable fame as a playwright grew even larger with his short-lived marriage to Marilyn Monroe.

Another talented playwright to emerge in the postwar years was Thomas Lanier "Tennessee" Williams, who produced two of his most significant works before the dawn of the fifties, *The Glass Menagerie* (1944) and *A Streetcar Named Desire* (1947). Blanche Du Bois and Stanley Kowalski of *Streetcar* were already two of the most widely known characters in American drama. But Williams's *Cat on a Hot Tin Roof* (1955) received critical praise; its popular success was second only to *Streetcar*. Set in the South, *Cat* probes the regional mores that promote the repression underlying the themes of alcoholism and sexual tension that also permeated *Streetcar*. Williams won the Pulitzer Prize for both plays.

In the early fifties, the musical was at the end of a wave of success. Two musicals by composer Richard Rogers and lyricist Oscar Hammerstein, one of the most successful teams in the American musical theater, won Tony Awards: *South Pacific* in 1950 and *The King and I* in 1952. *Guys and Dolls* by Frank Loesser won a Tony in 1951. Even as these classics won accolades, however, it was clear that musicals were in trouble. Production expenses had soared, and attendance had dwindled before the onslaught of television. Only nine new musical shows appeared in the 1950–51 season, and each of them had lost money. Other outstanding shows appeared later in the decade, by which time lyricist Alan Jay Lerner and composer Frederick Lowe had supplanted Rogers and Hammerstein as the dominant composer-lyricist team on Broadway. Among the most successful musicals in the latter part of the decade, Lerner and Lowe's *My Fair Lady* (1956) shared top billing with *West Side Story* (1957), Leonard Bernstein and Stephen Sondheim's tale of rival gangs in New York, and with Jule Styne and Stephen Sondheim's *Gypsy* (1959), in the tradition of lavish musicals of the thirties and forties, which hailed the passing of an era by featuring one of the grand dames of the musical theater, Ethel Merman, in her final role. The fifties were the last decade in which the musical was at center stage in American popular culture. A musical revolution was under way that would force show tunes to the periphery of American musical tastes.

Popular Music: Big Band Veterans and Country Stars

Popular culture in the early fifties reflected the larger society as a whole: calm on the surface, turbulent below. This is especially true in the realm of popular music, where the popular charts listed "hits" that ranged from pleasant but uninspired melodies to insipid ditties. Other genres—rhythm and blues, jazz, and country—showed greater vitality and creativity, and claimed loyalty of sizable portion of the music market.

In the fifties, popular instrumental music seemed to retreat from the central role it played in the big band era of the thirties and forties—and from the verve and vibrancy it brought to that role. Musicians who earlier found work in the big bands now worked in studios, recording "light music," or "mood music," as it variously became known. They backed popular singers, and recorded the instrumental forerunners of Muzak, or "elevator music." White singers controlled the *Billboard* pop charts; *Billboard* relegated African-American performers to the rhythm and blues listings.

A veteran singer of the big band era, Frank Sinatra became a teen idol in the later forties and the most popular American singer in the forties and early fifties. He carried his success into movies, where he usually portrayed a tough guy; he won an Academy Award as best supporting actor in 1953 for his non-singing role in *From Here to Eternity*. Sinatra's versatility was one of his strengths. As a singer, he could range from ballads to jazz.

Most vocalists in the fifties got their start in the big band era. Among the other male vocalists who enjoyed success in the fifties were Tony Bennett, Perry Como, and Eddie Fisher. Nat "King" Cole broke the color barrier that kept black singers off the pop charts. Singers became celebrities. Sinatra's private life became the subject of many news articles, and Eddie Fisher's marriages to actresses Debbie Reynolds and Elizabeth Taylor boosted public interest in his career. Like their male counterparts, many female vocalists had their start as singers for bands in the forties. Peggy Lee, Jo Stafford, and Rosemary Clooney were all veterans of the big band era who parlayed early success into recording careers.

Country music, relegated by the influential *Billboard* popular music ratings to its own corner of the music market, nonetheless climbed in popularity and seemed on the verge of breaking through to broader popular success. Hank Williams, its biggest star, recorded his biggest hit, "Your Cheatin' Heart," in September 1952, only to die three months later, on New Year's eve, a victim of alcoholism and undiagnosed spina bifida, months before his thirtieth birthday. Roy Acuff, who'd risen to stardom before Williams, now became the most prominent force in country music, reigning as "King of Country Music" at Nashville's Grand Ole Opry. A singer and fiddler, Acuff joined forces with Fred Rose to become a successful publisher of country music as well. Eddy Arnold and Gene Autry were other popular country stars, both known beyond the confines of *Billboard*'s country charts. Yet, even though Arnold had more than sixty top-ten hits on the country charts, *Billboard* listed only two on the pop ratings. Country hits found their way to the pop charts mainly through "covers"—recordings of their songs by mainstream artists.

A world unto itself, nestled in the heartland, Nashville defied the dominant cultural meccas of the East and West Coast. It was to country music what Hollywood was to film. Aspiring writers hung around the city's bars, hoping to make connections with artists. Country artists who'd achieved a measure of success performed at the Grand Ole Opry. And most of the noteworthy country songs came out of Music Row, a section of houses and apartment buildings along Seventeenth Avenue in downtown Nashville.

Men had long dominated country music, but that began to change in the fifties when Kitty Wells, whose songs often addressed the sexism inherent in the industry, broke the gender barrier. Wells recorded "It Wasn't God Who Made Honky-Tonk Angels," in which she responded to a popular Hank Thompson country hit that accused married women of wandering. Wells turned the tables vocally, alleging that too many married men acted like they were still single. Among those who heard Wells was Loretta Lynn, who later credited Wells with inspiring her to begin her own career in country music.

In the late fifties, Johnny Cash emerged as the leading country artist, and one whose songs could jump the wide gulf from country to the pop charts, particularly with the mid-fifties hit "I Walk the Line," which became his signature. Cash's deep, resonant voice was a signature in itself, as was his familiar opening greeting, "Hello, I'm Johnny Cash." His rise to stardom began when he caught the attention of record producer Sam Phillips and toured with Carl Perkins, the two men who launched Elvis Presley's career. Legend has it that Perkins told Cash to write "I Walk the Line" after Cash used the expression; Cash later told Perkins about an Air Force buddy who warned him not to step on his blue suede shoes. Thus their travels together inspired two of the most popular songs of the decade. Cash cultivated the image of an outlaw, dressing in black and singing about social outcasts, prisoners, and malcontents—and behaving like a malcontent himself. In the late fifties, he gave concerts at a frenetic pace, and started popping pills to keep up. His behavior began to reflect the pressure, and incidents in which he broke up motel rooms and concert stages led promoters to stop booking him.

The Black Roots of Popular Music: Blues, Jazz,
and Rhythm and Blues

Black music, which had in decades past vitalized much of American popular music, would serve as its most pervasive cross-pollinator during the fifties.
A migration of African Americans from the rural South to northern cities during the Depression, World War II, and postwar years was most responsible for
a blending of styles. Gospel music, the blues, and traditional African music
had already undergone their own blending, and the changes in the fifties were
a continuation of an ongoing process. One of the most common routes of
black migration led from Mississippi to Chicago. Thus Mississippi Delta blues
came to Chicago, which became a cauldron of musical experimentation.
Muddy Waters was one of those who followed this path; in the forties, he
began to play in jazz clubs on the South Side of Chicago. Adding piano, electric guitar, and drums to the traditional blues guitar, his band played a new
form of music some called the "urban blues." The general public had little understanding of the musical changes afoot in small city clubs in the fifties. Indeed, Waters was little known beyond the jazz joints where he played until the
sixties, but he exerted influence on Chuck Berry and other leaders of the revolution before the turn of the decade.

By the mid-fifties, record companies began to market black music as
"rhythm and blues," which itself was an amalgam of styles. The term came to
denote black music, but it had appeal far beyond the confines of the black
community. Lines of demarcation became less clear, and the emergence of
rock and roll in the mid-fifties owed much to these black roots.

Jazz, too, underwent significant change in the fifties. Unlike the blues,
which had rural roots, jazz remained the music of the city, and built on foun-
dations laid in earlier decades. Characteristic regional styles developed in New
Orleans, Chicago, Kansas City, and New York in earlier years, and in San Francisco in the fifties, contributed strains to the evolving art form. Alto saxo-
phonist Charlie Parker, a key performer in Kansas City during its jazz heyday
in the thirties and forties, was an influential force in the development of bebop
in the forties and of modern jazz in the fifties. Parker, pianist Thelonious
Monk, trumpeter Dizzy Gillespie, drummer Kenny Clarke, and others played
at jazz clubs in New York, where they developed the bebop strains that contributed to the cool jazz movement of the late forties and early fifties.

Jazz in the fifties continued to be a genre in the making, influenced by

1940s swing and the big bands of Duke Ellington and Count Basie, the vocals of Ella Fitzgerald, and the bebop movement. Trumpeter Miles Davis, whose middle-class origins and formal training at the Juilliard School of Music set him apart from most jazz musicians, influenced the emergence of cool jazz. His 1949 album *Birth of the Cool* built on his experience playing with bebop musicians Charlie Parker and Dizzy Gillespie. By the mid-fifties, Davis had earned a reputation as a leading composer, jazz musician, and bandleader, and the Miles Davis Quintet was the most influential jazz group of the late 1950s. New Orleans continued to be a mecca for jazz. Trumpeter and bandleader Louis Armstrong, a native of the city, was perhaps the most recognizable of all jazz musicians, so popular that he moved easily into film. New Orleans jazz was also enriched by two highly regarded white jazz musicians, trumpeter Al Hirt and clarinetist Pete Fountain; in California, white musicians would contribute to the West Coast cool jazz movement. Dave Brubeck's group helped to popularize jazz, particularly on college campuses, where his "Take Five" and "Time Out" became well known far beyond the usual audience for jazz.

The Birth of Rock 'n' Roll

The roots of rock 'n' roll extend deep into American popular music. Even the term "rock" had been around since the twenties, three decades before the new musical style of rock 'n' roll began to transform American musical tastes. When the musical revolution began in the fifties, Cleveland disk jockey Alan Freed was atop the barricades, and rock historians give him credit for being a catalyst present at the creation. In 1952, Freed called his radio show "a rock and roll session," even though the songs he aired were basic rhythm and blues (R&B). In the fall of 1954, Freed took his act to radio station WINS in New York, and the following January 14th and 15th, he sponsored a "Rock 'n' Roll Ball" in Saint Nicholas Arena. All the performers were black, but almost half of those attending were white. Freed's name was inextricably linked to rock 'n' roll, and at one point he even tried to trademark the term. Surely "rock 'n' roll" was preferable to the term "race music," which had been commonly applied to R&B.

By 1954, musical tastes among young consumers were shifting. The phenomenon that Freed had noticed, in which young white audiences were favoring R&B music by black artists over pop music by white artists such as Perry Como and Eddie Fisher, had become a national trend. Radio stations, ever sensitive to consumer tastes, began to shift their formats, or at least to alter their playlists. Some of the leading record companies responded by having white artists "cover" successful R&B singles, a tactic that had a short run of success. Soon, however, black performers "crossed over," and R&B hits recorded by black artists began to climb the pop charts.

Technology also influenced changes in musical tastes. As television gained popularity in the early fifties, it attracted audiences for radio programming that had been popular in the forties, particularly radio drama. As radio drama dwindled, and then virtually disappeared, radio stations began shifting to music formats. Alan Freed's popularity spawned imitators; by the end of the fifties, disk jockeys (DJs) like Murray the K and Wolfman Jack became as well known as earlier radio personalities. The adoption of music formats on radio gave a significant boost to record companies, and ultimately spawned a "play-for-pay" scandal.

The record companies also benefited from technological advances in their own industry. Until the late forties, the 78 rpm phonograph record was the industry standard. Then the two major record companies introduced new record formats. Columbia developed the $33\frac{1}{3}$ long-playing record, soon known simply as the "LP." Columbia saw its market as classical music: the new LPs offered greater fidelity and allowed entire symphonies to be recorded on one disk. RCA then introduced smaller 45 rpm records, ideal for single songs. Pop songs—and rock—began to appear on "45s," which began to displace "78s"; by 1957, these were phased out altogether. For the most part, classical and rock retained their distinct format identities until the end of the decade. Cheaper and more portable than LPs, 45s appealed to younger consumers. Rock singles continued to outsell LPs until well into the sixties, when promoters came to recognize the potential market for rock, pop, and jazz LPs.

The next herald of the revolution was an unlikely revolutionary. Bill Haley was white and nearly thirty. In the late forties, he fronted for a country group called the "Saddlemen," wearing a Stetson. The Saddlemen became the Comets; in the spring of 1954, Bill Haley and His Comets recorded "(We're Gonna) Rock Around the Clock." The song rose briefly to number 23 on the *Billboard* charts, and then faded. Haley had more success in the fall with a cover of a tune by Joe Turner, "Shake, Rattle, and Roll," which sold over a million copies. Then, in the spring of 1955, a movie about juvenile delinquency chose "Rock Around the Clock" as its theme song. *Blackboard Jungle* starred Glenn Ford and Sidney Poitier, but the movie's real star made its appearance with the opening riffs of Haley's song. "Rock Around the Clock" shot up the *Billboard* charts to number 1, and ultimately became—with Bing Crosby's "White Christmas"—one of the best-selling singles of all time. Reaction to the song provoked a generation gap almost as wide as the one provoked by reaction to the juvenile delinquency portrayed in the film: teenagers danced in the aisles of theaters and committed random acts of noise outside.

Other early rock 'n' roll hits showed the close connection to rhythm and blues. New Orleans native "Fats" Domino was already established in R&B circles when his "Ain't It a Shame" broke into the pop charts in the summer of 1955. Pat Boone, a young white singer, covered and took the song to number 1; the Fats Dominio original only made number 10. Chuck Berry's "Maybellene" and Little Richard's (Richard Penniman's) "Tutti Frutti" then helped solidify a sense that rock 'n' roll had its own distinct identity.

In 1954, Elvis Presley, a 19-year-old truck driver in Memphis who'd been singing for years in church and at revival meetings, went to the studios of Sun Records. When Carl Perkins and Colonel Tom Parker heard him sing "That's All Right (Mama)," they immediately recognized his talent. Not only could Presley sing the blues, he could also reshape a tune and make it his own. Parker bought out Presley's contract and became his exclusive manager. In Nashville in January 1956, just two days after his twenty-first birthday, Presley recorded "Heartbreak Hotel," which blended blues and gospel; Chet Atkins backed him on guitar, and Floyd Cramer added a blues piano line. The recording had technical flaws, but they hardly mattered.

Fueled by a series of television appearances and hit singles recorded in New York in January and early in February, the Elvis Presley phenomenon took off in 1956. Presley's television career started modestly, with appearances on *Stage Show*. His recording sessions in New York yielded songs that showed Presley's raw talent to full advantage, mainly covers of songs already established as part of the rock 'n' roll vocabulary: "Shake, Rattle, and Roll," Little Richard's "Tutti Frutti," and "Lawdy Miss Clawdy." Another, Carl Perkins's "Blue Suede Shoes," became Elvis's second million-seller. By the time Elvis made his two appearances on *The Milton Berle Show* in April and June, he was well known, which he hadn't been at the time of his earlier guest spots on television.

The televised appearances drew the battle lines in the Elvis culture wars. Young teenage girls swooned, and crusty puritanical New York critics wailed about his lack of talent, his vulgar "animalism," and the bad taste of his gyrations (which one critic compared to "an aborigine's mating dance"). Presley was a rebel, but he was a respectful rebel. He had a work ethic and a cooperative attitude uncharacteristic of rock stars in later years. He was polite, and didn't smoke or drink. Steve Allen asked Presley to make an appearance on his show wearing a tux with tails, singing "Hound Dog" to a hound dog. Despite his handlers' concern that the gimmick might be humiliating, Presley did as he was asked, with no repercussions. (The next day, Presley recorded a two-sided hit, "Hound Dog," backed by "Don't Be Cruel." Unrestrained by Allen's guidelines, he sang "Hound Dog" as an upbeat, pulsating wail, laying to rest the Steve Allen version. "Hound Dog" ultimately sold 7 million copies, which made it the biggest hit of the fifties.)

Presley touched something in the American psyche. His suggestive swiveling hip movements offended parents whose teenagers idolized him, but the reaction of critics and parents went deeper than merely taking offense. His overt sexuality was something new in a male performer. The male as sex object implied a role reversal that touched other American anxieties of the fifties. Commentators at the time worried about threats to masculinity, for women were entering the workforce, and men in corporations were working in "teams" rather than as rugged individuals, the traditional image of the American male.

The biggest television show in the late fifties was *The Ed Sullivan Show,* a variety show that sported everything from seals to ballerinas. Sullivan first turned up his nose at Presley, but shrewdly changed his mind after competitors' ratings soared when the young singer appeared. In the summer of 1956, Sullivan invited Presley to perform on his show, directing his cameramen to frame their shots above Elvis's waist. Even so, 54 million people tuned in to see Presley sing on September 9.

Presley's phenomenal career survived slumps that would have done in many singers, but he never again matched the energy, dynamism, and drive of 1956 and 1957. He switched labels, moving from Sun to RCA, the corporate major leagues, where image became as important as the music, diminishing the music. Drafted into the Army, he served a two-year stint from 1958 to 1960, during which his singles continued to sell. He made a succession of B-movies that celebrated cars, women, and the sun, of which *Jailhouse Rock,* made in 1957, was the first and perhaps the best. He would go on to make some thirty films, until it seemed that each new film was a parody of the last. Tom Parker overmanaged and overcontrolled his priceless property, shielding him from the media—to Presley's detriment. The quality of Presley's songs declined, and by 1962, it seemed clear he'd lost his edge. He spent the last years of his career as an overweight nightclub performer, a faded talent. But, at his peak, he had achieved the status of an icon, and gained public veneration that few entertainers of the fifties—perhaps only Marilyn Monroe and Frank Sinatra—could approach.

One of the keys to the rapid rise of rock 'n' roll was promotion. Rock tapped a new market—teenagers—at a time when their purchasing power had become significant, and when their younger brothers and sisters, the leading edge of the baby boom, had begun to buy records themselves. One of the most successful promoters in the late fifties was Dick Clark, the host of the late-afternoon television show *American Bandstand*. Telecast each weekday afternoon from Philadelphia, *Bandstand* had a bare-bones, low-cost format: Clark would play records, and teenagers would dance to the music. Teenagers from all over the country could identify with the dancers, who lined up each afternoon hoping to get in, and whom Clark treated as the stars of the show.

When Clark attracted some of the biggest recording stars to *American Bandstand*, the show became popular with industry insiders. Even though he could not afford to pay stars the kind of money Ed Sullivan did, stars came nonetheless, accepting minimum payment, aware of the popularity of the show and of the value of exposure to a young audience. Clark was no gambler, but he did take risks. He hosted performers like Jerry Lee Lewis, whose hits included the raucous "Great Balls of Fire," and who irritated adults. He also quietly began including blacks among the dancers on the show, and despite some misgivings, began interviewing them as he did white kids. The negative reaction that he anticipated never materialized.

Ultimately, both Dick Clark and Allen Freed became ensnared in rock's first scandal. Congress was investigating allegations that disk jockeys had accepted bribes from record companies to hype sales by playing selected singles repeatedly. The "payola" scandal broke in 1959, right on the heels of television's quiz show scandal. Clark and Freed were simply the two best-known DJs whose names came before the committee. Others also became targets, particularly DJs in larger markets. Some frankly admitted accepting a routine ten dollars with the receipt of a new record. Freed, who'd moved from WINS to WABC in New York, conceded that, although he'd accepted gifts *after* he'd played songs, he'd never accepted any bribes. Nonetheless, in late November 1959, when Freed refused to sign a statement that he had never taken money to promote a record, WABC fired him. He dismissed reporters who hounded him by saying that he didn't see anything wrong with taking gifts, even large ones, and that he was helping launch careers. Freed's glib responses, so effective on the radio, did not serve him well now. He claimed that, when someone asked him, if he received a Cadillac, would he send it back? he'd replied, "It depends on the color." Clark, for his part, preserved his calm, buttoned-down image and his career. Challenged to give up either *American Bandstand* or his outside music interests, he immediately divested himself of the outside business.

The payola investigation never reached the proportions of the quiz show scandals, and critics gave the investigation mixed reviews. To some, it revealed a materialistic sickness that pervaded American society. To others, it was simply another political act by another congressional subcommittee seeking publicity. Some considered it another manifestation of the growing gap between generations, with the adult world seeking to explain why their kids liked this new loud and grating music. Surely, it must be because bribed disk jockeys barraged them with repeated plays of noise that otherwise would have passed quickly into oblivion.

The payola scandal was only part of a crisis that besieged rock 'n' roll at the end of its first decade. The crisis was in part a defensive reaction to external pressure, in part a self-destructive impulse that at times seemed endemic. Public pressure mounted against the allegedly lewd content of rock 'n' roll lyrics and performance. The recording companies were rocked by the criticism, and rolled over. They began producing harmless ditties that used the rock form, but relinquished its raw edge in favor of the mild and inoffensive. Soon dubbed "schlock rock," this variant of teen music included songs like Paul Anka's "Put Your Head on My Shoulder" and Frankie Avalon's "Venus."

Rock's self-destructive tendencies and happenstance removed several of its key performers from the scene. Elvis Presley's departure for military service temporarily removed rock's biggest name. When Jerry Lee Lewis married his fourteen-year-old cousin (who may have been only thirteen—accounts varied), the negative public reaction forced him out of the business. Three of rock's premier stars, Buddy Holly, Richie Valens, and J. P. Richardson (the "Big Bopper") died in a plane crash in 1959. Little Richard nearly became another victim of an air disaster, after which he converted to Christianity and abandoned his revolutionary music. Chuck Berry, whose "Maybellene" was one of the first crossover hits from the R&B charts to the pop ratings and whose rock classics included "Roll Over Beethoven" and "Johnny B. Goode," was arrested and later convicted for a violation of the Mann Act for "transporting an under-aged girl across state lines for immoral purposes."

Folk music, a genre with deep roots in the American past, was rediscovered in the late fifties. It had served as a vehicle for the social protests of Depression-era singers such as Pete Seeger and Woody Guthrie, and would do so again in the sixties with singers such as Joan Baez, who made her debut as leading female folk vocalist at the 1959 Newport Folk Festival. But, as revived in the late fifties, and performed most notably by the Kingston Trio, folk music played no such role.

Popular music thus had undergone a radical transformation in the fifties, giving birth to new forms of music that would continue to evolve in the sixties. The popular music of 1950 had more in common with the music of the twenties than with music of the later fifties; by the early sixties, popular songs of a decade before seemed quaint or archaic. Although the transformation would continue in the decades to follow, the most dramatic break with the musical past occurred in the mid-fifties.

Recommended Reading

Jonathan Fineberg's *Art Since 1940: Strategies of Being* (Englewood Cliffs, N.J.: Prentice Hall, 1995) is an excellent survey of recent trends in American art.

One of the best treatments of popular music is Donald Clarke's *The Rise and Fall of Popular Music: A Narrative History from the Renaissance to Rock 'n' Roll* (New York: St. Martin's Press, 1995). Despite its misleading subtitle, the book concentrates on twentieth-century popular music, emphasizes American music, gives due credit to African-American influences, and offers personal, often acerbic commentary. James Miller's *Flowers in the Dustbin: The Rise of Rock and Roll, 1947–1977* (New York: Simon and Schuster, 1999) is more narrowly focused, but equally informed and effective. Nicholas Dawidoff's *In the Country of Country* (New York: Pantheon Books, 1997) takes a biographical approach to the roots of country music.

10

Foreign Policy at the Dawn of the Space Age, 1957–1960

THE COLD WAR DOMINATED the foreign policy of Eisenhower's second term as it had the first. By 1957, it had become clear that the rivalry with the Soviet Union would seldom involve direct confrontation between the super-powers, but rather crises in geopolitical hot spots around the globe. In the late 1950s, several of these problem areas were familiar: problems between China and Taiwan, turmoil in Vietnam, and Soviet agitation over Berlin. Latin America, and especially Cuba, emerged as a new area of concern. Vice President Nixon played a larger role in foreign affairs than he had in Eisenhower's first term, visiting Latin America and the Soviet Union. Eisenhower himself was more prominent in foreign policy, in part because cancer had weakened Secretary of State Dulles, and would take his life in 1959.

Vietnam under Diem: The Deepening American Commitment

During Eisenhower's first term, the French crisis in Vietnam brought Southeast Asia to the center of the administration's evolving foreign policy. In Vietnam, it drew a line against the expansion of Communism in Asia. It developed an approach to combatting Communism in the Third World, deciding in the process the limits to its commitment to fighting Communism in lesser-developed, marginal regions.

During Eisenhower's second term, events in Vietnam never demanded the administration's attention in the way that Dien Bien Phu, Geneva in 1954, and President Ngo Dinh Diem's decision in 1956 not to hold the national elections promised at Geneva had. Nonetheless, developments during Eisen-

12. President Dwight D. Eisenhower and Secretary of State John Foster Dulles (from left to right) greet South Vietnam's President Ngo Dinh Diem at Washington National Airport, May 8, 1957. Record Group 342: Records of U.S. Air Force Commands, Activities, and Organizations, 1900–1991, Special Media Archives Services Division (NWCS-S), National Archives at College Park, NAIL Control no. NWDNS-342-AF-18302USAF.

hower's second term were no less critical in determining the course of American involvement in the 1960s. The American commitment to the Diem regime deepened, even as Americans became increasingly uncomfortable with Diem's leadership. U.S. goals remained consistent—prevent the spread of Communism to other areas in Southeast Asia, weaken Communist influence in the region, strengthen the anti-Communist government in the South and the South's own defense forces, and reunify Vietnam under anti-Communist leadership.

The Eisenhower administration concentrated most of U.S. aid to Vietnam on the military and on purchasing imports for South Vietnam. In the late fifties, the United States consistently paid 85 percent of the costs to maintain the South Vietnamese military, and purchased over 75 percent of its imports. When American agricultural advisor Wolf Ladejinsky recommended a land transfer program, a program that might have brought economic improvement, Diem ignored it, and Washington demurred. Historian David L. Anderson described the South Vietnamese economy as a "tripod of rice, rubber, and relief in the form of U.S. aid." Modest early gains in rice and rubber production were reversed toward the end of the decade as Vietminh infiltration and rural violence increased. Vietnamese officials siphoned off most of the aid intended for urban development. When Diem did undertake reforms, they were counterproductive. In an effort to control the countryside, he initiated a resettlement program and replaced local officials with government appointees. Both reforms disrupted traditional patterns of life in the rural areas, and turned people against Diem's government.

In May 1957, when Diem visited the United States, the president greeted him at the airport; Diem met with Eisenhower, Dulles, and other members of the administration. The media feted him, applauding the "miracle" he had wrought in Vietnam. Diem's reception in private conferences was far less welcoming, however. His request that U.S. aid remain at its current level of $250 million received only polite attention. Faced with the costs of several crises in 1956 and committed to budget cuts, the Eisenhower administration wanted to reduce foreign aid. As the Vietminh campaign of disruption in the South became more active, Diem had responded with more repression rather than with more reform, and aid program administrators questioned whether it was wise to pump more money into Vietnam.

By the end of his presidency, Eisenhower could take little pride in what his administration had achieved in Vietnam. South Vietnam was nominally independent, but, if anything, less secure than it had been in 1954, when the French surrendered at Dien Bien Phu. The United States found itself supporting an unpopular repressive leader who had enemies in his own government. Although Eisenhower's defenders would praise him for keeping America out of the Vietnam quagmire into which his successors would so deeply sink, he had been the first president to move the country down that path.

Sputnik

The Cold War took a dramatic turn in the fall of 1957 when a new crisis burst on the scene, signaling its arrival with an unsettling "beep-beep" sound.

On October 4, 1957, the Soviet Union launched into earth orbit a 184-pound aluminum-paneled ball, 22 inches in diameter, named "Sputnik"—the earth's first artificial satellite. Its launch caught the United States by surprise, and had ramifications for American society that no one could have anticipated.

The immediate U.S. reaction was one of shock. Most Americans believed that the Russians were technological Neanderthals, capable of massive construction, but not sophisticated enough for more refined scientific endeavors. The Soviets' feat was doubly astonishing. Not only had they preempted the United States in one of the most dramatic technological achievements of the age, but they had launched a satellite that weighed more than fifty times as much as the three-and-a-half-pound satellite being prepared for launch by the United States. The national security implications of the achievement were staggering: if the Russians had developed the rocket thrust needed to launch an earth satellite, they could likely develop the capacity to deliver warheads to American targets as well.

Sputnik challenged Americans on several fronts. Were U.S. defenses adequate? Was American education in science and engineering falling behind that of the Soviet Union? Could the U.S. space program compete with the Soviet Union? President Eisenhower's news conference on October 9 sought to reassure people that Sputnik was no reason for hysteria. The fact that the Russians had put "one small ball" into space did not mean that the United States was imperiled. He described the U.S. space effort even as he denied that the United States was engaging in a space race with the Soviets. He minimized the military threat posed by Sputnik, insisting that both the Army's and the Navy's missile and space programs were progressing, and that the Soviet satellite amounted to nothing more than a psychological advantage. Having developed the rocket thrust to launch a satellite was a very different thing from developing the ability to control the path of an intercontinental ballistic missile (ICBM), he insisted.

Eisenhower's reassurances were to no avail. He underestimated the reaction of the American public. People's long-held confidence in the superiority of American technology had been badly shaken. The Russians had moved ahead in a critical area that seemed to threaten national security. Although Eisenhower had good reason for his equanimity in the aftermath of Sputnik, it was based on classified information he couldn't reveal. High-altitude Lockheed U-2 aerial reconnaissance spy planes flying over Soviet territory had returned information that gave the president confidence that the United States did not trail the Soviets in defense capability.

Over the course of the next two months, a series of aftershocks to the Sputnik earthquake only heightened the nation's anxiety. On November 3, the Soviet Union followed its first space spectacular with an even more astounding performance, launching a second artificial satellite, Sputnik II, that was six times as heavy as its predecessor and that also carried a passenger—a dog named "Laika."

The second aftershock came four days later. In details leaked to the press, a secret defense report warned that the Soviet Union was superior to the United States in nuclear weapons technology, and that, within two years, it could be capable of launching a massive ICBM attack on U.S. territory. The Gaither report was the product of a blue-ribbon panel commissioned by the president the previous April to study civil defense responses if the United States came under nuclear attack. Chaired by H. Rowan Gaither, who headed the Ford Foundation and the Rand Corporation, the panel included prominent American scientists, educators, businessmen, and public officials, most notably, former Secretary of Defense Robert Lovett; General James Doolittle, the head of the National Advisory Committee for Aeronautics (NACA); Dr. James R. Killian Jr. of the Massachusetts Institute of Technology; and Frank Stanton, president of CBS. The report indicated that, because of the dynamic expansion of its economy and its willingness to pour its resources into military spending, the Soviet Union was becoming an increasingly serious threat. The alarmist tone of the report fueled the burgeoning American hysteria, and became an important step in the perception that the Soviets had created a "missile gap," leaving the United States far behind. Although there was no missile gap, to refute such concerns, the president would have had to reveal the American aerial reconnaissance program, and he wasn't prepared to do so. The Gaither panel advised that the United States should respond by building civil defense fallout shelters, bolstering the defense capabilities of the Strategic Air Command, and pushing the development of American missiles. To finance such a program, the panel called for $40 billion in new defense spending over the course of the next five to eight years.

Early in December, post-Sputnik America endured its third aftershock. Hopes for a U.S. space launch rested with the Navy's Project Vanguard. Planned for launch as part of the International Geophysical Year, Vanguard was a global program of scientific investigation. Now it had the weight of U.S. prestige as an added burden. On December 6, as a national television audience watched, Vanguard exploded on its launch pad.

The failure set off a controversy. The Army Ballistic Missile Agency at the Redstone Arsenal in Huntsville, Alabama, had been developing rockets under the direction of German expatriate rocket engineers, who had developed the V-2 rocket for the German army during World War II under the leadership of Dr. Wernher von Braun. The engineers had come to the United States after the war as part of Project Paperclip, an U.S. Army program designed to bring the most talented German scientists and engineers to the United States. Working for the Army at Redstone Arsenal, von Braun's team had developed the Red-stone rocket, and now offered a modified Redstone called the "Jupiter-C" as an alternative to Vanguard, claiming it could be ready for launch sixty days after receiving approval to proceed. More than a year before Sputnik, on September 20, 1956, von Braun's group had launched a four-stage Jupiter-C capable of putting a satellite in orbit, but had remained within Defense Department constraints by filling the fourth stage with sand. Even so, the rocket had reached a speed of 13,000 miles per hour and risen to an altitude of 682 miles.

The Sputnik launch put the Eisenhower administration on the defensive. Although the president refused to be drawn into the hysteria that characterized the public response, he did take action to energize the nation's missile programs. He summoned officials from the Defense Department, and when Assistant Secretary of Defense Donald A. Quarles confirmed the capabilities of the Army's Jupiter-C, Eisenhower gave the green light to the Army project. The president appointed MIT president James Killian as his special assistant for science and technology and as chairman of the newly created President's Science Advisory Committee (PSAC). Killian thus had broad authority to examine the American space and missile programs, to limit interservice rivalry in missile development, and to review science education and research programs. An excellent administrator, Killian shared Eisenhower's view that Sputnik required a measured response, and that long-range planning was preferable to panic-induced programs.

The president soon faced two new challenges, however, the first both physical and political; the second purely political. On November 25, Eisenhower suffered a mild stroke. Not nearly as serious as his earlier heart attack—he resumed normal activity within days—the stroke nonetheless prompted concern over succession if the president were to be incapacitated. Eisenhower reached an understanding with Nixon about succession: he would keep the decision in his own hands unless he was incapable of acting, in which case the decision would rest with Nixon.

The political challenge came from Congress, where Democrats mounted an attack on the administration. Senate Majority Leader Lyndon Johnson, who chaired the Defense Preparedness Subcommittee of the Senate Armed Services Committee, announced that he would hold hearings about why U.S. space and missile programs lagged behind the Soviets'. Johnson promised bipartisan hearings, and although the hearings never became overtly partisan, critics alleged that the Texas senator was trying to position himself for a run at the presidency in 1960. Eminent scientists and defense experts, including Edward Teller, testified that the United States was in danger of falling behind the Soviets, and need a push not only in missile programs, but also in education.

On January 31, 1958, from Cape Canaveral in Florida, the Army's Jupiter-C, successfully launched into orbit Explorer, a satellite developed at Cal Tech in Pasadena. Before the end of March, two more successful American satellites launched, Explorer III (Explorer II had failed) and Vanguard, bringing new confidence to the U.S. space program.

The successful launches also focused attention on a study undertaken by Killian's advisory committee. PSAC recommended that scientific nonmilitary space projects be conducted by a new civilian space agency. On July 29, Eisenhower signed the act authorizing establishment of the National Aeronautics and Space Administration (NASA). The new agency was to be formed from the old NACA, which had been devoted to aeronautics research. The division of responsibility for U.S. space projects still had to be negotiated by NASA and the armed services. Negotiations involved not only money and programs, but also two military groups that NASA hoped to absorb, the Jet Propulsion Laboratory (JPL) in California and Wernher von Braun's Army Ballistic Missile Agency (ABMA) in Alabama. JPL went to NASA, but von Braun's ABMA remained with the Army until 1960, when it also joined NASA.

Bit by bit, Eisenhower gave ground before the clamor raised by Sputnik. He lifted his $38.5 billion budget ceiling on defense spending, granted the development of more intermediate range ballistic missiles (IRBMs), and finally gave support to federal assistance to education. The education issue was tricky. The federal government had entered the field reluctantly, for education was an area that the states and local communities had guarded jealously. In January, Eisenhower had proposed a relatively small federal program of scholarships, which grew in size as the debate over education went forward. Advocates avoided possible state or local opposition by tying the measure to defense concerns rather than presenting it as a straightforward education bill.

13. Triumphantly displaying a model of Explorer I, the first American satellite, are (from left to right) Jet Propulsion Laboratory (JPL) Director James Pickering, James van Allen of the State University of Iowa, and Wernher von Braun of the Army Ballistic Missile Agency (ABMA) in Huntsville, Alabama. JPL packed and tested the payload, a radiation detection experiment designed by van Allen. ABMA developed the Jupiter-C rocket that carried the satellite into orbit on January 31, 1958. History Office, NASA Marshall Space Flight Center.

The resulting National Defense Education Act (NDEA) passed in August 1958. The act supported in particular instruction in science, math, and foreign languages. It established a $295 million loan fund, which allowed needy students to borrow up to $1,000 a year for five years, and a $59.4 million fund for graduate fellowships in science, education, and foreign languages. The act also offered federal matching funds for the purchase of equipment useful in teaching in the target areas.

Sputnik thus prompted reforms in education, led to the formation of a national civilian space agency, and gave impetus to another round of the arms race. Eisenhower fought hard to maintain equanimity in the face of pressure for more dramatic action; in the end, he was able to assert considerable influence in all areas.

Nuclear Testing, Disarmament, and Fallout

During Eisenhower's second term, public concern about nuclear testing rose to a level that the administration could no longer ignore. Both the Soviet Union and the United States conducted test series in 1957. Soviet tests in the first four months of the year resulted in heavy fallout, and observations revealed that the fallout was traveling great distances in the upper atmosphere. In May, the United States conducted six tests, reportedly seeking a "clean" atomic trigger for H-bombs—one that would create a minimum of fallout.

The president himself had concerns about fallout and nuclear testing, and in June 1957 he met twice with Lewis Strauss, chair of the Atomic Energy Commission and his chief advisor on nuclear testing. Strauss, who not only had the president's ear himself, but who also controlled access to the White House on nuclear issues, insisted on more testing, even as opposition mounted. He brought three like-minded nuclear scientists to the second meeting, including Edward Teller, principally credited with developing the hydrogen bomb. The scientists sought to allay Eisenhower's concerns by telling him that they were closing in on technology that would produce "clean" weapons, by warning him that the Soviets were capable of evading any test ban agreement by carrying out undetectable tests in secret, and by reassuring him about possible peaceful uses of atomic weapons. Eisenhower confined his concerns to private discussions; in public, he continued to defend the testing program. When reporters questioned him about fallout and test ban proposals, he repeated the arguments he had heard from Teller.

The discovery that strontium 90, a radioactive by-product of nuclear testing, had found its way up the food chain into cow's milk stirred public concern. The Soviets, too, pressured the administration, completing a series of atmospheric tests in 1957 and then trying to preempt a planned series of American tests by declaring a moratorium on further testing early in 1958. As disturbed as Eisenhower was about atmospheric testing, he believed that he had little choice but to proceed with the tests. Sputnik cast a long shadow, and concern about Soviet nuclear delivery systems overmatched concern over strontium 90.

Lebanon, 1958: American Intervention

In the aftermath of the 1956 Suez crisis, the Middle East became a less stable region, more hostile to American interests, yet one in which American influence loomed larger than it had before. American policy in the region focused on preventing the spread of Nasser's influence. The Eisenhower Doctrine, approved by Congress early in 1957, technically aimed to halt the spread of international Communism, and promised aid to any nation that was threatened by it and that requested American aid. In the context of Middle Eastern politics, however, the Eisenhower Doctrine meant preventing the spread of Nasser's influence.

By late 1957, Washington feared that Syria was falling under Soviet influence. America's most trusted allies in the vicinity, Turkey, Iraq, and Lebanon, all would have agreed to American intervention, but none wanted to issue a request. Within months, pro-Nasser forces took Syria into union with Egypt, forming the United Arab Republic.

Lebanon's complex ethnic composition left it as vulnerable to nationalism as any country in the region. The nation's pro-Western president, Camille Chamoun, was the only leader in the region to have accepted the Eisenhower Doctrine, but he headed a government whose structure guaranteed conflict. He was a Maronite Christian governing a nation with a Muslim majority, which itself divided into competing factions. Under terms of an agreement that dated to 1943, Lebanon retained an uneasy stability by having a Maronite Christian president, a Sunni Muslim premier, and a Shiite Muslim speaker of the Chamber of Deputies.

Claiming that he feared an uprising, but wanting instead to prevent a takeover by pro-Nasser nationalists, Chamoun attempted to amend the constitution to give himself the right to run for reelection. People in Lebanon were outraged by the blatant bid for power, which threatened to jeopardize the uneasy Lebanese political balance. Radio broadcasts out of Cairo and Damascus encouraged rebels in Lebanon, and seemed to give credence to concerns that the United Arab Republic might be behind an anti-Chamoun rebellion. Opposition leaders in Lebanon traveled to Damascus to welcome the Nasserite victory, and some proposed that Lebanon join the United Arab Republic. Chamoun began raising government forces, and other ethnic and religious groups began raising militia units. When civil war broke out in May, Chamoun's government asked the United States how it would react to a request for assistance.

The Eisenhower Doctrine required evidence of Communist influence for the United States to act, and the administration did not believe such evidence existed in Lebanon. Only by assuming that Nasser-inspired activity was instigated by Communists, or at least influenced by Communists, could the administration justify action under the terms of the doctrine.

Dramatic developments in nearby Iraq in the summer of 1958 exposed Chamoun's vulnerability. On July 13, Iraqi nationalists sympathetic to Nasser took power, killing King Faisal and other members of the Hashemite royal family. The 70-year-old pro-Western prime minister, Nuri es-Said, escaped, only to be discovered and slain the next day. The coup shocked the Eisenhower administration; the CIA had no inkling that a rebellion was afoot. Chamoun once again requested U.S. assistance.

When Eisenhower's advisors met with him, they sensed that he'd already made his decision. "How soon can you start, Nate?" he asked General Nathan Twining, who answered, "Fifteen minutes after I get back to the Pentagon." The president responded, "Well, what are we waiting for?" The Iraqi coup swept aside Eisenhower's earlier reservations. Even though Iraq provided no greater indication of Communist activity, the coup had made the dangers of instability so clear that Eisenhower was willing to commit U.S. troops abroad, the only time he would do so during his presidency. When he explained his actions to the American public in a televised address the next day, however, Communism served as the principal justification.

American troops landed on the shores of Lebanon on July 15. It was no Inchon. Sunbathers watched as the marines came ashore unopposed. Lebanon was not the only Middle Eastern nation worried about the spread of nationalism; two days after the American landing, Britain sent 2,500 paratroopers to Amman to assist Jordan's King Hussein. By the end of the first week in August, the United States had more than 114,000 troops in Lebanon. The State Department dispatched Robert Murphy to Lebanon to mediate a settlement. He negotiated an agreement under which Chamoun left peaceably, and General Fuad Chehab, whom both sides accepted, took his place. On August 12, the marines began to withdraw.

China Redux: The 1958 Formosa Straits Crisis

After a lull of over three years, the unresolved issue of China's offshore islands rose again in August 1958, when the Chinese Communists again shelled Quemoy and Matsu. The situation now was more perilous than it had been in 1954–55, for Chiang now had stationed 100,000 troops on Quemoy and Matsu, one-third of his forces. Furthermore, the United States was now more committed to defend Chiang than it had been when the crisis began in 1954.

President Eisenhower dispatched units of the Seventh Fleet to the Formosa Straits, where they assisted the Nationalist Chinese forces resupplying the troops on the offshore islands by escorting them to within three miles of Quemoy. The Communist batteries forced the Nationalist supply vessels back several times before they completed their mission, but it was clear that the Communists were avoiding firing on American ships. The Communists, however, seemed more intent on carrying the attack to a conclusion. They blockaded the islands, and began air attacks that led Eisenhower to consider the use of tactical nuclear weapons against the mainland.

By September 4, when Eisenhower met with Dulles to confer on the crisis, the U.S. dilemma was clear. To defend the offshore islands too vigorously could risk war with China, perhaps even a nuclear war, and would encourage Chiang to attack the mainland. To back off would encourage the Communists to attack the islands, calling the U.S. commitment to question and risking a larger crisis later, perhaps an attack on Formosa itself, or the collapse of other Asian "dominos."

Dulles wanted to escalate, and brought a message from the Joint Chiefs of Staff indicating that they agreed. Dulles argued that, if the administration wasn't willing to use nuclear weapons in a crisis of such magnitude, it would render the weapons meaningless and force the nation to reevaluate its defense strategy. The military wanted authority to use tactical nuclear weapons shifted to the commander in the field. Chiang also wanted to step up the attack. Eisenhower, who had no intention of initiating what might become a nuclear exchange, refused to sanction Dulles's proposal.

The first break in the crisis came just two days later, on September 6. Chinese Premier Chou En-lai (pinyin: Jou En-lai) indicated that his government wanted to negotiate. Eisenhower left the door open, but, as in the 1954–55 Formosa crisis, he maneuvered to keep a range of options available. The Joint Chiefs reconsidered the situation, too, and advised the president that the offshore islands were probably not defensible, nor were they necessary for the defense of Formosa.

On September 11, the president spoke to the nation in a televised address, reiterating the administration's commitment to defend the islands. He warned of the dangers of appeasement, of another Munich, if the United States did not stand fast. The American public weighed in after the address. People were angry about the prospect of putting American lives on the line to defend islands that the U.S. military had deemed unnecessary to the defense of Formosa. American allies were no more enthusiastic. If there would be war, it would be a war no one wanted, except perhaps Chiang.

But how to end it? Both sides now began to seek ways to defuse the crisis. Secretary of Defense Neil McElroy discussed with the president the prospects for getting someone to replace Chiang. Eisenhower considered ways to get Chiang to reduce his own commitment to the islands. Dulles explored this approach in a press conference on September 30, backing off on the U.S. commitment to the islands, which he granted had no legal basis, and suggesting that a cease-fire might be a first step toward reduction of island fortification. The Communists responded, announcing a week-long cease fire if the United States agreed to halting resupply escort service, to which the administration consented.

The lull on both sides provided a way out of the crisis. At the end of the first week, the Communists extended the cease-fire for two more. Chiang, too, contributed to the relaxing tensions. He agreed to renounce the use of force as a means to regain the mainland, and pulled back some of his forces from the islands. When the Communists resumed shelling, they did so on an alternate days, and after a time the shelling stopped altogether.

The 1958 crisis thus ended much like the one of 1955—without much change, without any concessions, without resolution—but also without a broader war. Eisenhower had withstood criticism of a policy that placed Americans at risk, but had done so without directly putting any American lives on the line. And although the United States had increased its commitment to Chiang's government, Chiang had also made concessions that reduced the level of tensions in the Formosa Straits until the United States and China moved to establish diplomatic relations in the 1970s.

The United States and Latin America: The Nixon Trip

Midway through President Eisenhower's second term, relations with Latin America had fallen into a familiar pattern. The United States paid attention to Latin American nations when danger threatened to disrupt stability, but ignored them otherwise. Thus the 1954 coup in Guatemala was no aberration, but a continuation of a pattern established in the nineteenth century. In the early years of the twentieth century, under the mantle of the Monroe Doctrine and the "Roosevelt Corollary" of the early twentieth century, the "Colossus of the North" asserted its right to act as the police power of the Western Hemisphere.

Now in the mid-twentieth century, the United States viewed Latin America principally in the context of the Cold War. The aid that the United States sent to Latin America often took the form of assistance to repressive dictators such as Anastasio Somoza in Nicaragua, Rafael Trujillo in the Dominican Republic, and Fulgencio Batista in Cuba. Latin Americans resented the fact that the United States paid more attention to distant Asia than to its Latin American neighbors. That policy made good sense to Eisenhower. The Asian nations in question were on the front lines in the battle against Communism, whereas Latin America was relatively secure. The United States wanted to help Latin America, but through loans, not grants; through trade and private sector investment, not government aid. The administration established this pattern in its first year when the president rejected the advice of his brother Milton to increase aid to Latin America. The only significant change since then had been a decision to increase Import-Export Bank loans. Since the 1954 coup in Guatemala, Latin America had been stable, with no overt signs of Communist activity. The administration was pleased with its policy in the region.

Late in 1957, Assistant Secretary of State for Latin American affairs Roy Richard Rubottom challenged the administration's complacency about the region; he urged Secretary Dulles to visit Latin America. Dulles forwarded the recommendation to the president, pleading that his schedule was already full, but suggesting the vice president as a likely candidate for such a mission.

Nixon accepted the assignment, but without enthusiasm; it was scheduled for May 1958 to coincide with the inauguration of Argentina's President Arturo Frondizi. The State Department recommended expanding the itinerary to include most of the nations of South America. With little other than ceremonial appearances on the agenda, Nixon expected a routine trip.

On the first stops—in Montevideo and Buenos Aires—for the most part, the vice president encountered a warm response as he worked the crowds from his motorcade, stepping out of the car a few times to shake hands. Only occasionally were there indications of anti-American attitudes, when signs with "¡Fuera Nixon!" (Nixon Go Home!) would appear here and there. In Lima, at San Marcos University, the oldest university in the Western Hemisphere, students confronted him at the gate, some throwing oranges and stones. Although Nixon held his ground for a few minutes and demanded of the students, "Are you afraid of the truth?" he was finally forced to retreat. Crosstown at the Catholic University, he received a friendlier reception. But as he was walking back to his hotel, a hostile crowd yelled, threw things, and spat at him.

In Bogotá, Nixon learned of a possible attempt to assassinate him in Caracas, the last stop on his Latin American trip, although the Venezuelan government assured him it had things well in hand. Four months earlier, Venezuela had overthrown its dictator, Colonel Marcos Pérez Jiménez. Despite widespread popular resentment over long-term U.S. support for the Pérez Jiménez government, despite CIA reports of continuing Communist and anti-American activity, Nixon decided to go ahead with his visit to Venezuela. On May 13, a mob surrounded his plane at the Caracas airport and spat on the vice president and his wife, Pat, while they stood at attention for the Venezuelan national anthem.

On the way from the airport to the Panteón Nacional (National Cemetery), the Nixon motorcade was blocked by automobiles stopped across its route. Hundreds of angry people descended on the vice president's car. The motorcycle escort disappeared, leaving only Nixon's secret service officers to defend him. Rocks hit the windshield of the car, and splinters of the window showered Nixon and the Venezuelan foreign minister, who was riding with him. Pat Nixon and the foreign minister's wife watched from the car behind. One person attacked the vehicle with a pipe, trying to break the window. The mob began to rock the car, trying to overturn it. Nixon would later remember that, at that moment, he realized he might be killed. Finally, the driver found an opening, and sped through it, with the second car following. Once free of the crowd and again escorted by motorcycles, the motorcade drove on. Nixon told the driver to turn down a side street and let the motorcycles go on ahead, reasoning that the entourage would be better off without them, and traveling any route other than their expected one; they soon made it back to the embassy compound.

The Nixon party left the next morning to return to Washington. The president, the cabinet, congressional leaders, and the Nixons' daughters, Tricia and Julie, greeted them at National Airport. For the next few weeks at least, Nixon received a hero's reception everywhere he went.

Nixon Versus Khrushchev: The Kitchen Debate

A year later, in July 1959, Nixon undertook another foreign trip, this one to Moscow to open a United States exhibition at Sokolniki Park in Moscow, part of a cultural exchange and a convenient event around which to center a trip that had many purposes. Both nations hoped Nixon's visit would continue the good will surrounding the "spirit of Geneva" that characterized Soviet-American relations in the late fifties. Soviet Premier Khrushchev hope to use Nixon's visit to lay the groundwork for a return visit to the United States, which would culminate with a summit meeting between the leaders. Nixon, who planned to run for president in 1960, told Eisenhower before he left that he saw the trip as an opportunity to confront Khrushchev, and thereby strengthen his reputation as an anti-Communist. Nixon prepared diligently for the trip, learning phrases in Russian and meeting with area specialists. He conferred with Secretary Dulles, who was hospitalized with the cancer that would take his life only four days after Nixon's visit to the Soviet Union.

Nixon arrived in Moscow on July 22. Khrushchev and he met several times, sizing one another up, with Khrushchev alternately charming and challenging the vice president. Because Congress had passed the Captive Nations Resolution just before Nixon left Washington, criticizing Russia for its role in Eastern Europe, the mood of the meetings was more confrontational than it might otherwise have been. The most memorable encounter occurred as they toured the U.S. exhibition before its official opening. They talked briefly before a mock-up of an American television studio, where Khrushchev boasted that the Soviet Union had made more progress in its brief existence than the United States had in its one hundred and eighty years. The group moved on, and then stopped before a display of a modern American kitchen. The Soviet press had claimed that the kitchen was beyond the reach of the average American.

As they stood before the American kitchen, Nixon spoke of the diversity of American consumer goods, and of the right of Americans to choose. Khrushchev countered by claiming that such a system was inefficient. Nixon remarked that it was better to be comparing washing machines than rockets, but Khrushchev responded, "Yes, but your generals say, 'We want to compete in rockets. We can beat you.' " Nixon argued that neither side should threaten the other, or issue ultimatums. "Who is giving an ultimatum?" Khrushchev replied. "You want to threaten? We will answer threats with threats." The two men stood face-to-face, pointing fingers at one another, in a debate that historian Stephen Ambrose described as "an exchange of bluff, bluster, and near-buffoonery." Photographers crowded in, snapping pictures that appeared in the world press the next day. As contentious as the kitchen debate appeared, observers noticed that Khrushchev enjoyed it.

The vice president met with Khrushchev away from the public view, and carried on their debate about the differences in the two systems. Nixon and his wife toured the Russian hinterland, Nixon working crowds like an American politician, Pat visiting children in hospitals and youth camps. Before his departure, the Soviets allowed Nixon to make a television address to the Russian people. He called for a world not divided into two camps, a world in which each nation had the opportunity to choose its own political and economic system. Shortly before Nixon left, Eisenhower announced that he was extending an invitation to Khrushchev to visit the United States.

Nixon left the Soviet Union with a sense of what a formidable adversary the Soviet Union could be. "I knew my intuition had been right," he wrote in his memoirs. "Khrushchev would respect only those who stood up to him, who resisted him, and who believed as strongly in their own cause as he believed in his."

The United States and the Cuban Revolution

American interest in Cuba dated to the mid-nineteenth century, and its direct involvement, to the Spanish-American War in 1898, long associated in the minds of Americans with the highly publicized campaign of Theodore Roosevelt's Rough Riders. From that time on, the United States became as entrenched in Cuban affairs as in those of any other Latin American nation.

Cuba became the testing ground in the late nineteenth century for the concept of American Empire. The anti-imperialists achieved approval of the Teller amendment, which forbade annexation, only to have their adversaries pass the Platt amendment, which gave the United States control over a Cuban protectorate, a naval base at Guantanamo, and the right to approve or disapprove of Cuban treaties. Until 1934, the United States kept Cuba in protectorate status.

The year after the United States relinquished its protectorate, Fulgencio Batista emerged as a defender of the old order in Cuba. For the next twenty years, U.S. fortunes in Cuba would be tied to those of Batista, who served as president only briefly, but who was always near the seat of power. Batista encouraged U.S. investment on the island, and ultimately U.S. companies controlled 40 percent of Cuban sugar production. The United States treated Batista as a close friend, extended military aid to his regime, trained his constabulary, and relied on him to maintain order. The U.S. ambassador was so close to the Cuban leader that it became an embarrassment; in 1957, the Eisenhower administration replaced him with Earl E. T. Smith, a businessman who had the temerity to criticize Batista on occasion.

Havana became an American playground, where American organized crime operated with impunity, and where prostitution and vice flourished, often with direct American participation. Cuba seemed prosperous, but it was a superficial prosperity in which few of the Cuban people participated. Cuba's literacy rate had declined since Batista came to power, and its unemployment rate was three times that of the United States. Sugar required intensive effort only during part of the year, and most sugar laborers were seasonal workers who found it difficult to find employment in off-peak periods. Understandably, the Cuban people considered the presence of the United States to be oppressive.

Fidel Castro was a young law student at the University of Havana when he began his involvement in political activism. He led an ill-fated attack against army barracks at Moncada in Santiago on July 26, 1952, receiving a fifteen-year jail sentence for his efforts. Batista freed him in 1955, and Castro and his brother Raúl went into exile in Mexico City. There Raúl met Jacobo Arbenz, who had been ousted by the CIA-sponsored coup in Guatemala the previous year. With other Cuban expatriates, the Castro brothers planned their return to Cuba. In 1956, they landed with a band of supporters dedicated to overthrowing Batista, but again, the assault failed. Castro and the remnants of his revolutionary band retreated into Cuba's Sierra Maestra. For the next two years they successfully evaded authorities; they began organizing, increasing their numbers, and plotting against the government. No longer just a student protest, the 26th of July movement gathered support first among rural peasants, but ultimately from the cities and countryside alike, and from urban middle-class Cubans opposed to Batista.

As Castro's popularity increased, the Eisenhower administration found itself in a predicament, caught between supporting an unpopular dictator unwilling to relinquish power, and a young, untested, unknown revolutionary leader whose intentions were far from clear. Americans knew too little about Castro to make informed judgments about what he stood for. A *New York Times* reporter had interviewed him a year earlier, and Castro seemed to offer idealistic if fragmentary plans for reform. Eisenhower didn't trust him, but he no longer believed Batista merited continued U.S. backing.

By the end of December 1958, any support Batista may have had among the Cuban people had faded away. Castro marched into Havana; on New Year's Eve, Batista fled into exile. Castro in power was as enigmatic as he had been before. The Eisenhower administration replaced Ambassador Smith, whose previous criticism of Castro left him out of favor, with Philip Bonsal, a liberal who'd served as ambassador to Bolivia. Castro declared himself premier in February, ordered the execution of his opponents, and soon began to criticize the United States, still denying, however, that he was a Communist.

In April 1959, Castro came to the United States at the invitation of the American Society of Newspaper Editors. The president refused to meet with him, but Vice President Nixon conferred with the Cuban leader for three hours in the vice president's formal office. Nixon challenged Castro about why he did not hold elections, why he was continuing to execute former supporters of Batista. In a long memorandum to Eisenhower, Nixon explained that Castro had claimed to be following the will of the Cuban people. Nixon was more concerned about Castro's "almost slavish subservience to prevailing majority opinion" than about his possible Communist leanings. Castro, Nixon continued "is either incredibly naïve about Communism or under Communist discipline—my guess is the former." The vice president concluded that Castro clearly had the ability to lead, and that the United States should "at least try to orient him in the right direction."

The Eisenhower administration tried to work with Castro well into the fall of 1959. Castro initiated a land reform program, and began to nationalize large industries, none of which were U.S. businesses at this early point. The administration monitored Castro's actions, and even defended his right to nationalize. And when Castro's anti-American rhetoric increased, the administration withheld judgment. Ambassador Bonsal signaled Castro that the United States wanted to continue good relations with Cuba.

Signs of discontent in Cuba encouraged the administration to believe that Castro's support in Cuba was shallow. Early in 1960, the stream of refugees fleeing the island swelled. Wealthy landowners, the victims of seizure for land reform, were the first to leave. Then, as Castro broadened nationalization, people engaged in business departed, followed by professionals, students, and small property owners. Terrorists attacked government property, including sugar mills and power plants. The appearance of resistance to Castro was deceptive, however. After the departure of the more discontented Cubans, those who remained remembered the notorious corruption under Batista and felt loyalty toward the new leader. The sporadic terrorist attacks on government facilities only strengthened Castro's position.

In 1960, the United States began to move against Castro. Planning took place at the highest levels. In 1954, Eisenhower had approved a National Security Council directive, NSC 5412, that authorized covert operations against Communist activities. The following year top-level officials from the State and Defense Departments, the CIA, and the White House staff began meeting as the "5412 Committee" to discuss covert operations. On January 13, 1960, they took up the deteriorating situation in Cuba, and Allen Dulles suggested that the United States might not be able to tolerate Castro much longer.

The following month, the administration took another step closer to intervention when the Soviet Union announced that, under a trade agreement with Cuba negotiated by Vice Premier Anastas Mikoyan, it had agreed to buy a million tons of Cuban sugar per year for five years, and to extend credits to Cuba to purchase Soviet-made equipment. Having ranted against Castro in several meetings of the 5412 Committee over the following weeks, on March 17, Eisenhower authorized a covert operation to oust Castro. As formulated by the committee and by task forces in the CIA and NSC, the operation was to use propaganda, to enlist the Cuban opposition on the island and in exile, to undertake covert actions, and to develop "a paramilitary force outside of Cuba for future guerilla action."

The CIA helped small groups of exiled Cubans return to the island to conduct sabotage. Although CIA Director Allen Dulles and Richard Bissell, who took charge of covert action aimed at Cuba, hoped that these groups could begin to organize internal opposition to Castro, they weren't able to do so. The Eisenhower administration then imposed an embargo on Cuban sugar. That summer, the CIA generated plans to assassinate Castro, some of which were so far-fetched—such as injecting botulism toxin into Castro's favorite cigars—they subjected the agency to ridicule when Senate hearings uncovered them years later. The CIA contacted mafia bosses who'd done business in Havana during Batista's heyday in hopes that they might be able to carry out the agency's dirty work. Planners devised various cloak-and-dagger schemes to try to embarrass Castro. One such scheme was to spray disorienting chemicals into the radio booth from which Castro addressed the nation, believing that his speeches would become rambling, and he would lose the confidence of the Cuban people. Those who'd heard Castro's speeches, which often lasted several hours, wondered how anyone would ever be able to tell if the scheme had worked.

At the same time that the CIA began plotting to assassinate Castro, it began planning for an invasion of the island by Cuban exiles with CIA support. It constructed an airstrip in Guatemala for use by exiles and their trainers; it trained exiles there and in the Canal Zone in Panama. Bissell briefed Eisenhower, keeping his reports vague enough to preserve the president's "plausible deniability." Whatever hopes the CIA may have had of concealing U.S. involvement were dashed from the outset. Castro had sources within the exile community both in South Florida and in Guatemala. Covert planning became an open secret.

Eisenhower's defenders later insisted that he was never enthusiastic about the covert operation, but neither did ever indicate he no longer supported it. In the final months of his presidency, Eisenhower upped the ante against Castro, imposing a full trade embargo on Cuba in October 1960. The president progressively reduced the U.S. embassy staff in Havana. Then, on January 3, less than three weeks before leaving office, he broke off diplomatic relations with Castro's government. During his transition meetings with Kennedy, Eisenhower told the president-elect to do whatever was necessary in Cuba. Vice President Nixon was an outspoken advocate of the operation throughout, despite his campaign debate position to the contrary in October 1960.

There seemed to be every reason to believe that the operation would succeed. Many of the same people who'd been involved in planning the successful 1954 coup in Guatemala were involved in planning the Cuban operation, including Allen Dulles, Richard Bissell, and Tracy Barnes, who'd directed the ouster of Arbenz in Guatemala. The CIA's seemingly easy triumphs in Iran and in Guatemala had fostered a myth of agency invincibility in covert operations. What Third World nation could stand up against the accumulated expertise of the CIA?

The flaws in these assumptions didn't become clear until the operation was already under way, and by then it was too late. Planners made the mistake of assuming that Cuba was like Guatemala. Not only were the situations different, but Castro, too, had learned lessons from Guatemala. He did not tolerate opposition from any quarter in the Cuban military, as Arbenz had in Guatemala. The most critical misjudgment was the belief that the Cuban people would rise up to oppose Castro. CIA intelligence experts judged that Castro's popularity had peaked in 1959, and had been declining since, although those same experts also judged that Castro had been able to defuse internal opposition, and that he would likely be able to continue to do so. The most seemingly convincing evidence of Cuban opposition to Castro came from Cuban exiles, whose vested interests should have led analysts to treat their observations with skepticism—or at least with caution. Ultimately, the CIA ignored the assessments of its own intelligence estimates. The pessimistic estimates did have one effect on planning: as skepticism about a Cuban uprising against Castro increased, the CIA increased the size of its potential invasion force.

By the time the CIA executed its plan, Eisenhower was in retirement on his farm in Gettysburg, and Nixon was establishing an office in Southern California, where he would launch a bid for governor in 1962. The Bay of Pigs debacle in April 1961 was a disastrous début for the Kennedy foreign policy team. Many critics blamed the failure on Kennedy's own decisions, most notably the decision not to send a second air strike, and on an assumed consensus in which advisors were reluctant to challenge a president making his first major foreign policy decision. Kennedy accepted responsibility for going in with what proved to be inadequate air cover. But many of the mistakes rested with planning done under his predecessor. There was plenty of blame to be shared by both administrations.

Eisenhower, Khrushchev, and the Chances for Accommodation

In the years since Stalin's death, the Cold War had proceeded in fits and starts, with occasional opportunities for better relations between the United

States and the Soviet Union dashed by new crises. The last years of the Eisenhower administration would follow the same pattern.

The Soviet leader Nikita Khrushchev precipitated a new clash over Berlin when he issued an ultimatum in November 1958, demanding that the Western powers leave the city within six months. If they did not do so, he threatened to interrupt transportation across the zones of occupation, as Stalin had done in 1948, precipitating the Berlin airlift. Furthermore, Khrushchev threatened to conclude an independent treaty with the German Democratic Republic (East Germany), a provocative threat since the United States was supporting West German Chancellor Konrad Adenauer's plan to reunify Germany. The West insisted on a settlement for all of Germany, not just for Berlin, which the Soviets refused to consider.

The deadline for a settlement came in May 1959, within days of the death of Secretary of State Dulles. The date passed without incident, but Khrushchev railed at Averell Harriman, who visited him in Moscow, telling Harriman that he would liquidate U.S. rights in West Berlin. Khrushchev had been insisting on a summit meeting with Eisenhower, but his behavior made it difficult for Eisenhower to accede. The new secretary of state, Christian Herter, proposed a way out. Why not invite Khrushchev to the United States?

Khrushchev accepted; in September, he flew to Washington, where Eisenhower got the visit off to an auspicious start by meeting his plane. The next day, Eisenhower took his guest on a helicopter ride over Washington, where the Soviet premier saw cars streaming out of the city to their single-family homes in the suburbs. Khrushchev criticized the inefficiency of the American system, claiming that Soviet citizens preferred to live in more efficient apartments—but Eisenhower had made his point.

The American media followed Khrushchev's trip with great interest—to New York and the United Nations, to Iowa, where he talked shop with a farmer, and then to California. In California, Khrushchev witnessed a performance of the can-can, and made clear his disgust at the immorality of the performance, a sure sign of the degradation of the West. He asked to visit Disneyland, but authorities denied his request, fearing that it would be difficult to ensure his security. When he returned to Washington, Eisenhower took him to Camp David, where they had productive discussions. Observers noticed that Khrushchev seemed at ease, but that his demeanor stiffened when members of the Soviet delegation joined the meetings—suggesting that Khrushchev may have been under pressure from the Kremlin. The visit was a great success, and the leaders planned for a summit meeting in Paris in May 1960, to be followed with a visit by Eisenhower to the Soviet Union. Khrushchev, however, left the United States believing that he'd received assurances of a settlement on the status of Berlin. His disappointment over the continued absence of one was one of the factors leading to the demise of the spirit of Camp David.

U-2: Eisenhower's Last Cold War Crisis

During Eisenhower's first term, the administration sponsored development of the technology to monitor the Soviet Union from high above the earth. In 1954, the aircraft firm Lockheed developed an extraordinarily light, even fragile plane that could fly at extremely high altitudes, designating it the "U-2." The Air Force expressed no interest in the plane, but the CIA contracted to purchase twenty units. The following year, the administration authorized the Corona project, which eventually produced the first American spy satellite. Both systems depended on high-resolution cameras; the Soviets were able to compete with the United States on rocket technology in the 1950s, but the Russians had nothing to challenge the high resolution of American cameras. Ultimately, there were 147 Corona satellite missions between 1959 and 1972, when the program ended. The Corona satellite required that its film canisters be recovered, and thus also required precise timing and virtually flawless operation. Not until the fourteenth mission, on August 18, 1960, was a canister with film successfully recovered. Two more successful missions took place before Eisenhower left office, but the program was still in the early development stages, and yielded few results before his term ended.

The U-2 was another matter. It was a spectacular success, producing high-quality photographs that yielded excellent information about the Soviet missile programs and defense system. The U-2 flew at an altitude of 70,000 feet, above the range of Soviet fighters or surface-to-air missiles. The Soviets protested, but not publicly since their inability to shoot down the plane was an embarrassment. Both sides kept the U-2 secret, each for its own reasons. Even after the 1957 Sputnik launch, when Eisenhower's advisors recommended that he tell the American people about the U-2 to reassure them, Eisenhower refused.

But each flight was a risk: there was no question that the Soviets were working on technology to shoot down the U-2. The CIA assured the president that even if the Russians were able to shoot down a U-2, the pilot would not survive: the plane was equipped with a self-destruction device, and the pilot carried a suicide pill. Nonetheless, the president required the CIA to clear each flight with him.

In April 1960, the CIA flew a successful mission, and asked the president for permission for one more flight. Eisenhower was scheduled to meet with Khrushchev in Paris on May 16, and he did not want to jeopardize the summit. Nonetheless, he reluctantly approved another flight, to be flown no later than April 25. Weather delayed the flight until May 1, an unfortunate circumstance since that date had long been an international workers holiday, one of the most significant dates on the Soviet calendar, the date when the Kremlin paraded its new military hardware in Moscow. The U-2 took off from Pakistan, and flew over the Soviet Union. A Soviet missile exploded close enough to the U-2 to force pilot Francis Gary Powers to eject.

Khrushchev said nothing for the next four days, after which he announced that the Soviets had shot down an American spy plane. The United States attempted to cover up, announcing that a weather plane had strayed off course, and may have penetrated Soviet air space. Khrushchev then announced that not only had the plane been shot down, but the pilot had also survived and was in custody. Eisenhower refused to blame subordinates, and took personal responsibility for the flight. He admitted the existence of the spy plane, and defended it.

The Soviets indicated that they still wanted the Paris summit, and Eisenhower went to Europe hoping that the incident had blown over. It had not, and the meeting degenerated into charges and countercharges that prevented any progress on restricting nuclear tests. There would be no Eisenhower visit to the Soviet Union, and the remaining months of the Eisenhower presidency witnessed no crowning diplomatic achievements. Relations between the superpowers had taken a turn for the icy, and the Cold War would dominate the election campaign of 1960.

Recommended Reading

Many of the foreign policy issues that faced Eisenhower in his second term had their origins in his first term—or earlier.

Thus, on Vietnam, see the works recommended in chapter 5, particularly those by Karnow, by Herring, and by Anderson. On the Eisenhower administration's response to Sputnik, see Robert A. Divine's *The Sputnik Challenge: Eisenhower's Response to the Soviet Satellite* (New York: Oxford University Press, 1993).

On Cuba, see Thomas G. Paterson's *Contesting Castro: The United States and the Triumph of the Cuban Revolution* (New York: Oxford University Press, 1994) is a historian's perspective that considers the U.S. response during Castro's revolution and after he seized power. Wayne S. Smith's *The Closest of Enemies: A Personal and Diplomatic Account of U.S.-Cuban Relations since 1957* (New York: Norton, 1987) offers the perspective of a diplomat who served in Cuba during the revolution.

Two surveys of U.S. relations with China that examine the Formosa (Taiwan) Strait crises are Warren I. Cohen's *America's Response to China: A History of Sino-American Relations,* 4th edition (New York: Columbia University Press, 2000) and Michael Schaller's *The United States and China in the Twentieth Century* (New York: Oxford University Press, 1985).

Two books survey the U.S. high-altitude and space spy programs of the 1950s and their political ramifications, Michael Beschloss's *Mayday: Eisenhower, Khrushchev, and the U-2 Affair* (New York: Harper and Row, 1986) and Curtis Peebles's *The Corona Project: America's First Spy Satellites* (Annapolis, Md.: Naval Institute Press, 1997).

11

The End of the Ike Age

Eisenhower and Congress: Living with the Democrats

FOR THE LAST SIX YEARS of his presidency, Eisenhower had to contend with a Democratic majority in both houses of Congress. His last two years were extraordinarily difficult: after the Republican thrashing at the polls in 1958, the Democrats fell just short of veto-proof majorities in both houses. With Eisenhower prohibited by law from seeking reelection in 1960, Democrats were not reluctant to flex their political muscle. Senate Majority Leader Lyndon Johnson had presidential aspirations and sought to demonstrate his political clout.

Nonetheless, prospects were not as dismal as they might have appeared: the president often found his policies more closely aligned with conservative Democrats than with members of his own party. Democratic leadership in both houses often made common cause with the president. Speaker of the House Sam Rayburn and Senator Johnson were both Texans, and would often join Eisenhower for cocktails and discuss legislation. Eisenhower biographer Geoffrey Perret noted that Eisenhower liked to hark back to his birth in Denison, Texas, and joke, "There's no problem that three Texans can't solve." On social policy, civil rights, the budget, and international relations, the three men often found room for agreement. Their cooperation paid dividends. Congress passed 80 percent of the bills he introduced, reflecting favorably on his own administration and earning Johnson a reputation for effectiveness that few majority leaders in U.S. history could match.

One of Eisenhower's disappointments was that he hadn't been able to bring the Republican Party together. His "middle of the road" politics meant that his natural allies in Congress were usually moderate Republicans and conservative Democrats. His views on civil rights were closer to those of most Southern Democrats than either his Democratic predecessor's or successor's were. He believed that the South had to work out its own racial problems and once confided to Chief Justice Earl Warren that Southerners weren't bad people. Eisenhower despised conservative Republicans who had supported McCarthyist excess. He tried to move his party toward a more international foreign policy, and found that his most ardent foes were often Republican congressional leaders such as Senator Robert Taft of Ohio and Senator William Knowland of California. After Eisenhower's retirement and Nixon's defeat in the 1960 election, conservative Republicans gained ascendancy in the party and, in 1964, helped Barry Goldwater win the party's presidential nomination—only to be defeated decisively by Lyndon Johnson.

Even policies that, in retrospect, seem uncontroversial had political implications. The admission of Alaska and Hawaii as the nation's forty-ninth and fiftieth states came in rapid succession in 1959, but only after protracted delay. Democrats had been calling for their admission for many years, but Republicans had resisted, worrying that senators and members of Congress from both territories would likely be Democrats. Eisenhower and many Republicans believed that Alaska was too sparsely populated to merit statehood. Conservative Southerners considered the racial mixing of Hawaii's population to be troublesome, and Republicans feared union strength on the island. Nonetheless, polls suggested that some 80 percent of Americans supported statehood for both territories, and ultimately, Eisenhower set aside partisan political considerations and endorsed the policy.

The Battle of the Budget

As the Eisenhower administration entered its second term, the Democratic majority was only half of its problem with Congress. The other half lay in the Republican Party itself, and in the continuing divide between the Old Guard and the moderates. The Republican intramural struggle, simmering for years, had come to a full boil during the 1956 election campaign. Arthur Larson, undersecretary of labor, had written a campaign book entitled *A Republican Looks at His Party*, in which he lauded Eisenhower as the center of American politics, embodying a "New Republicanism" that balanced free enterprise with social welfare legislation. Eisenhower liked the book and on election night had boasted, "modern Republicanism has proved itself." Such a notion stuck in the craw of the Old Guard, to whom the president's policies, whether called "New Republicanism" or "modern Republicanism," represented a desertion of traditional Republican values, and were one reason why Eisenhower's coattails had been disappointingly short.

The Old Guard struck back when the president delivered his budget message in January. Conservative Republicans claimed that Ike's $71.8 billion budget was far too high, and that it violated the principles established in the Taft-Eisenhower agreement in 1952 setting $60 billion as the target ceiling for government spending. New Republicanism, the Old Guard complained, was beginning to look a lot like New Dealism.

The ensuing battle, which stretched on for months and did not reach resolution until early September, embarrassed the administration. Eisenhower's inept handling of the issue gave gleeful Democrats a chance to embarrass the administration. Confusion reigned from the first day, when, in a press conference after the president's message, Secretary of the Treasury George Humphrey joined Old Guard critics in calling the budget too high. He made matters worse by adding that, if expenditures weren't cut, "you will have a depression that will curl your hair"—a line that made headlines in newspapers around the country. And Eisenhower made matters still worse by agreeing with Humphrey, saying that Congress should cut the budget wherever possible. When it came to budgetary matters, however, Eisenhower's most serious problem in the cabinet was, not Humphrey, but Secretary of Defense Charlie Wilson, who speaking for the military, demanded $40 billion for defense even after Eisenhower insisted that $38.5 billion was his absolute ceiling.

Democrats and Republicans alike responded quickly to the president's invitation to cut his budget. Democrats sought to trim administration programs and to expand their own. Republicans, for their part, looked to trim New Dealism right out of the budget. Historian Stephen Ambrose commented that representatives and senators from both parties "tried to outdo each other in irresponsibility." Ultimately, Congress trimmed some $4 billion from the administration's budget in a struggle that did no one proud. Even Chief of Staff Sherman Adams acknowledged that the battle of the budget had been "a serious and disturbing personal defeat" for Eisenhower.

Conflict of Interest: The Fall of Sherman Adams

Sherman Adams was as close as anyone on the president's staff to being an indispensable man. The former New Hampshire governor was one of the first governors to support Eisenhower's candidacy in 1952. After managing Eisenhower's campaign, Adams took charge of the White House staff. Those who wanted to see the president had to go through Adams, who soon established a reputation as the "Abominable No-Man." He was much more than a gatekeeper, however. He helped plot political strategy, dispensed patronage, and executed unpleasant tasks the president wanted to avoid. Often a counterbalance to administration conservatives such as Secretary of the Treasury George Humphrey, Adams pushed Eisenhower toward more liberal policies on McCarthy, civil rights, and social policy. Adams's performance won him few friends outside the White House, and when he got into trouble, there were few people shedding tears.

President Eisenhower won election in 1952, in part, on the strength of charges of corruption in the Truman administration, promising that his administration would be "clean as a hound's tooth." So the Republicans were sensitive when similar charges came their way. No one was more aware of this than Adams, the administration's enforcer. Twice—in 1955 and early in 1958—Adams had demanded the resignations of appointed officials who'd used their influence to get favors for clients or friends. Later in 1958, a congressional subcommittee leveled similar allegations at Adams himself. First, the Legislative Oversight Subcommittee found that, in 1953, Adams had approached the Civil Aeronautics Board on behalf of Murray Chotiner, Vice President Nixon's former campaign manager. Then, in June and July, the same subcommittee accused Adams of accepting expensive gifts from a friend, Boston textile businessman Bernard Goldfine, and then using his influence to assist Goldfine in his dealings with the Federal Trade Commission (FTC) and the Securities and Exchange Commission (SEC).

The investigation revealed that Goldfine had given Adams a $2,400 Oriental rug and a vicuña coat, and had paid for over $3,000 worth of hotel lodgings for Adams and his family. The vicuña coat was a doubly embarrassing symbol since one of the key allegations against a Truman aide had been a gift of a mink coat, which Nixon had satirized in his Checkers speech when he referred to his wife's "respectable Republican cloth coat." Adams denied that he'd done anything improper, and insisted that his contacts with regulatory agencies on Goldfine's behalf were ordinary inquiries that were common practice in Washington. Eisenhower defended him in a statement to the press that acknowledged a "lack of prudence," but ultimately conceded, "I need him." With elections drawing near, however, and the Republican Old Guard pushing for Adams's departure in any case, Eisenhower could ill afford to dig his heels in too deeply. On September 22, the president accepted Adams's resignation.

The Democratic Sweep of 1958

Republicans entered the 1958 election campaign divided, demoralized, and on the defensive. The year had brought a series of difficult issues, and few had been resolved with unambiguous success. A foreign policy crisis in Lebanon that required the commitment of American troops abroad for the first time since Korea, an ongoing confrontation over Quemoy and Matsu in the Formosa Strait, the battle over the budget, inflation, Little Rock, Sputnik, and worries about a missile gap gave the Democrats enormous advantages. The Republicans were left wondering just how badly they would be defeated. The Sherman Adams debacle had been devastating since, in light of all of the party's other difficulties, Republican National Committee Chairman Meade Alcorn had designed the party's national campaign around Democratic corruption under Truman. Even though 1958 would be his last campaign, Eisenhower made few appearances. Many of the Republican candidates were from the Old Guard, senators who'd been elected six years earlier as part of the McCarthy sweep.

The election was a disaster of epic proportions for Republicans. The Democrats swept statehouses and Washington alike; their sweep of the Senate exceeded even the one that accompanied Franklin D. Roosevelt's landslide reelection in 1936. Democrats won 13 seats in the Senate, and 47 in the House, increasing their margins to 17 and 49, respectively. The gubernatorial returns were even more devastating for the GOP. Democrats now controlled 35 of 48 statehouses, including Vermont, which they hadn't won in a hundred years. Eisenhower had to face his last two years in the White House with a decisive Democratic majority ensconced at the other end of Pennsylvania Avenue.

Labor-Management Relations and the Landrum-Griffin Act

One of the key issues of Eisenhower's last two years in office was the reform of labor legislation. More than a decade had passed since the Taft-Hartley Act of 1947 had passed over President Truman's veto, and by the late fifties, several circumstances made leaders of both parties receptive to reform. Truman had vetoed the bill, at least in part, to win the support of labor in the 1952 election. Labor termed Taft-Hartley a "slave-labor law," and objected in particular to the provision for an 80-day cooling off period that could be granted upon presidential request. After Eisenhower's election in 1952, Republicans, too, found fault with Taft-Hartley, complaining, however, that it was too lenient toward labor. In the years that followed, labor learned to live with Taft-Hartley, and even Truman admitted that it was a good law.

The labor movement had boomed in the thirties and forties, benefiting from a rapid rate of growth and favorable legislation during the Roosevelt years. Labor membership continued to grow in the fifties, but the rate of growth slowed in comparison to the thirties and forties. Union membership began the decade at 14 million, increased to more than 18.5 million by mid-decade, but declined to less than 17 million by 1960, as unions were charged with corruption. The growth in the economy began a shift toward the service sector, and the slower rate of growth in manufacturing jobs affected union membership. The South remained hostile to unions, enacting "right-to-work" laws that put tight restrictions on union activity. Unions became more active politically, but even the 1955 merger between the AFL and the CIO failed to make a significant difference in the ability of the labor movement to effect legislative changes.

The public perception toward labor changed for the worse in the fifties. Most damaging to the image of the labor movement were repeated charges of corruption, many later proven in court. Teamster President Dave Beck appeared before the Senate Permanent Investigations Subcommittee, and committee counsel Robert Kennedy grilled him about allegations that he had used union funds for personal real estate purchases. In 1956, Beck became one of the first targets of Senator John McClellan (Democrat-Arkansas), chairman of the Select Committee on Improper Activities in the Labor or Management Field, investigating charges of embezzlement, theft of union funds, and fixing union elections. When charged with bilking his union out of $322,000, Beck invoked the Fifth Amendment 117 times before the committee. The AFL-CIO Executive Committee finally expelled him in 1956. His successor, Jimmy Hoffa, soon faced charges of his own for ties to organized crime. As majority counsel to the McClellan Committee, Robert Kennedy went after Hoffa with a determination that led critics to call Kennedy "ruthless." The AFL-CIO expelled the entire Teamsters Union in 1957. As attorney general in his brother's administration in the early sixties, Kennedy continued his pursuit of Hoffa, who went to prison in 1964 for jury tampering and fraud in 1963 and 1964.

By 1958, public and Congress alike were receptive to restrictions on union activity. Early in the year, in response to findings of the McClellan racketeering investigation, the president called for labor reform legislation. In April, Senator John F. Kennedy (Democrat-Massachusetts) proposed legislation to regulate union pension and welfare funds. After encountering considerable opposition, the bill became law, the Welfare and Pension Plans Act of 1958, in a watered-down version that relied on voluntary self-policing.

The 1958 law wasn't enough to satisfy those who had wanted stiff laws to curb racketeering, so the call for greater restrictions carried over into the next session of Congress. Labor cheered the results of the 1958 elections, and believed the results protected them against any punitive legislation in the new Congress. The public demanded reform, however. Senator Kennedy, whose standing among his colleagues had risen as a result of his efforts to pass labor legislation the previous year, drafted a second bill. The administration believed Kennedy's bill was too lenient. Eisenhower wanted harsher penalties for bribery, extortion, and embezzlement, as well as stiffer requirements for record keeping and financial reporting. Republicans and Democrats alike began submitting amendments, altering the Kennedy bill substantially. Although Kennedy's work made him a more credible candidate for president in 1960, his name would not be attached to the bill he introduced.

Labor found itself divided over the proposals circulating in Congress. Some were opposed to any reform legislation, while others recognized the inevitability of such legislation and wanted to restrict it to anticorruption provisions. Some wanted something akin to the Kennedy bill, but Hoffa and his supporters opposed it. Management was more unified, and wanted to strengthen the Taft-Hartley Act. One of the most strenuously debated issues was a proposal to broaden limits on secondary boycotts, which would prevent unions from pressuring employers to boycott companies targeted by the unions for boycotts or strikes.

The administration realized that it had to gain the support of Democrats in order to pass any labor reforms. Robert P. Griffin (Republican-Michigan), a second-term representative on the House Committee on Education and Labor who came to Congress with experience in labor law, became the administration's advocate. His colleague on the Education and Labor Committee, Philip M. Landrum (Democrat-Georgia), agreed to cosponsor legislation that mainly reflected the administration's goals. Neither Griffin nor Landrum had a reputation for being either pro-labor or antilabor, which made them well suited to serve as sponsors. To preserve the spirit of bipartisanship, Republicans listed the Democratic sponsor first in all references to the bill, which thus became know as "Landrum-Griffin."

The Labor Management Reporting and Disclosure Act, better known as the "Landrum-Griffin Act," passed both houses of Congress in early September. The president signed it into law on September 14. Even though his role had not been central, Eisenhower got virtually everything he wanted. The act set criminal penalties for corrupt practices by union officials, and established means to ensure that union elections would be democratic. It strengthened the provisions of Taft-Hartley in key areas, including the disputed issue of secondary boycotts, and extended Taft-Hartley's strike and picketing restrictions to cover additional groups of workers.

Landrum-Griffin, like Taft-Hartley before it, turned out to be less odious than labor had predicted, although labor historian R. Alton Lee considers it a fine example of how laws should *not* be written. The committee system broke down: drafted and amended largely in response to the actions of Beck and Hoffa, the law disproportionately reflected public opinion and fell prey to hastily conceived expedients.

Selecting Candidates for the Election of 1960

The election of 1960 promised to bring new faces to presidential politics. After two consecutive Eisenhower-Stevenson races, the electorate and the parties looked to new candidates. The Democrats had no desire to back Stevenson a third time, for he had been trounced twice and had the aura of a loser, as much as he may have retained respect of many voters. The Republicans had no choice. After the death of President Franklin D. Roosevelt, they had, in February 1951, pushed through the Twenty-second Amendment to the Constitution, which prevented a president from serving more than two full terms. They now found themselves the first victims of their own revenge. Despite the U-2 crisis and the continuing Cold War, President Eisenhower remained an enormously popular figure and, without the constitutional prohibition, almost certainly could have won reelection in 1960.

In the primary campaign, the drama rested with the Democrats. The race for the Republican nomination, it seemed, would be a contest between Vice President Richard M. Nixon, whose strength was rooted among conservatives, and New York Governor Nelson Rockefeller, one of the most liberal members of his party. But that soon turned out not to be the case. Although his name was well known nationally, the governor had been forced to concentrate on matters that seldom generated publicity outside of the Empire State. When he tested the political waters outside of New York, he found that his support was tepid at best. Rockefeller had international experience beyond that of most governors, especially in Latin America, but little of this had received national attention, and it paled beside Nixon's contacts abroad as vice president. Rockefeller's support for tax increases in New York won him few friends elsewhere. Thus, in December 1959, long before the first primary, he announced his "definite and final" decision not to seek the nomination.

The Democratic contest was wide open, with Adlai Stevenson seeking to gain a third nomination in an unusually strong field of candidates—the five main contenders included the party's standard-bearers in five consecutive elections, from 1952 through 1968. The Democrats had controlled the Senate as the majority party throughout the fifties with the single exception of the 83rd Congress (1953–54), and had a mature slate of potential candidates.

Senator Lyndon B. Johnson of Texas, the Senate majority leader since 1955, was the early favorite to unseat Stevenson, who had a loyal following but whom most Democrats believed could not win. Johnson was as ambitious as any politician, and as skilled as any legislator. Few could match his ability to pass legislation. He had masterfully gained the support of Democratic senators through his use of the prerogatives of his position as majority leader, and in the Senate operated as a skillful practitioner of the art of compromise. He had demonstrated his ability in particular after the launch of Sputnik by the Soviet Union, refusing to use the issue to embarrass the Republicans, and instead leading the national debate on the American space program. Among the electorate, however, Johnson had limitations. Despite his down-the-line support for the New Deal and the Fair Deal, Johnson was still a Southerner, which was still an obstacle to nationwide acceptance in the fifties and early sixties. He also had a reputation as a political manipulator. He operated best in one-on-one situations, where he could employ the "Johnson treatment" that became legendary during his presidency. He was less adept before crowds, and was the least talented public speaker of the Democratic hopefuls.

Senator Hubert Humphrey of Minnesota, a man of impeccable liberal credentials in an era when such a résumé carried weight, had a distinguished record on civil rights and civil liberties, farm politics, labor, and welfare issues. If Johnson's limitation was a lack of speaking ability, Humphrey's was in not knowing when to stop speaking. His energetic excitement about politics won many supporters, but seemed excessive to the point of naïveté in the eyes of critics. The logical heir to Stevenson's supporters, both because of his regional origin and his political views, Humphrey seemed to relish the give-and-take of campaigning.

If Humphrey had the Stevenson crowd, Senator Stuart Symington of Missouri had the Truman legacy in his corner. Truman took his fellow Missourian on as a protégé. Symington had served in the Truman administration as secretary of the Air Force, and since had played the difficult game of courting Truman's support while retaining independence. Symington looked presidential, but had not developed a national reputation to match those of his rivals. He gained visibility during the McCarthy hearings, when as a member of McCarthy's Committee on Government Operations, he challenged the Wisconsin senator in dramatic confrontations before television cameras. That his expertise was in defense issues increased his stature in the aftermath of the U-2 incident, and he remained the second choice of enough Democrats who favored other candidates that he appeared to be a logical compromise candidate in case of a deadlock.

Massachusetts Senator John F. Kennedy was another possible candidate to emerge out of a strong Democratic field. He came from a politically ambitious family, whose patriarch, Joseph Kennedy, had made a fortune in the liquor, film, and investment industries. Joseph Kennedy had educated and driven his sons to succeed, and had wanted his eldest son, Joe Jr., to seek the presidency. When Joe Jr., a Navy pilot, died on a wartime mission in 1944, Jack became the heir apparent. A sickly but attractive young man, John F. Kennedy accepted the road chosen by his father. In 1946, he parlayed his father's money, his own wartime heroics, and ethnic support in Massachusetts's Eleventh Congressional District to win election to Congress.

After serving three lackluster terms in the House, during which time he did not sponsor any major legislation, Kennedy defeated the popular Republican Senator Henry Cabot Lodge Jr. to win a seat in the United States Senate. Kennedy's first term as senator was little more distinguished than his tenure in the House, but he began to attract national attention nonetheless. His marriage to Jacqueline Bouvier in 1953 received extensive press coverage. In 1956, his book *Profiles in Courage* won the Pulitzer Prize for biography, which gave Kennedy credentials as an intellectual—although years later it became known that his aide Theodore Sorenson and others were more responsible for the book than Kennedy himself. Ultimately, the book may have done Kennedy as much harm as good, for there was in addition to the controversy over authorship the oft-repeated comment that Kennedy himself ought to show less profile and more courage. At the 1956 Democratic National Convention, he gave a dramatic nominating speech for Adlai Stevenson. After Stevenson won the nomination, he threw open the vice presidential nomination, and Kennedy nearly won on the strength of the speech.

In the years between Eisenhower's reelection in 1956 and the election of 1960, Kennedy began to receive a modicum of respect for his activities in the Senate. In 1957, he spoke out against French colonialism in Algeria and Southeast Asia. He won the admiration of his Senate colleagues for his hard work on labor reform, playing a central role in the debate over labor law, writing a bill that others rewrote into "Landrum-Griffin"—which in its final form bore little resemblance to his original draft.

By 1960, Kennedy had emerged as a rising star in the Democratic Party, well enough known that some polls named him as the most popular figure among potential Democratic nominees. His charm, his personal appeal, and his self-deprecating sense of humor all made him an attractive candidate. Most experienced Democrats discounted him nonetheless. He was too inexperienced, too young. If he were to be elected, he would become the youngest president in American history, replacing the oldest. Political wisdom of the day said that his Catholicism virtually disqualified him. No Catholic could be elected president, and Al Smith's loss to Herbert Hoover in 1928 provided a lesson for those who thought otherwise. Others distrusted Kennedy's father. Harry Truman claimed that it wasn't the Pope that worried him, it was the Pop. People remembered Joe Kennedy's conservative isolationism, which had been evident during his tenure as ambassador to Britain in the years leading to World War II. They also resented Joe's ability to use his wealth to influence elections, as he did again in 1958 when Jack won reelection to the Senate.

In 1960, primaries didn't carry the weight they would in later years. They served the interests primarily of those who weren't well entrenched with party regulars, who didn't have a national reputation, and who believed they had to demonstrate their ability to generate support. As the primary season began, besides Kennedy, only Humphrey, who had to prove that he was not too liberal for the electorate, saw advantage in entering most every primary. Stevenson was still engaged in his quadrennial vacillation about whether or not to run. Johnson saw his route to the nomination lay through his superlative party connections, and was content to watch from the sidelines as Kennedy and Humphrey battered each other in the primaries. Symington had little alternative but to hang around hoping for a deadlock that might lead to his selection as a compromise candidate.

Kennedy's strategy required him to take risks. He ran against Humphrey in the Minnesota senator's neighboring state, Wisconsin. Kennedy's victory there on April 5 proved the effectiveness of his campaign operation, his youthful energy, and the impact of ethnic voters, who supported Kennedy in large percentages. In West Virginia, Kennedy confronted the religious issue directly, for the state was 95 percent Protestant. Kennedy used his military record, his record on the separation of church and state, and his opposition to aid to Catholic schools to demonstrate that he was not a puppet of Rome. The first polls showed him trailing Humphrey, 60 to 40 percent. Kennedy more than reversed that tally on Election Day, when he received 61 percent of total votes, to Humphrey's 39 percent, in a victory that demonstrated his appeal to voters and forced Humphrey out of the race.

After West Virginia, Kennedy won other primaries, some of them unopposed, in Indiana, Nebraska, Oregon, and Maryland, and established his position as the favorite heading into the national convention in Los Angeles. Seasoned politicians—Johnson, Truman, and Stevenson—tried to undercut Kennedy as inexperienced, but it was too late. Kennedy was nominated on the first ballot.

The convention's major surprise was the selection of Lyndon Johnson as Kennedy's running mate. Johnson had finished second to Kennedy at the convention; he could aid the ticket's appeal in the South, where Kennedy had been weakest; and he could help in relations with Congress, where senators and representatives respected Johnson but still believed that Kennedy was out of his league. Johnson, however, had been saying that he wouldn't accept the second spot on the ticket, and both Kennedy and his brother Robert, the campaign's key strategist, expected Johnson to turn down the offer. Instead, he accepted. Labor and liberals, two of Kennedy's key constituencies, were outraged, and the Kennedy brothers briefly considered withdrawing the offer.

In contrast, the Republican campaign had been a placid affair. Once Rockefeller pulled out, Nixon's nomination was a foregone conclusion. The biggest problem for the Republicans was to attract attention, for they couldn't match the excitement on the Democratic side. For someone other than Nixon, the lack of publicity would have been a serious handicap. Nixon, however, had been in the public eye for eight years as vice president, and had a substantial edge on Kennedy in terms of experience. Even before his tenure as vice president, his investigation of the Hiss case had given him publicity and a reputation as a hard-edged anti-Communist. Kennedy couldn't begin to match Nixon's foreign policy experience, nor the stature Nixon's kitchen debate with Nikita Khrushchev alone had given him.

With the presidential nomination settled long before the Republicans began their convention in Chicago late in July, the vice presidential nomination was the only source of drama remaining. For Nixon, the selection was important in securing the broad support of the party, whose appeal was narrow enough at best. As Nixon noted in his memoirs, "my most serious liability was the weakness of my Republican Party base," since Democrats outnumbered Republicans by about 50 million to 33 million. Nixon securely held the support of Republican conservatives and moderates, but liberals were another matter. To reach the liberals, Nixon preferred Rockefeller as his running mate, but Rockefeller had made it clear that he wasn't interested. Nixon believed that it was necessary to meet with the New York governor in any case, particularly because Rockefeller had begun to criticize emerging platform language, which he considered too weak on civil rights and defense.

The July 22 meeting at Rockefeller's New York apartment culminated in what angry Republicans called the "Compact of Fifth Avenue," or the "Treaty of Fifth Avenue." The perception of a Nixon surrender was misleading, for, as historian Herbert Parmet points out, the vice president was already looking beyond the convention and the need to appeal to other than dedicated Republicans. Nixon and Rockefeller, meeting well into the morning of July 23, worked out an agreement on defense spending that included Nixon's wording "there must be no price ceiling on America's security." It wasn't hard to read that as criticism of Eisenhower and, indeed, the president did read it that way. Ignoring or perhaps forgetting the parallels to his own "Surrender at Morningside Heights" meeting with Senator Robert Taft eight years earlier, Eisenhower found the document "somewhat astonishing."

Nixon selected UN Ambassador Henry Cabot Lodge as his running mate. Lodge's name had last graced a ballot in 1952, when he'd lost a Senate race—to John F. Kennedy. The selection signaled Nixon's interest in foreign policy, and contrasted to the lack of such experience on the Democratic ticket.

Eisenhower's reaction to the Nixon-Rockefeller meeting was one piece of another campaign puzzle that reporters watched closely. While there was no question that the president preferred Nixon to Kennedy, there was a question about how enthusiastic Eisenhower was about Nixon's candidacy. Observers knew that the president and vice president had never been personally close. Nixon had to straddle the line, keeping Eisenhower in his corner, and yet reaching out to the Rockefeller Republicans. Eisenhower resented the fact that Nixon seldom sought his advice, and often ignored it when offered. During the campaign, reporters pressed Eisenhower about Nixon's role in the administration, and asked the president to give an example of one of Nixon's ideas that he had adopted. "If you give me a week, I might think of one," Eisenhower replied. Immediately recognizing that he had inflicted unintended damage on the Nixon campaign, he apologized to the vice president and, late in the campaign, offered to give a series of hard-hitting stump speeches. At the urging of Mamie and the president's physician, however, Nixon asked him not to risk his health. Nixon couldn't avoid speculating in his memoirs about what "might have been" had Eisenhower campaigned.

Passing the Torch: The Election of 1960

Television, which had come into its own in the fifties, played an important role in the campaign for the first time. Both candidates used television advertising extensively, but the new medium made its most dramatic impact in a series of televised debates in September and October. When Kennedy challenged Nixon to debate, Nixon's advisors recommended against accepting: their candidate was better known and had little to gain. For Kennedy, simply to appear on the same platform with Nixon as an equal would be a victory of sorts. Nevertheless, Nixon accepted, in the belief that he had more debating experience than Kennedy. Moreover, his previous experiences with television—most memorably, in the 1952 Checkers speech and the kitchen debate with Khrushchev—had been successful.

The first debate, on September 26, was the most significant turning point in the campaign. The prime-time debate received coverage from all three major television and radio networks. Some 70 million people watched the debates. Neither debater scored any significant points on substance. Both were articulate, if nervous. But the debate revealed the fickle nature of the medium. Those who scored the debate in traditional ways found it hard to separate the two men. Although people who listened to radio coverage gave Nixon a narrow victory, television favored Kennedy in unanticipated ways. He appeared tanned, rested, and more confident than Nixon, who appeared pale and tired. Nixon had refused to use any makeup other than a beard cover, which, under the hot television lights, melted and ran. Kennedy won, not because he was a better debater, but because he had acquitted himself well in a contest with a better-known rival, and because television had favored his youthful physical appearance.

Although Nixon may have won the third debate on points, the last two debates served merely to confirm the verdict of the first. Differences on policy emerged, but the candidates weren't far apart on the issues. Both considered foreign policy to be a strength of their campaign. Both men were ardent Cold Warriors, and believed that the United States had to be aggressive in defense of American interests abroad. Neither had given much thought to civil rights.

In an election in which the candidates had similar policy positions, style emerged as a significant factor, and the advent of television gave style extra points. Nixon seemed taciturn, angry, and guarded. He had always had an adversarial relationship with reporters, and the rigors of the campaign brought old suspicions out into the open, putting Nixon on the defense. Kennedy, in contrast, seemed to thrive on the attention he received, and bantered with reporters in a way that Nixon never could. Kennedy's sense of humor often bailed him out of tight situations, whereas when Nixon was cornered, he lashed out. When challenged about his father's wealth, Kennedy joked that the old man had told him he would not pay for a landslide. Kennedy had gifted speech writers—Theodore Sorenson and Arthur Schlesinger Jr. among them—who added eloquence to his wit. Both candidates had physical problems during the campaign, and both sought to suppress them. Appearances, however, favored Kennedy. The senator's aides later recalled how difficult it was for Kennedy even to get out of bed when his back began to hurt, yet by the time he appeared in public he was jaunty, and no one would ever have suspected. Nixon was equally courageous in seeking to overcome his maladies, but he often appeared worn down by the campaign ordeal.

Often the difference that emerged between the candidates was situational: Kennedy had the advantage of being able to attack, whereas Nixon had to defend. Both projected optimism, and used the images of moving America forward. This, of course, was easier for Kennedy to do since he could claim that the nation had been standing still under Eisenhower, whereas Nixon had to both defend the record of the Eisenhower-Nixon administration and yet make clear his own political identity.

Cuba emerged as one of the key issues of the campaign, and the way it evolved showed clearly the quandary facing a sitting vice president, defending policies that weren't always his own and sometimes unable to reveal those that were. For several months, the CIA had been plotting ways to get rid of Castro. No one in the administration pressed harder for aggressive action against the Cuban leader than Nixon. For national security reasons, the public could knew nothing of this.

Everything about the Cuban issue went wrong for Nixon, however. In September, a Senate Internal Security Subcommittee report that criticized the Eisenhower administration had not heeded warnings in Cuba. On October 6, Kennedy employed the report to allege that the administration had "lost" Cuba. When the administration imposed a full trade embargo on Cuba, Kennedy dismissed it as "too little, too late." In mid-October, just three weeks before the election, Castro began nationalizing American interests in Cuba, making the administration action seem all the more timid, embarrassing the vice president even further.

Then the issue took an unusual turn. CIA Director Allen Dulles had briefed Kennedy about Cuba, and although it isn't known how detailed the briefing may have been, there is reason to believe that Dulles did discuss administration aid to Cuban exiles. But publicly, Kennedy said that the administration ought to discard the policy of nonintervention, and assist Cuban exiles.

Kennedy's attack angered Nixon, who knew he had been impaled on the horns of a dilemma. Fundamentally, Nixon agreed with Kennedy, but to say so publicly would be to criticize Eisenhower, which was unthinkable, and would jeopardize plans then under way, which was unconscionable. Historian

Stephen Ambrose suggested that Nixon could have simply refused to respond, as Eisenhower had done when Stevenson attacked him on the issue of nuclear testing in 1956, but that ran contrary to Nixon's combative nature. The vice president devised a particularly Nixonian response. "In order to protect the secrecy of the planning and the safety of the thousands of men and women involved in the operation," Nixon explained in his memoirs, "I had no choice but to take a completely opposite stand and attack Kennedy's advocacy of open intervention in Cuba." He did so eloquently, attacking the premise of intervention on legal, ethical, and pragmatic grounds. He claimed such an intervention would force Cuba closer to the Soviet Union, and cost the United States friends in Latin America. The final irony, of course, would not be known for several months, and would unfold at the Bay of Pigs in April 1961; Nixon the debater, arguing against Nixon the vice president, had been right.

Another foreign policy issue placed Nixon in a similarly difficult position. Kennedy spoke often of a "missile gap," alleging that the United States had fallen far behind the Soviet Union in delivery systems. The missile gap arose both from exaggeration by the military of the Soviet threat and from "guesstimates" based on incomplete data. Nixon knew that the missile gap was a fiction, but his information came from reconnaissance photos, and he could not refute Kennedy's allegations without revealing classified information.

By 1960, civil rights had emerged as one of the key domestic issues in a campaign dominated by foreign affairs. The issue had many dimensions: moral, regional, and pragmatic. Since the New Deal, the black vote had traditionally gone to Democratic candidates. By 1960, however, the dynamics of race in American politics had changed. African Americans expected more from elected officials than they had previously. White Americans, whether or not they supported desegregation, for the first time since Reconstruction considered race to be one of the defining domestic issues, The events of the late fifties and the early months of 1960, from Little Rock to the sit-ins, required more than a pro forma response.

Neither Nixon nor Kennedy had established much of a record on civil rights. As a congressman, the Republican candidate had voted in favor of the Fair Employment Practices Commission. Nixon's record as vice president suggested comfort with the approach adopted by the Eisenhower administration, supporting civil rights with rhetoric and symbolic actions, but playing it safe in order to appeal to the white South. His record on civil rights was not that of a crusader, but it demonstrated awareness of an issue beyond that of most members of the Eisenhower administration. Kennedy had demonstrated no commitment to civil rights. Even his campaign staff acknowledged that he considered civil rights only in its political context. In balance, Nixon had stronger civil rights "credentials" than Kennedy at the start of the campaign.

The early course of the campaign gave little indication that either candidate would make much of an effort to appeal to African-American voters. Before the convention, Rockefeller's presence in the race forced Nixon to be more of an advocate for civil rights than after he received the nomination, and he had supported a civil rights plank in the party platform. Nixon avoided the issue on the campaign trail, hoping to capitalize on the Republican Party's nascent Southern strategy. When the Republican vice presidential candidate announced that, if elected, the Nixon-Lodge administration would name an African American to the cabinet, Nixon's staff forced an embarrassed Lodge to retreat.

Kennedy, too, had been little more than a symbolic supporter of civil rights. He had brought Johnson to the ticket mainly to secure the South, a goal that did not suggest appealing to black voters. Kennedy had two things going for him that Nixon did not: a record of traditional black support for his party, which meant that if both candidates were equally indifferent toward civil rights, Kennedy would likely win the black vote; and advisors such as Harris Wofford and Burke Marshall, who were sensitive to civil rights even if the candidate wasn't.

With both candidates focusing on foreign policy, civil rights became an issue only late in the campaign, and because of external events rather that the inclinations of either Nixon or Kennedy. On October 19, police in Atlanta arrested Martin Luther King Jr., who had been participating in a sit-in in a department store. King had a suspended sentence from an earlier violation for having an expired driver's license; the DeKalb County court sentenced him to four months of hard labor. King's supporters appealed to the Eisenhower administration for a reduced sentence. Attorney General William Rogers, a Nixon supporter, had a statement drafted that would have directed the Justice Department to "take all proper steps to join with Dr. Martin Luther King in an appropriate application for his release." Eisenhower decided not to use the statement. Nixon privately criticized King's arrest, but said nothing publicly despite urging from Rogers and other members of the administration.

In contrast, when Kennedy's advisors pressed him to act, he called King's wife, Coretta, and expressed his sympathy. Robert Kennedy called the judge, and secured King's release from prison. The contrast inspired King's father "Daddy King," a prominent preacher in his own right, to declare his support for Kennedy, saying that he had a "suitcase of votes" that he intended to dump in Kennedy's lap. The elder King's statement helped invest the two phone calls with a significance they might not have had otherwise, and helped to influence the black electorate. Kennedy used civil rights in other ways to attack the Eisenhower record, included a statement that he as president would be able to wipe out discrimination in federal housing "with a stroke of the presidential pen." The statement would haunt the first year-and-a-half of his presidency, as he found the act more difficult to fulfill than the promise was to make.

The religion issue continued to hang over the election like a cloud of uncertainty, and in September Kennedy decided to take it head-on. He appeared before a group of Baptist ministers in Houston. "I believe in an America where the separation of church and state is absolute," he told his audience. His courage and unequivocal statement won over the Baptist ministers, and minimized the impact of the issue on the outcome of the election.

The Kennedy-Nixon election was one of the closest in American history, and thus provided plenty of room for speculation about "might-have-beens." Nixon suffered a seemingly minor injury as he began his campaign in mid-August when he banged his knee while getting into a car. The knee became badly infected, and Nixon had to spend two weeks in the hospital recovering, losing precious time. Once he resumed campaigning, the pace wore him down, and he developed a fever that further inhibited his ability to make appearances. Nixon had promised to visit every one of the fifty states during his campaign; despite illnesses, and against the advice of his staff, he kept the promise. In doing so, however, he lost the chance to spend more time in closely contested states.

Late in October, columnist Drew Pearson wrote in his syndicated column that Donald Nixon, the vice president's brother, had accepted a $205,000 loan from business magnate Howard Hughes. In return, Hughes's enterprises, particularly Hughes Aircraft Company and Trans World Airlines (TWA), had received preferential treatment from federal officials. Nixon denied being the source of any influence, and although no concrete evidence turned up to prove or disprove his claim, the issue followed him to the end of the campaign.

Eisenhower's role in the campaign plagued Nixon more than any other circumstantial development. The two men never formed a friendship, and Eisenhower never really believed that Nixon was of presidential caliber. Despite Eisenhower's apology, his press conference comment rankled, and reflected the reality of their relationship more accurately than either would acknowledge. Eisenhower did not rely on Nixon for ideas, although he did rely on him in other ways: as a bridge to the Republican right, as a lightning rod to deflect criticism from the president, as an ambassador. Yet, once the two parties had named their candidates, Eisenhower's preference was clear. The president considered Kennedy too young, too liberal, and too inexperienced, and expected that he would also be too loose with the nation's checkbook. He distrusted Joe Kennedy, and had little respect for Lyndon Johnson. In the days before the election, Eisenhower planned an aggressive, expanded stump campaign for his vice president. Nixon painfully recounts in his memoirs that Mamie and the president's physician both worried about Eisenhower's health, fearing that Eisenhower's heart might not withstand the rigors of a more vigorous campaign. Eisenhower himself thought otherwise, and was ready to go. Nixon respected the wishes of the president's wife and doctor, but wrote in his memoirs, "In retrospect, it seems possible that if he had been able to carry out his expanded campaign schedule, he might have had a decisive impact on the outcome of the election."

Other last-minute issues also clouded the relationship between the two men. Stories about Kennedy's Addison's disease were circulating in the press, and Nixon intended to raise the issue of his opponent's health. Eisenhower, understandably troubled about raising the issue of the health of a candidate, refused to be a party to the project. Nixon had another late campaign inspiration, a pledge that if he was elected, he would send President Eisenhower on a goodwill mission to Europe. Again, Eisenhower refused to cooperate, and commented that he found the request astonishing and hysterical.

The popular vote was closer than any previous presidential contest in the twentieth century, with Nixon losing by only 118,000 votes, one-fourth of 1 percent of the more than 68 million people who cast ballots. Theodore Sorenson later calculated that if only 12,000 voters in five states changed their votes to Nixon, he would have won the election. The margin in the electoral college was wider, 303–219, but changes in large states where the result was close could have turned the election. Irregularities in some of those large states, particularly Illinois and Texas, were serious enough that they might have formed the basis for a recount, but Nixon chose not to demand one.

Religion played less of a role in the election than many had anticipated. Kennedy had addressed the issue forthrightly from the beginning. National reports of his speech to the Baptist convention in Texas, and of its reception, reassured many voters that Kennedy's Catholicism would play no political role in his administration. Harry Truman chided his fellow Baptists for giving any substance to fears of undue religious influence. Nixon did not make religion an issue in his campaign. Surely voters were influenced by religion, but most analysts believed that the issue was a wash; about as many people voted against Kennedy for religious reasons as voted for him on the same basis. The religious issue led many Democratic Protestants to desert their party and to vote for Nixon, but it also brought back Democratic Catholics who'd left the fold four years earlier to vote for Eisenhower instead of Stevenson.

Different constituencies read the results in different ways. Democrats rejoiced that the ship of state had righted itself, and that the Democratic coalition fashioned by Franklin Roosevelt had been restored. (Roosevelt's 1936 victory brought blacks, women, farmers, union workers, people in large industrial cities, intellectuals, and the Solid South into the Democratic fold.) Blacks in particular could make a case that they provided Kennedy with his margin of victory in key states such as Michigan and Illinois. Lyndon Johnson could argue that his influence prevented Nixon from "stealing" the South from the Democrats. The Republicans took only Florida in the South, although the Democrats also lost electoral votes in Mississippi, Alabama, and Oklahoma to Independent candidate Harry Byrd.

Transition: The Last Days of the Eisenhower Presidency

The election results were devastating to Eisenhower, who couldn't help feeling they were, at least in part, a repudiation of his administration. With two-and-a-half months left in his presidency, Eisenhower faced the plight of the lame duck; though still president, his power seemed to slip away day by day. He spent the transition preparing for private life, but also completing affairs of state. President-Elect Kennedy met with him on December 6. Eisenhower, impressed by Kennedy's receptive manner, told the younger man about mundane matters of how things operated in the White House, and about substantive matters of state, including the balance-of-payments issue.

On January 17, just days before he relinquished the presidency, Eisenhower delivered what would be his most memorable speech, his Farewell Address, speaking to the American people over television. It was a speech that only Eisenhower could have given, for it drew on his experiences in the military and as president, and particularly from his attempts to hold the line against unbridled military spending. He worried that the greatest threat to U.S. security came from within, but his warning was no McCarthy-like anti-Communist diatribe. The defense industry had broadened its influence by extending contracts to businesses in virtually every state, thus having people both in government service and in the private sector dependent on money from Washington. He described the recent advent of "the conjunction of an immense military establishment and a large arms industry." He spoke of how the process of military procurement had changed, and that large, federally funded research projects had replaced the solitary inventor working in a small laboratory. Universities, too, had become part of the intertwined relationship between government, industry, and education. "In the councils of government," he cautioned, "we must guard against the acquisition of unwarranted influence, whether sought or unsought, by the military-industrial complex." Carrying the thought one step further, he warned, "public policy itself could become the captive of a scientific-technological elite." He worried that American free inquiry would decline, he feared, if "a government contract becomes virtually a substitute for intellectual curiosity." This influence, he worried, could turn the United States into a garrison state. Even more sobering was the "potential for the disastrous rise of misplaced power." He raised the prospect that Americans had heard similar warnings since the end of World War II, but never from the president of the United States.

Snow blanketed Washington on the day before inauguration, and city crews worked through the night to clear streets. Inauguration Day dawned cold and windy, but the chill in the White House was considerably less than it had been during the Truman-Eisenhower transition eight years earlier. President-Elect and Mrs. Kennedy visited with the Eisenhowers and Nixons in the morning before leaving the White House together for the ride to the inauguration platform in front of the Capitol. Poet Carl Sandburg highlighted the inaugural ceremony, reading his poetry in the glaring Washington sunlight. Then Eisenhower and Nixon sat behind the incoming president as he delivered an inaugural address laden with aggressive Cold War rhetoric in which he promised that Americans would "pay any price, bear any burden" in the defense of liberty.

Eisenhower had paid his price, and borne the burdens of leadership in a lifetime of public service, and he now prepared to retire to his farm in Gettysburg. He lived for another eight years, engaging in golf, painting, and bridge, and writing his memoirs.

Ike and the Historians: A Rise in Reputation

In the years that followed, Eisenhower's reputation changed more dramatically than that of any other U.S. president. When he left office, most Americans considered him to have been a decent, honest man who'd been fortunate to preside over the nation in a time of prosperity. He'd been one of the nation's great military leaders during World War II, and came to the presidency on the strength of that record. Most believed that, although he'd been an exceptional wartime leader, he'd been a bit out of his league in the presidency. His press conferences seemed to meander; his sentences rambled and were often convoluted; and he often seemed to say little of any substance. At least he'd had the good sense to delegate major responsibilities to men better qualified to handle those tasks. When he ran into problems in the last year of his presidency with the U-2 debacle, it seemed to reinforce that impression; after all, John Foster Dulles had died, and was no longer around to keep Ike out of trouble.

Kennedy's presidential campaign reinforced such general impressions. Here was the youngest man ever to hold the office, inheriting the presidency from the oldest. Kennedy had stressed the theme of action in his campaign. He would get the nation moving again, for it had stagnated during Eisenhower's eight years in office. Eisenhower had often played golf while his subordinates were tending the shop. Eisenhower, so the impressions of the time ran, hadn't really done much in office, hadn't asserted U.S. power abroad, and had been something of a caretaker. Indeed, the grandfatherly figure who rode with Kennedy to the Capitol on Inauguration Day seemed to be a man from another era.

Two years later, when historians conducted a poll ranking U.S. presidents, Eisenhower tied for twentieth position with Chester Arthur, just above Andrew Johnson in the lower level of the "average" presidents. This placed him two spots below Herbert Hoover, still a convenient scapegoat for the Great Depression. Twenty years later, however, in a poll of historians similar to the one conducted in 1962, Eisenhower ranked eleventh, by far the largest rise for any president in the history of these rankings. He'd leapfrogged over the likes of James Polk, James Madison, and James Monroe, and even ranked two spots above the young martyred president who had succeeded him.

What had happened? The opening of his papers in the Eisenhower Library and the examination of those papers by scholars, the contrast of his record with that of his successors, the course of public policy in the sixties and seventies, and the evolving judgment of the American people of what they want in their leaders: all these factors figured into the remarkable elevation of Eisenhower's ranking.

The first wave of scholars to examine Eisenhower's presidency reflected the general view at the time he left office. Typical was James David Barber's influential *The Presidential Character*, which first appeared in 1972. Barber ranked twentieth-century presidents based on his evaluation of their level of activity on one axis and their self-perception and their attitude toward the office on the other. He greatly admired the "active-positives," who were self-confident and optimistic, and whose numbers included Eisenhower's immediate predecessor and successor. Barber classified Eisenhower as a "passive-negative" along with Calvin Coolidge, and described them as being involved in politics out of a sense of duty rather than enjoyment, and as men who avoided conflict and emphasized procedures.

Although there were earlier hints of a reevaluation, the most dramatic rise in Eisenhower's stock occurred with the publication in 1982 of Princeton political scientist Fred Greenstein's *The Hidden-Hand Presidency: Eisenhower as Leader*. Greenstein surveyed new papers opened for research in the Eisenhower Library, the most important of which were the files of Eisenhower's personal secretary Ann Whitman. The papers revealed that Eisenhower had not been the disengaged delegator that historians had supposed. Eisenhower was not only engaged; he was in charge. Even the formidable John Foster Dulles looked for direction from Eisenhower, and took it. Eisenhower's marginalia reveals an ability to summarize arguments concisely, and to establish a position in a straightforward, no-nonsense manner. He was content to allow his subordinates to be on the front lines, to take the heat, while he remained in the background, preserving his options, controlling policy with his "hidden hand." Greenstein demonstrated that, on foreign and domestic policy, Eisenhower had the last word. Even those confusing press conferences were part of Eisenhower's style, maintaining flexibility with circumlocution. The previously cited incident with press secretary James Hagerty illustrated this point; when last-minute news arrived just before Eisenhower headed out for a press conference, Hagerty tried to pass the news on to the president. Eisenhower told him not to worry, if the issue came up, he would just confuse them. And he did.

Greenstein's book launched a cottage industry in Eisenhower revisionism, and led even skeptical historians to like Ike. For the next decade, books on Eisenhower were full of praise, and his reputation rose in dramatic fashion. Stephen Ambrose's biography appeared two years after Greenstein's. He acknowledged the disappointments, but showed his admiration, praising Eisenhower for his ability to manage crises, and for presiding over eight years of peace and prosperity. Recent scholarship has also acknowledged that Eisenhower was in command, but in subjecting that authority to closer scrutiny while not greatly diminishing his ranking, it has found Eisenhower wanting in areas such as civil rights, his response to McCarthy, and U.S. policy in areas of the Third World.

Recommended Reading

The *History of American Presidential Elections,* volume 4, edited by Arthur M. Schlesinger Jr. (New York: Chelsea House, 1971) provides a succinct overview of this and other elections covered in this volume, along with pertinent documents and party platforms. Journalist Theodore H. White's *The Making of the President, 1960* (New York: Atheneum, 1961), one of a series he wrote on presidential elections and a classic of election reportage, is available in several reprint editions.

On labor legislation, see R. Alton Lee's *Eisenhower and Landrum-Griffin: A Study in Labor-Management Politics* (Lexington: University Press of Kentucky, 1990).

Fred Greenstein's pathbreaking *Hidden-Hand Presidency: Eisenhower as Leader* (New York: HarperCollins, 1982) started the wave of Eisenhower revisionism.

Index